GW00771685

The Muslim-Croat Civil War in Central Bosnia

Number Twenty-three:
Eastern European Studies
Stjepan Meštrović, *General Editor*

Charles R. Shrader

The
Muslim-Croat
Civil War
in Central Bosnia
A Military History,

1992–1994

Texas A&M
University Press
College Station

The paper used in this book
meets the minimum requirements
of the American National Standard
for Permanence of Paper
for Printed Library Materials,
Z39.48-1984.
Binding materials
have been chosen for durability.
∞

Shrader, Charles R.
   The Muslim-Croat civil war in Central Bosnia : a military history,
1992–1994 / Charles R. Shrader.—1st ed.
      p. cm.—(Eastern European studies ; no. 23)
   Includes bibliographical references and index.
      ISBN 1-58544-261-5 (cloth : alk. paper)
      1. Yugoslav War, 1991–1995—Campaigns—Bosnia and Herze-
govina. 2. Bosnia and Herzegovina—History, Military. I. Title. II.
Eastern European studies (College Station, Tex.) ; no. 23.

   DR1313.3 .S54 2003
   949.703—dc21

                                                        2002153967

Excerpt from Rebecca West, *Black Lamb and Grey Falcon: The Record of
a Journey through Yugoslavia in 1937,* courtesy Macmillan Publishers
Ltd., London, 1946.

To those who suffered

English persons, therefore,
of humanitarian and reformist disposition
constantly went out to the Balkan Peninsula
to see who was in fact ill-treating whom,
and, being by the very nature
of their perfectionist faith
unable to accept the horrid hypothesis
that everybody was ill-treating everybody else,
all came back with a pet Balkan people
established in their hearts as suffering
and innocent, eternally the massacree
and never the massacrer.

—Rebecca West,
Black Lamb and Grey Falcon:
The Record of a Journey
through Yugoslavia in 1937

Contents

Illustrations

Figures

Tables

Maps

Foreword

Charles Shrader's book on the war in Bosnia-Herzegovina focuses primar- xiiiily on the Muslim-Croat civil war within a larger war waged by Serbia in the 1990s. It brings to mind the kind of detailed, expert analyses one sees on C-Span by authors who are military experts on various historic battles such as the Battle of Plattsburgh. Shrader, a retired army lieutenant colonel, brings a similar military expertise, an eye for detail, and an objectivity that only an American officer with no ax to grind could bring. I can also envision Shrader's book being important for the international community as it continues to struggle with the issue of post-Nazi war crimes. This is because, in addition to or perhaps because of the detailed military analysis that he offers, he also sheds light on the origins, nature, and eventual resolution of ethnic conflict in a limited geographic area. In this regard, he also offers a sociological analysis. Students of ethnic conflict in diverse academic disciplines will also benefit from this analysis.

The war in Bosnia-Herzegovina was widely covered but is still poorly understood, especially from the military point of view. Most of the other books on the conflict were written by journalists and constitute little more than testimonies of people's suffering. That is what journalists do: they cover events. But they are seldom equipped, conceptually or by training, to delve into the military, sociological, or legal aspects of them. Shrader uses the military history perspective as a vehicle for offering a much more comprehensive understanding of what really happened in Bosnia. In particular, he focuses on the military strategies of the Bosnian Muslim armed forces, which were not unequivocally defensive. I do no believe that Shrader's approach should be dismissed as an example of "blaming the victim." Bosnian Muslims were undoubtedly and primarily victims in the various wars in Bosnia-Herzegovina. Yet it is important to keep in mind that several civil wars raged simultaneously: Serbs against Croats, Serbs against Muslims, Croats against Muslims, and also Muslims against Muslims (Fikret Abdic led a failed secessionist movement against the government of Alija Izetbegovic). The macabre drama of the dissolution of Yugoslavia began with the Serbs as the clear and primary victimizers of other ethnic groups, and then became grotesquely twisted into tales of the primary victims (Croats and Muslims) victimizing each other. The unfolding of the process by which some victims become victimizers is horrifying from psychological, sociological, and legal perspectives. This ambivalent emotion is captured by the epigram that

Shrader uses from Rebecca West's *Black Lamb and Grey Falcon*. Even when well-meaning people wanted to help stop the bloodshed in Yugoslavia, they were paralyzed by not being able to discern clearly the victims from the victimizers, historically, as well as in relation to the events of the 1990s. The metaphor I would use to capture the overall picture is the following: The Belgrade regime acted as prison guards to prisoners (Bosnian Muslims and Croats) who tried to break out, and who turned on each other in the process. The war in Bosnia-Herzegovina was chaos. An ideal-type "normal" observer would have expected the victims to remain allies against the aggressor, but instead, the allies turned on each other. Shrader attempts to bring an orderly perspective to this seemingly psychopathological state of affairs.

For example, Shrader argues that the fall of the town of Jajce was the true origin of Muslim-Croat tensions in Bosnia-Herzegovina. One will never know whether the Serbs used the fall of Jajce as a deliberate military strategy to cause chaos and conflict among their victims, but it certainly had that effect. As streams of refugees began to flow into predominantly Croat towns and villages, the overcrowding caused competition for already scarce resources necessary for survival. Under similar conditions replicated among laboratory animals, psychologists find that the result is aggression. Aggression became exacerbated among Belgrade's victims, and some of it was turned toward the Serbs and some toward fellow victims. The Croats and Muslims created disorganized defense forces drawn primarily from a pool of able-bodied men who were traumatized and bent upon revenge. Seventy percent of Bosnia was already under Serbian control. Shrader notes that there is no "smoking gun" evidence that proves the Croats and Muslims rationally planned to "ethnically cleanse" the other ethnic group from the remaining thirty percent of Bosnia. Nevertheless, he argues that from a military point of view, the Bosnian Muslim forces had the necessary means, motive, and opportunity, whereas the Bosnian Croats had far less of each. This is a controversial argument. It flies in the face of the prevailing conclusions reached by journalists. It is up to the reader to assess Shrader's objectivity and evidence.

Lieutenant Colonel Shrader's credentials and reputation as an author and military expert speak for themselves. He conducted intensive research in Bosnia-Herzegovina that involved primary evidence in addition to reading secondary evidence based upon reports by European Community, United Nations, and other Western monitors. By this I mean that he climbed up the actual hills, went into the villages, and interviewed the company and battalion commanders involved in the war in Bosnia. He examined the situation from the perspective of a military historian: what types of weapons were used by various factions, the location of the front lines, the trails used for the evacuation of the wounded, the proximity of the battle lines, the location of villages that fell, the location of the checkpoints, the availability of instruments and mechanisms for command and control, and so on. Clearly, Shrader conducted painstaking and detailed research for this book. Yet the military issues that he raises expose social and sociological issues that will be of interest to a much broader audience, namely: the fighting was at extremely close quarters, most of the fighters were neighbors and former civilians, and neighborly love turned into the most brutal hatred practically overnight. He shows through this detailed analysis that the Serbs were the main aggressors in Bosnia-Herzegovina and they used both the conventional warfare techniques learned in the Yugoslav National Army as well as guerrilla tactics and other unconventional techniques. One of these unconventional strategies was to "help" both the Croats and the Muslims—who were initially allies against the Serbs—in devious ways such that the two allies became paranoid and suspicious of each other's motives. Shrader shows that all sides eventually came to use this blend of conventional as well as unconventional military strategies. In my opinion, the net result came to resemble the symptoms of mental illness: extreme paranoia, hatred, deceit, the projection of blame onto other parties, and a desire for revenge. Shrader cites Sefer Halilovic's memoir *Shrewd Strategy* as an illustration of the means, motive, and opportunity of the Bosnian Muslims. Halilovic—who was Alija Izetbegovic's chief of staff—certainly does disclose these things, but his book can be rationalized as the memoirs of one of Izetbegovic's enemies. In contrast to Halilovic, Shrader offers an objective analysis of military facts to document not only the strategies used by that the disorganized strategies were commensurate with the paranoia, deceit, projection of blame, and desperation that is evident to anyone who is familiar with the war in Bosnia. It is an open question whether other war crimes in other settings, from the My Lai massacre to the crimes in Rwanda are similar to the psychotic blend of organization and chaos uncovered by Shrader. Nonetheless, it is an important question.

In summary, this is an extremely detailed, well-documented analysis of an important historical event. A significant function of academic communities and the university presses that serve them is to bring to light diverse perspectives, even if controversial, so long as these perspectives are well documented. The answer to the "big question" in any field is often found in the small details. By examining the minute details of what happened in the Bosnian conflict, Shrader offers an uncomfortable yet haunting picture of that tragic war.

Stjepan G. Meštrović
Series Editor on Eastern Europe

Preface

Everyone loves an underdog, real or imagined, particularly if that under- xvii dog can be portrayed as the thoroughly innocent victim of sinister and numerous attackers following a premeditated plan of conquest and anni- hilation. Such a simplistic, Manichean explanation of complex events is both easy to construct and easy to understand. Thus, the portrayal of the Bosnian Muslims and the fledgling Republic of Bosnia-Herzegovina (RBiH) as the blameless victims of both Bosnian Serb "Chetniks" and Bos- nian Croat "Ustashas" during the devolution of Yugoslavia in the early 1990s has gained currency despite the patent inaccuracies and lack of so- phistication of such a portrayal and the obvious efforts of the Muslim- dominated RBiH government to concoct a sophisticated, wide-reaching, and ultimately successful propaganda campaign to paint their rivals, both Serb and Croat, as war criminals and themselves as the innocent victims. The acceptance of this manufactured myth by the international media and western governments has served to cover effectively the Bosnian Muslims' own sins of commission and omission.

While it is undoubtedly true that the ill-prepared Bosnian Muslims were the victims of a vicious attack by the Bosnian Serbs, the usual por- trayal of them as innocent prey of their erstwhile Croat allies during the 1992–94 civil war in central Bosnia is far less accurate. In both the numer- ous media accounts and the plethora of testimony and decisions in the United Nations–sponsored war crimes trials in The Hague, the salient facts of the Muslim-Croat conflict in central Bosnia have been distorted thor- oughly by the ideological, political, social, and personal agendas of various government leaders, journalists, war crimes prosecutors and witnesses, and other observers—few of whom were properly equipped or inclined to analyze and report the facts of the matter accurately, thoroughly, or out- side the commonly accepted but faulty framework of a story in which the Bosnian Muslims appear to be the victims of overwhelming forces intent on their destruction.

Grounded in the myth of the Bosnian Muslim community as underdog, most existing versions of the story portray the Bosnian Croats as having waged, at the behest of Croatian president Franjo Tudjman, a campaign of unprovoked military aggression against the innocent and unsuspecting Muslims for the purpose of "ethnically cleansing" central Bosnia as a first step toward its annexation by the Republic of Croatia. Convincing evidence to support such far-reaching assertions has yet to be made public, although those who promote such a version of events have repeated their assumptions and assertions loudly and frequently. The question of political or ideological bias aside, this version of what happened suffers from having been cobbled together hastily either by participants in the events, who were seldom in the best position to observe their overall pattern with a critical eye and who were committed to one cause or another; by commentators far removed from the scene and thus in an even weaker position to discern what actually occurred; by prosecutors desperate to find a basis for their charges; or by witnesses seeking revenge for injuries both real and imagined. In fact, what many commentators allege were planned and sinister actions by the Croats in central Bosnia frequently turn out, on closer examination, to have been accidental or the result of a misinterpretation based on faulty assumptions, ignorance, biased witnesses, and pure speculation.

The obvious question is why so many presumably intelligent and experienced observers, as well as many of the actual participants in the events, have been taken in by the myth of the Bosnian Muslims as underdogs. The answer is quite clear and rather prosaic. One of the most basic rules adhered to by historians—indeed, by police detectives and others who seek to reconstruct past events—is that the number of interpretations of what, when, how, and why something happened usually exceeds the number of witnesses. Each participant in an event brings to it certain preset patterns of thought, biases, and propensities, and each participant has a different level of experience and skill to help him make sense of the scene. Then, too, each observer makes his observations from a slightly different viewpoint, and no one observer is likely to have all of the facts at his disposal. This Rashomon effect—the acknowledged curse of historians—is well known, so it is somewhat surprising that so many observers of the events in Bosnia-Herzegovina appear to have abandoned all sense of skepticism and critical thought and instead chosen to rely on hearsay, propaganda, rumors, and speculation as the bases for their stories of how the Muslim-Croat conflict arose, how it progressed, and what it implied.

A number of factors disposed the United Nations, western governments and diplomats, journalists, war crimes prosecutors, and others to accept an interpretation of events favorable to the Bosnian Muslims. For the governments of the European Community—and to a lesser degree of the United States—historical biases and contemporary national interests played a major role. Residual distrust and hatred of the Croats stemming from their alliance with Nazi Germany during the Second World War—the fact that the Bosnian Muslims also cooperated actively with the Nazis notwithstanding—colored the attitudes of the principal western European governments and their representatives on the ground in Bosnia-Herzegovina. The Persian Gulf War of 1990–91 and the continuing need to court Islamic states in the Middle East made it expedient to appear pro-Muslim, the more so in that several of the European Community states, notably France, Germany, and the Netherlands, had substantial and often restive Muslim minorities at home and lucrative trade relationships with Muslims abroad.

Such considerations also influenced journalists and other observers covering the war in Bosnia-Herzegovina, although the practical day-to-day aspects of covering their beat and the usual dynamics of contemporary media competition probably played a greater role. Most of the journalists covering the war in Bosnia-Herzegovina were focused on Sarajevo and the besieged cities in eastern Bosnia-Herzegovina (Srbrenica, Goradze, and so forth). They normally entered the country through Sarajevo and were reliant on the Muslim-led central government, United Nations agencies, or nongovernmental organizations (NGOs) for information, transport, interpreter services, and other necessary support. Consequently, there was a tendency for them to see and hear only what the Bosnian government wanted them to see and hear. In any event, the competitive nature of contemporary journalism reinforced their natural propensity to opt for the most striking and titillating version of events and to ignore the very concrete, but often complex and dull, reasons for the military conflict between Croats and Muslims in central Bosnia: the struggle for control of military production facilities and lines of communication in the region, as well as the need to resettle the large number of Muslim refugees created by the Bosnian Serb aggression.

The military aspects of the Muslim-Croat conflict in particular have been misrepresented in the international media and before the International Criminal Tribunal for the Former Yugoslavia (ICTY). The military organization, capabilities, and strategies of the opposing sides—as well as their intentions and the course of military operations in central Bosnia between November, 1992, and March, 1994—can be made clear only by a detailed and unbiased analysis of the conflicting evidence and commentary. Such careful analysis is made more difficult by the selective nature of the factual data made public by the United Nations and the governments concerned, all of which have national interests to protect. The massive amount of uncritical and largely anecdotal commentary in the popular press and in books by journalists and participants in the events described is also of little use in finding the truth because of their own biases and because the bulk of such material does not address the military aspects of the Muslim-Croat conflict in any substantial way.

A correct assessment of the Muslim-Croat civil war in central Bosnia requires an unbiased consideration of the facts, the rejection of unwarranted conjecture, and the determination of what patterns, if any, can be imputed to the events. The following brief military history of the Muslim-Croat civil war in central Bosnia attempts to provide such an assessment, and in doing so differs in many significant respects from the accepted version of the story based on the myth portraying Bosnian Muslims as the victims of unprovoked aggression by their Bosnian Croat allies. In the first instance, this study rejects the distorted, counterfactual, and anecdotal evidence that underlies the underdog myth in favor of documentary evidence and direct participant testimony as to the events in question. Secondly, this analysis focuses on the military aspects of the story to the exclusion of its political, diplomatic, and sociological dimensions. It also concentrates on the Muslim-Croat conflict in central Bosnia to the exclusion of events elsewhere in the region. The focus is thus primarily on events in the Lasva, Kozica, and Lepenica Valleys—wherein are the major towns of Travnik, Novi Travnik, Vitez, Busovaca, and Kiseljak—and the mountainous regions to the immediate north and south, an area that generally corresponds to the assigned boundaries of the Croatian Defense Council (HVO), Operative Zone Central Bosnia (OZCB), and the Army of Bosnia-Herzegovina's (ABiH) III Corps. However, it should be noted that the much larger III Corps's southern boundary incorporated the towns of Bugojno, Gornji Vakuf, and Konjic, which were not part of the OZCB—a fact that has caused considerable confusion among commentators. Accordingly, events in comparatively distant areas, although technically under the purview of the OZCB commander, are not developed in detail except insofar as they directly affect events in the Lasva-Kozica-Lepenica Valley enclave. In any event, those outlying areas (Zepce, Kakanj, Visoko, Vares, and Sarajevo) were isolated from the OZCB commander's command and control by virtue of their physical isolation and the inadequate telephone and radio communications available. Similarly, the key towns on central Bosnia's border with Herzegovina (notably Kupres, Jablanica, Prozor, Bugojno, Gornji Vakuf, and Konjic) as well the Mostar region, which were under other HVO commands, figure in this narrative only insofar as they directly affected events in central Bosnia. Thus, the intense Muslim-Croat fight for Mostar is generally excluded, as are events in the far north of the country.

The restriction of this study to a narrow focus on central Bosnia as defined above is also required by a more important consideration. There was a substantial difference in the Muslim-Croat conflict in central Bosnia and elsewhere. The Muslim-Croat civil war in central Bosnia was unique with respect to ends, means, and methods. What may have been true of the conflict in Herzegovina was not necessarily true of the conflict in central Bosnia, especially with respect to the motives and goals of the two sides, the resources available, or the involvement of outside forces. Neither the HVO nor the ABiH were totally integrated monolithic structures, and one cannot simply assert that attitudes and actions common to HVO leaders in Mostar were reflected unaltered by HVO leaders in Vitez or Busovaca. Similarly, the attitudes and actions of the ABiH's III Corps leaders in Zenica were not necessarily the same as those of Bosnian government leaders in Sarajevo. Moreover, the resources available to the OZCB commander were severely restricted compared to those available to the HVO commanders in Herzegovina, just as the operational situation was far different. Facile interpolations based on the situation in Herzegovina are thus very misleading and should be avoided. In the end, the Muslim-Croat civil war in central Bosnia must be judged on its own terms.

The reader familiar with the Bosnian-Croat-Serb (BCS) language will notice, too, that I have not included the usual diacritical marks to indicate the special phonetic value of certain letters in place and proper names or in the words in the very few BCS phrases included in this volume. The decision to omit such marks in the text was dictated by several factors including the inconsistency of the sources, particularly the English translations prepared by the staff of the International Criminal Tribunal for the Former Yugoslavia; my own imperfect knowledge of the BCS language; and editorial economy and simplicity. I believe the omission of the usual BCS diacritical marks will cause no problems as most English readers are familiar with the unmarked forms of the places and persons named and unfamiliar with the proper values associated with the various diacritical marks.

The complexity of events, the nature of the available sources, and the usual problems of reconstructing and interpreting the past guarantee that even the most conscientious historian is sure to make errors of both omission and commission. Such errors as may be found here are mine alone. They would have been far more numerous without the generous assistance and helpful comments of my friends and colleagues, among whom I wish to thank particularly Turner Smith Jr., Steve Sayers, Mitko Naumovski, Bob Stein, Chris Browning, Barbara Novosel, Ksenija Turkovic, Bruno Gencarelli, Stjepan Meštrović, Jim Sadkovich, Milan Gorjanc, and Miles Raguz. Special thanks are due to Bill Nelson who drew the maps. I am particularly indebted to Zeljana Zovko, Joanne Moore of the ICTY Public Information Service, and Kevin O'Sullivan of AP/Wide World Photos for their assistance in finding the photographs used to illustrate the text. I am also grateful for the cheerful assistance of Denis Bajs, Jadranka Berkec, Teri Dabney, Sonja Domjan, Tristan Kime, Ivica Kustura, Goran Selanec, and Erica Zlomislic. As always, my wife Carole deserves commendation for enduring my prolonged absences, both physical and mental, during the preparation of this study.

The Muslim-Croat Civil War in Central Bosnia

Prologue

In October, 1992, Jajce, an important town northwest of Travnik on the
main road to Banja Luka, had been under siege by the Bosnian Serb Army
(BSA) for nearly five months. A mixed garrison of Croatian Defense Council and Army of the Republic of Bosnia-Herzegovina soldiers defended
the town and its two important power stations. They were supported from
Travnik over a tenuous, narrow, twenty-five-mile-long corridor through
Serb-held territory. Reinforcements, food, ammunition, and other vital
supplies were brought forward by truck, usually at night. Constantly under
fire, the nightly convoys that snaked from Travnik along the primitive road
through rough mountain terrain barely sufficed to keep Jajce's beleaguered
garrison and civilian population alive. On October 27, 1992, the BSA's I
Krajina Corps acted to end the siege of Jajce with an all-out attack preceded
by several air strikes. The following day, Jajce's HVO defenders evacuated
their sick and wounded along with the Croat civilian residents before abandoning the town that evening. The Muslim soldiers and civilians soon followed when, on October 29, the BSA entered the town and began a program of "ethnic cleansing" that resulted in what has been called "the largest
and most wretched single exodus" of the war in Bosnia-Herzegovina.[1]

For many of the thirty thousand refugees who fled over the mountains
or down the by-then notorious "Vietnam Road" toward the relative safety
of Travnik, it was not the first time they had been forced to flee before the
BSA. Many had fled earlier to Jajce from Banja Luka, Prijedor, Sanski Most,
Kotor Varos, and other towns and villages in the Bosanska-Krajina region.
For the most part, the HVO soldiers and Croat refugees who fled Jajce filtered down into the relative safety of Herzegovina or even into Croatia itself. The twenty thousand or so Muslim refugees, on the other hand, had
no place else to go and therefore remained in Travnik, Novi Travnik, Vitez,
Busovaca, or villages near Bila and Zenica. Amidst mutual accusations of
having abandoned the defense of the city, both the HVO and the ABiH were
forced to repair the substantial military damage suffered while their respec-
tive civilian authorities were faced with the problems caused by a major influx of refugees into the central Bosnia area.

Therein lay the seeds of the coming conflict. The Muslim refugees from
Jajce posed both a problem and an opportunity for Alija Izetbegovic's government. The problem was where to relocate them. The opportunity was
a military one: the large number of military age males, well motivated for

revenge against the Serbs and equally ready to take on the Croats, provided a pool from which the ABiH could fill up existing units and form new mobile ones that would then be available to undertake offensive missions. Until the last months of 1992, the lack of mobile units trained and motivated for offensive operations had prevented the ABiH from mounting a sustained offensive action—against the BSA or anyone else.[2] However, the influx of refugees from Jajce, combined with large numbers of military-age refugees from eastern Bosnia and the arrival of fundamentalist Muslim fighters (mujahideen) from abroad, made it possible for the ABiH to form such mobile units and to contemplate offensive action on a large scale for the first time.[3]

Thus, contrary to the commonly accepted view, it was the fall of Jajce at the end of October, 1992, not the publication of the details of the Vance-Owen Peace Plan (VOPP) in January, 1993, that precipitated the Muslim-Croat conflict in central Bosnia. It was the Muslims, who had both the means and motive to strike against their erstwhile ally. The United Nations–backed VOPP proposed the division of Bosnia-Herzegovina into ten provinces, each of which—except for the one surrounding Sarajevo—would be dominated by one of the three principal ethnic groups. The plan's details were announced in December, 1992, and the supporting map was released the following month. The common but nevertheless erroneous argument is that the Muslim-Croat conflict in central Bosnia arose from the Bosnian Croats' premature and ruthless efforts to implement the plan in the central Bosnian provinces assigned to them.[4] However, that argument rests on faulty *post hoc propter hoc* reasoning unsupported by convincing factual evidence as to means, motive, and opportunity. Nor does it take into account the time required to plan and execute an offensive campaign. Open conflict between the Muslims and Croats in Central Bosnia broke out on January 14, 1993, just two days after the VOPP cantonal map was finalized in Geneva but two and one-half months after Jajce fell.

On the other hand, the temporal and causative connections between the massive influx of Muslim refugees into central Bosnia following Jajce's fall and the outbreak of the Muslim-Croat conflict are clear. Their disruptive presence in central Bosnia's towns and villages, their incorporation into the ABiH's new mobile offensive units, and the urgent need to find them living space are well-known and widely accepted facts. The role they played as the catalyst for the Muslim-Croat conflict was pointed out by Franjo Nakic, the former HVO Operative Zone Central Bosnia chief of staff, and many other witnesses appearing before the International Criminal Tribunal for the Former Yugoslavia in The Hague. As Nakic succinctly stated, "the Croats and Muslims, the local ones, would never have entered into a conflict were it not for the influx of these refugees who sought a space for themselves, having lost their own in Western and Eastern Bosnia."[5]

1 *The Operational Milieu*

Both the historical context and the physical environment in which military conflicts take place combine to shape them. The historical context—a product of the past interaction of such elements as ethnicity, religious belief, political ideology, economic conditions, and social relationships—influences both the causes and the objectives of military campaigns as well as their intensity. The physical realities of terrain, climate, prevailing weather patterns, and the nature of the man-made infrastructure, particularly the lines of communications (roads, rail lines, inland waterways, ports, and airfields), determine the nature of plans and influence their execution. Like many other conflicts, the Muslim-Croat civil war in central Bosnia in 1992–94 was shaped by both historical and physical factors, some patent and immediate, some obscure and remote.[1]

The Historical Context of the Muslim-Croat Civil War in Central Bosnia

The Muslim-Croat civil war in central Bosnia from 1992–94 arose in the immediate context of the dissolution of the Socialist Federal Republic of Yugoslavia following the death of Marshal Tito in 1980. The roots of ethnic, religious, economic, and ideological division were, of course, much deeper, and nowhere were such divisions so pronounced as in Bosnia-Herzegovina, the historic borderland between East and West. In an era in which the entire region was dissolving into its component parts, it should not have come as a surprise that the long-standing enmities existing between Muslims and Croats in Central Bosnia should have bubbled to the surface once again to fuel the fires of civil war.

The Roots of Conflict

The political and cultural division of the South Slav tribal groups destined to become the modern Slovenes, Croats, and Serbs began in the sixth and seventh centuries A.D., soon after the completion of their migration into the former Illyrian provinces of what had been the Roman Empire. All fell under the domination of more powerful cultures—Germanic, Magyar, and Byzantine Greek—which they resisted to greater or lesser degrees, but which ultimately determined their basic orientation. The Slovenes and Croats adopted the Western, Roman Catholic ways of their Germanic and Magyar overlords. The Serbs, on the other hand, adopted the Eastern, Orthodox Christian mores of the Byzantine Empire.

In the sixth century, the Slovenes' ancestors moved into the southeastern region of Germanic territory as far as what is today central Austria. Dominated by the Bavarians and the Franks from 745 to the twelfth century, they fell under the rule of the Austrian Hapsburgs in the thirteenth century and remained a constituent of the Austro-Hungarian Empire until 1918. The Croats' forefathers reached the area of modern Croatia in the sixth century. In the early tenth century, the Croat leader Tomislav established an independent Croat kingdom that incorporated most of present-day Croatia, Slavonia, Dalmatia, and Bosnia-Herzegovina. Tomislav was crowned king of the Croats by Pope John X in 925, but the unified Croat kingdom was short-lived, being subject to attack from its neighbors and riven by in-fighting among the Croatian nobles. Defeated by Hungarian king Ladislas I (1077–95) in 1091, the Croats accepted his successor, Kalman the Bookman (1095–1116) as king of both Hungary and Croatia in the so-called Pacta Conventa in 1102. Following the Battle of Mohacs and the extinction of the Arpad dynasty in 1526, the Croats chose Hapsburg prince Ferdinand (later Ferdinand I, Holy Roman Emperor, 1531–64) as king. Thenceforth, with only brief periods of quasi-independence until 1918, the Croats were ruled as part of the Austro-Hungarian Empire. Croatia retained a degree of autonomy but was generally under Hungarian control except for the so-called Military Frontier (Krajina) in eastern Croatia created by the Hapsburg emperors in 1578 as a bulwark against the Ottomans. Ruled directly from Vienna according to its own customs and laws, the Military Frontier was populated by peasants, including many Germans, Magyars, and Serbs as well as Croats, who were granted land in return for military service.

The ancestors of the modern Serbs and Montenegrins settled in the mountainous regions of the eastern Balkans in the seventh century and were nominally subjects of the Byzantine Empire, thus giving their culture an Eastern orientation. However, Serbian tribal leaders (the *zupans*) frequently sought to throw off Byzantine rule and establish an independent Serbian state. The weakness of the Byzantine Empire in the late twelfth century allowed Serbian *zupan* Stjepan Nemanya to establish an independent Serbian kingdom in 1168, which he ruled until his death in 1196. The medieval Serbian kingdom reached its apogee under Stjepan Dushan (Stjepan Urosh IV, 1331–55).

Bosnia-Herzegovina, the borderland between the Croats and the Serbs, was contested ground throughout the Middle Ages, as the Croats, Serbs, Hungarians, and finally the Ottoman Turks vied to control it. The Bosnians gained independence from Serbian domination in the mid-tenth century only to fall under Hungarian influence in 1254. In 1376, the greatest of the Bosnian rulers, King Tvrtko I (1353–91), aided by the Ottoman Turks, expanded his rule into western Serbia and took most of the Adriatic coast. However, the Bosnian kingdom created by Tvrtko I disintegrated after his death in 1391, and in 1393, the Hungarians recovered those portions of Croatia and Dalmatia that they had lost.

The invasion and eventual conquest of the Balkans by the Ottoman Turks, which began in the fourteenth century, added further complexity to the region's ethnic, political, religious, and cultural rivalries. On June 28, 1389, the Ottoman Turks under Mursad I and his son Bayazed soundly defeated a coalition of Serbs, Bosnians, Albanians, and Wallachians led by Serbian prince Lazar I in the Battle of Kosovo-Polje—"the Field of Blackbirds"—but it took the Turks until 1459 to complete their conquest of Serbia and incorporate it into the Ottoman Empire. In 1463, the Ottomans extended their conquests into Bosnia, and in 1483 they took Herzegovina. Zeta (modern Montenegro) fell in 1499.

The conquest of the Balkans by the Ottoman Turks also established the basic tripartite religious division of the Balkan peoples that still exists today. The South Slavs had been converted to Christianity by the end of the tenth century, with the Serbs in Serbia and eastern Bosnia generally accepting the Greek formulation, and the Slovenes and Croats adopting the Latin version. Religious differences between Serbs and Croats were solidified by the Great Schism of 1054 that divided Christendom into competing western Roman Catholic and eastern Greek Orthodox branches; by the domination of the Croats by the Roman Catholic Magyars; and by the nomination in 1219 of Rastko (later Saint Sava), the son of Stjepan Nemanya, as the Orthodox archbishop of the Serbs. Further dissension among the Christian populations of the region was created by the adoption of the Bogomil heresy as the official religion of the medieval Bosnian kingdom.[2]

The third major religious competitor arrived with the influx of Muslim Ottoman rulers and administrators in the fourteenth and fifteenth centuries and the subsequent conversion to Islam of many Christians desiring to preserve their political and economic status. Converts to Islam—notably the Bogomil heretics—were rewarded by their Ottoman masters with land and administrative positions, thereby establishing a pattern of political and economic power relationships that persisted into the nineteenth century as a major cause of strife in areas under Ottoman rule. Although changed and attenuated over time, the pattern was one in which a primarily agricultural population of Catholic Croats and Orthodox Serbs were dominated politically and economically by Muslim landowners, merchants, and government officials.

The Rise of Nationalism

The Slavic peoples of the Balkans were caught up in the romantic nationalist movements of the nineteenth century, movements that had as their principal goal the incorporation of culturally and linguistically similar peoples into independent nation states. Led largely by intellectuals, romantic nationalism in the region manifested itself in several forms. There was, in the first instance, a movement for the creation of a South Slav nation state that would incorporate all of the South Slav groups, but there were also more strident variants based on narrower definitions of religious and cultural identity.

Thoroughly dominated by the Germanic Roman Catholic culture of the Hapsburgs, the Slovenes nevertheless retained elements of their Slavic cultural identity that were revived in the mid-nineteenth century. Although they generally favored the concept of South Slav unity, the Slovenes remained committed until 1918 to the idea of Slovene political autonomy within the Austro-Hungarian Empire.

The unity of Roman Catholic Croats was promoted in the mid-nineteenth century by the liberal bishop of Djakovo, Josip Strossmeyer, as part of a broader program that advocated the unification of all the South Slavs. The Croatian Party of Rights—founded in 1880 by Ante Starcevic, who espoused the Croats' complete autonomy and scorned the Serbs and other South Slavic peoples as inferior—espoused a more virulent version of Croat nationalism. Starcevic's strident vision of Croat nationalism was reflected in the Ustasha movement of the 1930s and 1940s and revived again in the early 1990s with an even stronger anti-Serb bias.

The Serbs also dreamed of a "Greater Serbia," one that would gather all of the Orthodox Serbs scattered throughout the Balkans under a single independent government. Although its roots lay in the nineteenth century romantic Serbian cultural nationalism of Vuk Karadzic and the claims for Serbian leadership of the movement for South Slav unity put forward by Ilya Garashanin in the 1840s, the "Greater Serbia" movement soon took on violent and xenophobic overtones. This more virulent and exclusionary form of Serb nationalism was promoted by Kosta Pecanac in the 1920s and 1930s, refined by Stjepan Molsevic and Nikola Kalabic in the early 1940s, and resurrected by Dobrica Cosic and other prominent members of the Serbian Academy of Arts and Sciences in Belgrade in the late 1980s.

Bosnia-Herzegovina, with its mixed population of Croats (mainly in Herzegovina), Serbs (mainly in northern and eastern Bosnia), and Muslims (mainly in central Bosnia and in urban areas), failed to develop a unique national cultural identity of its own in the nineteenth century. Instead, both the advocates of "Greater Croatia" and the advocates of "Greater Serbia" coveted it. The latter also yearned to incorporate the substantial Serb population of the Croatian Krajina.

The growing sense of cultural nationalism among the South Slavs was accompanied by efforts to achieve political independence from their Ottoman and Austro-Hungarian overlords. The Croats supported the Austrian Hapsburgs in the suppression of the Hungarian revolution of 1848 and briefly obtained their independence from Magyar domination. However, the Croats were poorly paid for their efforts, and with the Compromise of 1867 and the creation of the Dual Monarchy, they were returned to Hungarian control. The Serbs were more successful. Beginning with a revolt in 1804, the Serbs—led by the competing houses of Milosh Obrenovich and Alexander Karageorgevich—achieved autonomy in 1830, followed by practical independence from their faltering Ottoman masters. Serbia's and Montenegro's formal independence was recognized on July 13, 1878, in the

Treaty of Berlin, which ended the 1877–78 war between Serbia (aided by Russia) and Turkey. Milan Obrenovich became king of the new Serbian monarchy in March, 1882, and his dynasty was replaced by that of the Karageorgevichs in 1903.

With the decay of Ottoman power in the nineteenth century, the Austro-Hungarian Empire extended its influence eastward into Bosnia-Herzegovina, for which it competed with Serbia. The Treaty of Berlin recognized the Hapsburg claim in 1878, and Bosnia-Herzegovina was occupied by Austro-Hungarian troops. Bosnia-Herzegovina was formally annexed to the Austro-Hungarian Empire in October, 1908, but the Hapsburgs left the exploitive system of Muslim landowners and administrators in place, thereby arousing the nationalist and religious animosity of Bosnian Serbs and Bosnian Croats alike. However, it was the Serbian nationalists who led the opposition to Hapsburg domination, the Croats being closer in culture and religion to the Austrian overlords.

On June 28, 1914, Gavrilo Princip, a Bosnian Serb nationalist aided by the Serbian intelligence service, assassinated Austrian archduke Franz Ferdinand and his wife in Sarajevo, thereby precipitating the First World War. Following three abortive Austrian attacks on Serbia in 1914, the Austrians, this time with German assistance, soundly defeated the Serbs in 1915. Forced to evacuate their country under fire, the Serbian government and the remnants of the Serbian Army were able to regain the lost ground with substantial aid from the western Allies operating from Salonika in 1916–18.

With the defeat and collapse of the Austro-Hungarian Empire in 1918, the resurgent Serbs annexed Bosnia-Herzegovina, and representatives of the Yugoslav peoples declared for the union of Slovenia, Croatia, and Serbia. King Nicholas of Montenegro was deposed in November, 1918, and Montenegro's national assembly declared in favor of union with Serbia. On December 4, 1918, the United Kingdom of the Serbs, Croats, and Slovenes was formally proclaimed under the regency of Serbian prince Alexander Karageorgevich. It soon became clear the Serbs would dominate the new monarchy—giving Croats, Montenegrins, Bosnians, and other minority groups reason to oppose the new state. The constitution was approved by only a slim majority of the delegates to the constitutional convention after the Croats, led by Stjepan Radic and members of his Croatian Peasants Party, and others walked out.[3]

With the death of King Peter in 1921, Alexander Karageorgevich assumed the throne as King Alexander I. He dissolved the parliament in 1929 and subsequently ruled as a dictator, renaming his realm the Kingdom of Yugoslavia. Alexander's harsh rule, coupled with preferential treatment for the Serbs, the dispossession of Bosnian Muslims in favor of Serbian war veterans, and the suppression of political opposition, prompted the creation of groups such as the Ustasha. The latter, a proto-fascist Croat independence movement formed by Ante Pavelic in 1929, drew support from Italy and was linked to similar violence-prone nationalist groups. A Macedonian nationalist linked to the Ustasha subsequently assassinated King Alexander in Marseilles in 1934, and a regency was established to rule on behalf of his eleven-year-old son, Peter.

The Second World War

The creation of an independent South Slav kingdom in 1918 fulfilled the romantic dreams of generations of South Slav nationalist intellectuals but ignored the very real differences among the new kingdom's 12 million inhabitants. Centuries of ethnic and religious hatred, economic and political exploitation, and cultural conflict had left their mark, however. The result was that the Yugoslavian kingdom was beset by internal strife from the beginning. Led by Vladimir Macek after the assassination of Stjepan Radic in 1928, the Croatian Peasants Party finally obtained the concession of Croat autonomy within the Yugoslav kingdom in 1939. That achievement did much to tamp down Croat dissension, but the Serbs resented it, and it provoked demands for similar status by other minority groups.

In March, 1941, the Yugoslav government was forced to sign the Tripartite Pact with Nazi Germany and Fascist Italy. The government's actions provoked a successful coup by Yugoslav army officers on March 27. King Peter was subsequently declared of age, and Prince Paul's regency ended. Although the new Yugoslavian government did not renounce the treaty with the Axis powers, Germany sought to further ensure the protection of its southern flank as it went to the aid of Italy in Greece and mounted its attack against the Soviet Union. Accordingly, Germany, Italy, Hungary, and Bulgaria invaded Yugoslavia on April 6, 1941. Quick to seize upon the divisions in Yugoslavian society, the Axis powers successfully played one group against another, and an armistice favorable to the Axis was signed on April 17, 1941.

Slovenia was divided up among the Axis powers, and Ante Pavelic and the Ustasha, interned by Italy since 1934, were put in charge of the newly created Independent State of Croatia (Nezavisna Drzava Hrvatska [NDH]). Opposed by Vladmir Macek and the Croat Peasant Party, which controlled the rural areas, Pavelic's fascists annexed Bosnia, ceded a large part of the Dalmatian coast and other areas to Italy, and focused on eliminating their Serbian enemies.

Yugoslavian Muslims also collaborated enthusiastically with the Nazis, a fact often suppressed by today's Bosniaks and their supporters. Many Muslims joined the Ustasha, and three divisions of Muslim volunteers served with the German forces, the best known being the 13th Waffen-SS Mountain Division "Handschar," raised primarily in Bosnia-Herzegovina.[4]

Although many Croats and Muslims supported the Axis powers, most Serbs favored the anti-Croat and anti-Communist Chetnik forces led by Col. Dragoljub "Draza" Mihailovic, sometime minister of war in the Yugoslavian government in exile. The British supplied Mihailovic's Chetnik guerrilla army until they decided to shift their support to Croatia-born Josip Broz Tito and his Communist partisans. The British view was that Tito's partisans, most of whom were Croats, were more effective in opposing the Axis occupation forces. Even so, the partisans devoted a good deal of their effort to destroying their Chetnik and Ustasha rivals. Indeed, the fascist Ustasha, the royalist Chetniks, and the Communist partisans murdered, imprisoned, and otherwise oppressed each other with equal zeal and abandon, thereby exacerbating the existing divisions and hatreds. According to one estimate, some 1.8 million Yugoslavs were dead by 1945, about 11 percent of the pre-war population.[5]

The Rise and Fall of the Socialist Federal Republic of Yugoslavia

Given the existing divisions within the Yugoslavian state, the discipline and focus of Tito and his Communist partisans won out, and they emerged as the dominant force after World War II. On November 29, 1945, Tito proclaimed the Socialist Federal Republic of Yugoslavia (SFRY) and quickly moved to suppress ethnic and religious nationalism and enforce socialist unity on his fractious countrymen. The Tito-led government subsequently created six republics—Slovenia, Croatia, Serbia, Montenegro, Macedonia, and Bosnia-Herzegovina—as constituent parts of the Yugoslav federation. In 1971, Tito recognized the Muslims of Bosnia-Herzegovina as a distinct ethnic group, and Yugoslavia's 1974 constitution established the autonomous regions of Vojvodina and Kosovo.

Despite Tito's strong efforts to suppress ethnic separatism and internal strife, the conflict between Serbs, Croats, and Muslims simmered just beneath the surface, fueled by the fevered dreams of exclusionist Serbian and Croatian nationalists, the deteriorating economic conditions, and demands for political reform. Speculation was rampant about the possible disintegration of Yugoslavia that was sure to follow Tito's demise. Yet the reality proved to be worse than anyone had feared. With Tito's death in 1980, the long-suppressed nationalism of the SFRY's component elements exploded. Resurgent Serbian nationalism, fanned by the revival of the "Greater Serbia" ideology of Dobrica Cosic and his ilk, was compounded by the machinations of Slobodan Milosevic, who skillfully manipulated the frustrations and anxieties of the Serbs—which were attributable to the fact that Serbia, with 40 percent of the population, had only one-eighth of the republic's voting power.[6] Nevertheless, the Serbs generally supported the continuation of central control embodied in the SFRY, as did the Serbian-dominated Yugoslavian National Army (JNA), often described as "the last bastion of Titoism."[7] At the same time, the Slovenes, Croats, Macedonians, and Muslims, spurred on by nationalist aspirations for independence, were all eager to throw off the Serbian yoke. This centrifugal trend coincided with the ferment of the revolution sweeping the Communists from power in Eastern Europe, but the Yugoslavian elections in early 1990 returned six new presidents for the six constituent republics of the SFRY, only one of whom, Alija Izetbegovic of Bosnia-Herzegovina, was not a former Communist. Slobodan Milosevic, an advocate of "Greater Serbia," became president of Serbia, and Franjo Tudjman, an advocate of "Greater Croatia," became president of Croatia.

The SFRY's dissolution began with the Republics of Slovenia and Croatia declaring their independence on June 25, 1991. Both new republics were recognized by the European Union (EU) in January, 1992, and by the United States that April. However, the Serbian-dominated rump Federal Republic of Yugoslavia (FRY) was unwilling to let either state go without a fight.[8] Slovenia, distant from Belgrade and without significant minorities, was prepared to defend her independence by force, and after the Serbian-led JNA lost several skirmishes to the well-armed, well-trained, thirty-five-thousand-man Slovenian territorial defense force, the withdrawal of JNA troops was negotiated.[9] Slovenia then proceeded to make good its independence and fortunately remained outside the bloody conflict that engulfed first Croatia and then Bosnia-Herzegovina.[10]

The new Republic of Croatia was less well prepared to resist the Serbian onslaught, particularly in view of its significant Serbian minority population in the eastern Krajina region. In the summer of 1991, the Serbs in Croatia, aided directly by Serbia, the rump FRY, and the JNA, rebelled, seized 30 percent of Croatia's territory by September, 1991, and proclaimed their own independent "Republic of Serbian Krajina."[11] The fighting was horrific, and both sides committed atrocities—although the Serbs showed themselves to be masters of massacre, rape, concentration camp operations, and the techniques of ethnic cleansing.

Under pressure from the United Nations, the United States, and the states of the European Union, the JNA agreed to withdraw from Croatia at the end of 1991. Unfortunately, the UN/U.S./EU intervention served mainly to confirm the Serbian rebels' seizure of territory, a situation that was not corrected by the temporary peace agreement brokered by UN envoy Cyrus Vance and signed in February, 1992.[12] In accordance with UN Security Council Resolution (UNSCR) 743, United Nations Protective Force (UNPROFOR) I was deployed to Croatia in March, 1992, to enforce the cease-fire. Four UN-controlled Protected Areas (UNPA)—Sectors North, South, East, and West—were established, heavy weapons were turned over to the UNPROFOR by both sides, and the open conflict subsided. However, the Krajina Serbs continued to engage in the ethnic cleansing of Croats in the areas under their control (the so-called pink areas), and fighting continued between the Krajina Serbs and Croatian forces. In January, 1993, President Tudjman, fed up with the UN peacekeeping forces' ineffectiveness and angered by continued Serbian/FRY interference, launched rearmed Croatian forces on a one-hundred-kilometer front in northern Dalmatia, and the Croatian army regained sovereign control over Sectors North, South, and West.[13]

Meanwhile, in Bosnia-Herzegovina, independence was proclaimed on March 3, 1992, following a referendum on February 29 supported by Bosnian Muslims and Croats. On April 7, the United States recognized the new Republic of Bosnia-Herzegovina (RBiH). The Bosnian Serbs boycotted the referendum on independence, however, and their leader, Radovan Karadzic, immediately demanded national self-determination and the right to join with Serbia. With the overt aid of Serbia, the rump FRY, and the JNA, the Bosnian Serbs quickly formed the Bosnian Serb army and proceeded to seize some 70 percent of Bosnia-Herzegovina's national territory by force of arms accompanied by a terror campaign of ethnic cleansing against the Muslim and Croat populations in the newly proclaimed "Serbian Republic of Bosnia-Herzegovina."[14] By the middle of 1992, the BSA, aided by the JNA, had surrounded Bosnia-Herzegovina's Muslim and Croat defenders and begun slowly compressing them into a number of slowly shrinking enclaves.

A conference was held in London on August 26 to coordinate UN and European Community (EC) efforts to pressure the Serbs to abandon their support of the aggressive actions of ethnic Serbs in Croatia and Bosnia-Herzegovina. In October, UNPROFOR II forces were deployed to Bosnia-Herzegovina ostensibly for the purpose of facilitating the delivery of humanitarian relief supplies to the victims of the ongoing conflict between Bosnian Serbs and the Muslim-Croat alliance. At the same time the EC deployed a force of unarmed observers, for the most part military officers with intelligence backgrounds, to monitor the situation and, where possible, facilitate cease-fire arrangements. Focused on preventing the breakup of Bosnia-Herzegovina into its three natural constituent parts, the UN, the United States, and the EU supported a series of peace plans for Bosnia-Herzegovina—most notably the Vance-Owen Peace Plan revealed in January, 1993—none of which met the wholehearted approval of all the warring factions. Indeed, only the Bosnian Croats supported all of the peace proposals advanced by the UN and the EU.

From March, 1992, until the end of the year, Alija Izetbegovic's RBiH government in Sarajevo struggled to get organized, form an effective military force, and establish some defense against the Serb onslaught. During that period, it was expedient for the Muslim-dominated central government to cooperate with the Bosnian Croats (who had organized themselves as the Croat Community of Herceg-Bosna) against the common enemy. Such an alliance was all the more desirable in that, with admirable foresight, the Bosnian Croats—forewarned by the earlier JNA attacks on Slovenia and Croatia—had already begun to form a military force, the Croatian Defense Council, to defend their territory from expected Serb/JNA aggression.[15] However, by the end of the year, relations between the two allies had begun to deteriorate at an ever-accelerating pace. Radical Muslims in central Bosnia, frustrated by the Serbs but emboldened by the growing strength of the Army of Bosnia-Herzegovina and reinforced by Muslim refugees from the fighting in the Krajina and eastern Bosnia as well as by fanatical mujahideen from abroad, were planning an open attack on their erstwhile ally, the Bosnian Croats.

The Physical Environment of Central Bosnia

Central Bosnia's terrain and climate had a definite impact on the planning and conduct of military operations during the Muslim-Croat conflict of 1992–94. Moreover, the region's transportation and industrial infrastructure, both the lines of communication and the factories for military production, were themselves primary objectives for both sides and thus became the principal focal points of the conflict.

Terrain and Climate

Some 70–80 percent of the former Yugoslavia is mountainous, the highest point in the northwest being some twenty-nine hundred meters above sea level.[16] In general, there are three landforms: the northern plains, the interior highlands, and the Adriatic coast. The Republic of Bosnia-Herzegovina falls almost entirely in the interior highlands region, which extends some 970 kilometers from northwest to southeast and some 550 kilometers from east to west. Central Bosnia's topography is very similar to Korea or West Virginia, with high mountains covered with birch, ash, oak, and a variety of coniferous trees; steep *karst* hills and ridges; narrow, well-watered valleys; and numerous deep ravines. The major watercourses in the region (the Una, Vrbas, Bosna, and Drina Rivers) drain northward into the Sava River and thence via the Danube to the Black Sea. Their upper courses lie in parallel valleys running from southeast to northwest and dividing central Bosnia into a number of compartments.

In general, the climate of most of the former Yugoslavia is similar to that of the northern continental United States, with warm, rainy summers and cold winters. The winters in central Bosnia are normally quite harsh with significant snowfall and ice. The mean summer temperature at lower elevations is in the low seventies to low nineties Fahrenheit, while the mean winter temperature at lower elevations ranges from the middle teens to the low fifties Fahrenheit. The interior highlands are, of course, cooler in both summer and winter. Relative humidity is highest in autumn and winter and lowest in summer, ranging from 60–95 percent in the mountains. Surface winds are normally light and variable, but the cold winter wind known as the Bora can significantly lower temperatures, and drifting snow and blizzard conditions can occur any time in the mountains during the winter.

Central Bosnia's rugged topography and harsh climate, coupled with a road net largely restricted to the main valleys and passes, make military operations difficult in any season. Cross-country vehicular movement is limited throughout the year, although movement for both wheeled and tracked vehicles is generally easier in the summer and fall than in the winter and early spring—when ice, deep snow, mud, flooding streams, and landslides restrict vehicular traffic even on the few available improved roads. A 1954 U.S. Army historical study of World War II German counter-guerrilla operations in the Balkans noted: "The most important physical

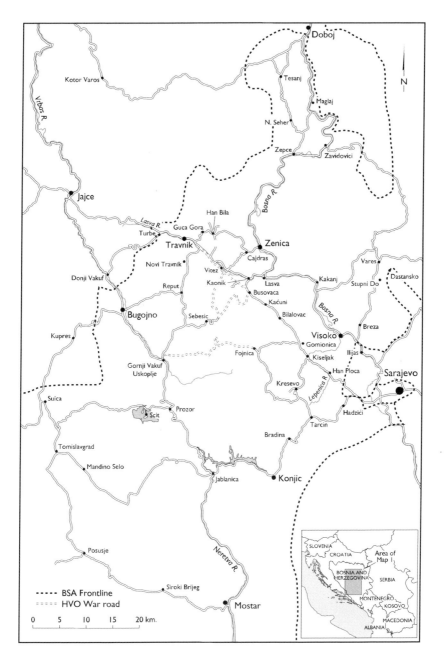

Map 1. Central Bosnia. *Map by Bill Nelson.*

feature of the Balkans as a scene of military operations is its wild terrain. The brushy mountain country, craggy peaks, and roadless forest areas offer irregular troops numerous places to hide, opportunity to shift forces unseen even from the air, and locations for ambush."[17]

The Lasva Valley

The focal point of the fighting between the Bosnian Croats and Muslims in central Bosnia in 1992–94 was the Lasva Valley. The valley itself is quite small, ranging from six-tenths to three miles (one to five kilometers) in width, and some eighteen miles (thirty kilometers) in length from Travnik to Kaonik. The Lasva River, from which the valley takes its name, is really only a creek or stream in American terms. It rises in the mountains north and west of Travnik to flow from northwest to southeast, emptying at its eastern end into the Bosna River. The Lasva is joined at Kaonik by the Kozica River, which flows from the southeast and along which are situated the key towns of Busovaca and, at its junction with the Lepenica River, Kiseljak. Within the Lasva Valley—or adjacent to it— are the towns of Travnik, Novi Travnik, and Vitez, as well as a large number of small villages both on the valley floor and on the slopes of the surrounding mountains.

When first viewing the Lasva Valley, the student of military history is immediately struck by the similarity of the Bosnian Croat positions on the valley floor in 1993 and the entrenched French camp at Dien Bien Phu in 1954. In fact, the valley of the Nam Yum is only about half as long as that of the Lasva (ten miles versus eighteen miles) but is generally twice as wide (three and one-half to five miles versus six-tenths to three miles).[18] The most striking correspondence, however, is the tactical disadvantage at which some eight thousand Croat combatants on the valley floor dominated by much more numerous Muslim forces holding the surrounding heights found themselves, just as the fifteen thousand French Union troops at Dien Bien Phu were dominated by some fifty thousand Vietminh soldiers on the surrounding hills. The major difference, of course, is that the French Union forces at Dien Bien Phu were not defending their homes and hearths. Everyone knows what happened to the French when they failed to root out the Vietminh in the heights. One can hardly blame the Croat defenders for wanting to avoid the same fate and thus acting aggressively to clear the hills surrounding the Lasva Valley of Muslim forces.

Population

The population of Bosnia-Herzegovina in March, 1991, was some 4,364,000 people—slightly less than the state of Georgia—and its population density was some 85.6 souls per square kilometer.[19] The limestone composition of the mountains in central Bosnia makes farming difficult and unable to support a large population. Settlement is sparse outside of towns, and villages tend to be small and relatively isolated.

In 1991, the ethnic distribution of Bosnia-Herzegovina's population was approximately 44 percent Bosniak (Muslim), 33 percent Serb, and 17 percent Croat.[20] In general, Bosnian Croat villages and towns occupy the valley floors, whereas Muslim villages are located on the slopes of nearby mountains and hills. Given such conditions, the few major lines of communications passing through the valleys and their populated areas assume great importance—as do passes, bridges, and other choke points.

Key Strategic Features

Like many other conflicts, the civil war in central Bosnia in 1992–94 was a war of logistics. The principal objectives for both sides were logistical in nature: the control of military industrial facilities and of the key lines of communications (LOCs). Both were of overwhelming importance for the HVO and ABiH. Following the arms embargo imposed on the former Yugoslavia by the UN Security Council in September, 1991, the obtaining of necessary arms, ammunition, and other military equipment needed to fend off the Serbian aggression was a main preoccupation of the RBiH government, and it became a major consideration for the HVO as well. The vital LOCs connecting central Bosnia with the Dalmatian coast and the outside world thus assumed critical importance, the more so in that they also linked the principal military production facilities of the former Yugoslavia located in central Bosnia and northern Herzegovina. Thus, the military factories in the region and the LOCs through central Bosnia became the principal prizes over which the Croat and Muslim forces contested.

Military Industrial Facilities The majority of the military production facilities in Bosnia-Herzegovina were in the Lasva Valley or arrayed on its periphery.[21] All had been established by the JNA before Yugoslavia disintegrated, and they formed a military industrial chain, most of which was concentrated in central Bosnia. For the most part, these plants for the manufacturing of war matériel fell into the ABiH's hands in 1991 and 1992, but the most important of them remained in the HVO's hands throughout the period.

Arrayed north and south of the Lasva Valley were a number of military factories, all controlled by the ABiH. The Zenica Ironworks manufactured castings for all calibers of shells and charges. The IGM factory in Konjic manufactured ammunition from 7.62-mm to 12.7-mm as well as shells for 20-mm and 40-mm antiaircraft guns. A factory in Bugojno produced antitank and antipersonnel mines, fuses for projectiles and mines, and hand grenades. Among the former JNA manufacturing facilities in or on the edge of the Lasva Valley itself and controlled by the ABiH, the Bratstvo factory in Novi Travnik manufactured artillery pieces ranging from 60-mm to 152-mm, 128-mm rocket launchers, and Oganj and Vatra rocket systems, as well as the improved 152-mm gun-howitzer known as "NORA." The Technical and Maintenance Institute at Travnik manufactured signal equipment and command and control vehicles for use at brigade level. Also in Travnik were a communications repair shop and a factory that produced uniforms, military boots, and other equipment.

The most important of the military production facilities in central Bosnia was the Slobodan Princip Seljo (SPS) factory in Vitez. The SPS factory manufactured military explosives essential for the production of mortar and artillery shells. It was the only such manufacturing facility in the Balkans, and it was the only important military production facility controlled by the HVO forces. The Vitez explosives factory, located just west of the town in a draw flanked by the villages of Donja Veceriska and Gacice and mostly underground, was the key to the entire chain of military production in Bosnia-Herzegovina. Without it, the other arms manufacturing facilities were largely useless. The importance of the SPS explosives factory to the ABiH was signaled during talks in Bonn, Germany, between Pres. Alija Izetbegovic of Bosnia-Herzegovina and Pres. Franjo Tudjman of Croatia in January, 1993. In a message to the UN secretary general, negotiator Thorvald Stoltenberg noted: "In the talks he had with Tudjman in our presence, Izetbegovic insisted the Croats must leave Vitez because it had an ammunition plant that the Muslims must have. Tudjman replied that the Muslims will never have the plant and will never be able to take Vitez militarily. However, if they did, the plant would be blown up."[22] Although the SPS explosives plant was the main objective of ABiH offensives in the Lasva Valley throughout 1993, it was never taken and remained in the HVO's hands at the time of the Washington Agreements in February, 1994.

Lines of Communication Both the ABiH and the HVO depended heavily on the lines of communication from the Adriatic coast to and through central Bosnia not only for the importation of war matériel, but for food and other supplies for the civilian population as well. Of vital importance to both the ABiH and the HVO, these LOCs were few in number, vulnerable to interdiction, and often steep and difficult to negotiate. In Roman times the Via Bosnae, the most important Roman route across the Balkans from Ljubljana in the northwest to Thessalonika in the southeast, ran through the Lasva Valley from Travnik to Sarajevo. As shown on Map 1, the Lasva Valley sits astride the principal routes from the coast and Herzegovina to northern and eastern Bosnia. Through it runs the only east-west route through central Bosnia from Travnik via Vitez, Kaonik, Busovaca, and Kiseljak to Sarajevo. Thus, for both the HVO and the ABiH, control of the Lasva Valley was the key to controlling the vital lifelines to the outside world.

Entry into the Lasva Valley from the north can be accomplished by four routes: the main road from Banja Luka via Jajce and Turbe to Travnik (the old Roman Via Bosnae); the road from Poljanice via Han Bila that connects with the main route through the Lasva Valley just to the northeast of Stari Bila; the road from Zenica via Cajdras and Sivrino Selo that joins the Lasva Valley road at Dubravica just east of Vitez; and the road from Zenica along the Bosna River that turns west at the junction of the Lasva and Bosna Rivers and enters the valley via Grablje, Strane, and Kaonik.

During the Muslim-Croat conflict in 1992–94, central Bosnia could be reached from the Dalmatian coast and Herzegovina to the south by five routes, all except one of which passed through Jablanica.[23] From Split, the principal port of entry for Bosnia-Herzegovina, the main route for all traffic to Jablanica (Route CIRCLE) ran via Brnaze and Kamensko to Tomislav-grad and thence to Mandino Selo. From Mandino Selo the main road continued to Jablanica and thence to Prozor (Route SQUARE), but it was also possible to go directly from Mandino Selo to Prozor (Route TRIANGLE). The easternmost (Konjic–Hadzici–Sarajevo–Visoko) and westernmost (Bugojno–Donji Vakuf–Turbe–Travnik) routes from Jablanica into central Bosnia were both in the BSA's hands for most of the period under consideration and were thus not available to either the HVO or the ABiH. The route from Jablanica through Bugojno via Reput to Novi Travnik was apparently little used even before the ABiH took Bugojno thereby closing that route to the HVO altogether. Once the ABiH took Konjic, a significant portion of the route from Jablanica via Konjic, Kresevo, Kiseljak, Busovaca, Kaonik to the Puticevo intersection (Route PACMAN) was also denied to the HVO, which in turn blocked the road south of Kresevo thereby denying its use to the ABiH as well. Thus, the route from Jablanica via Gornji Vakuf (Uskoplje) and Reput through Novi Travnik to the Puticevo intersection with the road running down the Lasva Valley (Route DIA-MOND) was the main supply route from Herzegovina to central Bosnia over which flowed the bulk of UN relief cargo as well as a small amount of commercial traffic. It was also the principal resupply route for UNPRO-FOR forces, and the British Royal Engineers improved and maintained it during the entire period.[24] From April 14, 1993, neither the ABiH nor the HVO had free use of this critical LOC because each held various segments of its length. The HVO held the termini at Gornji Vakuf and Novi Travnik, and the ABiH held the center section.

During the course of the Croat-Muslim conflict in central Bosnia, both sides constructed a number of alternative "war roads" to replace routes lost to the enemy or unusable because they were under direct observation and fire from the other side. The HVO built two such routes into the Lasva Valley from the south. The first ran from Prozor to Gornji Vakuf and then across the mountains to Fojnica. Called the "Road of Hope" by the HVO, this road was known to UNPROFOR as Route SALMON. Another HVO resupply route ran from Gornji Vakuf over the hills northeast to Sebesic, where it split— one path continuing on to Vitez and another to Busovaca.[25] Not suitable for vehicular traffic, the HVO used this route primarily to move essential supplies on horses and mules.

The main route through the Lasva Valley itself was used extensively during the war, but because it was vulnerable to attack from the hills north of the road, the HVO built a war road on the south side of the Lasva River running from Novi Travnik via Vitez to Busovaca. Despite sustained attempts by the ABiH to interdict it, this route remained open to HVO vehicular traffic from Vitez via Rijeka and Rovna to Busovaca as late as mid-January, 1994. Both sides constructed numerous other local war roads because they were needed to support particular locations and operations.

2 *Organization of the Opposing Forces*

The Muslim-Croat conflict in central Bosnia in 1992–94 was fought by two newly formed militia armies, neither of which had appropriate experience; sufficient training; sound organization; effective command, control, and communications (C³); established doctrine; or adequate logistical support. Both armies were primarily light infantry forces with minimal combat support (artillery, air defense, engineers, signal). Both had only rudimentary combat service support (logistical) systems that were barely a step above living off the land. Transportation and medical services were barely adequate, and neither side could boast of air support or aerial transport worthy of the name. Both the Croatian Defense Council forces and the forces of the Army of Bosnia-Herzegovina evolved from the Territorial Defense (TO) organization of the former Yugoslavian National Army (JNA). They thus shared elements of a common defense policy, strategic and tactical doctrine, organizational structures, administrative methods, and other holdovers from the JNA. To the degree that any of their officers had formal military training or experience, it had been obtained in the JNA, usually in the form of brief active duty training followed by service in the TO forces. On the whole, there were few officers in either the HVO or the ABiH who had risen much beyond captain first class in the JNA, although each army had a sprinkling of career JNA officers in its ranks. Formal military training of any kind was at a premium at all levels. When open conflict broke out between Croat and Muslim forces in central Bosnia in January, 1993, neither the HVO nor the ABiH had been in existence as a separate entity for a full year. Armies take time to work out organizational and administrative problems, to develop an effective combat style and competency, and to develop and impose rules and regulations. That time was not available either to the HVO or to the ABiH, and the consequences were all too obvious.

Comparative Manpower

The surviving public documentation for determining the comparative strength of HVO and ABiH forces in central Bosnia during the Muslim-Croat conflict between November, 1992, and March, 1994, is sparse and unreliable. Equally hard to find is documentation concerning the deployment of those forces with respect to the front lines against Bosnian Serb aggression. In late February, 1993, the European Community Monitoring Mission (ECMM) estimated the HVO's overall strength in Bosnia-

Herzegovina at some 45,000–55,000 men well-equipped with both armor and artillery.[1] The ABiH forces were estimated to be only slightly larger: 50,000–60,000 men in five corps areas, to which were added an unspecified number of militia and paramilitary forces. At the same time, active Bosnian Serb forces were estimated to be some 70,000–80,000 strong, divided into six corps, and equipped with some three hundred tanks and six hundred artillery pieces, as well as short-range surface-to-surface missiles and extensive air assets that included MiG-21 fighters.

Other estimates placed the relative numbers somewhat higher. For example, military historian Edgar O'Ballance, relying on a German intelligence estimate, put the comparative numbers in November-December, 1992, at 30,000 HVO militiamen supplemented by about 40,000 mobilized policemen; around 100,000 men in the ABiH; and a Bosnian Serb army of some 90,000 "regulars" and 20,000 paramilitary troops.[2] The normally reliable International Institute for Strategic Studies (IISS) in London, probably working with UN and ECMM figures, estimated that the HVO had 50,000 men and the ABiH 30,000–50,000 in the 1992–93 edition of *The Military Balance*.[3] In the 1993–94 edition, the HVO numbers remained the same (50,000 men in some thirty infantry brigades and one special forces brigade), but the ABiH figures were revised upward to some 60,000 men organized under five corps headquarters with some fifty-nine infantry brigades, four mechanized brigades, seven mountain brigades, a special forces brigade, an artillery brigade, and two air defense regiments.[4] The IISS figures included only "regular" forces. The HVO Main Staff itself put the ration strength of the HVO on February 23, 1993, at 34,080 officers and men, including some 6,000 in Operative Zone Southeast Herzegovina, 8,700 in Operative Zone Northwest Herzegovina, 8,750 in Operative Zone Central Bosnia, and 10,630 in other locations.[5]

The ABiH's strength as reported by the IISS and various journalists and commentators may have been underestimated by a significant amount inasmuch as their primary of source of data was the government of Bosnia-Herzegovina, which had an interest in understating the number of men under arms so as to encourage sympathy for the embattled republic. In fact, Sefer Halilovic, the ABiH commander, put his army's total military strength, including Territorial Defense and reserve forces, at about 168,500 in August, 1992, and 261,500 in January, 1993.[6] According to Halilovic, the overall total remained at about 261,500 throughout 1993, but by the end of 1994 casualties, desertion, and leaves had reduced the total to about 228,368, of whom 130,050 were on the front lines, 58,089 in other designated positions, and 19,126 on leave. The remainder were sick, abroad, deserted, or absent without leave (AWOL).[7]

The correlation of forces with respect to manpower was somewhat less favorable to the HVO in central Bosnia. The HVO's estimates place the comparative strengths of the two forces in the spring of 1993 at 8,000–8,200 for the HVO Operative Zone Central Bosnia (OZCB) to 82,000–84,000 for the

ABiH III Corps, a ratio of more than 10:1 in favor of the ABiH.[8] However, the actual disproportion was probably considerably less. In fact, the ABiH III Corps's headquarters (HQ), reported in 1997 that its authorized strength during the period November, 1992, to April, 1993, was approximately 26,182 officers and men.[9] As noted above, the OZCB's ration strength was 8,750 on February 23, 1993. Using those figures, a quick calculation yields a ratio of about 3:1 in favor of the ABiH. Although the HVO was able to muster favorable force ratios on a local basis, the ABiH III Corps had a significant advantage in manpower resources throughout the Muslim-Croat conflict in central Bosnia. The III Corps area of operations was larger than that of the HVO OZCB, and some III Corps units were deployed against HVO forces in Operative Zone Northwest Herzegovina. On the other hand, troops from those units, as well as Muslim forces from the other ABiH corps areas (particularly the I, VI, and VII Corps) were frequently deployed against the HVO in central Bosnia. Nonetheless, HQ, OZCB, could still muster near equivalence with III Corps on a place-by-place basis at various times. For example, in February, 1993, HQ, OZCB, reported ratios of forces in contact in the Busovaca area as 1,500 ABiH to 1,395 HVO (1.1:1); in the Novi Travnik area as 1,800 ABiH to 1,160 HVO (1.6:1); in the Travnik area as 4,000 ABiH to 1,701 HVO (2.4:1); and in the Vitez area as 2,000 ABiH to 2,279 HVO (1:1.2).[10] However, such favorable force ratios are apt to be misleading in that the reserves not in contact available to the ABiH III Corps were substantial, whereas the HVO was fully committed.

As time went on, the basic disproportion grew in favor of the Muslims as the ABiH increased in strength while the HVO forces in central Bosnia declined in number due to casualties and other losses. While the HVO was unable to find replacements, the ABiH was constantly being augmented by the influx of large numbers of Muslim refugees entering central Bosnia after having been expelled from eastern Bosnia and the Krajina by the BSA. For example, at the end of 1992, some twenty thousand Muslim refugees from the Jajce area settled in central Bosnia, providing a large number of well-motivated military-age men to fill out ABiH units and create several new, mobile brigades that could be used for offensive operations outside a given territorial home base. Despite the lack of HVO manpower throughout Bosnia-Herzegovina and particularly in central Bosnia, the Croatian Defense Council's headquarters in Mostar did not declare full mobilization until June 10, 1993.[11]

In light of the later Muslim-Croat conflict, a good deal of controversy has arisen as to the exact proportion of effort dedicated to the defense against the BSA applied by the HVO and the ABiH, particularly on the western front, first in the Jajce area, and after the fall of Jajce on October 30, 1992, in the Turbe-Travnik area. Croatian Defense Council authorities have charged that the Muslims refused to participate fully on the front lines against the Serbs in part because they were focused on organizing, arming, and training the forces needed to pursue their strategic plan for an offensive to clear the Bosnian Croats from central Bosnia.[12] For their part, the Muslims made similar accusations against the HVO and also accused the HVO of abandoning the fight against the Serbs altogether, at Jajce and elsewhere.[13]

Neither the HVO's claims nor those of the ABiH are entirely correct or entirely wrong. In 1993, the greater portion of the ABiH forces in central Bosnia deployed against the BSA were stationed on the Visoko-Sarajevo front, while the HVO forces deployed against the BSA were stationed primarily on the Turbe-Travnik front.[14] However, a substantial portion of the ABiH III Corps was deployed in positions surrounding the Croat enclaves in the Travnik–Novi Travnik–Vitez-Busovaca-Kiseljak area, far from the BSA's front lines. As for Muslim charges that the Croats abandoned the line against the Serbs at Jajce and elsewhere, it is true that HVO forces in Jajce in October, 1992, recognized that the town was on the verge of falling to the BSA and withdrew first. However, HVO forces on the Turbe-Travnik line did not abandon their positions to the BSA in June, 1993, as the Muslims have charged. In fact, they were attacked from the rear by the ABiH and forced to abandon their positions and flee across the front lines into the hands of the BSA.[15]

The actual number of troops stationed on the Travnik front by the HVO and the ABiH at any given time in 1992 and 1993 varied from day to day, and the proportion of the defense provided by each force cannot be determined with any accuracy. Brigadier Ivica Zeko, the former HQ, OZCB, intelligence officer, said that until April, 1993, the ABiH III Corps—with some 80,000 troops at its disposal—put only a minuscule number, some 1,500–1,700 men, in the lines against the BSA in the Travnik area, but added that there was not really much room on the front for many more Muslim troops.[16] Meanwhile, another HVO veteran of the fighting on the Travnik front noted that by April, 1993, the HVO had one three-battalion brigade and one two-battalion brigade, a total of some 2,500–3,000 men, on line, whereas the ABiH had two local brigades (the 306th and 312th Mountain Brigades), the 1st and 17th Krajina Mountain Brigades, and elements of the 7th Muslim Motorized Brigade on the Travnik line under the control of Gen. Mehmed Alagic.[17]

Assuming that the ABiH brigades were manned at roughly the same level as the HVO's, the total number of Muslim soldiers in the Travnik defenses would have been at least eight thousand to ten thousand. In any event, the one thing the ABiH had plenty of was manpower, and the number of men available to the commander of the ABiH III Corps were sufficient to man the Muslim portion of the Travnik defense line while simultaneously undertaking a program for the organization, arming, and training of mobile forces for a possible offensive against the Croats in central Bosnia.

Organization of the Croatian Defense Forces

The organization, arming, and military training of the Croat community in Bosnia-Herzegovina began in 1991 when the Bosnian Croats realized that they were next on the Serb agenda and that the newly independent Republic of Bosnia-Herzegovina's government, led by Alija Izetbegovic, and its Muslim population were either incapable of or unwilling to take decisive defensive measures against a probable attack by the Bosnian Serbs and their allies.[18] At the time, the Muslim-dominated government in Sarajevo was declaring that "it is not our war," and HVO veterans later charged that Izetbegovic was actually cooperating with the Serbs. Even the ABiH's chief of staff, Sefer Halilovic, has expressed disgust with Izetbegovic's coterie of Serbian agents, confidence in the JNA's good intentions, and refusal to take even the most basic steps to organize his country for defense.[19] Moreover, the apparent emphasis Izetbegovic placed on Islam as the foundation of the new Republic of Bosnia-Herzegovina was taken as a threat to the continued existence and freedom of the Catholic Croat community in Bosnia-Herzegovina.

Creation of the HVO

The civilian element of the Croatian Defense Council of the Croatian Community of Herceg-Bosna (HZ HB) was formally established on April 8, 1992, to coordinate the work of the local municipal Bosnian Croat military forces. The civilian element of the HVO was envisioned as the highest executive and administrative authority of the HZ HB's territory, but it was intended as only a temporary expedient, necessary until the RBiH government assumed responsibility for protecting all of the new nation's citizens.[20] The legal justification for the formation of an autonomous military force was seen in the provisions of the laws of the former Socialist Federal Republic of Yugoslavia that authorized the citizens and their civic organizations to organize for their own self-defense when their government could not or would not defend them adequately. Bosnian Croat political leader Mate Boban later claimed that the HVO was formed because "thirteen Croatian villages in the municipality of Trebinje—including Ravno—were destroyed and the Bosnian government did nothing thereafter."[21] The creation of the HVO was thus a protective reaction rather than an aggressive step toward the dissolution of the RBiH.

The HVO's military element came into existence formally on May 15, 1992, with the establishment of the HVO Department of Defense, although some elements, including the HVO Main Staff, the Main Logistics Base at Grude, the Military Police, and the Personnel Administration, had been created earlier, and some HVO combat units had already been formed.[22] The emerging HVO defense organization generally followed the old JNA Territorial Defense pattern both at the higher (regional) level and at the local level. Figure 2–1 shows the overall organization of the Croatian Defense Council in its developed form.

Inasmuch as the Bosnian Muslims had taken over the old JNA Territorial Defense organization and then allowed the JNA to disarm it, the Bosnian Croats had to set up local defense units from scratch, evolving them from so-called crisis staffs, flowing from the extant Croatian

Fig. 2-1. Organization of the Croatian Defense Council (HVO)

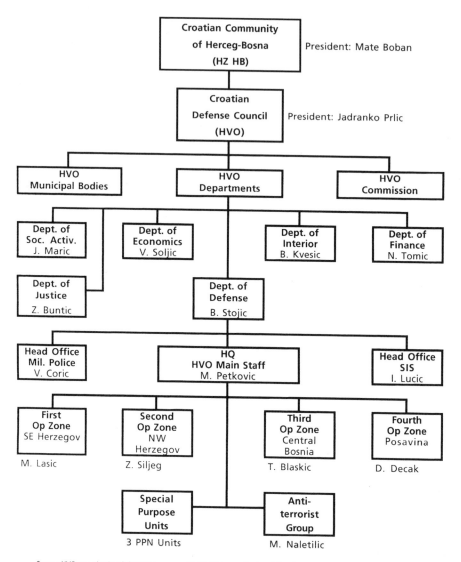

Source: HVO organizational chart (n.a., n.p., n.d.), B D497; organizational chart "Structure of the HZ H-B. 1992–1993" (n.a., n.p., n.d.), B D251. Note that the Military Police and the Security Information Service (SIS) were controlled directly by the HVO Department of Defense, whereas the Special Purpose Units (PPN) were controlled directly by the HQ, HVO Main Staff (in fact by the HVO chief of staff personally).

Democratic Union of Bosnia-Herzegovina (HDZ-BiH) Party and municipal political organizations.[23] In April-May, 1992, organization and training activities quickened, and the local HVO crisis staffs were redesignated as Municipal HVO Commands and subordinated to the HVO Main Staff in Mostar.[24]

The HVO Operative Zones

At first, each political district (*opcina*) in the HZ HB was responsible for its own defense preparations. Later, the HVO divided responsibility for defense of the territory of Herceg-Bosna among four Operative Zones (OZ), the headquarters of which were at Tomislavgrad, Mostar, Vitez, and Orasje. The OZ boundaries were determined by the existing *opcina* boundaries rather than by major terrain features, the idea being to keep the HVO military organization parallel to the civilian governmental structure. The key municipalities of Livno, Tomislavgrad, Kupres, Bugojno, Gornji Vakuf (Uskoplje), and Prozor fell in the Operative Zone West Herzegovina and those of Jablanica and Mostar in the Operative Zone East Herzegovina. The principal towns in Operative Zone Central Bosnia, the organization of which is shown in Figure 2–2, were Travnik, Novi Travnik, Vitez, Busovaca, Kiseljak, Zenica, Kakanj, Vares, Zepce, Zavidovici, and Sarajevo. Although effort was made to coordinate the operations of the four OZs, coordination and cooperation between them was never very good.

The territorially based Operative Zone was the principal HVO administrative and operational entity. Roughly equivalent in function to a U.S./North Atlantic Treaty Organization (NATO) corps headquarters, the HVO OZ headquarters controlled a varying number of subordinate tactical brigades and supporting forces but had under its command far fewer combat troops and fewer organic combat support and combat service support units than did a U.S./NATO corps headquarters. Moreover, the HVO OZ headquarters itself was far smaller. The proposed "authorized" staffing for HQ, OZCB, prescribed in November, 1992, called for only forty-one officers and slightly more than sixty enlisted personnel. Even that staffing level was never reached: in April, 1993, the HQ, OZCB, had only twenty-five staff officers—only three of whom had any substantial military training for the tasks they were assigned.[25]

In July, 1992, the HVO command in central Bosnia established four subordinate territorial commands to control the operations in the various municipalities and later those of the tactical brigades.[26] With the redesignation of the Central Bosnia Armed Forces Command as the Operative Zone Central Bosnia, the OZCB commander reorganized the subordinate territorial commands, then also called Operative Zones, and redesignated them as Operative Groups (OG).[27] Municipalities subordinate to the old 1st OZ headquartered in Gornji Vakuf were transferred to the Operative Zone Northwest Herzegovina. The new 1st OG (formerly 2d OZ) was given responsibility for the municipalities of Travnik, Novi Travnik, Vitez, Jajce, and Zenica. The 2d OG (formerly 3d OZ) took over the municipalities of Kiseljak, Kresevo, Busovaca, Fojnica, Vares, Kakanj, and Sarajevo. The 3d OG (formerly 4th OZ) was made responsible for the municipalities of Zepce, Zavidovici, Maglaj, Teslic, and Tesanj.

Types of Forces Available to the HVO

The actual military forces available to the commander of the Operative Zone Central Bosnia in 1992–93 were all essentially territorially based static

Fig. 2-2. HVO Third Operative Zone (Central Bosnia)

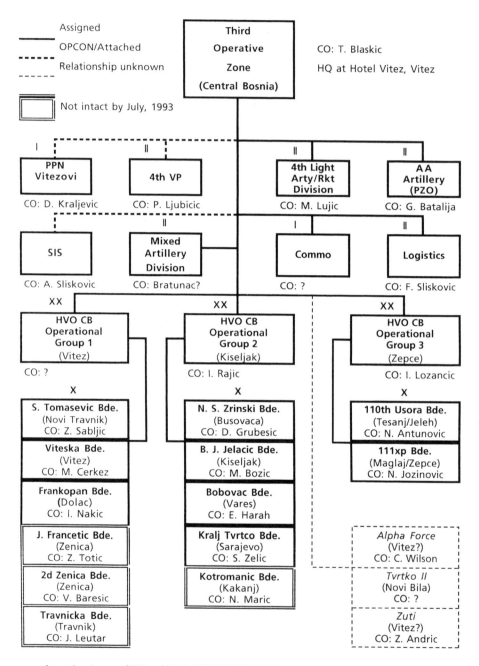

Sources: Organigramme of HVO, as of July 20, 1993, KC Z1148.2; HQ, BHC, UNPROFOR, *Bosnia-Herzegovina Warring Factions*, 6th ed.

reserve forces based on the old JNA Territorial Defense model. They ranged from old men armed with shotguns assigned to village defense tasks to organized, uniformed, and well-equipped brigade-sized formations that nevertheless employed part-time soldiers. As time went on, the HVO forces became increasingly better organized and more "professional," but it was not until early 1994, at the very end of the Muslim-Croat conflict, that the HVO began to form the so-called guards brigades—mobile units manned by full-time professional soldiers.[28]

Village Guards As fighting spread in Croatia and Bosnia-Herzegovina in 1991 and 1992, the inhabitants of many central Bosnian villages spontaneously formed so-called village guard formations to defend against possible BSA attack and growing criminal mischief. The village guards were local men who served on a volunteer basis, did not wear uniforms, and were armed with a hodgepodge of pistols, shotguns, hunting rifles, and old military weapons.[29] For the most part, the village guards were old men, boys, and the disabled, although some able-bodied men did participate when not otherwise engaged. The village guard formations were often multiethnic and included Croats, Muslims, and even some Serbs. Village guards elected their own leaders and served primarily as sentries and a weak reaction force in case of trouble. Although not officially a part of the HVO, the village guards formed a recruiting pool of potential volunteers for HVO military formations. Able-bodied members of the village guards often served voluntarily as members of the "shifts" manning the frontline against the BSA, and many of them were absorbed into the HVO brigades under the control of HQ, OZCB, after the Muslim attacks began in April, 1993. The HVO Home Guard organizations formed in 1993 assumed many of the village guards' area defense functions.

Shifts The OZCB commander relied on local leaders to organize groups of volunteers who agreed to serve repetitive shifts of seven to ten days in the front line against the BSA.[30] The shifts were controlled by HQ, OZCB, and consisted of fifty to sixty men from a given area, such as Vitez. The available military weapons were kept on the frontline position and transferred to the relieving shift. The men participating in the shifts were only skimpily supplied with uniforms and other equipment and were considered soldiers only during the time they were actually on shift. Shifts going on duty usually formed up a day or two in advance at some convenient location in their home locality, underwent some refresher training, drew additional equipment, and were then transported to the front line, where they relieved the shift that was on duty.[31] Given their limited manpower and armament, the HVO shifts were capable of only very limited local offensive action and were thus for the most part relegated to conducting a static defense in place against the BSA. Following a Muslim attack on HVO frontline troops in the Travnik area in June, 1993, many of the men who had volunteered previously for shift duty were incorporated in the HVO brigades in central Bosnia.

HVO Brigades The core of the HVO's military power in central Bosnia consisted of brigades formed in late 1992 and early 1993. The brigades were reserve formations manned by part-time soldiers who, when not on duty, lived at home and pursued their civilian occupations. Compared to other HVO military elements, the men in the HVO brigades were relatively well-organized, well-armed, and well-equipped but were capable of only limited, local offensive action and were employed primarily to defend their home territory. With the onset of the Muslim-Croat conflict in January 1993, the HVO brigades became the mainstay of the Bosnian Croat defense forces and bore the brunt of the fighting against the ABiH.

The HVO brigades were territorially based and took their designation either from a historical personality or the area in which they were located, although two OZCB brigades, the 110th Usora and the 111xp, were numerically designated. Municipal defense forces in the OZCB area of operations were first organized in late November, 1992.[32] Initially, nine brigades were proposed, with headquarters to be located in Usora, Travnik (two brigades), Vitez, Zenica, Zepce, Busovaca, Kiseljak, and Vares. A total of thirteen brigades were eventually formed, five of which were destroyed, captured, or disbanded in the course of the Muslim-Croat fighting in the first half of 1993. By July of that year, there were only nine HVO brigades on the active list in the OZCB, as shown in Figure 2–2.

The organization of the HVO brigades was based on a modification of the old JNA Type "R" reserve brigade tables of organization and equipment and had a planned strength of 2,841 officers and enlisted men (OEM), as shown in Figure 2–3.[33] However, the authorized strength of HVO tactical units was seldom achieved. For example, in mid-May 1993, the Frankopan Brigade in the Guca Gora–Travnik area had an actual strength of only 1,376 OEM.[34] In the fall of 1993, the Viteska Brigade, with four battalions, was one of the larger HVO units, yet it could muster only 2,423 OEM—of whom 80 percent were home guardsmen.[35] In early February, 1994, at the very end of the Muslim-Croat conflict, the principal HVO units in the Lasva Valley enclave under the control of HQ, OZCB, included the Stjepan Tomasevic Brigade in Novi Travnik (1,981 OEM); the Viteska Brigade in Vitez (2,909 OEM); the Nikola Subic Zrinski Brigade in Busovaca (2,238 OEM, plus another 1,429 men in the 3d Battalion in Fojnica); and remnants of the Frankopan Brigade (1,214 OEM), the Jure Francetic Brigade (57 OEM), and the Travnicka Brigade (1,074 OEM).[36]

Essentially light infantry forces, the HVO brigades were normally organized with three or four subordinate infantry battalions and a minimal combat support and combat service support structure, as shown in Figure 2–3. Most of the HVO brigades in the OZCB had three organic infantry battalions; however, the 110th Usora Brigade and the 111xp Brigade each had five battalions and, as noted, the Viteska Brigade had four.[37] Each infantry battalion had three infantry companies, a reconnaissance platoon, an antitank platoon, an escort troop (equipped with 120-mm and 82-mm mortars and recoilless rifles), a logistics platoon, and a communications section.[38]

Fig. 2-3. HVO Brigade Stucture, April–May, 1993

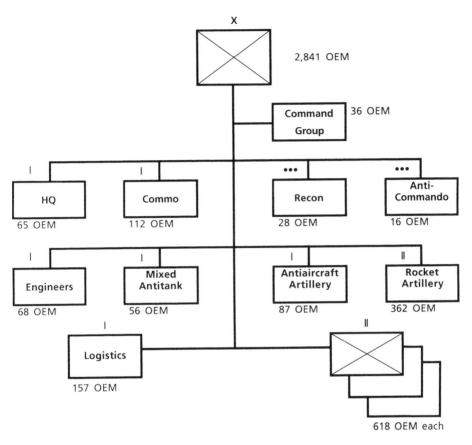

Sources: See HQ, Vitez Brigade, no. 10–123–293, Vitez, Apr. 10, 1993, subj: Elements of Extract from the Mobilization Plan—Vitez Brigade, KC Z636.1; commander, Frankopan Brigade, to commander, OZCB, Guca Gora—Travnik, May 17, 1993, subj: (Organization and Strength of Frankopan Brigade), B D246; HQ, Central Bosnia Armed Forces Command, no. 01–4–36/93, Vitez, Apr. 3, 1993, subj: Extract from Mobilization Department—Kotromanic Brigade, Kakanj, KC Z597.

The HVO Home Guard To supplement the organized HVO brigades' slender resources, in early 1993 the HZ HB government established a Home Guard (HD) organization.[39] This territorially based defense force was intended to provide support for the "regular" HVO forces and to provide armed control of territory; protect areas and facilities of special significance to the defense of HVO territory, such as reservoirs and waterworks, power plants, telecommunications facilities, hospitals, factories for the production of food and military goods, and vital storage facilities; to fight infiltrating sabotage-terrorist groups; counter enemy air strikes; secure law and order; and prevent any activity aimed at undermining the defense system.[40] Each municipality in Herceg-Bosna was ordered to establish an HD command by February 10, 1993, with the mobilization and organization of units to follow. Home Guard companies were to be set up in municipalities with few or no facilities of special significance, HD battalions in municipalities near the frontlines with the BSA or with a large number of special facilities, and an HD regiment in Mostar. An assistant chief of the HVO General Staff in Mostar was appointed to oversee HD activities, and each OZ was instructed to appoint an assistant commander for HD affairs. Home Guard units within a given Operative Zone were to be subordinate to the OZ commander, and in effect provided the extant HVO military forces with a reserve. Zonko Vukovic was named assistant commander for the OZCB's Home Guard, and orders establishing the OZCB's HD units were issued in March, 1993.[41]

The exigencies of the Muslim-Croat conflict in central Bosnia in 1993 precluded completion of the organization of the Home Guard. Following the conflict's end in February, 1994, and the subsequent creation of the Muslim-Croat Federation Army, the existing HVO brigades were redesignated as Home Guard regiments. The existing HVO brigades in the Vitez Military District (formerly the OZCB) were redesignated as follows:[42]

Stjepan Tomasevic Brigade	Novi Travnik	90th HD Regiment
Francopan Brigade	Novi Bila	91st HD Regiment
Viteska Brigade	Vitez	92d HD Regiment
Nikola Subic Zrinski Brigade	Busovaca	93d HD Regiment
Ban Josip Jelacic Brigade	Kiseljak	94th HD Regiment
Bobovac Brigade	Vares	96th HD Regiment
110th Usora Brigade	Tesanj	110th HD Regiment
111xp Brigade	Zepce	111th HD Regiment

A new HVO unit, the 95th HD Regiment, was also created in Kresovo. At the same time, the HVO set up a new General Staff Mobile Command to control the newly formed "professional" guards brigades. The General Staff Mobile Command had its headquarters at Capljina and consisted of the 1st Guards Brigade (Capljina), 2d Guards Brigade (Rodoc Helidrome), 3d Guards Brigade (Vitez), 4th Guards Brigade (Orasje), 116th Special Forces (PPN) Battalion "Ludvig Pavlovic" (Capljina), and the 56th HD Regiment (Konjic).[43]

Organization of the Army of Bosnia-Herzegovina

The Republic of Bosnia-Herzegovina began its existence in March, 1992, without an effective national armed force to protect its fragile independence. The Bosnian Croat community, which had long recognized the threat posed by Bosnian Serb ambitions, reacted by forming the Croatian Defense Council, the military wing of which was established officially in May, 1992. Bosnia-Herzegovina's Muslim political leadership, on the other hand, had been slow to recognize the threat. As a consequence, the Bosnian Muslim community generally lagged behind the Bosnian Croat community in the creation of defense forces. Given the RBiH government's reluctance to act, the lead in organizing the Bosnia Muslims for defense was taken by private citizens and Muslim-led "patriotic" organizations. Muslim activists had gained control of the existing Territorial Defense organization in many localities and used the TO structure as the framework for the creation of a national army. Beginning in mid-1991, the Muslim-led Patriotic League of Bosnia-Herzegovina had raised, organized, and equipped a considerable armed force to provide the manpower and matériel to augment the TO organization. Although the Muslims had far greater manpower resources, they initially tended to be less well armed, less well led, and less effective as a military force on a man-to-man basis than either the BSA or the HVO, but they improved substantially in all areas by January, 1993.

The Creation of the Army of Bosnia-Herzegovina

By the time Bosnia-Herzegovina declared its independence on March 3, 1992, the Izetbegovic government had begun to realize that there was a real threat to the new Republic of Bosnia-Herzegovina posed by the JNA's six corps and the eighty thousand to 120,000 men in the paramilitary forces of the Serbian Democratic Party (SDS), the main Bosnian Serb political party.[44] On April 8, 1992, the same day the HVO was formed, the presidency of the Republic of Bosnia-Herzegovina declared that a "state of imminent threat of war" existed and moved to create a new Territorial Defense organization based on district staffs and to incorporate the armed forces of various groups such as the Patriotic League into the formal defense structure.[45] The ABiH's first units were established by the RBiH presidency on May 27, 1992, and included thirteen infantry brigades, twelve separate platoons, one military police battalion, one engineer battalion, and a presidential escort company.[46]

The structure of the newly formed ABiH was based primarily on the old JNA TO organization, which grouped the forces of several municipalities together in Territorial Defense districts.[47] In January, 1991, the JNA had ordered the disbandment of all TO units in Bosnia-Herzegovina, and Alija Izetbegovic, the president of Bosnia-Herzegovina (then still a part of the Federal Republic of Yugoslavia), complied, allowing the JNA to disarm the TO units and redistribute their weapons to the Bosnian Serbs.[48] However, Bosnian Croat and Muslim patriots in many municipalities ignored the order to disband their TO units and successfully took over the existing TO structure, its facilities, and many of its weapons.

Initially, Bosnia-Herzegovina's TO forces included both Croats and Muslims, but as the RBiH government began to emphasize its Islamic character, Croat members left to join the HVO or were expelled. For example, Ivica Zeko, who later served as the intelligence officer of the HVO OZCB, left the TO organization in Travnik when it became apparent that only Muslim members would receive promotions and positions of responsibility.[49]

In any event, the organization did not lack for manpower. The Muslim-dominated Territorial Defense forces operated under the laws and regulations that had governed the TO of the former Yugoslavia and were generally tied to the location in which they were recruited. However, the influx of Muslim refugees from eastern Bosnia and the Bosanska-Krajina region at the end of 1992 provided large numbers of well-motivated military age men to fill out the TO force and to create new mobile units suitable for offensive operations.

The military forces organized by the Muslim-dominated Patriotic League played an important role in the RBiH's early defense against BSA aggression and in the creation of the ABiH. In June, 1991, Bosnian Muslims formed the National Defense Council to prepare the Muslim community to defend itself against the actions of the Bosnian Serbs, and in September, Sefer Halilovic, a former JNA officer, began to organize a secret armed force, the Patriotic League, to "defend Bosnia-Herzegovina and the Muslim people," and the following month, the Patriotic League in the Sarajevo area established a regional military headquarters, logistical facilities, and mobile, static, and special purpose units.[50] Following a meeting on December 2 in conjunction with the First Congress of the Party of Democratic Action (SDA, the dominant Bosnian Muslim political party), Alija Izetbegovic ordered Halilovic to expand the Patriotic League throughout Bosnia-Herzegovina.[51] The Patriotic League subsequently established a military council in the village of Mehurici near Travnik, developed a plan for the league's regional military headquarters, assigned tasks to the regional military staffs, and prepared a defense plan entitled "Directives for the Defense of the Sovereignty of Bosnia-Herzegovina."[52] The Patriotic League's main headquarters eventually controlled nine regional military headquarters, 103 municipal military headquarters, and a large number of static (local defense), mobile, and special purpose units—a total of some 120,000 men.[53]

By the beginning of August, 1992, the ABiH had grown to 170,000 men in twenty-eight brigades, sixteen independent battalions, one armored battalion, and two artillery divisions, plus 138 other units.[54] Formed by the integration of the existing Patriotic League and Territorial Defense forces, the ABiH was augmented by a number of Muslim paramilitary groups such as the so-called Muslim Armed Forces (MOS) and the "Green Berets," as well as by a large number of fundamentalist Muslim fighters, the mujahideen, from throughout North Africa, the Middle East, and Afghanistan, who had been invited into the country by Alija Izetbegovic. In addition, after their mobilization in April, 1992, the ABiH was augmented by Ministry of the Interior police forces (MUP), which had some seventy thousand men scattered throughout the country but mostly concentrated in the Sarajevo area.[55] The Muslim-led MUP was armed mainly with small arms and had few vehicles but was generally well equipped and well trained.

ABiH Corps Organization

On August 18, 1992, the existing RBiH Territorial Defense districts were transformed into five ABiH corps areas.[56] At the same time, the various District Defense Headquarters were subordinated to the new corps headquarters as follows: Sarajevo to I Corps; Doboj and Tuzla to II Corps; Banja Luka and Zenica to III Corps; Mostar to IV Corps; and Bihac to V Corps. Although the presidential decision directing the formation of the ABiH corps was issued on August 18, it was some time before the decision could be put into effect. The ABiH III Corps with headquarters at Zenica, for example, was not formally organized until December 1, 1992. The ABiH subsequently created two additional corps in the second half of 1993: VI Corps, headquartered at Konjic (responsible for the municipalities of Igman, Jablanica, Visoko, and Kalinovik), and VII Corps, headquartered in Travnik.[57] All seven ABiH corps headquarters are shown in Figure 2–4.

The corps was the ABiH's basic administrative unit and corresponded in function to the HVO Operative Zone even though the ABiH corps had more manpower and a larger area of responsibility. For example, the HVO OZCB controlled approximately eight thousand men whereas the ABiH III Corps controlled as many as eighty thousand. Moreover, the ABiH III Corps area of responsibility overlapped that of the HVO OZCB. The northern boundary of both was roughly the same, but the III Corps area extended farther south to include Bugojno, Gornji Vakuf, and Kupres. The ABiH corps had a varying number of assigned tactical brigades and supporting artillery, engineer, signal, and logistical troops as well as other forces, such as MUP, that were attached to, or under the operational control (OPCON) of, the corps headquarters.

ABiH Operational Groups

Toward the end of 1992, the ABiH corps began to group their brigades to form Operational Groups (OG) in much the same way as the HVO had done. However, unlike the HVO OG, which were semipermanent organizations with a fixed geographical base, the ABiH OG were temporary organizations designed to facilitate the conduct of operations and command and control in combat. They were formed as required for specific operational situations, and their composition and strength varied depending on the mission. Normally, brigades and other units were assigned in their entirety to a given OG, but individual battalions could be attached to an OG while its parent brigade remained in position, and units from the various corps might be cross attached for duty in a given OG. In essence, the ABiH OGs were small divisional task forces, and the number and size of the Operational Groups in existence at any given time varied with the situation.

In March, 1993, Enver Hadzihasanovic, commander of the ABiH III Corps, directed the reorganization of the brigades assigned to the corps into four Operational Groups, noting that in order "to strengthen all defence structures . . . new organizational modes should be adopted."[58] The missions assigned the four new OGs are uncertain, but based on their positioning and subsequent utilization it would appear that OG Bosanska-Krajina, headquartered in Travnik, was oriented primarily toward the BSA threat in the Turbe-Travnik area; OG Zapad (West), headquartered at Bugojno, was

Fig. 2-4. ABiH Corps Headquarters and Commanders

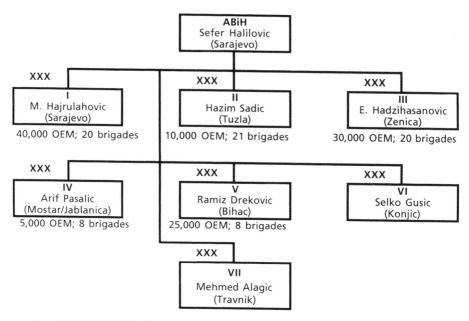

Sources: Based on Sefer Halilovic, *Lukava strategija*, 14. The strength and number of brigades is for the period before the creation of the VI and VII Corps and is based on International Institute for Strategic Studies, *The Military Balance, 1993–1994*, 74–75.

oriented toward the BSA threat from the west-southwest; and OG Bosna, headquartered in Zavidovici, was oriented toward the BSA threat in the Maglaj salient. Operational Group Lasva, headquartered at Kakanj, appears to have been oriented principally toward the Bosnian Croat enclaves in the Lasva-Lepenica Valleys (Vitez, Busovaca, and Kiseljak).

The composition of the four III Corps OGs created in March, 1993, as well as the corps support units and those brigades retained under the direct control of III Corps headquarters are shown in Figure 2–5.

ABiH Brigades

The Territorial Defense detachments in the various municipalities developed into brigades in the fall of 1992. Thereafter, the brigades constantly evolved as more men and material became available. After the fall of Jajce in October, 1992, the ABiH was able to use Muslim refugees to fill out existing units and to form a number of new brigades that were not tied to a specific locality and that could be deployed as desired. As in the HVO, the brigade was the ABiH's principal tactical unit, and each was organized with three or four infantry battalions and some supporting forces. Most ABiH brigades in the III Corps area (central Bosnia) were organized as so-called mountain infantry brigades, the model for which was the JNA's partisan

Fig. 2-5. ABiH III Corps Organization

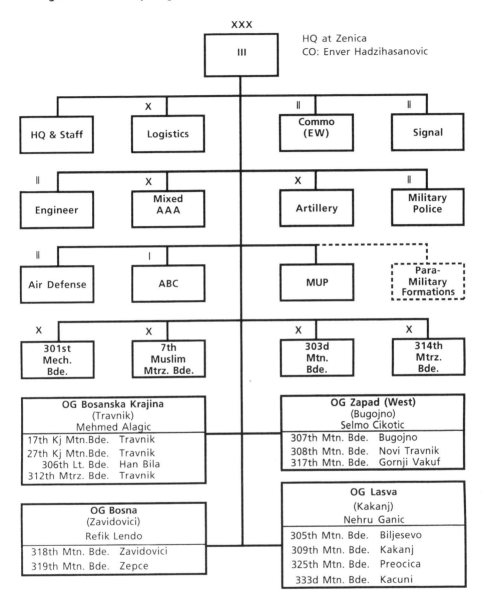

Note: Data is as of July 20, 1993, unless otherwise noted.
Sources: HQ, BHC, UNPROFOR, *Bosnia-Herzegovina Warring Factions,* 6th ed.; 1 PWO, "Order of Battle for HVO Operative Zone Central Bosnia" (hand drawn), n.d. (ca. July, 1993), B 378.

Fig. 2-6. Typical ABiH Mountain Brigade Organization

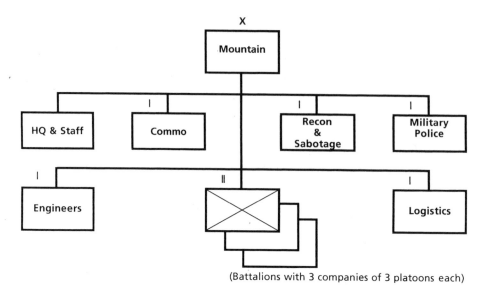

(Battalions with 3 companies of 3 platoons each)

Source: This diagram is based on the organization of the 7th Muslim Motorized Brigade, an elite unit. However, its general organization was representative of other ABiH brigades. See Col. Asim Koricic, Blaskic trial testimony, June 10, 1999.

battalion. Figure 2–6 shows the organization of a typical ABiH mountain brigade. A few were also designated light infantry brigades, and as time went on the III Corps reorganized several of its mountain brigades as motorized brigades and the light infantry brigades became mountain brigades. The 301st Mechanized Brigade was essentially an armor formation, although it boasted only six tanks.

As was the case with the HVO brigades, the ABiH brigades were perpetually understrength: at the end of 1993 there were an estimated fifteen hundred men per brigade in III Corps.[59] First-line ABiH forces (the brigades) were supplemented by Territorial Defense (militia) units in the various Muslim villages and towns.

Reorganization of the ABiH

On April 24, 1993, the ABiH General Staff proposed a number of organizational changes aimed at improving the efficiency of leadership and operations, but more than two months passed before the issues were discussed in the RBiH presidency.[60] On June 2, 1993, Izetbegovic placed before the presidency an alternative plan for reorganizing the ABiH that aroused strong opposition from Halilovic and other members of the General Staff.[61] The plan proposed to establish ranks in the ABiH beginning with the appointment of general officers and colonels as brigade commanders; instituted the extraconstitutional post of commander of the General Staff and appointed to that position Gen. Rasim Delic with Stjepan Siber and Jovan Divjak as deputy commanders while retaining General Halilovic, without defining his duties, as chief of the General Staff; reduced the size of the General Staff and the headquarters of corps and brigades substantially; created the VI Corps, to be commanded by Col. Selko Gusic, with its headquarters at Konjic and responsible for the area of Igman, Jablanica, Visoko, and Kalinovik; and set up two commissions to deal with lifting the blockade of Sarajevo. Halilovic objected strongly, but the proposal went forward nonetheless.[62]

3 *Command, Control, and Communications*

Neither the HVO nor the ABiH in central Bosnia can be said to have had fully developed, effective command, control, and communications (C^3) systems during the 1992–94 conflict. For both sides, C^3 was a major problem, particularly with regard to control of criminal and extremist elements and of special operating forces that did not answer through the normal chain of command. Lieutenant Colonel Robert Stewart, commander of the British UNPROFOR battalion in the Lasva Valley, stated that the HVO OZCB commander, Col. Tihomir Blaskic, "had effective command and control" because when he "said something, it happened lower down."[1] However, it is apparent that Stewart failed to grasp the realities of Colonel Blaskic's C^3 difficulties—indeed, of the complexities of C^3 in general—so his comments on the matter are superficial at best. This is surprising, as he was a professional military officer who, had he given the matter more than cursory consideration, would have recognized that the chaotic conditions in central Bosnia in 1992–94 were scarcely such as to facilitate *effective* command and control. Colonel Blaskic may well have been *in command,* but the real question is: Was he *in control?* Withal, the questionable definitions of "effective command and control" used by Stewart and others leave a great deal to be desired.

Consistently effective C^3 is always difficult to achieve, even in well-trained and well-disciplined armies with good communications facilities and equipment. Given the situation in central Bosnia in 1992–94, however, it was almost impossible to achieve. Among the factors inhibiting the effective exercise of command and control by commanders on either side were the comparative youth of their organizational structures; the heavy reliance on volunteer officers and soldiers; the influence of local political authorities on the selection and dismissal of subordinate commanders; the presence in the area of operations of independent units not in the local chain of command; the chaos attendant upon a desperate defensive war and the resulting growth in common criminality; the presence of UN peacekeepers and European Community monitors; and, above all, poor communications.

The Problem of Newly Formed Volunteer Forces

Neither the HVO nor the ABiH had been in existence for more than a year when the Muslim-Croat conflict in central Bosnia erupted in January, 1993. All of the institutions and norms of both armies were still in the formative stage, and there had been insufficient time to work out suitable regulations and standards—much less to impart them effectively to all personnel. A good deal of time is required to achieve consensus on institutional processes and norms and to insure that all members of the organization know the rules, accept them as valid, and act accordingly. That time was simply not available to either the HVO or the ABiH.

Another factor serving to degrade command and control in both the HVO and the ABiH was that both armies were composed predominantly of part-time "citizen" soldiers, who in effect served pretty much when and even where they pleased. Most units were composed of comrades from the same village, lower-level leaders were often elected, and command authority had to be earned. Consequently, as Brigadier Slavko Marin, the operations officer at HQ, OZCB, has pointed out, many of the lower-level HVO commanders in central Bosnia were not fully respected by their subordinates, their peers, or their superiors.[2] Moreover, particularly in the HVO, the part-time soldiers mixed civilian and military duties. When they were not on the frontlines against the Serbs, they were in their home villages pursuing their normal occupations, and the lack of barracks exacerbated the lack of discipline. The HVO soldiers in central Bosnia were also prone to select for themselves the unit in which they wished to serve, requiring the commander of the HVO Viteska Brigade, for example, to issue a specific order forbidding "transfers from one unit to another on one's own initiative."[3] Although common around the world, such part-time and "voluntary" military service under the command of one's friends and neighbors is not conducive to the acceptance of strict discipline and accountability.

The Impact of Political Influence

The lack of consistent political guidance from above and the strong influence of local political authorities on such matters as the selection and dismissal of commanders also weakened the command and control systems of both the HVO and the ABiH. Brigadier Marin addressed the problem directly in his testimony in the Blaskic trial before the ICTY:

> By way of an example, if you wanted to appoint a brigade commander, before doing anything else, the commander of the Operative Zone had to reach agreement with the municipal authorities and to come to an agreement as to the name of the person who would be proposed. When such agreement was reached, information about that commander would be submitted through the brigade commander to the commander of the Operative Zone and further on to the highest level, the president of the Croatian Community of Herceg-Bosna. After which, when all these steps were taken, a document would be drafted on the appointment of this commander. Throughout this chain, a key role was played by the political authorities in the municipality.[4]

The necessity for military commanders to consider seriously the views of local political authorities can be considered normal in neonate armies and
continues to exist in even highly evolved military systems. For example, a
major effort was required by the U.S. government at the beginning of the
twentieth century to eliminate the baleful influence of local political authorities on the militia forces of the various states, even when they were
called into federal service. Even today, few decisions can be made regarding
promotions or assignments of National Guard personnel without consult-
ing the political powers of the state in question. Yet, however strong such
political influence may be on personnel matters and even on national policy, it seldom extends to operational matters.

Although there was certainly dissension in the higher levels of the HZ HB
government and the HVO over matters of military policy, organization, and
strategy, the principal point at which political influence affected the exercise of effective command and control by HVO military leaders was at the
local level. The best illustration of this problem is the case of the relief of
Stjepan Tuka, commander of the 3d (Fojnica) Battalion of the Ban Josip
Jelacic Brigade in April, 1993. In response to the ABiH III Corps's attack in
the Busovaca and Kiseljak area, on April 18, the commander of the OZCB,
Col. Tihomir Blaskic, ordered the 3d Battalion of the Jelacic Brigade to attack Muslim forces southeast and northwest of Fojnica to relieve pressure
on HVO forces in the Gomionica, Sebesic, and Busovaca areas.[5] At that
point, the town of Fojnica was not yet under direct attack, and the Bosnian
Croat political and military authorities in Fojnica were unwilling to precip-
itate such a conflict. The result was that Stjepan Tuka, the Fojnica Battalion
commander, refused to have his forces attack as ordered, and at 11:20 A.M.
on April 20, Colonel Blaskic dismissed Tuka and appointed Drago Simunic
in his place, transferred the 3d Battalion to the Zrinski Brigade, and ordered
it to carry out its mission forthwith.[6] What ensued was essentially a mutiny.
Tuka, backed by Fojnica's Bosnian Croat community, refused to give up his
command or to carry out the attack as ordered. Due to the chaos attendant
on the ABiH offensive, little could be done immediately by Colonel Blaskic
to enforce his orders, and about a month passed before Tuka was, in fact, relieved of his command. The lesson was that, without the assent of the local
civilian authorities, even the major regional commander might find it difficult to relieve a subordinate commander for cause. It was even harder for
an HVO commander to relieve or otherwise discipline a subordinate who
might not only be a local favorite but his cousin or brother-in-law as well.

Unlike the HVO, which appears to have had a fair degree of unanimity
and cohesion in the higher echelons, the ABiH's high command was divided
on basic issues of defense policy, organization, and objectives. For most of
the period under consideration, Alija Izetbegovic, the president of the RBiH,
was at odds with the army's chief of staff, Sefer Halilovic, over such fundamental questions as whether the RBiH ought to defend itself from Bosnian
Serb aggression at all. In his memoir of the wartime period, Halilovic related

his many disagreements with President Izetbegovic and outlined the division between the more or less passive and inept (if indeed not treasonous) supporters of Izetbegovic and his own enthusiastic, nationalist supporters.[7] The situation was further complicated by the introduction of a fundamentalist Islamic faction, generally favored by Izetbegovic, which sought to radicalize the ABiH and thereby alienate whatever good will and cooperation there may have been among other factions and among the Bosnian Croats and Serbs who remained loyal to the central government and its program of a multiethnic state. Halilovic also inveighed in his memoir against Fikret Muslimovic, Zijad Ljevakovic, and other ideologues who sought to replace strategy with religious schools and mosques and the national army with an SDA party-controlled, ideologically oriented army.[8]

Izetbegovic and Halilovic also quarreled over integrating the twenty thousand well-armed and trained men of the Ministry of the Interior police reserve into the ABiH structure. In his memoir, Halilovic noted that the RBiH would have realized a much more favorable defense situation if the issue had been resolved early on, as it had been in Croatia, where the MUP was made "a pillar of the defence." After much delay and acrimonious debate, Izetbegovic finally signed a decree subordinating the MUP reserve to the ABiH General Staff, but the decision was never carried out, and, as Halilovic noted, "the well-armed members of the Interior Ministry reserve forces have never been made operational for the carrying out of combat duties . . . [although] individuals and individual Interior Ministry units . . . went to the frontlines."[9]

The Role of Military Police and Special Purpose Units

For the commanders of both the HVO's OZCB and the ABiH's III Corps, the most significant and direct challenge to their exercise of effective command and control was the presence in their area of responsibility of military police and special purpose units under the control of national-level authorities and thus not obliged to answer through the local chain of command. Moreover, the III Corps commander was also forced to deal with a number of quasi-private military forces, such as the Muslim Armed Forces, the Patriotic League, the Green Berets, the "Sosna," and the various mujahideen units operating in central Bosnia. The command and control problems in this case were especially critical because extremist groups on both sides were often accused of war crimes, and their leaders often were not under the jurisdiction of the HVO or ABiH commander in whose area they operated.

The HVO special purpose units (PPN) and military police (VP) posed special command and control problems for the commander of the Central Bosnia Operative Zone. Elements of these forces were often placed under the OZ commander's operational control (OPCON), however, they remained under the HVO Department of Defense for administration and military justice.[10] That is to say, Colonel Blaskic, the OZCB commander, could in theory assign operational tasks to OPCON VP and PPN units, but he could not dismiss or discipline their commanders. In practice, the OZ commander's powers to task OPCON PPN, VP, and Security Information Service units were even more limited, and it was usually necessary to negotiate the assignment with their commanders before formally assigning tasks to their units. At the same time, the HVO Department of Defense could (and often did) task such units directly—with or without notifying the OZ commander in whose area of responsibility they might operate.

The UNPROFOR intelligence officer based in the Lasva Valley acknowledged that the HVO special purpose units were "not effectively under Blaskic's command," and ECMM monitors likewise admitted that the HVO military police were not under tight control.[11] Lower-level HVO commanders had similar problems. For example, in May, 1992, Borivoje Malbasic, commander of the Bobovac Brigade in Vares, stated that although he was the superior of Zvonko Duznovic, a radical and the commander of the local element of the HVO Military Police, he was unable to give him any orders.[12] Even HVO Defense Department headquarters in Mostar had great difficulty in controlling the actions of the PPN and Military Police units in the field.[13]

An HVO special purpose unit known as the "Vitezovi" ("Knights") was formed on September 10, 1992, and on September 19 stationed at the elementary school in Dubravica-Krizancevo near Vitez.[14] The unit was composed of some 120 men from the municipalities of Vitez, Zenica, and Travnik. It later received refugees from those municipalities into its ranks, bringing its strength to 140-180 men. Commanded by Darko Kraljevic, the Vitezovi reported directly to the HVO Department of Defense in Mostar and had the whole of central Bosnia and Herzegovina as its area of operations. The principal tasks assigned to the unit were the retaking of lost positions, breaking through enemy lines, deep reconnaissance and raids behind the enemy lines, and similar commando-type operations. It was first employed in the Jajce area on September 22, and continued operations until November, 1993. From time to time in late 1992 and early 1993, the other two official HVO special purpose units (PPN "Ante Bruno Busic" and PPN "Ludvig Pavlovic") also operated in the OZCB.[15] The Vitezovi and the other PPN units responded to orders from Minister of Defense Bruno Stojic in Mostar, but the OZCB commander could do nothing other than request they participate in operations at certain times and places.[16]

The HVO's more than three thousand military policemen were organized in four (later eight) battalions, each of which had companies specializing in antiterrorist and assault operations, guarding headquarters and other key installations, traffic control, and investigating crimes committed by or upon military personnel.[17] Given their status as a quasi-national police force and their direct participation in operations as assault troops, HVO VPs were more like the Italian *carabinieri* than U.S. Army military policemen in both organization and function.[18] The HVO VP units reported directly to the VP office at the HVO Department of Defense headquarters in Mostar. Military Police units were normally placed under the operational control of the

Operative Zone commander, who could direct their operations but had no administrative or military justice powers over them. The 4th (later 7th) Military Police Battalion, organized as shown in Figure 3-1, was OPCON to the OZCB for most of the period under consideration, but in mid-August, 1993, the OZCB commander was given full authority over the battalion and those military policemen attached to HVO brigades in the OZCB answered to his brigade commanders.[19]

The Role of Paramilitary Forces

Homegrown paramilitary forces also posed a significant command and control problem for both the HVO and the ABiH. Several of the Bosnian political parties sponsored their own armed forces, and there were also a number of small, private armies raised by Croat and Muslim leaders. Such groups, some of which were little more than heavily armed bandit gangs, were impossible to restrain, short of mounting an all-out campaign to annihilate them.

The principal paramilitary organization posing a control problem for HVO authorities in central Bosnia was the Croatian Defense Force (HOS), the military arm of the ultra-right wing Croatian Party of Rights (HSP), which had branches in both Croatia and Bosnia-Herzegovina.[20] The HOS forces, dressed in black and sporting a variety of fascist insignia, included both Muslims and Croats and cooperated enthusiastically with the HVO and the ABiH in the fight against the Bosnian Serbs.[21] The HOS headquarters was in Ljubuski, and its principal area of operations was in the southern areas of Bosnia-Herzegovina. Extremist in their orientation, HOS soldiers were responsible for numerous excesses—including the operation of notorious detention centers for Serb prisoners in Capljina and Mostar.[22]

Initially, both HVO and RBiH authorities tolerated the unpredictable and unruly HOS forces for their value in fighting the Serb aggressors. Relations between the HVO and HOS soured quickly, however, after the HVO was implicated in the ambush and death of Blaz Kraljevic, a HOS commander, and seven other HOS members at a police checkpoint in the village of Krusevo on August 9, 1992.[23] Soon thereafter, HOS forces in western Herzegovina were disarmed by the HVO, and on August 23, HOS and HVO officials in Herzegovina agreed that the HOS would be absorbed by the HVO. The remaining HOS units were subsequently recognized by the government of Bosnia-Herzegovina as part of the ABiH (as was the HVO). Those HOS forces operating in central Bosnia under the command of Mladen Holman were later merged with the HVO in central Bosnia on April 5, 1993.[24] The HOS units in the Zenica area, along with their vehicles, weapons, ammunition, and other matériel, were integrated into the HVO and placed under the command of the Jure Francetic and 2d Zenica Brigades.

The OZCB commander had several other small paramilitary groups under his nominal control. Among them was the so-called Alpha Force, a thirty-five-man reconnaissance and sabotage group formed on April 6,

Fig. 3-1. Organization of HVO 4th Military Police (VP) Battalion

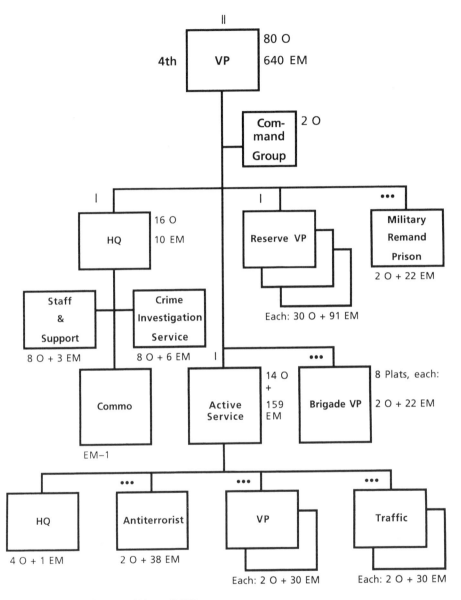

Note: Organization shown is as of February 15, 1993.
Source: Commander, 4th Military Police Battalion (Pasco Ljubicic) to Military Police Administration, Mostar, no. 02–4/3–07–190/93, Vitez, Feb. 15, 1993, subj: (Military Police Payroll), KC D321/1.

1992. Kris Wilson, a Briton, led the Vitez-based organization.[25] Another shadowy paramilitary force operating in the Lasva Valley was the so-called Tvrtko II, which appears to have been a locally sanctioned PPN-type unit. It, too, apparently operated under at least the nominal control of the OZCB commander inasmuch as it is listed on the distribution list for some HQ, OZCB, orders and messages. There were several similar local special purpose units under the HVO 111xp Brigade in the Zepce area.

For Enver Hadzihasanovic, commander of the ABiH III Corps, the problem included "authorized" units acting independently, as well as a number of private armies and armed extremist groups operating in the corps area of operations. Some of them were little more than criminal gangs continuing the long Balkan tradition of the mountain bandit.

Although a regularly constituted unit of the ABiH, the 7th Muslim Motorized Brigade posed many of the same command and control problems for the commander of the ABiH III Corps that the Vitezovi and 4th Military Police Battalion posed for the commander of the HVO OZCB. Created in November, 1992, the 7th Muslim Motorized Brigade was an elite mobile unit made up of Bosnian Muslims particularly devoted to Islamic fundamentalism.[26] The brigade was normally dispersed, and its battalions, companies, or even platoons were employed in critical areas as assault troops or to stiffen other units. The brigade's officers and men tended to be radical and independent in outlook, and it appears that the unit had a close relationship with the mujahideen and received some funding from Emir Mahmut Efendija Karalic's Islamic Center in Zenica.[27] The III Corps commander was apparently able to exercise only nominal control over their operations, although Col. Asim Koricic, the brigade's commander from its formation to July, 1993, testified at the Blaskic trial that the brigade was totally subordinate to the III Corps commander.[28]

The private armies and other armed Muslim extremist groups operating in the region were also troublesome from the standpoint of effective command and control by the III Corps commander. Chief among those paramilitary units were elements of the Patriotic League not already integrated into the ABiH; the Muslim Armed Forces, made up primarily of Muslims who previously had been members of the HOS and based at the Bilmisce School in Zenica; and Ahmed Demirovic's Green Berets.[29] The ABiH also employed several armed gangs raised and led by private individuals as special purpose units. These included the hundred-man Sosna Detachment in Novi Travnik, and two sixty- to eighty-man units—one in Nanetovi and one in Mercici.[30]

Criminal Activities

The state of general chaos engendered by the defensive war against the BSA, the internal conflicts in central Bosnia, and the general availability of weapons significantly increased the opportunities and rewards for common criminal activity in the region, a factor that further degraded the HVO and

ABiH commanders' ability to exercise effective command and control.[31] Croatian Defense Council authorities recognized the situation in a mid-1993 report, which noted: "The law and order situation in the HZ H-B has reflected the state of war on the greater part of its territory. Under such conditions we evaluate the law and order situation as exceptionally complex, since war operations bring in their train various phenomena such as theft and increase in all types of crime, fights, violent behaviour, the insulting and disparagement of law-enforcement officers, arguments, shooting with firearms in public places, etc."[32]

The frequent "holdups" of UN and private humanitarian aid convoys passing through central Bosnia were a particular problem. Such crimes were often blamed on HVO or ABiH military units when in fact they were the work of organized criminal gangs whose members may only coincidentally have been soldiers in one or the other army. Although both the HVO and the ABiH took some "official" action with respect to interference with the aid convoys, many of the incidents had nothing to do with actions authorized by either the Croat or the Muslim military or civilian authorities.

Although many of the crimes of violence against persons and property were the actions of individuals, the most serious threat to law and order was posed by some of the smaller paramilitary groups, both Croat and Muslim. These heavily armed criminal gangs engaged in wholesale murder, robbery, arson, extortion, black marketeering, and other criminal activity and thus were almost impossible for HVO and ABiH commanders to control. Among the most active Croat gangs operating in the OZCB area of operations were the "Zuti" in Travnik, led by Zarko "Zuti" Andric, and the "Maturice" and "Apostoli" gangs controlled by Ivica Rajic (aka Victor Andric) in the Kiseljak area.[33] Among the more active Muslim gangs was the "Fish Head Gang" led by "Paraga," which preyed upon the UN humanitarian convoys on Route DIAMOND between Gornji Vakuf and Novi Travnik.[34]

The Role of Outside Forces

Real or imagined, the presence in central Bosnia of armed forces from outside the country also posed significant problems for both the Operative Zone Central Bosnia commander and the commander of the ABiH III Corps. Allegations of Croatian Army (HV) intervention in central Bosnia posed a political and public relations problem, but the presence of fundamentalist Muslim mujahideen and of other foreign mercenaries and the presence of UNPROFOR troops and both United Nations and European Community monitoring teams constituted a substantial challenge to effective command and control by commanders on both sides.

The Alleged Croatian Army Intervention

Although not involving a direct command and control problem for the OZCB commander, the issue of whether or not HV forces operated in central Bosnia was of great political and legal significance. Although it is quite clear that the HVO in central Bosnia benefited directly from the logistical support provided by Croatia and may have benefited indirectly from the intervention of HV units in southern Bosnia-Herzegovina, the actual presence of HV combatants in central Bosnia remains unproved. Despite persistent rumors, the accusations of Bosnia-Herzegovina's Muslim-led government and of Muslim witnesses before the ICTY, a great deal of speculation on the part of UNPROFOR and ECMM observers, and a straightforward statement by the UN Security Council, there is, in fact, no convincing public evidence conclusively proving that the Croatian Army ever intervened in the Muslim-Croat conflict in central Bosnia. Those making such allegations generally fail to make two key distinctions: first, between the HVO/ABiH fight against the BSA and the Muslim-Croat conflict; and second, between the situation in central Bosnia and the situation elsewhere in Bosnia-Herzegovina. What may have been true in one conflict or location was not necessarily true in another.

Peacekeeping force officers and ECMM monitors were prone to see an HV soldier in every foxhole and an HV tank battalion around every curve in the road. In fact, their bases for making such assertions were ridiculously thin: secondhand reports from Muslim authorities; an encounter at the HVO headquarters in Novi Travnik with an obnoxious young major who "was alleged to be" a Croatian officer; an HVO order to report any HV officers or men in the ranks of HVO units; the wearing of HV uniforms and insignia by Bosnian Croat veterans of the war in Croatia; and the questionable judgment that "the HVO couldn't have done it on their own."[35] The latter speculation was particularly specious, and is worth quoting in its entirety:

> HVO forces have, during the past four months, proved capable of mounting military operations well inside the Bosnian Serb/Croat front-line with a strength and subsequent success which would have been unlikely had they been alone in their struggle.
>
> Indeed, the HVO have been involved in sustained combat with two foes and have managed to make gains against Moslem BiH forces while still being able to resist strong, competent and persistent Serb offensives. With such an extended front-line with the Serbs and limited resources in manpower, equipment and munitions, their effort has been supreme.[36]

A formal accusation by the UN Secretary General was of greater moment. On February 1, 1994, UN Secretary General Boutros Boutros-Ghali formally notified the Security Council that, based on UNPROFOR reports, "the Croatian Army has directly supported the HVO in terms of manpower, equipment and weapons for some time," and that the UNPROFOR estimated that, as of the date of the report, the Croatian Army had the equivalent of three brigades (some three thousand to five thousand men) of regular HV personnel in "central and southern Bosnia and Herzegovina."[37] Yet, one must ask where the secretary general got his information. It could only have been from UNPROFOR observers on the ground or from Bosnia-Herzegovina's Muslim-led government, which, once conflict had broken out between Muslims and Croats, had a vested interest in blaming the situation on Croatian intervention. In any event, what constituted HV intervention? A few HVO soldiers wearing old HV uniforms and insignia, or a thousand-man HV brigade with all its authorized weapons and vehicles? The former there were aplenty; the latter existed in central Bosnia only in the imagination of some overwrought observers.

In an undated statement signed by Hadzo Efendic, the government of the Republic of Bosnia-Herzegovina charged that the government of Croatia had "openly supported 'unlawful' actions of the HVO in Mostar and Central Bosnia" and that "reliable information" indicated that there were two units of the regular Croatian military establishment "in the Lasva region": the 114th Splitska Brigade and the 123rd Varazdinska Brigade.[38] The presence of the two HV units was never confirmed, and even the ECMM acknowledged that "the many reports [of HV involvement in BiH] provided by the BiH Armija have seldom been confirmed by ECMM, UNMOs or UNPROFOR."[39]

On June 11, 1993, Mate Granic, the Croatian deputy prime minister and minister of foreign affairs, stated that Croatia had no armed formations in Bosnia-Herzegovina, and shortly thereafter Maj. Gen. Slobodan Praljak of the Croatian Ministry of Defense formally acknowledged that Croatia had provided logistical support to the HVO but denied HV combat forces had any direct involvement in the Muslim-Croat conflict in central Bosnia.[40] Senior HVO officers in central Bosnia also consistently denied under oath that HV forces were ever present or took part in the Muslim-Croat conflict there.[41] Under questioning by a member of the Trial Chamber in the Blaskic trial, even Col. Bob Stewart acknowledged that "generally BRITBAT did not believe there was any HV presence in Central Bosnia," and the UNPROFOR chief of staff, Lt. Gen. Sir Roderick Cordy-Simpson, also stated that UNPROFOR had not confirmed such reports and that he personally had never seen any HV troops in the Kiseljak area.[42]

The Mujahideen

The Muslim "private armies" in central Bosnia were particularly difficult for the ABiH III Corps commander to control, but the mujahideen were the principal problem. Perhaps as many as four thousand Islamic fundamentalist fighters from throughout the Muslim world flocked to Bosnia-Herzegovina on the open invitation of Alija Izetbegovic to help ensure the creation of the only fundamentalist Islamic state in Europe.[43] Extremists in both religious and political orientation, the mujahideen cared little for the interests of Bosnia-Herzegovina's Muslim-led government, and even less for the commanders of the ABiH. Moreover, their combat methods tended to include the inculcation of terror as a primary aspect. Even central Bosnia's Muslim inhabitants feared the mujahideen and would have preferred to see them leave.[44] As for the Bosnian Croats, they believed the mujahideen were devils incarnate.

The first mujahideen arrived in central Bosnia in mid-1992, and were integrated into the Territorial Defense structure in Travnik, with camps in the old town and in the Medresa facility.[45] Subsequent increments went to separate camps in the villages of Mehurici (near Travnik), Duboka (near Novi Travnik), Ravno Rostovo (where they had a training center), Podbrezje and Arnauti (on the outskirts of Zenica), and Podgorica (near Kiseljak).[46] Several mujahideen units, such as the "Abdul Latif" Detachment in Kakanj and the "El Mujahid" Detachment, were formed and made part of the ABiH 7th Muslim Motorized Brigade.[47] With their beards, Muslim skullcaps, and refusal to eat pork or drink alcohol, the mujahideen, as one wit put it, "stuck out like penguins in the desert."[48] Despite their fearsome reputation, on the whole they seem to have lacked the respect of the Bosnian Muslim combatants. As one put it: "Arab man is strange man, he no eat pig and he no drink sljivovic." Nor were ABiH leaders enthralled with the presence of organized units of armed foreign fanatics over which they exercised only nominal control. Finally, almost all Bosnian Muslims—Westernized, liberated, and notorious for their lack of orthodoxy with respect to Islamic custom and ritual—were distinctly uncomfortable with the presence in their midst of a group of strict observers who made a point of proclaiming the coming of a fundamentalist Islamic state in Bosnia-Herzegovina.[49]

The mujahideen were supported by various Muslim countries as well as by "cultural and humanitarian" groups and private citizens in central Bosnia.[50] The mujahideen assigned to the 7th Muslim Brigade received money and other support from the Islamic Center in Zenica headed by Emir Mahmut Efendija Karalic.[51] Similarly, the 8th Muslim Brigade, formed in October, 1993, from the "El Mujahid" unit of the 7th Muslim Brigade, was allegedly funded by Halic Brzina, a wealthy Muslim businessman from Zenica.[52] The tragic attacks on the World Trade Center and the Pentagon on September 11, 2001, and America's subsequent "war on terrorism" have revealed the connection between Osama bin Laden's al-Qaeda terrorist organization and various Islamic businessmen and humanitarian organizations. Although no clear linkage has yet been established, it seems probable that al-Qaeda played a prominent role in sending the mujahideen to Bosnia-Herzegovina in 1992-93 and in supporting them there.[53]

Other Mercenaries

Aside from the mujahideen, a number of foreign mercenaries fought for both the HVO and the ABiH in Bosnia-Herzegovina. The deputy commander of the Operative Zone West Herzegovina was an ex-patriot Croat named Nicholas Glasnovic, who had been a soldier in the Princess Patricia's Canadian Light Infantry Regiment, and a number of Germans and Scots also worked for the HVO.[54] Lieutenant Colonel Bob Stewart, commander of the UNPROFOR unit in central Bosnia, also recorded meeting a number of British and Danish mercenaries serving with the Muslim forces in the Travnik area.[55] Two British mercenaries, Ted Skinner and Derek Arnold, were shot by the mujahideen.[56] Skinner, who worked with the Territorial Defense forces, was from Cheshire and had served in the New Zealand army.[57] The circumstances surrounding the execution of Skinner and Arnold by the mujahideen are unclear, but it is not unlikely that they were British Special Air Service (SAS) operatives whose identity was discovered, or even just suspected.

Intervention by UNPROFOR and the ECMM

From the point of view of the commanders on both sides of the Muslim-Croat conflict in central Bosnia, the presence of UN peacekeepers and EC monitors constituted yet another factor inhibiting effective command and control. Peacekeeping troops and ECMM teams often interfered with the employment of both Muslim and Croat forces; passed on to the other side sensitive information on deployments, positions, and intentions; and provoked incidents in which lower-level commanders engaged in emotionally charged confrontations with UN and EC personnel contrary to the orders and intentions of the senior HVO and ABiH commanders. Moreover, some UNPROFOR personnel were involved in black-market and other criminal activities adding to the disruption of law and order in the region.[58]

As Yugoslavia began to tear itself apart in the early 1990s, Western observers became obsessed with the need to stop the near genocidal level of bloodshed and "ethnic cleansing" and to provide humanitarian relief to the victims. Western governments, equally obsessed with a policy of "stability at all costs," were unable to endure the growing instability in the former Yugoslavia and took action to stabilize the situation, even at the cost of imposing artificial and temporary solutions on the warring factions. A cease-fire and withdrawal of JNA forces was brokered in Slovenia in 1991, and in Croatia in early 1992. United Nation's Security Council Resolution 770 of August 13, 1992, called upon all member nations to facilitate the delivery of humanitarian aid by the UN high commissioner for refugees (UNHCR) in Bosnia-Herzegovina, and pursuant to Security Council Resolution 776 of September 14, 1992, a separate Bosnia-Herzegovina Command (BHC) was established and UNPROFOR II forces were deployed, ostensibly for the purpose of facilitating the delivery of humanitarian relief supplies to the victims of the ongoing conflict between the Bosnian Serbs and the Muslim-Croat alliance.[59] As the Bosnian Serb aggression against Sarajevo and other Muslim enclaves in eastern Bosnia increased in 1993, the UN Security Council designated Bihac, Tuzla, Sarajevo, Srbrenica, Zepa, and Gorazde as so-called safe zones and authorized the deployment of additional UNPROFOR troops to defend them.[60] By May, 1994, UN efforts to deliver humanitarian aid in the former Yugoslavia involved over thirty-three thousand UN military troops, six hundred UN military observers, three thousand UN civilian administrators and staff, and hundreds of private aid workers.[61] Of the total, some 16,300 UNPROFOR troops were in Bosnia-Herzegovina, five thousand of them in the Sarajevo area alone.[62]

The UNPROFOR units operating within the boundaries of the HVO Operative Zone Central Bosnia in 1992–94 included British infantry battalions stationed in Novi Bila; the Dutch/Belgian transportion battalion in Busovaca; and the UNPROFOR Bosnia-Herzegovina Command headquarters (HQ, BHC) in Kiseljak.[63] Three reinforced British infantry battalions served successive six-month tours as the principal UNPROFOR force in the Lasva Valley.[64] Lieutenant Colonel Stewart's 1st Battalion, 22d (Cheshire) Infantry Regiment, arrived from Germany in October, 1992, and established the British battalion (BRITBAT) base in the school at Novi Bila just off the main route through the Lasva Valley. The Cheshires deployed one company in Gornji Vakuf and the HQ and remaining three companies at Nova Bila and immediately began to use their *Warrior* armored vehicles to protect the humanitarian aid convoys transiting the area.[65] The Cheshires were relieved in May, 1993, by the 1st Battalion, Prince of Wales's Own Regiment of Yorkshire, commanded by Lt. Col. Alastair Duncan.[66] The Prince of Wales's Own was replaced in November, 1993, by the 1st Battalion, Coldstream Guards, commanded by Lt. Col. Peter G. Williams.[67]

The UNPROFOR Dutch/Belgian transportion battalion at Busovaca was commanded by Lt. Col. Johannes de Boer from November, 1992, to April, 1993, and by Lt. Col. Paulus Schipper from April to November, 1993.[68] The battalion had the mission of providing transportation support for UNHCR humanitarian convoys and for UNPROFOR units in central Bosnia.

The UNPROFOR forces deployed in Bosnia-Herzegovina have been criticized for their general lack of training, discipline, and suitable equipment, as well as a poorly conceived mission statement.[69] Confined mainly to protecting the aid convoys, and later the UN "safe areas," UNPROFOR units were continually frustrated by restrictive rules of engagement (ROE) that prohibited them from actually intervening to prevent or stop the fighting or offenses against civilians. Even so, they established roadblocks and checkpoints, frequently interfered in on-going operations, and even fired upon Bosnian forces from time to time.[70] Croatian Defense Council commanders complained bitterly of UNPROFOR bias in favor of the Muslims, charging that UNPROFOR was being deceived by the high proportion of Muslim interpreters they employed and that UNPROFOR personnel supplied arms and ammunition to the ABiH, facilitated the movement of ABiH combat forces in UNPROFOR vehicles, discriminated against the Croats in the movement of wounded soldiers and civilians to hospital, and revealed HVO plans to the ABiH.[71] On the surface, however, UNPROFOR commanders in central Bosnia tried to maintain good relations with both Muslims and Croats, and they worked diligently to broker and oversee cease-fires and to reduce the level of violence in the area.

Although unarmed and fewer in number, the ECMM teams in central Bosnia were a much greater nuisance, particularly to HVO commanders, than were the UNPROFOR soldiers. The ECMM was established to oversee the cease-fire provisions of the Brioni Agreement of July 9, 1991, which ended the hostilities in Slovenia. The first group of ECMM monitors arrived in Slovenia on July 15, 1991, and the EC monitoring program was subsequently extended into Croatia and then, in late 1992, into Bosnia-Herzegovina.[72] The ECMM in the RBiH was managed from a Regional Center in Zenica with Coordinating Centers at Travnik, Tuzla, and Mostar. The actual monitoring work was done by teams composed of two monitors, usually military officers seconded to the ECMM for a six-month tour from one of the EC or Conference on Security and Confidence-Building in Europe (CSCE) countries, an interpreter, and a driver. The function of the monitoring teams was to patrol their assigned area and observe ongoing activities; maintain contact with local civil and military authorities as well as local and international aid agencies; facilitate and monitor cease-fire arrangements; investigate serious incidents and human rights violations; and encourage the improvement of relations between the warring parties. For reasons that are not entirely clear, the ECMM monitors in central Bosnia generally favored the Muslims, even to the extent of minimizing Croat charges of "ethnic cleansing" by the Muslims and accusing the HVO of using women and children to rob UN aid convoys.[73] Given their known biases, the HVO did not trust ECMM monitors, and they were not well received in areas controlled by HVO commanders. As a result, there were frequent incidents in which ECMM monitors were threatened by HVO troops and denied access to certain areas. In turn, the monitors were quick to blame the HVO for any incidents that occurred.

Communications

Perhaps the greatest impediment to effective command and control by either side was the lack of adequate communications.[74] Although both the ABiH and HVO were equipped with a variety of communications equipment—including radios, telephones, facsimile machines, and computers (linked with radios in the so-called packet system)—neither had such equipment in sufficient quantities, and neither could ensure the security of the communications means at their disposal. Both sides had fairly effective electronic warfare units, and all of the available modes of communication were subject to interception and constant monitoring. Thus, sensitive orders and information often could not be transmitted to subordinate elements. Moreover, maintenance deficiencies and enemy countermeasures often interrupted communications with higher headquarters, particularly for the HVO, which was surrounded and had to communicate by indirect means with the HVO Main Staff in Mostar. Achieving secure courier communications was seldom possible. Without reliable, secure communications, neither the HVO OZCB nor the ABiH III Corps commanders could exercise effective command and control over their often-fractious subordinate units. Strict adherence to the established laws of land warfare was impossible under such circumstances, as the atrocities committed by both sides attest.

1.
Colonel Tihomir Blaskic (*left*), commander of the HVO OZCB, conducts a joint press interview with Gen. Mehmed Alagic (*right*), commander of the ABiH III Corps.
(ICTY Photo)

2.
Croatian Defense Council chief of staff Gen. Milivoj Petkovic (*left*) and HVO OZCB commander Col. Tihomir Blaskic (*right*) visit the HVO hospital at Novi Bila. (ICTY Photo)

3.
The HVO OZCB's senior officers: Col. Tihomir Blaskic (*center*) with Col. Filip Filipovic (*right*) and Col. Franjo Nakic (*left*). (ICTY Photo)

4.
Dario Kordic, an HVO political leader (*left*), and former HVO Viteska Brigade commander Mario Cerkez (*right*) consult with their defense counsel in an ICTY courtroom in The Hague, February, 2001. (AP/Wide World Photo)

5.
Dusko Grubesic, commander of the HVO Nikola Subic Zrinski Brigade in Busovaca. (ICTY Photo)

6.
Darko Kraljevic, commander of the HVO "Vitezovi" special purpose unit. (ICTY Photo)

7.
Pasko Ljubicic, commander of the HVO 4th Military Police Battalion, monitors a UN relief convoy transiting central Bosnia. (ICTY Photo)

8.
General Sefer Halilovic, former ABiH chief of staff, appears before the ICTY in The Hague, September, 2001. (AP/Wide World Photo)

9.
Colonel Dzemal Merdan, deputy commander of the ABiH III Corps. (ICTY Photo)

10.
Senior officers of the ABiH: (*from left*) Gen. Mehmed Alagic, commander of the ABiH III Corps in 1993; Gen. Enver Hadzihasanovic, commander of the ABiH III Corps in 1992–93; and Col. Amir Kubura, commander of the infamous ABiH 7th Muslim Motorized Brigade in 1992–93. (AP/Wide World Photo)

11.
The Hotel Vitez, wartime headquarters of the HVO Operative Zone Central Bosnia. (ICTY Photo)

12.
The Vitez recreation center, wartime head-quarters of the Viteska Brigade. (ICTY Photo)

13.
This mosque in Ahmici was used as a Muslim defensive strong point and destroyed in the fighting on April 16, 1993. (ICTY Photo)

14.
A UN officer and
vehicle in front of the
"Bungalow" in Nadioci.
The "Jokers" launched
their attack on Ahmici
from here on April 16,
1993. (ICTY Photo)

15.
Remains of the HVO truck
bomb that exploded in
Stari Vitez on July 18,
1993. (ICTY Photo)

16.
View of the village of
Gacice following the HVO
clearing operation con-
ducted in April, 1993.
(ICTY Photo)

17.
United Nations soldiers protect the Roman Catholic church in Guca Gora following its desecration by mujahideen in June, 1993. (ICTY Photo)

18.
View of Vitez with smoke rising from Stari Vitez in the distance. (ICTY Photo)

19.
Intersection on the main Lasva Valley road near the British Battalion base in Stari Bila. The area depicted is typical of the built-up areas in which much of the fighting in central Bosnia in 1993 took place. (ICTY Photo)

20.
Two HVO soldiers approach a hastily constructed barricade typical of the ad hoc field fortifications found in central Bosnia in 1992–94. (ICTY Photo)

21.
A friend joins HVO soldiers as they celebrate a victory. (ICTY Photo)

4 *Training, Doctrine, and Logistics*

Being newly formed armies, both the Croatian Defense Council and the Army of Bosnia-Herzegovina were seriously deficient in individual, unit, and specialist training, had no well-defined and clearly communicated operational doctrine, and lacked both matériel and adequate logistical systems. Such deficiencies contributed to the problems of poor discipline and inadequate command, control, and communications systems, and made the conduct of sustained and efficient operations extremely difficult.

Training

The difficulties with C^3 in both the HVO Operative Zone Central Bosnia and the ABiH III Corps were in part the product of the low level of individual, unit, and specialist training. Training and discipline were weak in both armies except in the elite special purpose and military police units whose personnel apparently received extra training, were better armed, and exhibited a higher level of discipline and cohesion. The short duration of the Muslim-Croat conflict and the comparatively short existence of both the HVO and the ABiH, compounded by the exigencies of the war against the Bosnian Serb army, made the attainment of a high level of individual, unit, and specialist training all but impossible. Nevertheless, both the HVO and the ABiH attempted to provide at least rudimentary individual combat training for all personnel, and in some cases were able to offer officer training courses, specialist courses for engineers and snipers, and other forms of formal training. The HVO in central Bosnia published formal training schedules, although they seem to have been more a reflection of what commanders hoped would happen than they were realistic plans that could be and were actually carried out. Both sides also appear to have given their troops instruction in the laws of land warfare. For example, a leaflet on the subject prepared by the Croatian Red Cross was distributed to the HVO units in the OZCB.[1]

The ABiH early on contemplated the establishment of a war college to train officers and noncommissioned officers (NCOs), but it apparently did not come into being during the period under consideration. Courses for detachment commanders were organized at brigade level, and officers from other corps areas were sent to Zenica for training in engineering and other matters.[2] Soldiers in the elite 7th Muslim Motorized Brigade apparently received at least fifteen days of individual training, including the use of individual weapons, automatic rifles, and mortars.[3] They no doubt also received considerable instruction in the tenets of Islam. The mujahideen also conducted rather extensive training exercises at their various camps in central Bosnia.

Few officers in either the ABiH or HVO had been career officers in the Yugoslavian National Army or had received training adequate for the level of their posting. Indeed, there were only three officers in the OZCB, including the commander, Tihomir Blaskic, and the intelligence officer, Ivica Zeko, who had any additional training to qualify them for the positions they held in the HVO.[4] However, quite a few officers in both organizations had undergone training as reserve officers and NCOs in the JNA and then went on to serve in the JNA Territorial Defense structure for several years.[5] In most cases, that training and experience barely qualified them for duty as a captain first class or as a company commander.

Doctrine

The former Federal Republic of Yugoslavia relied on a national defense policy closely modeled on the Communist Chinese concept of "people's war."[6] The JNA's defense policy and military doctrine focused on defending against an invasion by either NATO or Warsaw Pact forces and thus stressed the mobilization of the entire population. In the event of an invasion of Yugoslavian territory, the policy envisaged the conduct of a "total defensive battle [that] would involve all the forces of the nation, the entire population, and all aspects and material resources of the society."[7] Accordingly, Yugoslavian defensive military doctrine was based on a relatively small but well-equipped national army (the JNA) whose job was to delay an invader by engaging him in conventional combined arms operations while the larger Yugoslavian Territorial Defense forces were mobilized. The TO forces would operate in conjunction with the JNA until the latter's combat power was exhausted. At that point, the TO would assume responsibility for large-scale guerrilla operations throughout the country to defeat and eject the invader. This doctrine was adapted in one form or another by all three warring factions during the war in Bosnia-Herzegovina.

The keystone of Yugoslavia's defense doctrine was the Territorial Defense force, which was destined to carry the battle through to its successful conclusion. The TO forces were organized into mobile, brigade-size elements designed to operate over wide areas and local regional forces designed to protect their home territory. Territorial Defense forces were equipped and trained to fight with light antitank and air defense weapons as well as mortars and machine guns. Finally, they were designed to operate in a decentralized and independent manner, and although organized in brigade strength, they were trained to fight in company-size or smaller units.

The JNA's maneuver concepts were, as Charles R. Patrick has noted, "focused almost exclusively on what Baron Antoine Henri de Jomini called the 'Grand Tactical Level of Battle.'"[8] They were, in fact, a blend of Soviet operational and tactical concepts and methods (for example, the use of special operations forces to degrade the enemy's command and control capabilities and heavy reliance on artillery firepower in both the offense and defense) with those of the U.S. Army (for example, the "active defense"). To these were added uniquely Yugoslavian elements based on their own combat experience and exercises and combining the use of regular, partisan, and irregular TO forces. Inasmuch as the JNA's defense doctrine envisioned a rather short period of conventional warfare followed by an extended guerrilla campaign, emphasis was placed on the conduct of both large- and small-scale guerrilla raids, ambushes, and terrorist actions throughout enemy-held territory. Consequently, territorial defense personnel received a good deal of training in small-unit tactics, special operations, and the employment of snipers—all of which figured prominently in the war in Bosnia-Herzegovina.

The JNA's doctrine also emphasized the use of checkpoints to control movement along important lines of communications.[9] Sited on or near key terrain features, natural choke points, and the front lines, checkpoints featured the use of antitank and antipersonnel mines laid on both sides of the roadway, antitank mines laid on the surface of the roadway (for easy removal in order to permit friendly vehicles to pass through), iron tetrahedron obstacles, concertina barbed wire, and light antitank weapons and machine guns. Usually manned by up to ten men, such checkpoints could also be used to extort fees for passage. Both sides in central Bosnia employed checkpoints as an important operational method. Even the elderly civilian inhabitants of some villages along the main supply routes found that the establishment of a checkpoint could provide a lucrative source of income, and such unofficial "geezer" checkpoints were common.

Armament and Logistics

Commentators on the war in Bosnia-Herzegovina have stressed the desperate straits in which the RBiH found itself as a result of the UN arms embargo and the closure of its ground links to the outside world by the BSA and the HVO. The Bosnian Serb army was by far the best equipped and supplied of the three warring factions, having taken over the bulk of the armament and equipment of JNA and TO forces in Bosnia-Herzegovina and enjoying the full support of Serbia and the rump Federal Republic of Yugoslavia. The HVO, too, was relatively well equipped overall, particularly in Herzegovina, thanks to Croatia's support.

Although the ABiH experienced great difficulty arming and supplying its forces, by early 1993 many of its logistical problems had been overcome—to the point where, during the Muslim-Croat conflict in central Bosnia in 1993, the ABiH had a clear advantage over the HVO in arms, ammunition, and other equipment.[10] For example, the ABiH in the Travnik was poorly organized and poorly equipped until after Jajce fell in October, 1992, at which point units began to receive weapons and equipment so that by June, 1993, the ABiH in the Travnik area not only outnumbered the HVO (by about eight to one), it also had four or five times as many weapons.[11]

In 1990, the FRY not only purchased arms from many other nations, it was one of the world's leading arms exporters to Third World countries. Yugoslavian military factories produced a full range of weapons: tanks, infantry fighting vehicles, armored personnel carriers, artillery pieces, multiple-barrel rocket launchers, and mortars, as well as a wide range of other military equipment and supplies.[12] Consequently, the principal source of arms, ammunition, and other military equipment for both the HVO and the ABiH was the system of arsenals and depots operated by the JNA in Bosnia-Herzegovina.

Although Alija Izetbegovic allowed the JNA to disarm the existing TO forces in 1991–92, and the JNA subsequently contrived to hand over those weapons as well as the bulk of its other arms and equipment in Bosnia-Herzegovina to the Bosnian Serbs, both the HVO and ABiH were able to obtain enormous quantities of matériel by raiding or outright seizing the remaining JNA stockpiles. Indeed, during the course of 1992, several armed squabbles between the Muslims and Croats in central Bosnia arose over the distribution of that booty. Yet, for the most part, the HVO and ABiH shared the available equipment and supplies equally, just as they did the remaining weapons coming from the Bratstvo factory in Novi Travnik in December, 1992. According to one authority, of twenty-four D-30J 122-mm howitzers produced by the Bratstvo plant, the ABiH obtained twelve and the HVO obtained twelve, of which only one remained in central Bosnia; and, of eighteen M-84AB 152-mm "NORA" gun-howitzers produced by the Bratstvo facility, the ABiH obtained nine and the HVO obtained nine, of which only two remained in central Bosnia.[13]

Despite the UN arms embargo, both the HVO and the ABiH obtained substantial quantities of arms, ammunition, and other military supplies from abroad. Some of it was obtained on the international black market, but the Republic of Croatia also supplied considerable amounts of arms, ammunition, and other equipment items to both sides.[14] Almost all of this matériel had to be funneled through Croatia, which thus controlled the types and amounts reaching the two forces in conflict in central Bosnia.[15] That the Croatian government allowed any military supplies at all to pass through Croatia for the ABiH can be attributed to their belief that it would be used against the Serbs, who continued to threaten Croatia as well. In some cases, the Croatian government refused to permit the transit of arms for the ABiH. For example, in September, 1992, Croatian officials discovered and confiscated some four thousand weapons and a million rounds of ammunition aboard an Iranian aircraft in Zagreb.[16] The aircraft was ostensibly delivering humanitarian supplies.

The transit of arms for the ABiH through Croatia is not consistent with the theory that Croatia planned to carry out an ethnic cleansing campaign against the Bosnian Muslims. Nor is it consistent with an alleged deal between

Croatia and Serbia to divide Bosnia-Herzegovina between them. One of the most curious aspects of the Croat-Muslim conflict in central Bosnia is the degree to which both sides communicated with each other and continued to cooperate in the common struggle against the Bosnian Serb army. Even at the height of the internal struggle in 1993, the ABiH requested, and the HVO approved, the movement of weapons and ammunition through the areas controlled by the HVO to areas threatened by the Serbs.[17] Moreover, many leaders in Bosnia-Herzegovina's Muslim-led government, including President Izetbegovic himself, parked their families in the relative safety of Zagreb to avoid the wartime dangers of Sarajevo. That the Croatian government and the HVO would permit such activities is scarcely consistent with the policy of separatism, persecution, genocide, ethnic cleansing, and wanton murder, rape, and destruction charged against HVO leaders in central Bosnia.

The transfer of arms, ammunition, and other military supplies from Croatia to the HVO and ABiH, as well as the transit of war matériel purchased on the international arms market through Croatia to Bosnia-Herzegovina violated the UN arms embargo. There was also a three-way black market that dealt in armaments and civilian consumer goods within Bosnia-Herzegovina itself. Both the HVO and the ABiH obtained small but often significant amounts of weapons, ammunition, and other supplies from the BSA, and both the HVO and the ABiH also benefited from illegal black market arrangements with UNPROFOR personnel. For example, the Ukrainian UNPROFOR unit in Sarajevo did a brisk trade with the HVO in the Kiseljak area, French UNPROFOR engineers supplied the ABiH with fuel, and the Dutch/Belgian UNPROFOR transport battalion in Busovaca sold fuel to the HVO.[18]

Both the HVO and the ABiH internally produced some of the arms and equipment they needed. The HVO produced various types of ammunition as well as some improvised weapons such as the infamous Bébé ("Baby"): a kind of bomb launcher, the ammunition for which was manufactured from fire extinguisher canisters.[19] Even refrigerators were turned into improvised mines.[20] Although the ABiH controlled the principal former JNA arsenals and military production facilities in Bosnia-Herzegovina (except for the critical SPS explosives factory in Vitez), the RBiH government was slow to establish programs to maximize production for use in the defense against the BSA, preferring instead to hope that the UN arms embargo would be lifted. In his memoir, ABiH chief of staff Sefer Halilovic frequently mentioned the difficulties encountered in financing, arming, and supplying the ABiH that resulted from inadequate mobilization of resources by the Izetbegovic government, speculation by government officials charged with military supply, the lack of raw materials for internal production, and the closure of lines of communications by the BSA and HVO.[21] In fact, a good deal of the ABiH's ammunition was home-produced. During the war's first year and one-half, some twenty-five thousand mortar and artillery shells and more than two hundred thousand bombs and grenade launchers were produced in Sarajevo alone. Obtaining raw materials was always a problem, and at one point the factory in Konjic, which produced infantry ammunition, was idle due to the lack of brass stock, and more than two hundred thousand artillery shells were awaiting explosive filler.[22]

Despite the UN embargo and other restrictions, both sides in central Bosnia had sufficient quantities of small arms and automatic weapons. The main deficiency was in artillery and mortar ammunition inasmuch as the lack of raw materials precluded any substantial internal production. Clothing and boots were also a problem for both sides, perhaps more so for the ABiH, which had significantly greater numbers of troops for which to provide.[23] Former HVO intelligence officer Ivica Zeko noted that the ABiH was far more concerned with the supply of arms and ammunition than with clothing its soldiers.[24]

The 1993–94 edition of *The Military Balance* credits the HVO (throughout the RBiH) with some 50 main battle tanks (including T-34 and T-55 models) and around five hundred artillery pieces, and the ABiH with some 20 main battle tanks (including T-55 models), thirty armored personnel carriers, and "some" artillery.[25] However, *in central Bosnia*, the ABiH appears to have had a significant advantage in armor and artillery. The ABiH III Corps had at least six tanks incorporated in the 301st Mechanized Brigade, and although there were rumors that the HVO had eight tanks in the Maglaj salient and another nine in the Kiseljak area, there appear to have been no HVO tanks in the critical Travnik-Vitez-Busovaca enclaves.[26] With respect to artillery, the ABiH actually surpassed the HVO in mortars (60-mm–120-mm) and artillery (122-mm and 155-mm). The Muslim forces also had 128-mm multiple-barrel rocket launchers, although they lacked ammunition. During the fighting in April and June, 1993, the ABiH III Corps was supported by a hundred 120-mm mortars; ten 105-mm, 122-mm, and 155-mm howitzers; eight to ten antiaircraft guns; twenty-five to thirty antiaircraft machine guns; two or three tanks; and two or three ZIS 76-mm armored weapons.[27] In October, 1993, the commander of HVO forces in central Bosnia assessed the relative strength of the ABiH and HVO forces in the Busovaca, Novi Travnik, Travnik, and Vitez area noting the artillery and armor holdings shown in Table 4–1.

Despite UN restrictions, both the HVO and the ABiH made limited use of helicopters for medical evacuation and resupply. United Nations Security Council Resolution 816, issued on March 31, 1993, banned flights over Bosnia-Herzegovina by all fixed- and rotary-wing aircraft. This "no-fly zone" was subsequently enforced by NATO aircraft in Operation DENY FLIGHT, which lasted from April 12, 1993, until December 20, 1995. However, stopping unauthorized helicopter flights was extremely difficult, and between November, 1992, and July, 1995, UN authorities recorded over fifty-seven hundred violations of the flight ban.[28]

For the HVO, the use of helicopters to evacuate casualties and to bring in even small quantities of medical supplies, repair parts, and other critical

Table 4-1. Comparison of HVO and ABiH Heavy Weapons Holdings

Item	HVO	AbiH
Antitank Gun, ZIS	1	3
Mortar, 82-mm	14	9
Mortar, 120-mm	12	21
Howitzer, 105-mm	0	2
Howitzer, 122-mm	1	10
Gun-Howitzer, 152-mm, *Nora*	2	1
Rocket Launcher, 107-mm	1	1
Rocket Launcher, 128-mm	6	4
Multiple Rocket Launcher, 122-mm	2	0
Tank	0	5
Armored Combat Vehicle, BOV	1	0

Source: HQ, Vitez Military District, Vitez, n.d. (February 2), 1993, subj: Assessment of the Situation (Table, "Ratios of Forces and Equipment by Locality"), 21, KC D59/2.

items was a very important, if limited, part of the logistical chain. Prior to the outbreak of the Muslim-Croat conflict, HVO forces in central Bosnia were relatively well supplied by road from HVO logistical bases at Grude and Posusje in Herzegovina. With the ABiH attacks in April, 1993, the main land lines of communication to the south—Route DIAMOND in particular— could no longer be used to evacuate casualties from central Bosnia or to bring in supplies. The need for casualty evacuation was critical, and Drago Nakic, a manager of the SPS explosives firm stationed in Split, arranged and coordinated the legal use of Croatian Army helicopters for the evacuation of casualities from the HVO hospital in Novi Bila.[29] The HV helicopters operated from their base in Divulje under UNPROFOR and ECMM supervision, but their use was discontinued in July, 1993, due to the danger arising from heavier ABiH attacks and the shrinking of the Lasva Valley pocket. Nakic then arranged for the use of commercial helicopters with Russian and Ukrainian civilian crews to make the flights from Grude and Posusje, and the evacuation flights continued at a rate of two or three per week until early 1994.[30]

Although authorized helicopter flights brought in some medical supplies for the HVO in central Bosnia until July, 1993, for all practical purposes the OZCB was entirely cut off from Herzegovina from early July until the fall of 1993, and no significant amounts of military supplies were received.[31] However, the unauthorized commercial helicopter flights from Grude and Posusje did bring in limited amounts of critical items, such as ammunition, spare parts, and communications equipment, and there may well have been other unauthorized parachute drops and helicopter deliveries.[32]

Thus, while the HVO forces in Herzegovina may have been well equipped with tanks, artillery, food, fuel, clothing, ammunition, and other supplies provided by the Republic of Croatia and other outside sources, the situation in central Bosnia was vastly different. The HVO in central Bosnia was not only outnumbered, it was outgunned as well. As the conflict dragged on, the HVO's logistical situation became even worse, despite attempts to open alternate lines of communication and the use of helicopters. The measure of the HVO's resources poverty is that at the time of the Washington Agreement cease-fire in February, 1994, the on-hand stocks of artillery ammunition in the OZCB had fallen to six 122-mm shells and four 155-mm shells.[33]

5 Prelude to Civil War in Central Bosnia

The fall of Jajce to the Bosnian Serb army on October 29, 1992, marked the beginning of open conflict between the Muslims and Croats in central Bosnia. Until that time, the two communities had maintained an uneasy alliance against the BSA, but the tension between them grew during the course of 1991–92. The HVO and ABiH squabbled over the distribution of arms seized from the JNA, and there were numerous local incidents of violence by one group against the other. However, only in the last quarter of 1992 did Muslim-Croat disagreements begin to rise to the level of civil war.

In January, 1993, the building animosity transformed into open conflict as the ABiH, strengthened by large numbers of Muslim refugees and the arrival of the mujahideen, mounted a probing attack against their HVO allies. Muslim extremists, abetted by the Izetbegovic government and fervent nationalists within the ABiH, planned and initiated offensive action against their erstwhile ally in the hope of securing control of the key military industries and lines of communication in central Bosnia and clearing the region for the resettlement of the thousands of Muslims displaced by the fighting against the BSA elsewhere in Bosnia-Herzegovina.

There is, of course, no "smoking gun"—no operations plan or policy decision document—that proves beyond a doubt the ABiH planned and carried out an attack on the Croatian enclaves in central Bosnia with such objectives. The time and place at which the plan was approved, and who proposed and who approved it, remain unknown. Did a written document outlining the plan ever exist? Probably. Does a copy of that document still exist? Probably deep in the ABiH's archives. Will it ever be produced for public scrutiny? Probably not—for rather obvious reasons. On the other hand, neither does such clear evidence exist to support the oft-repeated hypothesis of journalists, UNPROFOR and ECMM personnel, and Muslim propagandists that the HVO planned and carried out such an offensive against the Muslims. The answer to the key question of who planned and initiated the conflict between Muslims and Croats in central Bosnia can only be determined by carefully evaluating the thousands of fragments of evidence and fitting them into a coherent pattern showing means, motive, and opportunity in the same way a detective arrives at a viable reconstruction of a crime. The process is tedious, but it produces reliable results. When applied to the events in central Bosnia between November, 1992, and March, 1994, it leads to just one conclusion: only the ABiH had the necessary means, motive, and opportunity; it was, in fact, the ABiH, not the HVO, that developed a strategic offensive plan and attempted to carry it out.

HVO-ABiH Cooperation in the Battle against the Serbs

At the beginning of the conflict with the Bosnian Serbs, the HVO attempted to strengthen coordination in the Muslim and Croat alliance. In mid-April, 1992, the HVO requested that RBiH president Alija Izetbegovic create a joint military headquarters to govern both the HVO and the Muslim-led Territorial Defense forces, but Izetbegovic ignored the request and the issue was never put on the agenda of any meeting of the RBiH Presidency, despite repeated pleas from Croat members of the Presidency. Efforts to improve coordination at the local level also met with Muslim indifference and obstruction. In central Bosnia, the HVO and TO attempted to form a joint military unit to defend against the BSA onslaught. In early 1992, the Vitez Municipality Crisis Staff proposed the establishment of a joint Vitez Brigade made up of a battalion from the HVO and one from the TO. A Croat, Franjo Nakic, would serve as commander, and a Muslim, Sefkija Didic, would be both deputy commander and chief of staff. The rest of the staff would be composed of both HVO and TO officers.[1] However, the Muslims' foot-dragging and quibbling regarding the proposed brigade antagonized the Croats, who increasingly left the Territorial Defense forces for the HVO, which was farther along in its preparations to defend against the Serbs.

Nevertheless, by mid-1992, the hastily assembled and armed HVO and TO forces, with some assistance from the Croatian armed forces, managed to establish a defensive line against the more numerous and much better equipped Bosnian Serb army. However, the BSA had surrounded Sarajevo, the RBiH capital, and the scratch Muslim and Croat forces faced the superior Serb forces on several fronts ringing the newly declared state. The cooperating HVO and Muslim forces faced significant BSA threats in both eastern and western Herzegovina, and a predominantly Muslim army struggled to retain control of several eastern Bosnia towns invested by the BSA. Of principal concern to the commanders of the HVO OZCB and the ABiH III Corps in central Bosnia were an eastern front running from Hadzici north to the Visoko-Ilijas area; a northern front in the Maglaj-Doboj-Teslic-Tesanj area; and a western front in the area extending from Jajce southward to Donja Vakuf and Bugojno. In all three areas, the RBiH's HVO and Muslim forces struggled to hold back the BSA advance.

The Growth of Muslim-Croat Hostility, March, 1992–January, 1993

Tensions between Muslims and Croats increased steadily throughout the course of 1992 as the two sides vied for political power in the various municipalities in central Bosnia; squabbled over the division of the spoils left by the JNA, which abandoned Bosnia-Herzegovina in May, 1992; sought to gain control over key localities and facilities; and acted to protect their communities from all comers. Despite growing tensions and a number of armed confrontations, the HVO and ABiH continued to cooperate in the defense against the Bosnia Serbs backed by the rump Yugoslavia (Serbia and Montenegro) and the remnants of the JNA. However, three essentially unrelated incidents in late October—just before Jajce fell to the BSA—signaled the coming conflict: the Novi Travnik gas station incident, the assassination of the HVO commander in Travnik, and the Muslim roadblock at Ahmici. These incidents led to a flare-up of small-scale Muslim-Croat fighting throughout the region that was tamped down by an UNPROFOR arranged cease-fire. Tensions and incidents increased substantially following Jajce's fall and the consequent influx of Muslim refugees, many of them armed, into the Lasva-Kozica-Lepenica region. At the same time, the mujahideen presence in central Bosnia began to make itself felt, and the ABiH began to infiltrate armed cadres into the villages and to position regular ABiH units in the Lasva-Kozica-Lepenica valley in preparation for the planned offensive.

Following numerous Muslim-Croat disagreements and confrontations in the Busovaca area, HVO authorities took over the Busovaca municipal government on May 10, blockading the town, demanding the surrender of weapons by the Muslim-dominated TO units, issuing arrest warrants for prominent Muslims, guaranteeing the security and eventual evacuation of JNA elements from the Kaonik area, and mobilizing the Croats in the town.[2] Moreover, the Croat authorities announced that the Busovaca HVO would take over all JNA weapons, equipment, and barracks in the local area. The Muslim-led Bosnian government was incensed by the Croats' seizure of control in Busovaca and on May 12 openly condemned the HVO authorities for not handing control of the town over to the central government on demand.[3]

The tensions in the Busovaca area were intensified by the Muslim failure to hold to the agreed upon plan for the distribution of arms from the former JNA arsenal in the area.[4] Several similar incidents occurred elsewhere, resulting in small fights between Muslims and Croats over the distribution of the spoils resulting from the JNA's withdrawal. There was a Muslim-Croat confrontation at the Bratstvo armaments factory in Novi Travnik on June 18 when HVO elements attempted to prevent Bosnia-Herzegovina's Muslim-led government from removing from the factory arms the government intended to sell abroad.[5] Two months later, in August, HVO and Territorial Defense elements forced the turnover of the JNA arsenal at Slimena in Travnik.[6] The arsenal had been mined by the JNA, and while the HVO tried to negotiate a surrender and the removal of the mines, TO elements broke into the factory and exploded them. In the aftermath of the debacle, the TO soldiers gathered up undamaged weapons parts, which they subsequently reassembled to make whole weapons. One result of the consequent increase in the numbers of weapons in Muslim hands was an increase in confrontations in the area.

Representatives of the various Croat communities in central Bosnia met in Busovaca on September 22 to discuss the situation, particularly the growing tensions between Muslims and Croats resulting from one municipality or the other coming under the exclusive control of either Muslim or Bosnian Croat authorities.[7] The conferees enumerated a number of general observations regarding the situation throughout the region. They noted in particular the need to revive the local economy and speed up preparations for winter in case they were totally cut off from Herzegovina and Croatia. They called for better coordination between HVO military and civilian authorities and uniformity of policy. Complaints were also made regarding the behavior of Muslims who acted "as if they have an exclusive right to power in B and H and as if they are the only fighters for B and H," and regarding Muslim attempts to enforce their policies through the use of Croatian Defense Forces (HOS) elements. Special concern was articulated regarding the daily arrival of new Muslim refugees in the area, as well as the increasing presence of Muslim forces in the various towns while HVO forces were busy holding the lines against the BSA and HVO military authorities were being urged to prepare defense plans in case of confrontations with the Muslims.

In mid-October, three apparently unrelated incidents led to open fighting between Muslims and Croats in central Bosnia. The first of these occurred in the town of Novi Travnik on October 18, and involved a dispute that began at a gas station near HVO headquarters. By mutual agreement, Muslims and Croats were sharing the region's fuel supplies. The conflict apparently broke out when Croats manning the gas station in Novi Travnik refused to provide gasoline to a Muslim Territorial Defense soldier.[8] A squabble began, the Muslim was shot dead, and within minutes HVO and TO forces in Novi Travnik were engaged in a full-scale firefight in the town center. The fighting, led by Refik Lendo on the Muslim side, continued for several days despite the efforts of British UNPROFOR officers to bring it to a halt.

News of the fighting in Novi Travnik spread quickly throughout the region. Both Muslims and Croats erected roadblocks, mobilized local defense forces, and in some areas fired upon each other. Even so, the conflict remained localized and uncoordinated, the Muslim and Croat forces in each town and village acting according to their own often faulty assessment of the situation. However, the situation worsened two days later when the commander of the HVO brigade in Travnik, Ivica Stojak, was assassinated on October 20 by mujahideen near Medresa, apparently on the orders of Col. Asim Koricic, commander of the 7th Muslim Motorized Brigade.[9] From about the time Jajce fell, the newly arrived mujahideen had begun to appear in the Travnik area, and the number of small incidents between Muslims and Croats had risen substantially. Nevertheless, Stojak's assassination may have been personal rather than part of some larger Muslim plot against the HVO in Travnik.

Perhaps the most serious incident of the October outburst was the establishment of a roadblock by Muslim TO forces near the village of Ahmici on the main road through the Lasva Valley. The roadblock was established on October 20, and the TO forces manning it refused to let HVO forces en route to the defense of Jajce pass.[10] The TO commander in the Ahmici area, Nijaz Sivro, was young and inexperienced, as was his deputy, Muniz Ahmic. Sivro had gone to the front lines against the Serbs in Visoko just before the roadblock at Ahmici was set up, and Ahmic was entrusted with the task of establishing the roadblock by the "Coordinating Committee for the Protection of Muslims." One Muslim officer characterized the setting up of the barricade as "ill-prepared and disorganized," and the initial confrontation at the Ahmici roadblock resulted in one Muslim soldier killed and several wounded.[11] Two days later, October 22, the roadblock was removed without a fight, and HVO forces could again use the Lasva Valley road for moving troops to the Serb front.[12] During the course of the altercation, the Muslim TO commander in Vitez told the UNPROFOR's Lt. Col. Bob Stewart that Muslims had established the roadblock at Ahmici to prevent the HVO from reinforcing their forces then fighting in Novi Travnik.[13] In fact, the establishment of the roadblock had been ordered by the ABiH zone headquarters in Zenica (later HQ, III Corps).[14]

After several days of fighting and almost fifty casualties in the Lasva region, officers of the British UNPROFOR unit managed to negotiate a cease-fire on October 21 in the Vitez area that was then extended to Novi Travnik and the rest of the region. The Muslim-Croat fighting had been widespread, but it appears to have been spontaneous rather than the result of a coordinated action by either side. Although a planned provocation by the Muslims, in and of itself the October 20 roadblock at Ahmici was a minor event. As far as the HVO authorities at the time were concerned, it was not a serious incident.[15] It took on much greater significance, however, after HVO forces assaulted the village on April 16, 1993. Those who wished to portray the HVO as the aggressor in the Muslim-Croat conflict in central Bosnia have painted the October incident as a cause of the April, 1993 events, although the only real connection between the two is that they occurred in approximately the same location: the point at which the village of Ahmici touches the Vitez-Busovaca road at the narrowest part of the Lasva Valley.

One historian has characterized the period from January, 1992, up to the outbreak of Muslim-Croat hostilities in late January, 1993, as one in which "there was some 'pushing and shoving' between Croats and Muslims, and a lack of wholehearted cooperation as each group sought to stabilise and strengthen its own territory."[16] Indeed, one can point to numerous small-scale local confrontations between Muslims and Croats in central Bosnia during the course of 1992 designed to gain control over stockpiles of arms, munitions, and other military supplies; to gain control of key facilities or lines of communications; and to test the other side's will and capabilities to resist. Such incidents increased in frequency and intensity after Jajce fell on October 29, 1992, but they do not appear to have been part of a coordinated plan by either party. Indeed, they appear to be random, unconnected, and short-lived episodes resulting from the increasing level of tension and distrust between the two communities in central Bosnia. Even the buildup of Muslim forces, the infiltration of armed ABiH soldiers and mujahideen into key villages and towns, and the suggestive positioning of ABiH units in central Bosnia went largely unnoticed by the HVO at the time.[17] Only in retrospect do they appear to be part of a pattern of actions taken by the ABiH to prepare for the opening of an all-out Muslim offensive against the Croatian community in the Lasva-Kozica-Lepenica region.[18]

The ABiH Strategic Offensive Plan

Although its author and the date of its creation remain uncertain, events clearly reveal the existence of an ABiH strategic offensive against the HVO in central Bosnia that began in mid-January, 1993, and continued in several phases until the signing of the Washington Agreements in late February, 1994. The strategic objectives of the plan were:

1. To gain control of the north-south lines of communication (LOCs) passing through the Bosnian Croat enclave in central Bosnia, thereby linking the ABiH forces north of the Lasva-Kozica-Lepenica Valleys with those to the south and securing the Muslim lines of communication to the outside world.

2. To gain control of the military industrial facilities in central Bosnia (the SPS explosives factory in Vitez and factories in Travnik and Novi Travnik) or on its periphery (factories in Bugojno, Gornji Vakuf, Prozor, Jablanica, Konjic, and Hadzici, among others) so as to facilitate the arming of the ABiH in the war against the Serbs.

3. To surround the Bosnian Croat enclave in central Bosnia and divide it into smaller pieces that could then be eliminated seriatim, thereby clearing the Croats from central Bosnia and providing a place for Muslim refugees expelled by the Serbs from other areas to settle.[19]

Achieving the third objective would also ensure that the Muslims retained political control of central Bosnia so they could continue to dominate the RBiH's central government. There was probably also an anticipation of a peace agreement that would result in a partition of Bosnia-Herzegovina among the Serbs, Muslims, and Croats, in which case possession of the Lasva-Kozica-Lepenica region would probably be tantamount to its inclusion in the Muslim area under any settlement, regardless of the area's former ethnic composition, a principle that was observed subsequently in areas seized by the Serbs. In fact, the area in question was part of Canton 10 under the Vance-Owen Peace Plan and was assigned to the Croats, but at the time the Muslim offensive plan was devised and set in motion the issue was still undecided.[20] In any event, occupation by the ABiH of the Lasva-Kozica-Lepenica region would probably be cause for revision of the VOPP. In a larger and less sinister context, the Republic of Bosnia-Herzegovina's

infant central government may simply have been eager to exert its authority over such territory as had not already been taken by the Bosnian Serbs.
It should also be noted that the Croat enclaves in northern Bosnia posed no
threat politically or militarily to the Muslim-led government and were useful for propaganda purposes to show the multiethnic composition and cooperation in the Muslim-led RBiH.

Such a complex and far-reaching plan could only have been worked out
in the ABiH General Staff under the direction of Chief of Staff Sefer
Halilovic, and further elaborated in Enver Hadzihasanovic's III Corps headquarters. Only they had the resources and expertise to prepare such a plan,
and there are some indications that they had considered such a plan much
earlier. By the time Jajce fell at the end of October, 1992, the ABiH's logistical situation was near collapse. The Izetbegovic government had failed to
induce the United Nations to cancel its arms embargo or to intervene militarily, and, despite Chief of Staff Halilovic's persistent entreaties, had done
little to mobilize the Bosnian economy for war. Too weak to seize the arms
and equipment it needed from the far more powerful Bosnian Serb army,
the ABiH still had sufficient strength to overpower its erstwhile ally, the
HVO—at least in the central Bosnia area. Success in such an endeavor
would solve two of the most pressing logistical problems. First, it would provide an immediate gain in arms and other equipment, which could be
quickly turned against the Serbs. Second, it would open the ABiH's lines of
communications through central Bosnia, thereby facilitating the more effective deployment of available ABiH troops, armaments, and supplies, as
well as the importation of arms, ammunition, and other vital supplies obtained on the international arms market. Moreover, General Halilovic's as-
sociates on the ABiH General Staff had long since identified Kiseljak, Busovaca, Vitez, and Vares as the site for refugee settlements. In the summer of
1992, two of Halilovic's subordinates, Rifat Bilajac and Zicro Suljevic, attended a meeting at SDA headquarters in Sarajevo to discuss the refugee situation. Halilovic relates that they returned to the headquarters infuriated,
Bilajac stating angrily: "I was informed about everything in the SDA headquarters. There were some 10–12 members of the executive committee present, and when I suggested that refugee settlements should be built in Kiseljak, Busovaca, Vitez and Vares, Behmen tells me nicely: 'It can't be there, as
that's Croat national territory.' The other members were silent. Then we
quarreled and left the meeting. Well, what are we dying for if this is Croat
national territory?"[21]

As to the question of when such a plan might have been conceived, it is
important to note that the ABiH III Corps first openly attacked HVO forces
in the Lasva Valley in late January, 1993. A significant amount of time,
probably not less than two months, would have been required to assemble
and prepare the forces necessary for an offensive on the scale of the January
attacks. Thus, the basic plan needed to have been completed no later than
November 1, 1992, suggesting that the necessary planning was already in

progress even before Jajce fell. It seems likely, therefore, that the concept of the ABiH strategic offensive against the HVO in central Bosnia was developed in the late summer or early fall of 1992 and that the "go–no go" decision was probably made in early November—soon after the fall of Jajce.

The HVO Reaction

While the ABiH was clearly the aggressor in the Muslim-Croat civil war in central Bosnia, the HVO commanders did not sit idly by waiting to be overrun by their more numerous Muslim opponents. Instead they adopted what is known in U.S. military parlance as an "active defense," that is, a defense in which the defender actively and continuously seeks to improve his defensive posture by seizing and controlling key terrain and lines of communication, degrading the enemy's offensive capabilities, and acting aggressively to spoil enemy attacks and keep the enemy off balance.[22] To an observer on the ground who did not understand the overall strategic situation—particularly one prone to rash judgments and broad inferences—the HVO's conduct of the active defense might well appear to have been offensive in nature. Yet, the fact is, it was largely reactive and preventive.

Thus, from an HVO perspective the strategic battle was entirely a defensive one, albeit marked by selective use of preemptive spoiling attacks (*preventivi*), counterattacks, and other offensive actions designed to support the Croat defensive strategy by the conduct of an "active defense" rather than a purely positional defense in the Lasva-Kozica-Lepenica Valleys. Surrounded, heavily outnumbered (by as much as eight or ten to one according to some accounts), and logistically bankrupt, it would have been completely illogical for the Croats to try to mount a systematic campaign to expand the enclave or to ethnically cleanse Muslims from the Lasva Valley, much less from all of the proposed Canton 10. One former HVO officer has said that an HVO commander would have had to be "insane" to have contemplated an offensive against the Muslims given their tenuous manpower, logistics, and full deployment against the Serbs.[23] They were barely able to repel the repeated Muslim attacks and were certainly too weak in numbers, arms, and ammunition to attempt a major offensive. Nevertheless, the hard-pressed HVO forces did manage to mount a number of small offensive actions to secure better defensive positions, prevent the Muslims from obtaining their objectives, and to clear their rear areas of troublesome Muslim enclaves. Generally, a clear military necessity can be shown for each of those offensive actions. More commonly, the HVO forces simply took up defensive positions and repelled a series of increasingly heavy Muslim attacks that inexorably whittled away the territory held by the HVO, inflicted casualties, and slowly asphyxiated the Bosnian Croat defenders.

6 *The ABiH Probing Attack, January, 1993*

Even before Jajce fell, the ABiH appears to have been planning some sort of offensive against the Bosnian Croats in central Bosnia. After October 29, 1992, the increasing numbers of able-bodied military-age Muslim refugees entering the region were organized, armed, and trained for offensive operations; mujahideen, ABiH soldiers, and armed refugees were infiltrated into key villages in groups of three or four men and hidden in Muslim homes or mosques; and by the end of 1992, the ABiH had positioned a number of its combat brigades in key locations throughout the Lasva, Kozica, and Lepenica Valleys.[1] In retrospect, the latter actions were particularly significant.

The first phase of the ABiH offensive plan began on January 20–21, 1993, and took the form of a probing action designed to seize key terrain and position forces for the coming main attack; to test HVO resistance and uncover HVO defensive plans and methods; and probably to test the reactions of UNPROFOR forces to an open conflict between the Muslims and Croats. This stage of the campaign, which was preceded by an ABiH III Corps attack on the town of Gornji Vakuf in an attempt to seal off the central Bosnia battlefield by closing the vital Route DIAMOND supply route, lasted only a few days, in large part because the HVO was able to repulse the main Muslim probes and quickly force a stalemate. The ABiH subsequently drew back and reformed in preparation for the main offensive in mid-April, 1993. The ABiH planners probably viewed the UNPROFOR's lack of response as a "green light" for the planned main attack in April.

The ABiH achieved tactical surprise with its January probing operations. Brigadier Ivica Zeko, the OZCB intelligence officer at the time, said in retrospect that it is clear the Muslims were positioning their units for an offensive, but that neither he nor anyone else in the HVO had a clear indication of it before the Muslims launched their attack.[2] The HVO was working with the Muslims against the Serbs, and no one was looking for Muslim perfidy. For example, the HVO headquarters in central Bosnia apparently did not target the ABiH for intelligence purposes before mid-January, 1993, although the Muslim intelligence services targeted the HVO.[3] But even had the HVO known in advance of the Muslim attack, there is little that could have done in terms of repositioning its forces, which were heavily committed on the lines against the Serbs.

Despite Zeko's disclaimer, the OZCB apparently did have some indications that something was about to happen. The attack on Gornji Vakuf and fighting in the Prozor area were clear signs that a major ABiH operation was in the offing in central Bosnia, and there were probably warnings from the HVO Main Staff in Mostar. On January 16, 1993, HQ, OZCB, ordered all subordinate units to raise their combat readiness to the highest level, including the cancellation of all leaves, the collection and redistribution of weapons in private hands, the disarming and isolation of Muslim members of the HVO who disobeyed orders, and an increase in the security posture of various Croat villages in the Operative Zone.[4] The HVO brigades in Zenica and Busovaca were directed to organize surveillance of the area between Zenica and the Lasva Valley, and the HVO brigade in Novi Travnik was instructed to monitor the area toward Gornji Vakuf and be prepared to act on order. The 4th Military Police Battalion was ordered to secure the HVO's military and political headquarters, control traffic, and confiscate weapons and other equipment from Muslim transports. The PPN "Vitezovi " and "Ludvig Pavlovic" were employed from January 19 on reconnaissance and intelligence-gathering missions to track the movement of ABiH units in the OZCB area of operations.[5]

The ABiH Attack on Gornji Vakuf

While the town of Gornji Vakuf (usually called Uskoplje by Croats) was in the Operative Zone Northwest Herzegovina rather than the OZCB, it was of vital importance to the defenders of the Croat enclaves in central Bosnia inasmuch as it was the southern terminus of the vital Novi Travnik–Gornji Vakuf supply route. Before the conflict in January, 1993, Gornji Vakuf's population included about ten thousand Croats and fourteen thousand Muslims.[6] Many of the surrounding villages had a Croat majority, and in the town itself the Croats and Muslims lived in mixed areas. When the Serbs attacked Croatia in 1991, the HVO in Gornji Vakuf started making military preparations, and by the time of the Battle of Kupres in 1992 had formed one HVO company. There were few problems in the town; the Muslims and Croats had parallel governmental and military structures, and the two communities coexisted warily. In August, 1992, the Muslim Green Berets paramilitary group established a headquarters in Gornji Vakuf, and they, rather than Territorial Defense troops, began to patrol the nearby Muslim villages. However, there were no serious incidents between the Muslims and Croats until January 8–10, 1993, when, as a prelude to the ABiH attack on the town, about a hundred Croats were expelled from their homes in the Muslim sections of town. On January 10, the main road was blocked for the first time, and the Muslims refused to allow HVO troops on their way to the BSA front to pass.

On January 13, the 305th and 317th Mountain Brigades of the ABiH III Corps, under the command of V. Agic, attacked the HVO forces in Gornji Vakuf. The attack's apparent objective was to test the mettle of the Croat defenders and, if possible, to cut the road to Novi Travnik, thus sealing central Bosnia off from Herzegovina. The town was defended by elements of the

Ante Starcevic Brigade, a unit subordinate to Brigadier Zeljko Siljeg's OZ Northwest Herzegovina. There were some three hundred HVO fighters in the town and about two thousand in the surrounding area, reinforced by some seventy HVO military policemen and about 150 men of the PPN "Bruno Busic."

Once the conflict began, a front line was established through the center of town, with the area south of the HVO military police headquarters under Muslim control. Following the initial clashes, the Muslims took positions on the surrounding hills, and the local HVO forces, lacking sufficient manpower to hold a continuous line, established a forty-five-kilometer line of strong points on key terrain facing the Muslims holding the surrounding high ground. Among the key positions the HVO held was the pass on the road between Gornji Vakuf and Prozor. A temporary cease-fire was arranged with UNPROFOR assistance on the afternoon of January 13, and the Croats could again use the road, but there continued to be many problems due to the Muslim checkpoints.[7]

At the time, the OZCB intelligence staff saw the attack on Gornji Vakuf as an isolated "local action" intended to disrupt traffic on the Gornji Vakuf–Novi Travnik road. Only in retrospect was it clear that the Muslims wanted to seal central Bosnia off from Herzegovina and to provoke the HVO into some offensive action to clear their lines of communication, an action that could then be used as a casus belli and proof of Croat perfidy.[8] The fighting around Gornji Vakuf subsequently intensified and assumed even greater significance as the ABiH continued its attempts to secure control of the southern end of the vital Gornji Vakuf–Novi Travnik corridor.

The ABiH Attacks at Kacuni and Busovaca

The two principal objectives of the Muslim probing attacks launched from the villages of Merdani, Lasva, and Dusina in January, 1993, were the village of Kacuni on the important Busovaca–Kiseljak road and the town of Busovaca itself. The intent of the ABiH attackers was to seize Kacuni and thus sever the connection between Kiseljak and the rest of the Croat enclave in central Bosnia. Busovaca was a key Croat political center and controlled the road net west to Vitez and Travnik, east to the Bosna River and thence north to Zenica or south and east to Kakanj, Visoko, and Sarajevo, and southeast to Kiseljak. By taking Busovaca, the ABiH could ensure control of the principal lines of communication in the Lasva, Kozica, and Lepenica Valleys. By definition, a probing attack is one, which, if it encounters only light resistance, can be pressed on to some major goal. In the case of the January, 1993, attack in the Busovaca-Kacuni area, the major goal was to lower Croat morale and divide the Croat enclave in central Bosnia into two segments. In fact, the latter objective was achieved.

The ABiH offensive operation in central Bosnia began on January 19 with the establishment of a checkpoint at Kacuni on the Busovaca–Kiseljak road by elements of the ABiH III Corps.[9] This marked the first open clash between the ABiH and the HVO in the area, and, just as the attackers intended, interrupted communications between Busovaca and Kiseljak. Meanwhile, efforts were made to open a road across the Hum-Kula massif leading to the Busovaca-Kacuni area for the purpose of facilitating the movement of ABiH forces into the contested areas. Elements of ABiH Operations Group (OG) Lasva, under the command of Nehru Ganic, attacked and seized the villages of Lasva and Dusina, and the 333d Mountain Brigade established a line from Lasva through Dusina to Kacuni.[10] In the course of taking control of Dusina, elements of the 2d Battalion, 7th Muslim Motorized Brigade—commanded by Col. Serif Patkovic—massacred a number of Croat soldiers and civilians in the village. They also executed the local Croat commander, Zvonko Rajic, and cut out his heart.[11] On January 23–24, elements of the 301st Mechanized and the 303d, 314th, and 333d Mountain Brigades, supported by part of the 310th Mountain Brigade from the Fojnica area, a battalion of the 7th Muslim Brigade, units of the Mobile Detachment, and a company of military police from the ABiH III Corps, continued the attack from Kacuni toward the village of Bilalovac which was taken thereby linking the ABiH's OG Istok (East) with OG Zapad (West).[12] The villages of Nezirovici, Oseliste, Gusti Grab, and Donje Polje were attacked on January 25–26, and their Croat populations "cleared up."[13] An accidental result of the Muslim seizure of Kacuni was that the HVO OZCB commander, Col. Tihomir Blaskic, was cut off from his headquarters in Vitez. A native of the Kiseljak area, Blaskic was paying a Sunday visit to his parents when the Busovaca–Kiseljak road was cut at Kacuni. It was some time before he was able to return to his headquarters, so he had to direct operations from the Ban Jelacic Brigade's headquarters in Kiseljak.

Although Muslim-Croat tensions were high, the January attack came as something of a surprise to the HVO soldiers and authorities in the Busovaca area. In December, 1992, armed Muslim refugees from Jajce and the fighting in the Krajina had begun to move into the Busovaca area, and in January, 1993, they were augmented by Muslim troops who had left the front lines against the Serbs and were taking over a building at a time in Busovaca and other towns and villages in the Lasva, Kozica, and Lepenica Valleys.[14] On January 6, the Intelligence Section of the HVO Nikola Subic Zrinski Brigade in Busovaca issued an estimate of Muslim capabilities and intentions that pin-pointed ABiH units and noted that they were in position to cut the Busovaca–Kiseljak road at Kacuni, the Busovaca–Vitez road at Ahmici, and the Busovaca–Zenica road at Grablje.[15]

There were numerous incidents in the Busovaca area in the days immediately preceding the Muslim attack, including the confiscation of weapons and the arrest of Croats by Busovaca Muslim authorities. The ABiH attempted to arrest Ignaz Kostroman, a local Bosnian Croat politician on January 22, and two HVO soldiers were killed and barricades were erected by Muslims in Busovaca two days later.[16] A sudden exodus of Muslims from

Busovaca, many of whom headed to the hospital in Zenica, occurred immediately before the attack on January 25.

Operating from assembly areas in the Merdani-Lasva-Dusina area to the northeast, ABiH forces moved up along the east bank of the Kozica River and launched a probing attack—preceded by heavy and indiscriminate shelling by 82-mm and 120-mm mortars and "Lancers"—on Busovaca itself in the early morning hours of January 25.[17] Some six hundred to seven hundred men from the Nikola Subic Zrinski Brigade's 1st and 2d Battalions defended the town. The Zrinski Brigade was still untried, having just been formed on December 19, 1992, but the HVO troops quickly occupied defensive positions around the town and forestalled a successful attack by the ABiH infantry.

The ABiH Attacks in the Kiseljak-Fojnica-Kresevo Area

Another important objective of the Muslim attackers in January, 1993, was to gain control of the Fojnica junction on the Busovaca–Kiseljak road near Gomionica in order to control access southward to the town of Fojnica, another important Croat stronghold. The Kiseljak-Fojnica-Kresevo area had long been surrounded by ABiH and Territorial Defense forces, and as early as August, 1992, the Muslim-dominated TO staff in Kiseljak had issued instructions for local TO units to prepare for a conflict with the HVO.[18] The Muslim's probing attack began in the Kiseljak area at about 6 A.M. on January 25 with a random artillery/mortar attack. The HVO defenders occupied defensive positions wherever they could, having not prepared any positions in advance. The Muslim forces, including Muslim military police elements, attacked from northeast to southwest across the Busovaca–Kiseljak road, but were stopped by an HVO force consisting of two battalions from the Ban Jelacic Brigade led by an acting commander named Zamenic, reinforced by a company of the HVO 4th Military Police Battalion. Many were wounded during the daylong clash, which ended at about 7 or 8 P.M. The HVO troops were able to improve their positions overnight and counterattacked on January 27, digging in at the end of the day. After five days of fighting, a cease-fire agreement was negotiated and signed. The Muslims attackers thus failed to seize their primary objective, the Fojnica intersection, but they did succeed in gaining control of the villages northeast of the road (Svinjarevo, Behrici, and Gomionica) and established their headquarters in Gomionica, occupying the area with about seven hundred ABiH soldiers. Most Muslim civilians in all of the villages south of Kiseljak and six villages north of the town subsequently left the area, although some remained, hoping the ABiH had sufficient power to protect them in a hotly contested area. Their decision was a fateful one, as the ABiH launched another unsuccessful attack in the heavily defended Gomionica area in April. Thereafter, the struggle in the Kiseljak enclave focused on an ABiH attempt to roll up the HVO positions around Kiseljak from the east and south.

The February–March Pause

With a typical rush to judgment, Lt. Col. Bob Stewart, the UNPROFOR commander in the Lasva Valley, misread the situation on January 25, opining that "both sides were having a go at each other; Croats in Busovaca; Muslims in Kacuni."[19] In fact, it was the Muslims who were "having a go" at the Croats in Kacuni, in Busovaca, and in the Kiseljak area. When all was said and done, the HVO and Croat population in the area paid the heaviest toll for the January fighting: the Croat villages of Nezirovici, Besici, Lasva, Dusina, Gusti Grab, Svinjarevo, Behrici, and Gomionica had been attacked and destroyed or occupied by the ABiH, the vital Busovaca–Kiseljak road had been cut at Kacuni, the southern end of the vital Novi Travnik–Gornji Vakuf line of communication was under attack, and more than forty-four HVO soldiers and Croat civilians had been killed and eighty-two wounded.[20]

The fighting in central Bosnia died down during the last week of January, and a temporary cease-fire was arranged under UNPROFOR and ECMM auspices. However, there continued to be numerous minor incidents as the ABiH consolidated its positions on the heights of the Hum and the Kula overlooking the Busovaca–Kiseljak road, and in the villages of Merdani, Dusina, and Besici. Meanwhile, the HVO, determined not to be surprised again, strengthened its defensive positions in the central Bosnia area and began to monitor ABiH movements more closely. Both sides continued to eye each other warily, and there were frequent violations of the cease-fire agreement as both sides jockeyed for position and advantage.

On January 29, HQ, OZCB, issued a situation report to its subordinate units and higher headquarters noting: "In the course of today the lines of defence have remained unchanged. A 45-kilometer long front has been established. Our defence is positioned and well-entrenched, further entrenchments are being completed, a fire system [i.e.-plan for the employment of artillery and other weapons] has been organised and the situation is under control."[21] The report goes on to note numerous violations of the temporary cease-fire by Muslim units; the excellent morale of HVO fighters and their determination to repel "this brutal aggression"; and the fact that "the BH Army, until yesterday our allies, continued their brutal aggression from the municipalities of Kakanj and Visoko" in the Kiseljak area, and also established a checkpoint in the village of Bilalovac that cut off communications with HVO forces in the village of Jelenov Gaj.

On January 30, 1993, ABiH and HVO leaders met in Vitez under the aegis of UNPROFOR, UNHCR, ICRC, and ECMM personnel to discuss a more permanent cease-fire in the central Bosnia area. Dzemal Merdan, deputy commander of the ABiH III Corps, and Franjo Nakic, the OZCB chief of staff, agreed to a cease-fire to begin at 8 A.M., January 31. In his report to the OZCB commander, Colonel Blaskic, who was isolated in Kiseljak, Nakic noted that Colonel Stewart had stated during the meeting that "he did not blame any side for the violation of the cease-fire [that is, the temporary cease-fire arranged earlier], but the reports he received indicated that it was the HVO who were the ones who started it." Nakic also noted the rather one-sided comments at the meeting by the ECMM representative, Jeremy Fleming, who "was full of praise for the 3rd Corps Command," even stating that "They are doing great things for peace."[22] It seems clear that both the UNPROFOR and the ECMM had already made up their minds—on the basis of who knows what information—to charge the HVO with initiating the January fighting in central Bosnia. However, under cross-examination in the Blaskic trial, Colonel Stewart confirmed that he had visited the ABiH III Corps headquarters in Zenica on January 25, 1993, and complained to its commander, Enver Hadzihasanovic, that the Muslims had started the conflict then raging in central Bosnia.[23]

The cease-fire arranged by UNPROFOR went into effect at the agreed upon time, and the situation in the Lasva-Kozica-Lepenica area returned to a semblance of calm as commanders of both HVO and ABiH units sought to enforce the cease-fire and prepare their troops for the next round of the conflict. In early February, international attention focused on Srbrenica and the continuing siege of Sarajevo. Meanwhile, central Bosnia remained relatively peaceful throughout the winter months of February and March as the ABiH assessed the results of its January probing attacks and prepared to launch a full-scale offensive against the HVO in the spring. For its part, the HVO, now alerted to the danger posed by its perfidious ally, began to make its own preparations for defending the Croat population and key facilities in central Bosnia.

On February 1, the commander of UNPROFOR in Bosnia-Herzegovina, French general Philippe Morillon, hosted talks at the Bila school base of the British UNPROFOR battalion attended by Enver Hadzihasanovic, the ABiH III Corps commander, Thiomir Blaskic, the commander of the HVO OZCB, and others to discuss implementing the cease-fire and the withdrawal of external forces from the Busovaca-Kacuni area.[24] It was agreed that all such forces should be removed no later than 1 P.M. the next day, and that all routes in the area—particularly the Vitez–Zenica and Kiseljak–Visoko roads—should be opened immediately, with the main barricade blocking the Vitez–Zenica road to be removed by 2 P.M., February 2.

On February 11, the HVO Main Staff issued orders announcing a joint agreement between the chief of the ABiH General Staff, Sefer Halilovic, and the chief of the HVO Main Staff, Milivoj Petkovic, to prevent further "disagreements and conflicts" between the ABiH and the HVO, and "to organise a joint struggle against the aggressor [the BSA]."[25] The same order directed the HVO OZCB commander and the ABiH III Corps commander to create a joint commission composed of HVO and ABiH officers, the purpose of which was to supervise and coordinate efforts to minimize Muslim-Croat conflict in the central Bosnia area. The joint commission was to oversee implementation of the cease-fire agreement with respect to the withdrawal of forces, the removal of barricades, the filling in of trenches and bunkers, and the opening of roads to all traffic, as well as the release of detainees and the investigation of incidents should they arise. The existing ABiH-HVO coordinating teams in Gornji Vakuf and Mostar were instructed to carry out the same actions prescribed for the joint commission in central Bosnia, and all commanders were ordered to ensure that lines of communication in their area of responsibility were open and functioning normally.

The HVO OZCB commander and the ABiH III Corps commander subsequently issued orders implementing the joint agreement of the HVO and ABiH chiefs of staff. A series of joint orders issued by the two commanders on February 13 from Kakanj referred to the joint agreement and ordered the withdrawal of units from forward positions by the fourteenth; the opening of roads by the fifteenth; the filling in of trenches and bunkers sited against the HVO by the twentieth; the establishment of coordinated checkpoints and roadblocks with a view to the eventual establishment of joint checkpoints; and the establishment of the joint commission to control and investigate incidents.[26]

Despite the cease-fire and occasional cooperation with the ABiH in the defense against the Serbs, the HVO forces remained wary and prepared for a resumption of open conflict with the Muslims in central Bosnia. On February 4, Colonel Blaskic issued orders instructing subordinate commanders to strengthen security and control crime, desertion, and unsatisfactory duty performance by HVO personnel, and also directed that the Operative Zone's logistics system be reorganized. On February 13, he issued orders to increase security and prepare defensive positions in anticipation of a possible resumption of hostilities with the Muslims.[27] The measures to be taken immediately and completed by February 21 included the preparation of defensive bunkers; the registration and assignment of all conscripts; shooting tests for all civilian and military police units and their formation into operative groups and intervention platoons; additional training and live-fire practice for snipers; control of unidentified individuals moving about the defense lines; the distribution of humanitarian aid to the Croat population; the continued assessment of the situation in cooperation with HVO civilian authorities; increased security and intelligence-gathering activities; and the definition of combat assignments for all Croatian personnel in the region.

The OZCB commander's attention also turned to dealing with an increasing number of troublesome incidents of violence by HVO personnel occasioned by the chaotic conditions and the large number of armed men in rear areas. On February 2, an HVO 4th Military Police Battalion investigative team reported on an incident that occurred between 9:30 and 10 P.M., February 1, in which three explosive devices were thrown at the intersection of the main Travnik–Vitez road near the Impregnacija Company's administration building and the house of Djevad Mujanovic.[28] The powerful explosions broke windows in the neighborhood and made a hole in the roof of Mujanovic's garage. The perpetrators were not identified, but they may have been Croats. On February 6, the OZCB commander reminded his subordinate commanders of their duty to carry out earlier orders regarding the suppression of incidents involving murder, the disturbance of public order and peace, threats with firearms, indiscriminate firing in public places, and similar unauthorized actions by HVO personnel.[29] Nevertheless, on February 10, a Bosnian Croat from Novi Travnik, Zoran Jukic, was killed by HVO military policemen while resisting arrest after stabbing a Muslim named Sarajlija in the Kod Dure Café in Novi Travnik.[30] Another bombing incident occurred at 6:10 P.M. on March 15 in front of the Maks store in downtown Vitez.[31] A few nearby cars were damaged, several persons were slightly wounded, and one seriously injured person was taken to the hospital in Travnik. On March 1, the HVO SIS office in Vitez issued an extensive report on the criminal activities of various Croat criminals active in the Travnik, Novi Travnik, Vitez, and Busovaca area. The list included Zarko "Zuti" Andric, the military police chief in Travnik, and Ferdo Gazibaric and Pero "Klempo" Krizanac, both of whom were also from the Travnik area.[32] Additional instructions regarding the treatment of HVO personnel engaged in criminal and destructive conduct were issued on March 17 and disseminated to battalion level.[33] The measures prescribed to suppress such activity included disarming and removing the uniforms of HVO personnel found committing such acts, as well as their arrest and subjection to disciplinary action.

The Muslims initiated a number of serious incidents and cease-fire violations. On February 4, Lieutenant Colonel Stewart traveled to Katici and Merdani to investigate and stop a fight there at the request of Dario Kordic, the HVO political leader in Busovaca.[34] At 9:30 A.M. on February 6, members of the ABiH and Muslim Armed Forces (MOS) arrested seven HVO soldiers in Kruscica.[35] Among those making the arrest were an ABiH soldier from Kruscica and three MOS members from Vranjska. The seven HVO soldiers were questioned about HVO positions in Ribnjak and Lovac and released unharmed at 7 P.M. the same day, although their insignia and personal documents were not returned to them. On March 13, the commander of the HVO N. S. Zrinski Brigade in Busovaca issued a letter of protest addressed to the ECMM, the nearby Dutch-Belgian UNPROFOR transport battalion, and HQ, OZCB, claiming that the cease-fire had been broken at 8:40 P.M. on March 12 by an ABiH M48 tank that had fired its machine gun on HVO positions in the village of Kula.[36]

On the evening of March 16, two HVO soldiers from Travnik were killed at an HVO checkpoint in the village of Dolac on the main Travnik–Vitez road.[37] The soldiers, Zoran Matosevic and Ivo Juric, attempted to halt a Lada automobile. The four occupants, probably mujahideen, were heavily armed and got out of the car with their weapons. An argument ensued, and a brief firefight erupted during which Matosevic and Juric were killed and their weapons taken by the car's occupants. Earlier that evening, the same car drove through an HVO checkpoint at Ovnak and its occupants made threatening gestures with their automatic weapons at the personnel manning the HVO checkpoint. A similar incident occurred at 9:40 P.M. on March 28 at an HVO VP checkpoint in the village of Cajdras.[38] Two HVO VPs attached to the Jure Francetic Brigade, Bernard Kovacevic and Ivan Laus, were murdered, apparently by members of the ABiH 7th Muslim Motorized Brigade. Two weeks earlier, on March 15, a group of Muslims led by Ferhet Haskic stopped and searched people traveling to Donja Veceriska.[39] A tractor belonging to an unknown person—presumably a Croat from Novi Bila—was stopped, the owner mistreated, and the tractor's tires punctured. Haskic was also suspected of throwing an explosive device in the front of the HVO headquarters in Donja Veceriska at 12:55 A.M. on March 16. The ABiH VPs subsequently helped HVO authorities apprehend Haskic.

The only major violation of the January cease-fire in central Bosnia occurred in mid-March, when the ABiH IV Corps's 1st Operational Group attacked north along the Neretvica River toward Fojnica with the objective of seizing control of some twenty Croat villages in the Neretvica Valley and linking up with the ABiH OG Bosanska-Krajina, thereby joining the ABiH III and IV Corps.[40] The attack stalled before reaching the Fojnica area, and Croat residents expelled from the area fled to areas still under HVO control—some toward Kiseljak and some toward Herzegovina. A description of this attack as well as an agreement between the ABiH and RBiH Ministry of the Interior regarding military operations against the HVO was issued March 20.[41]

The Muslim-Croat cease-fire in central Bosnia held through the first weeks of April despite numerous minor incidents, endemic lawlessness, and the organized ABiH offensive in the Neretvica Valley aimed at Fojnica. Although apparently random and probably initiated by extremist individuals or lower-level commanders, some of the more serious incidents suggest a pattern of intelligence gathering by the ABiH, the clandestine movement of Muslim forces throughout the region, and provocations by mujahideen and other Muslim extremists, all of which may have been continuations of the probing action initiated by the ABiH III Corps in January and preparation for the all-out Muslim offensive that began on April 15–16, 1993.

7 The ABiH Main Attack, April, 1993

The Vitez Area

Tensions were high throughout central Bosnia on April 15, 1993. Resent- ment over the ABiH's January probing attacks and the increasing number of clashes between Muslims and Croats had created an atmosphere of fear, hatred, and distrust heightened by the kidnapping on April 13 of four officers from the HVO Stjepan Tomasevic Brigade in Novi Travnik, apparently by Muslim extremists. The ABiH blockaded the Novi Travnik–Gornji Vakuf (Uskoplje) road, the main supply route to Herzegovina, on April 14, and at 7:15 on the morning of the fifteenth, Zivko Totic, commander of the HVO Jure Francetic Brigade, was kidnapped near his headquarters in Zenica during a brutal attack that left his four bodyguards and a bystander dead. That afternoon, Lt. Col. Bob Stewart, commander of the British UNPROFOR battalion stationed in the Lasva Valley, traveled to Zenica for a meeting with Muslim, HVO, ECMM, UNHCR, and International Red Cross representatives regarding the Totic kidnapping. The meeting was continued until the next morning, and Lieutenant Colonel Stewart spent the night in Zenica rather than return to his headquarters in Stari Bila. At about 5:30 A.M. on the sixteenth, he was awakened by an urgent telephone call from his second in command, Maj. Bryan Watters, who informed him "all hell was breaking loose in Vitez and the Lasva Valley." Indeed, it was; the main ABiH offensive against the Croat enclaves in the Lasva Valley had begun.

The HVO Intelligence Estimates

Stewart later testified that he did not expect the outbreak of a major conflict between the Muslims and Croats in the Lasva Valley.[1] However, the HVO authorities, having been caught flat-footed by the ABiH probing attack in January, were not surprised. The targeting of the ABiH for intelligence purposes began soon after the January 20–21 attacks, and on March 25 Ivica Zeko, the intelligence officer at HQ, OZCB, issued an intelligence estimate that accurately forecasted the nature, direction, and objectives of the April offensive.[2] A trained intelligence officer, Zeko's analysis of the situation led him to conclude that extremists in the ABiH and SDA, together with Muslim fundamentalists in the Zenica region and military experts, had "devised a plan to destroy the HVO and take control of the territory of Central Bosnia," which "might enable them to ensure living space and safety for the Muslim population" while producing fewer casualties than an offensive against the BSA."[3] According to Zeko, the detailed plans for the Muslim offensive were prepared by Refik Lendo for the Bugojno–Gornji Vakuf–Novi Travnik–Vitez area; by Vehbija Karic for the Kiseljak-Fojnica-Kresevo-Kakanj-Vares area; and by persons unknown in Zenica for the Zenica-Busovaca area.

According to Zeko's estimate, the offensive would open with action by sabotage teams against HVO command posts, communications and wire-tapping centers, logistics bases, and artillery positions. The ABiH would avoid a direct confrontation with HVO forces in the Tesanj-Maglaj-Zavidiovici–Novi Seher–Zepce area, where HVO troops held significant portions of the defense lines against the Serbs. However, the ABiH would seek to blockade HVO population centers, isolate HVO units, and overturn HVO civilian control through the establishment of checkpoints, the positioning of troops near critical installations, and direct attacks or sabotage operations directed against HVO command and control elements. Zeko noted that Muslim forces already surrounded the important population centers of Kiseljak, Fojnica, Kresevo, Kakanj, and Vares. However, he believed a larger conflict might be avoided by determined confrontation inasmuch as the majority of ABiH forces in the area occupied defensive lines to protect the vulnerable towns of Visoko, Breza, Olovo, Pazaric, and Tarcin from the Serbs. Due to HVO defensive preparations, Vares might be "a hard nut to crack," but the ABiH might achieve some success with selective attacks in the Kakanj, Kiseljak, and Fojnica area. For both the northern (Zepce) and eastern (Kiseljak) areas, Zenica was to be the command and control center, and any operations would be carried out by units from occupied areas then quartered in Zenica as well as MOS, "Green League," Green Berets, and Patriotic League forces.

According to Zeko, the main battles would occur in the crucial Vitez-Busovaca area and would involve direct offensive action by the ABiH along three main axes of attack: Kacuni-Busovaca-Kaonik-Vitez; Zenica-Kuber (Lasva)-Kaonik-Vitez; and Zenica-Preocica-Vitez. These attacks would be supplemented by forces attacking toward Vitez from Kruscica; from the areas of Vranjska and Poculica toward Sivrino Selo; and from the area of Han Bila through Stari Bila to cut the Travnik–Vitez road and complete the encirclement of HVO forces in the Vitez area. The main part of the ABiH forces carrying out this portion of the plan would come from Zenica, Kakanj, and Visoko. Having surrounded Vitez, the Muslim forces would then continue the attack until gaining full control of the town. In the event HVO forces were able to stall the advance on the Han Bila–Vitez axis, the attacker might divert his forces toward Gornja Gora and thereby enable the ABiH forces in Travnik to leave the town and advance toward Vitez. However, ABiH operations in the Travnik–Novi Travnik area would not take the form of a direct attack but would involve small-scale actions to control the HVO units there and keep them from intervening in the Vitez area.[4] Should Busovaca and Vitez fall to the attacker, Travnik and Novi Travnik would gradually be forced to surrender. Muslim forces in the areas of Bugojno, Gornji Vakuf, and Fojnica would play an essential role in the offensive by blocking the approach routes to central Bosnia from Herzegovina and by providing manpower, equipment, and supplies for the attacking forces.

Zeko concluded his analysis by noting that the Muslim forces were already occupying the territories in question piece by piece, displacing the Croat population and taking full control, and that they would be likely to continue to do so unless "it is made clear to [them] that the initiation of clashes in broader areas with well-planned attacks in the least expected places will not be tolerated." He then went on to state: "A possible attack by the BH Army will be relentless and it is necessary to take all measures and actions to repel the attack and completely destroy the military strength wherever possible."[5]

On March 14, Zeljko Katava, the Nikola Subic Zrinski Brigade's intelligence officer, had also warned of a possible ABiH attack. He believed the attackers would avoid the HVO position in Cajdras by advancing through Muslim territory from Zenica via Vrazale, Dobriljeno, and Vrhovine to launch an attack from Ahmici in order to cut the Vitez–Busovaca road and then continue via Donja Rovna to link up with Muslim forces in Vranjska.[6] Katava noted in an earlier (January 6, 1993) estimate that ABiH forces had already constructed a road from their positions on Mount Kuber through Vrazale to Zenica, and on April 10, a week before the Muslim offensive began, HVO intelligence officers obtained additional information that the ABiH was indeed making preparations to carry out military operations in the Lasva Valley.[7]

The HVO intelligence estimates were remarkably accurate in predicting the objectives, direction, and participating units of the ABiH offensive that began in mid-April, 1993. The situation remained quiet in the northern sector and around Vares, as well as in Travnik and—following a brief flare-up to pin down HVO forces and cut the road to Gornji Vakuf—Novi Travnik. The ABiH did not mount a general attack from all directions in the Kiseljak area, but again concentrated on trying to seize the critical road junction in the vicinity of Gomionica, which it had failed to do in January. Vitez, the SPS explosives factory, and the town of Busovaca were the primary ABiH objectives, and it was on them that the heaviest blows were struck. Elements of the 303d, 306th, and 325th Mountain Brigades, the 17th Krajina Mountain Brigade, and the 7th Muslim Motorized Brigade—with ABiH military police and antisabotage units (PDO)—participated in the attack in the Vitez area, while elements of the 333d Mountain Brigade attacked toward Busovaca.[8] The objectives, as Zeko had predicted, were to cut the Travnik–Busovaca road at Kaonik, at Ahmici, at Stari Bila, and at the Pucarevo turnoff to divide the Travnik-Vitez-Busovaca enclave into smaller parts and isolate the HVO units in Vitez and Busovaca; to take the SPS factory; and to clear Croat civilians from their villages in the area. At the same time, action was taken to eliminate the two HVO brigades in Zenica and to clear Croat civilians from the town and the surrounding villages.

The plan nearly succeeded: the HVO forces in Zenica were eliminated; all ground contact between the Travnik-Vitez-Busovaca enclave and the Zepce and Vares areas as well as with Herzegovina was severed; the HVO brigade in Kakanj was eliminated; the center of Vitez was held by Muslim fighters; and hundreds of Croat civilians were driven from their homes in the region. However, the ABiH failed to achieve its main objectives. This was due in large part to aggressive preemptive attacks and counteraction by the heavily outnumbered HVO forces in the Lasva-Kozica-Lepenica area. At the end of the Muslim offensive's first push, Travnik, Novi Travnik, most of Vitez, Busovaca, Kiseljak, Fojnica, and Kresevo were still under HVO control; the SPS factory remained in HVO hands; and hundreds of Muslim civilians had fled or been temporarily removed from Muslim villages in the Vitez-Busovaca-Kiseljak area, which had been the target of HVO military action to clear key terrain along the lines of communication and in its rear areas.

Preparatory Operations

The ABiH's April attack in the Lasva Valley was preceded by a number of incidents that call to mind the classic Spetsnaz operations prescribed by Soviet and JNA offensive doctrine and which serve to clarify the fact that, contrary to the usual opinion, the ABiH, not the HVO, initiated the fighting in central Bosnia on April 16, 1993. These incidents were designed to probe and fix local HVO defensive positions, gain control of terrain features critical to the success of the planned operation, sow confusion and fear, and disrupt command and control by decapitating the HVO leadership. The number of minor incidents involving clashes between Muslims and Croats increased during the first two weeks in April. Then, immediately prior to the launching of the Muslim offensive, there were two serious incidents that had all the hallmarks of the classic Spetsnaz operation: the kidnapping of three HVO officers and their driver near Novi Travnik on April 13, and the bloody kidnapping of Zivko Totic, commander of the HVO Jure Francetic Brigade in Zenica, on the morning of April 15.

During the period April 1–11, the HVO 4th Military Police Battalion reported a number of minor incidents including assaults, murders, "carjackings," bombings, and armed clashes involving Muslim and Croat civilians and military personnel.[9] Although many of these incidents were purely criminal or "private" in nature, some were no doubt provocations by the ABiH or extremist Muslim organizations designed to destabilize the situation, spread fear and confusion, and test the reaction of both HVO units and UNPROFOR and ECMM monitors. Typical incidents in the latter category included the March 29 murder of Slavko Pudj, a member of the Zenica HVO who was on guard duty, by three unknown persons in snow camouflage uniforms. The perpetrators escaped in the direction of Preocica, where a number of ABiH units were based. On April 4, someone threw a grenade or similar explosive device into the fenced storage yard of the Orijent Hotel, the HVO military police headquarters in Travnik. On April 9, three ABiH soldiers stopped Vlado Lesic near the Novi Travnik fire station and took his Golf automobile. Lesic was then taken to the Stajiste quarry, where he was abused, forced to bow in prayer, and made to speak in Arabic. The perpetrators fired in front of his feet and then forced him to jump into the quarry. They continued to fire at him, but failed to score any hits.

Several of the incidents in the Travnik area appear to have involved mujahideen or members of the extremist Muslim Armed Forces. On April 2, all HVO checkpoints in Zenica, Travnik, Vitez, and Busovaca were reinforced following an announcement by mujahideen in Zenica that they would attack the HVO military prison in Busovaca unless three MOS members were released. The same day, HVO military police reported that MOS members and mujahideen in Travnik were engaged in provocative and threatening behavior that included the singing of Muslim songs disparaging the Croat people and HVO military units. The Vitez civilian police arrested three armed mujahideen at a checkpoint on April 7, and the following day in Zenica, a van loaded with MOS members or mujahideen passed through the town as the occupants stuck their automatic rifles out the windows and threatened passersby. On April 9, HVO military police in Novi Travnik received telephone calls from someone who stated: "Do you know that there will be no Herceg-Bosna? Things have started in Travnik, now they will start here." That same day, some seventy prominent Croats from the Travnik area were arrested and held by the ABiH.[10]

The HVO did little to avoid provoking such incidents, and a serious outburst of violence began in Travnik when a Muslim soldier fired on some HVO soldiers erecting a flag.[11] Heavily armed soldiers from both sides prowled the streets of Travnik on the evening of April 8, and the conflict over the display of Croat flags continued the following day with armed clashes involving the HVO military police, the Vitezovi, and ABiH soldiers.[12] The April 9 firing began when a group of Muslims attempted to tear down the flag at the Orijent Hotel. Warned to desist, they pressed on, and a small firefight ensued. There were no Croat casualties, but a number of Muslims were apparently killed or wounded. Following the firefight in Travnik, HVO military police reported the arrival in Travnik of five trucks and several other vehicles carrying mujahideen and members of the Green Legion from Zenica.[13] The conflict continued until Easter Sunday, April 11, with numerous sniper and bombing incidents, arrests and abuse of HVO officers and policemen by ABiH soldiers and mujahideen, and general unrest in the town.[14]

Two additional incidents, far more serious and far more evocative of classic decapitation operations to disrupt the enemy's command and control system, occurred in the days immediately preceding the April 16 ABiH attack. On April 13, four members of the Stjepan Tomasevic Brigade were kidnapped by mujahideen outside Novi Travnik.[15] The four kidnapped personnel included Vlado Sliskovic, deputy commander of the Tomasevic Brigade; Ivica Kambic, the brigade SIS officer; Zdravko Kovac, the brigade intelligence officer; and their driver, Mire Jurkevic. The kidnapped HVO soldiers were bound, gagged, and blindfolded and remained so for most of their captivity. Early on they were beaten frequently and severely every day and interrogated frequently. They were also moved from place to place daily for a time, but were finally hidden at a hotel on the Ravno Rostovo plateau.

Kovac and the others learned much by listening to their captors, who openly bragged of their feat. Apparently the kidnapping was planned well in advance: the perpetrators had waited two days at the kidnap site hoping to take the Tomasevic Brigade's commander. The kidnap team consisted of four mujahideen: "Abu Hamzed" from Tunisia, the leader; "Abu Zafo," also from Tunisia; "Abu Mina" from Egypt; and "Abu Muaz" from Saudi Arabia. Twenty to thirty local Muslims assisted them. During the course of the kidnapping, the mujahideen did not cover their faces and did not hesitate to use their names, but the locals wore hoods. The kidnappers showed contempt for Dzemal Merdan, the deputy commander of the ABiH III Corps, and for the ABiH in general. They communicated by Motorola radio with the deputy commander of the 7th Muslim Motorized Brigade, whom they consulted several times regarding the disposition of the prisoners and who clearly had life-or-death power over them.

The kidnapping near Novi Travnik generated an intensive manhunt throughout the region. ABiH headquarters, feigning shock and surprise, joined HVO authorities in the hunt, which continued without success for some time. On April 14, the OZCB commander issued instructions for all of the HVO 4th Military Police Battalion's units to join in the search for the missing personnel.[16] On April 18, Zeljko Sabljic, the Tomasevic Brigade commander, reported on the progress of the joint ABiH-HVO commission investigating the case, noting that it had identified Vahid Catic from the village of Drvetine (Bugojno municipality) as the driver of the truck used in the kidnapping.[17]

On April 14, in the wake of the Novi Travnik kidnapping, Muslim forces blocked the main supply route (MSR) to Herzegovina south of Novi Travnik. Thenceforth only UNPROFOR, UNHCR and other relief convoys, and ABiH-HVO teams looking for the kidnapped personnel were allowed to pass. Muslim villagers living along the MSR had operated checkpoints at various points on the route before April 14; ABiH soldiers manned the checkpoints after that date. The closing of the Novi Travnik–Gornji Vakuf road effectively cut off the Croat communities in central Bosnia from all supply and reinforcement from their compatriots in Herzegovina and forced a search for alternate routes over the mountains. Those alternate routes were subsequently closed in early July, 1993, and the surrounded Croats had to make do with the matériel on hand, minuscule amounts of critical items brought in by helicopter, and whatever they could manufacture themselves, seize from Muslim forces, or obtain from relief convoys en route to Sarajevo, Srbrenica, Gorazde, and other Muslim-held areas.

At 7:50 on the morning of April 15, Zivko Totic, commander of the HVO Jure Francetic Brigade in Zenica, was ambushed while en route to his headquarters. His four bodyguards and a bystander were brutally killed, and Totic himself disappeared without a trace. The ambush—subsequently determined to have been carried out by mujahideen—had all the hallmarks of a classic Spetsnaz "decapitation" operation, and it indeed had the intended effect. The Francetic Brigade's command and control system was severely disrupted, and the commander of the other HVO brigade in Zenica, Vinko Baresic, was placed under severe stress. A meeting to discuss the Totic kidnapping was held by EC ambassador Jean-Pierre Thebault, UNPROFOR, ECMM, UNHCR, Red Cross, ABiH, and HVO representatives on the afternoon of April 15 without substantive results. The senior ABiH representative, Dzemal Merdan, denied any ABiH involvement in the Totic affair and appeared otherwise unresponsive.[18] The complicity of the ABiH III Corps headquarters in the Novi Travnik and Totic kidnappings remains uncertain in view of the subsequent identification of the perpetrators as mujahideen and Muslim extremists—some or all of whom may having been acting on the orders of the commander of the 7th Muslim Brigade, who was known to act independently. In any event, the two decapitation operations certainly served the III Corps commander's ends with respect to preparing the field for the April 16 offensive.

The three officers from the Tomasevic Brigade and their driver, as well as Zivko Totic, were subsequently exchanged for eleven mujahideen and two Muslim drivers arrested by the HVO between February 16 and early April, 1993.[19] The exchange took place in Travnik, Kaonik, and Zenica on May 17, following the appearance in Zenica on April 19 of two mujahideen who claimed to be holding Totic and the others and who demanded the release of certain mujahideen prisoners held by the HVO for various offenses. The automobile the two mujahideen used while making the exchange demand was later spotted in the III Corps headquarters parking lot. The mujahideen released in Zenica on May 17 were greeted by at least a hundred masked and heavily armed soldiers, probably from the 7th Muslim Brigade, accompanied by a three-barrel 20-mm antiaircraft gun mounted on a five-ton truck, and numerous antitank and antiaircraft shoulder-launched missiles.

The Active Defense in the Vitez Area

In the early morning hours of April 15 the ABiH launched an attack on HVO positions on Mount Kuber north of Busovaca that resulted in three HVO soldiers killed in action (KIA).[20] In view of the increase in incidents, the kidnapping of the four HVO personnel in Novi Travnik and of Zivko Totic, and the ABiH attack on Mount Kuber, Col. Tihomir Blaskic, the commander of Operative Zone Central Bosnia, made an estimate of the situation and issued a series of orders on April 15 preparing his forces for defensive action. The HVO forces in the immediate area of Vitez were very limited.[21] The Viteska Brigade was still in the process of being formed. Only

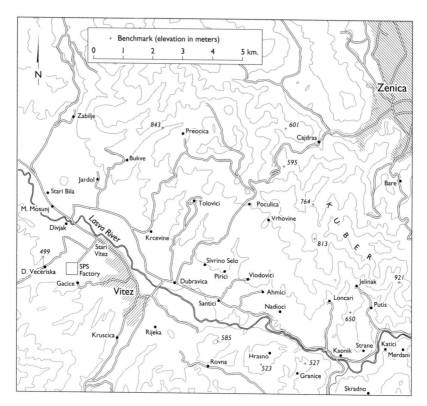

Map 2. The Vitez Area. *Map by Bill Nelson.*

the 1st Battalion (formerly the Stjepan Tomasevic Brigade's 2d Battalion) was even partially organized, and it had a maximum potential of only about 270 men. In fact, on April 16 the Viteska Brigade was able to deploy only about 80 men. Another sixty men were on shift duty on the Turbe front against the BSA, and an additional 50 were at the hotel in Kruscica preparing to relieve the shift then at the front. The additional forces available to Colonel Blaskic included an unknown, but relatively small, number of HVO village guards; the Vitezovi PPN (about 120 men); the Tvrtko II PPN (probably less than 30 men); and a portion of the 4th Military Police Battalion (probably less than 100 men).[22] The Vitezovi, the "Tvrktovici," and the military policemen constituted the best organized, best equipped, and most experienced combat forces available to the OZCB commander in the Vitez area, and thus naturally were deployed to face the greatest perceived threats.

At 10 A.M. on the fifteenth, the 4th Military Police Battalion was ordered to increase security of the HQ, OZCB, command post, to ensure that the Travnik-Vitez-Busovaca road was open to all traffic, and to expect "a rather strong attack by the Muslim extremist forces from the direction of the villages Nadioci-Ahmici-Sivrino-Pirici."[23] The Vitezovi were assigned responsibility for blockading the Muslim forces in Stari Vitez and preventing an attack from Stari Vitez toward the OZCB headquarters. The Viteska Brigade's 1st Battalion was assigned the mission of blocking any ABiH advance on Vitez from the Kruscica-Vranjska area.[24] In view of the fact that the Viteska Brigade was not yet fully operational, Mario Cerkez, the brigade commander, deployed his remaining forces in a sector defense arrangement with several small combat groups assigned to each sector.[25] All combat forces in the OZCB were ordered to carry out the defense of their assigned zones of responsibility to "prevent the extremist Muslim forces from effecting open cleansing of the territory, the genocide over the Croatian people, and the realization of their goals."[26]

During the course of the day, Colonel Blaskic received additional information regarding a possible attack by the ABiH and accelerated the preparation and positioning of his available forces.[27] At 3:45 P.M., he issued orders to all subordinate units to take additional measures to increase combat readiness, prepare for defensive action, and initiate increased antiterrorist, intelligence-gathering, and security measures. The ostensible purpose of such actions was to deter or counter aggressive actions by the 7th Muslim Brigade, the forces of which "have intensified their diversionary terrorist activities within the Operational Zone of Central Bosnia, and have been acting in a most brutal way. . . . These activities are planned, organised and promptly executed with the purpose of causing confusion within the HVO units and in order to prepare preconditions for offensive action and for capturing Croatian territory."[28]

By the early morning hours of April 16, Colonel Blaskic had alerted and deployed his limited available forces to meet the anticipated ABiH attack. In the ensuing battle, the HVO, significantly outnumbered and still not fully organized, successfully defended its lines against heavy and repeated ABiH assaults. The successful HVO defense in the Vitez area was due in large part to good intelligence work and the aggressive use of "active defense" measures to disrupt the ABiH offensive. The use of preemptive and spoiling attacks as well as blocking forces and clearing operations—often initiated and carried out by subordinate elements based on local assessments of the situation—prevented ABiH forces attacking the Vitez area from gaining their principle objectives: cutting the vital Travnik–Busovaca road, and seizing the SPS explosives factory.[29]

The aggressive actions of HVO forces in the Lasva Valley on April 16 were, in fact, mainly blocking operations and spoiling attacks intended to disrupt the ABiH offensive, prevent the breaching of HVO defensive positions and the loss of key positions such as OZCB headquarters and the SPS explosives factory, and retain control of the Travnik–Busovaca road. The HVO subsequently mounted a number of limited counterattacks and small clearing operations to regain or seize control of key terrain in the area of operations and to strengthen defensive positions by eliminating pockets of ABiH forces with direct observation and fields of fire on HVO positions. Four such HVO actions during the April fighting in the Vitez area merit special attention: the spoiling attack on the village of Ahmici; the clearing operations in the village of Donja Veceriska and in the village of Gacice, both of which overlook the SPS factory just west of Vitez; and the attempt to contain and then reduce the Muslim pocket in the Stari Vitez-Mahala section of the town of Vitez.

Ahmici

The HVO attack on the village of Ahmici on April 16 and the subsequent massacre of many of its Muslim inhabitants is perhaps the most notorious incident of the Muslim-Croat civil war in central Bosnia and has been at the center of at least five cases before the ICTY in which Bosnian Croat military and political leaders and HVO soldiers have been charged with war crimes.[30] Although later portrayed by ICTY prosecutors as the epitome of Croat atrocities in central Bosnia, the events at Ahmici on April 16 seem to have aroused little comment at the time—other than on the part of Lt. Col. Bob Stewart, the BRITBAT commander—and apparently did not become an issue for the Muslims until 1994–95.[31] However, despite investigations by the United Nations and the governments of both Bosnia-Herzegovina and Croatia, voluminous testimony before the ICTY by both Muslim and Croat witnesses, and the conclusions of ICTY prosecutors and judges, what actually happened in the village of Ahmici on the morning of April 16, 1993, and why, remain unclear. The most common interpretation is that the innocent Muslim inhabitants of the village were subjected to an unprovoked attack by HVO military police special operations forces. However, the available facts suggest a less fanciful alternative explanation: that Ahmici was a legitimate military target; that the village was defended by armed Muslim forces; that the OZCB commander, anticipating an attack by ABiH forces through the village, ordered a justifiable spoiling attack; and that the unit responsible for carrying out that attack, an element of the HVO 4th Military Police Battalion, either by premeditated design or in the heat of battle or both, went on a mindless rampage that included killing civilians and burning most of the Muslim section of the village.

The village of Ahmici was undoubtedly a legitimate military target for an HVO spoiling attack at the time by virtue of both its location and its probable use as an ABiH staging area. The village lies approximately three and one-half kilometers east of Vitez and on high ground some two hundred meters north of the main Travnik–Busovaca road. It is thus in a position to control the key route through the Lasva Valley at one if its most restricted points by direct and indirect fire.[32] Muslim TO forces from Ahmici set up a roadblock near the village in October, 1992, to prevent the passage of HVO forces headed toward Jajce, and it was clearly identified by HVO intelligence sources at various times in March and April, 1993, as being astride the planned ABiH axes of attack into the Vitez area from the north and east.[33] Given the proximity of the village to the Travnik–Busovaca road, it was the most likely assembly area for elements of the ABiH 325th Mountain Brigade and other ABiH forces tasked to make the attack across the road toward the Kruscica area on April 16.

Despite the repeated denials of senior ABiH commanders, on April 16 the village of Ahmici was clearly defended by local Muslim Territorial Defense forces as well as by ABiH elements staging for the attack across the Travnik–Kaonik road.[34] The village is clearly marked on a captured ABiH operational map as being occupied by ABiH forces in January, 1993, and on April 11, 1993, Enes Varupa, a Muslim TO commander, recorded in his notebook that a TO company of at least eighty-five men was in the village on that date.[35] Muslim TO members also met at their headquarters in the Zumara elementary school in Ahmici on April 11 to discuss plans for defending the village.[36] Muslim forces in Ahmici were assigned "clearly defined tasks . . . to secure the line toward Nadioci," and trenches and a number of dugouts had been prepared.[37] An HVO intelligence estimate dated April 10 placed elements of the ABiH 325th Mountain Brigade in the village, and elements of the ABiH 303d Mountain Brigade were also ordered to support the Muslim forces in Ahmici.[38] Croatian Defense Council sources also reported that the ABiH infiltrated thirty exceptionally well-armed soldiers into the village on April 14. On the evening of the fifteenth, the Muslim forces in Ahmici increased their level of security. In addition to the regular guards, ten men were on standby in the lower part of the village, and the guard force in the upper part of the village was doubled. During the course of the fight for the village on April 16, the Muslim forces in the village were reinforced from Vrhovine, and reinforcements from Poculica and the 325th Mountain Brigade were promised but failed to arrive in time to affect the situation.[39] The HVO assault forces encountered resistance, including shelling by the ABiH, and after the action they recovered weapons and large amounts of ammunition, including 7.62-mm and 12.7-mm machine gun ammunition and RPG-7 rocket propelled grenades.[40]

The HVO spoiling attack on Ahmici was planned on the afternoon and evening of April 15, and Pasko Ljubicic, commander of the 4th Military Police Battalion, briefed members of his command in the Hotel Vitez, noting that a Muslim message had been intercepted saying that the ABiH would attack in the morning on April 16 and that to forestall the attack the HVO would attack first. Ljubicic then issued orders for elements of the 1st Company to join the 4th Military Police Battalion's Antiterrorist Platoon (known as the "Jokers") at the "Bungalow," a former restaurant close to the road in Nadioci.[41] At 1:30 A.M. on the sixteenth, Colonel Blaskic, the OZCB commander, issued written orders for the 4th Military Police Battalion to block the Ahmici–Nadioci road (where he expected the Muslim attack) by 5:30 A.M. and to crush the enemy offensive.[42] Further briefings were conducted at the Bungalow, and Ljubicic's second in command noted that several mujahideen had infiltrated into Ahmici during the night.[43]

The seventy-five-man assault force consisting of the "Jokers" and other elements of the 1st Company, 4th Military Police Battalion, augmented by a few local HVO members was divided into assault teams and moved out from the area of the "Bungalow" between 4:30 and 4:45 hours on the morning of the sixteenth.[44] At 5:30, a single artillery round was fired—the agreed upon signal to start the assault—and the ground assault on the Muslim section of Ahmici was launched from the village's southeastern quadrant. Muslim forces in the lower part of the village resisted vigorously, and the attacking HVO troops immediately came under heavy Muslim fire.[45] Muslim defenders barricaded in the mosque and the elementary school were supported by ABiH artillery, by light fire from the villages of Vrhovine and Pirici, and by snipers firing constantly from the woods and clearings above the village.

The Muslim fire was intense, killing three HVO military policemen and wounding three more.[46] The HVO countered with intense mortar, small arms, and automatic weapons fire. Many buildings were set afire by tracers. At some point, whether by chance or by premeditated design, the responsible HVO commanders surrendered control of the situation, and what had been a legitimate, well-justified HVO spoiling attack deteriorated into a mindless rampage by the attacking HVO military policemen. Angered by earlier confrontations with the Muslims, the HVO attackers worked their way through the village using automatic weapons and grenades and killing men, women, and children in a cruel and indiscriminate manner.[47]

Unable to stem the HVO advance and failing promised reinforcements from Poculica and the 303d and 325th Mountain Brigades, the Muslim defenders evacuated the remaining civilians toward Vrhovine. They briefly considered a last-ditch stand in the upper village (Gornji Ahmici) before withdrawing at about 4 A.M. on April 17 to establish a defensive line at Barica Gaj, some 150 meters north of Ahmici, where the Muslim line remained until the Washington Agreements in March, 1994.[48] Those Muslim inhabitants remaining in the village after the HVO assault were subsequently taken to the camp in Donja Dubravica and held there for some time.

From a purely military point of view, the HVO spoiling attack at Ahmici was very successful. The planned Muslim attack across the Travnik–Busovaca road in the Ahmici area was completely disrupted and could not be resumed. However, the destruction in the village was horrific, and civilian casualties were appalling. Most of the Muslim houses in the lower village were burned, some with the inhabitants inside. Many houses were set afire by incendiary ammunition and grenades used in the assault, but others were no doubt deliberately "torched." According to some accounts, as many as 109 Muslim civilians, including women and children, died or were missing as the result of the combat action and deliberate killing by the enraged and out of control HVO assault troops.[49] Once the events in Ahmici on April 16 became known, the behavior of the HVO troops was justly characterized as a massacre, and a great deal of effort subsequently has been expended to bring the perpetrators to justice. Although the HVO forces' actions on April 16, particularly with respect to the unarmed Muslim civilians in the village, undeniably merit condemnation regardless of the emotional state engendered by active combat, the fact remains that the assault began as a legitimate military operation: a spoiling attack to disrupt the planned ABiH attack through Ahmici to cut the Travnik–Busovaca road. To have ordered such a spoiling attack was no war crime, although the events that ensued may have reached that level of culpability. It seems clear that the tragedy resulted not so much from the design of senior HVO leaders but rather from the working of that fear, anger, and madness attendant on many combat operations. In that respect, at least, the tragic events at Ahmici bear a far stronger resemblance to those at My Lai than to those at Lidice or Oradour-sur-Glane.[50]

Donja Veceriska

Even with good planning and near-perfect execution, collateral damage is inevitable during military operations in built-up areas. However, the HVO spoiling attack on the village of Ahmici was clearly an aberration, causing disproportionate destruction and wanton killing of noncombatants. The HVO clearing action in the village of Donja Veceriska on April 16–18, 1993, was much more representative of HVO operations conducted to foil the ABiH offensive in the Vitez area.[51]

The village of Donja Veceriska is located on a hill about one and one-half kilometers northwest of the center of Vitez and immediately overlooking the SPS explosives factory. In 1993, the population of the village was about 580 souls, of whom about 60 percent were Muslim and about 40 percent were Croats. The village dominated the factory and was thus very much "key terrain," since the SPS explosives factory was a major ABiH objective throughout the Muslim-Croat conflict in central Bosnia. Until late 1992, the village's Croat and Muslim inhabitants worked together to protect it from a possible attack by Bosnian Serb forces. However, in October and November there was an influx of Muslim refugees from Jajce and elsewhere, tensions grew, and the joint Muslim-Croat village guard forces were disbanded. The Muslims began digging trenches in the village, and the number of provocations by Muslim extremists increased. In mid-March, 1993, the Croats in Donja Veceriska began planning to defend the village against possible action by Muslim extremists. The HVO reserve forces (essentially the Croat village guard) were organized, the evacuation of the Croat civilian population in the event of conflict was planned, and demands were issued for the filling in of trenches and the cessation of provocations.[52]

In April, the Muslim Territorial Defense forces in Donja Veceriska included a platoon of forty to fifty men, one machine gun, two automatic rifles, eleven miscellaneous small arms, and various vehicles.[53] According to one Croat resident present at the time, the number of armed and uniformed Muslim soldiers plus armed Muslim refugees in Donja Veceriska may have been closer to a hundred, and their armament included AK-47s, "Gypsy" assault rifles, an M40 sniper rifle, Molotov cocktails, and other arms as well as a quantity of explosives obtained from the SPS factory by Boro Josic.[54] They also had "Motorolas" (handheld radios) to communicate with ABiH commanders in Stari Vitez. At the same time, the HVO Home Guard forces in the village numbered less than fifty men armed with AK-47 assault rifles, shotguns, and rocket-propelled grenades (RPGs). They, too, were equipped with Motorola radios that enabled them to communicate with higher-level commanders.

The whole Lasva Valley was on alert on evening of April 15, and Ivica Drmic, the HVO leader in Donja Veceriska, received information that the Muslims would attack at 9 A.M. on April 16, 1993, although Colonel Blaskic did not assign any of the OZCB regular forces to defend the village. The Croat families left at the first sign of trouble, and some Muslim civilians were evacuated in a different direction. Both groups of evacuees subsequently mixed at the "train station" on April 17. At around 5:30 A.M. on April 16, the Muslim forces in Donja Veceriska opened fire and attempted to gain control of the village and thus be in a position to dominate the SPS factory and to fire on HVO positions in Vitez. There was a great deal of confusion on all sides, but shortly before 8 A.M. an HVO assault force was organized consisting of ten to twelve local men augmented by twelve to fifteen members of the Tvrtko II special purpose force. Their task was to gain control of the village, suppress the Muslim firing, and take the house of Midhat Haskic, a radical Muslim, which was being used to store arms.[55] Fighting from house to house from the top of the village down, the HVO "assault force" succeeded in clearing Muslim fighters from ten to fifteen houses before being stopped at the Muslim strong point at Haskic's house

in the middle of the village. All the armed Muslim refugees in Donja Veceriska joined in the fight, and the firing continued all day long, stopping
only after midnight on April 17. United Nations Protection Force elements
entered the village on April 16 and 17 but did nothing to stop the fighting.
During the early morning hours of April 18, UNPROFOR evacuated the remaining Muslim villagers from Donja Veceriska.[56] The fighting in Donja
Veceriska resumed on April 18, and shortly after noon the HVO mounted
a determined house-to-house push that finally cleared the village.[57] The
remaining Muslim fighters, having expended their ammunition, withdrew
to Grbavica.[58]

During the fighting in Donja Veceriska from April 16–18, the HVO forces
suffered seven or eight wounded in action (WIA), including one who died
of his wounds. The Muslims had six or seven KIA, and the HVO took nine
Muslim prisoners. The latter were held overnight in Vitez and then released. Some Muslim civilians were also detained in Vitez, but all were released within three days.

By taking quick action to forestall Muslim seizure of the village, the HVO
forces in Donja Veceriska eliminated a serious threat to the SPS explosives
factory and the engagement of HVO forces in Vitez from the rear. The casualties inflicted were entirely proportionate to the ends of the operation,
which appears in every way to have been a straightforward and quite legitimate clearing action with minimal military and civilian casualties and destruction of property.

Gacice

Events on April 16–19 in the village of Gacice, located on a hill two kilometers southwest of the center of Vitez and immediately to the southeast of
the SPS explosives factory, paralleled those in Donja Veceriska and culmi-
nated in an HVO clearing operation to take the village.[59] Gacice overlooks—
and therefore dominates—the SPS factory and is also well within mortar
and recoilless rifle range of the center of Vitez. For a time in late 1992, the
headquarters of the ABiH 325th Mountain Brigade was located in Gacice's
middle school, the so-called Yellow House.

In April, 1993, Gacice numbered about 378 souls, evenly divided between Muslims and Croats. The upper village was mixed, but the lower village near the cemetery and the explosives factory was mostly Muslim. Almost everyone in the village worked in the explosives factory. Some two
hundred Muslim refugees from the Krajina moved into Gacice during 1992,
perhaps as part of a centrally directed plan to infiltrate Muslim refugees into
critical areas in order to change the ethnic balance. Tensions grew between
the two ethnic groups that summer, and for a time the Muslims blocked the
road by the school.

The Muslims in Gacice had few weapons until August, 1992, when
the HVO and TO tried to take over the JNA armory at Slimena in Travnik.
The armory was mined, and the Muslims broke in to get arms and exploded

the mines while the HVO was negotiating with the JNA.[60] The Muslims subsequently took the pieces and reassembled them into whole weapons. By mid-April, 1993, the Muslim TO forces in Gacice consisted of perhaps sixty well-organized and well-armed men.[61] According to Enes Varupa, they had at least one machine-gun, a radio transmitter, some twenty-eight small arms, and various vehicles.[62] Most were armed with AK-47 and "Gypsy" automatic assault rifles. They also had handheld Motorola radios to communicate with ABiH commanders. Once they were armed and organized, the Gacice Muslims became much more aggressive, and a number of clashes with the Croat inhabitants occurred.

Before the outbreak of fighting in the Lasva Valley on April 16, the HVO had no indication that the ABiH planned an armed takeover in Gacice.[63] Once the fighting started on the sixteenth, the Muslims in town, lacking a clear superiority over the Croat inhabitants, sought reinforcements from the ABiH 325th Mountain Brigade in Kruscica and negotiated with the HVO in order to extend the time needed for reinforcements to arrive. The HVO recognized the stalling for what it was, but before attempting to clear the village the HVO gave the Muslims a chance to give up their arms and surrender without a fight. The Muslim response was to start digging in.[64] The HVO then assembled an assault force consisting of a few policemen, about twenty village guards from Gacice and a few from nearby Kamenjace, and ten to fifteen members of the Vitezovi special purpose force.[65] At about 6:30 in the morning on April 19, the HVO initiated an assault intended to clear the village of the armed Muslim forces and to halt the firing on Vitez.[66]

The HVO forces attacked in six or seven groups; the Muslims defenders were in three groups. One group of five to seven Muslims surrendered at 4:30 P.M. Others escaped, setting fire to Croat homes on the way out. However, the Muslims were willing to sacrifice their civilians, and although most stayed in their homes, none were killed. The Muslim soldiers fleeing from Gacice took advantage of the roughly six-hundred-meter-long escape route near the SPS factory purposefully left open for Muslim civilians by the HVO. Following the battle, which ended by 5:30 P.M. on the nineteenth, the HVO rounded up Muslim civilians and moved them to Vitez, where they were held until after the fighting in the area ended. They were then returned to their homes the following day.

In the Gacice clearing operation the HVO lost one KIA, and the Muslims lost three KIA (including a man they themselves killed because he did not wish to fight his Croat neighbors).[67] The Viteska Brigade reported taking forty-seven prisoners. Two Muslim 82-mm mortars (without ammunition) and an M-84 machine gun were found after the action ended.

The contest for Gacice appears to have been a straightforward fight for control of a key piece of terrain following Muslim firing on Vitez, unsuccessful negotiations, and an offer by the HVO to resolve the situation without a fight. People were killed and things were broken—but certainly not disproportionately, and the HVO apparently did take positive action to ameliorate the effects of the battle on civilians by offering to accept surrender before the assault and by providing an escape route for Muslim civilians, although it should be noted that the usual Muslim pattern of retaining civilians in the battle area was practiced at Gacice.

Stari Vitez

Some of the most vicious fighting in the weeklong battle in the Vitez area focused on the Muslim enclave in the Stari Vitez–Mahala section of Vitez. Stari Vitez was a Muslim stronghold barely two hundred yards from the HVO OZCB headquarters. Beginning in November, 1992, the ABiH moved in experienced fighters, dug trenches, warehoused ammunition, and shifted an antiaircraft gun from the SPS factory to Stari Vitez.[68] By April, 1993, the TO headquarters in Stari Vitez commanded at least 350 Muslim combatants.[69] They were well-armed with small arms and automatic weapons; an antiaircraft gun; two 60-mm mortars; one M-84 heavy machine gun; three to six 7.62-mm light machine guns; ten rocket-propelled grenade launchers; and three sniper rifles, along with some 360 mortar shells.[70] The Muslim forces were deployed in trenches and shelters constructed around Muslim houses, with strong points in Mahala-Rakite near Otpad, in the community center, in the Metal Borac shop near the cemetery, and in Donja Mahala.

In anticipation of an attack on OZCB headquarters in the early morning hours of April 16, Colonel Blaskic ordered the Vitezovi to prevent any attack from Stari Vitez.[71] When OZCB headquarters came under fire on the morning of April 16, HVO forces acted immediately to isolate the Muslim forces in Stari Vitez. The Vitezovi, supported by military and civilian police and troops from the Viteska Brigade, encircled the enclave. A siegelike fight ensued as HVO forces first blockaded and then attempted to reduce the enclave and eliminate a serious cancer in their midst. Meanwhile, Muslim forces attacked repeatedly from north of the Travnik–Busovaca road to break through and reinforce their embattled comrades in Stari Vitez.

The battle for the Stari Vitez enclave continued long after the April 18 cease-fire agreement, with frequent shelling of the enclave by the HVO, intense sniper fire from both sides, and occasional attempts at ground assaults by both the Muslims in Stari Vitez and the HVO troops surrounding the enclave.[72] Throughout the so-called siege, Muslim forces in Stari Vitez continued to receive limited amounts of supplies by infiltration through the HVO lines, from humanitarian organizations, with the help of UNPROFOR, and allegedly from the HVO.[73] The battle produced heavy casualties on both sides, but the Muslim stronghold proved too hard a nut for the HVO to crack.[74] Finally, on February 27, 1994, UNPROFOR forces mounted Operation Stari Simon and broke into the enclave to evacuate the Muslim sick and wounded.[75]

Assessment

The HVO forces were under legal and moral obligations to conduct their military operations in accordance with the accepted laws of land warfare and the international treaties governing the conduct of military operations, but they were under no obligation to remain inactive and permit Muslim forces to attack them with impunity. Thus, having learned of the planned Muslim attack, Colonel Blaskic laid out an aggressive plan of active defense to foil the Muslim offensive. Except for the deplorable conduct of his subordinates in Ahmici, Colonel Blaskic's employment of the meager forces at his disposal was admirable. He correctly assessed the main threats and assigned his strongest forces to deal with them. Thus, elements of the 4th Military Police Battalion carried out a successful spoiling attack on the presumed ABiH assembly area in Ahmici, an attack that unfortunately deteriorated into a massacre of Muslim civilians. The Vitezovi blocked the strong Muslim forces in Stari Vitez, and the half-formed Viteska Brigade prevented a Muslim advance out of Kruscica and Vranjska. When Muslim forces in Donja Veceriska and Gacice posed a threat to Vitez and to the SPS factory, HVO assault forces composed of village guards augmented by small special purpose force detachments conducted successful clearing operations. Elsewhere in the Vitez area, local Croat forces, primarily village guards, held the line against advancing ABiH troops.[76] Again with the exception of Ahmici, all of these operations were conducted within the bounds of expected norms. Although casualties were heavy, they were not disproportionate to the legitimate military objectives sought.[77]

8 The ABiH Main Attack, April, 1993

Busovaca, Kiseljak, Zenica, and Elsewhere

Although the principal objectives of the April, 1993, Muslim offensive—the SPS explosives factory, OZCB headquarters, and the vital Travnik–Kaonik road—were in the Vitez area, the attack extended, as HVO intelligence officer Ivica Zeko predicted, to the Busovaca, Kiseljak, and Zenica areas. Elsewhere—in Travnik, Novi Travnik, Zepce, and Vares—the ABiH elected to avoid an all-out attack in order to concentrate their forces in the critical Vitez-Busovaca-Kiseljak-Zenica area. The HVO mounted a strong active defense and repelled the Muslim attack in Busovaca and Kiseljak. But Muslim attackers in the Zenica area succeeded in destroying the HVO forces and expelling the Croat population from the town and many of the surrounding villages.

The ABiH Attack in the Busovaca Area

The town of Busovaca and the road junction at Kacuni were important ABiH objectives during the probing attacks in late January, 1993. Although elements of the ABiH 333d Mountain Brigade seized control of the Kacuni intersection and took up positions overlooking Busovaca from the east, they were unsuccessful in taking either the Kaonik road junction north of Busovaca or the town itself, both of which the HVO vigorously defended. In the Muslim offensive that began on April 16, Busovaca and the critical Kaonik intersection were important Muslim objectives, and the fighting in the HVO Nikola Subic Zrinski Brigade's defensive zone was intense and sustained, punctuated by sequential Muslim attacks and HVO counterattacks that flowed back and forth over the hapless villages north and east of the Vitez–Busovaca road. The more numerous ABiH aggressors gained ground and inflicted heavy casualties on the HVO defenders, but they were ultimately unsuccessful in obtaining their principal objectives.

The ABiH forces committed to the offensive in the Busovaca area in April, 1993, consisted of elements of five mountain brigades (the 302d, 303d, 305th, 309th, and 333d), the 301st Mechanized Brigade, and the 7th Muslim Motorized Brigade, supported by the 2d Antisabotage Detachment–Zenica (2d PDO–Zenica), RBiH Ministry of the Interior police, Territorial Defense troops from Rovna, Kruscica, Busovaca, Fojnica, and Kakanj, Muslim Armed Forces units, and other troops.[1] In all, the attacking ABiH forces probably totaled over five thousand men.

Unlike the HVO defenders in the Vitez area, who had to defend against a Muslim attack on a broad front but from only one direction (albeit with

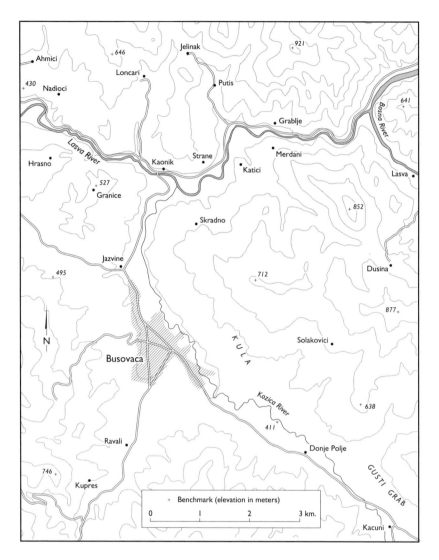

Map 3. The Busovaca Area. *Map by Bill Nelson.*

significant pockets in the center of Vitez and to their right and left rear), the Zrinski Brigade in Busovaca was compelled to adopt an all-around defense with significant "fronts" to the northwest, north/northeast, east/southeast, and south. The 3d Battalion, 333d Mountain Brigade, reinforced by elements of the 2d PDO-Zenica, was deployed northeast of Busovaca on a front extending from the village of Putis south across the Kaonik–Lasva road to a point just southeast of the village of Skradno.[2] The battalion command post was located in Grablje. The 2d Battalion, 333d Mountain Brigade—with its command post near Bozevic—was deployed to the southeast of the 3d Battalion, extending east of the village of Krcevine to run parallel to (and north of) the Busovaca–Kiseljak road to the Kacuni intersection. The area southwest of the Kacuni intersection was occupied by the 1st Battalion, 333d Mountain Brigade with its command post co-located with the Brigade command post near Benchmark (BM) 455 just northwest of the village of Mehurici and reinforced by the 4th Company, 3d Battalion, 7th Muslim Motorized Brigade. The 1st Battalion, 333d Mountain Brigade's zone began at the Kacuni intersection and ran southwest to Prosje, then northwest to Ocehnici, and then southwest again to link up with a 180-man detachment of Muslim TO forces from Fojnica in the vicinity of BM 751. The Muslim line extended farther to the southwest in an area occupied by elements of the 305th Mountain Brigade's 1st Battalion (about 170 men), extending from a point northeast of BM 1138 and running southwest to BM 1410. To the west of Busovaca, HVO forces were opposed by an eighty-man detachment from the Rovna TO forces deployed just west of the village of Kovecevac and a small ABiH pocket just to the northwest of the village of Bare. The area directly north of Busovaca, from the village of Nadioci east to the Loncari-Jelinak-Putis area was assigned to elements of the ABiH 303d Mountain Brigade from Zenica.

The area to the rear of the 333d Mountain Brigade's 2d and 3d Battalions in the vicinity of the villages of Merdani, Dusina, and Lasva was occupied by elements of the 305th Mountain Brigade, which maintained its command post in Biljesevo near Kakanj.[3] The ABiH forces in the Busovaca area were also supported by several tanks from the 301st Mechanized Brigade in Zenica. Later in the battle, elements of the 302d Motorized Brigade from Visoko were also committed in the Busovaca area.[4]

The HVO defenders in the Busovaca area consisted of the three battalions of the Nikola Subic Zrinski Brigade, commanded by Dusko Grubesic from a command post at "Sumarija" in Busovaca. The 3d Battalion was deployed northwest of Busovaca in the vicinity of the village of Bare, facing local Muslim forces from the Ravno and Kruscica area. The 2d Battalion, commanded by Anto Juric from a command post just south of the Kaonik intersection, was deployed north of Busovaca astride the road guarding the vital Kaonik intersection, with forward elements forming a thin screen in the Kuber area north of the intersection from the vicinity of Nadioci east to include Loncari, Jelinak, and Putis then southeast to the vicinity of BM 366 across the road from the village of Katici. The headquarters of the 1st Battalion, commanded by Anto Dusic, was located just west of the center of Busovaca and northwest of the road to the village of Kupres, and the battalion manned a line in the Kula area running southeast from the Strane area to Mejdani then just west of Solakovici south to the Busovaca–Kiseljak road in the vicinity of Krcevine. The 1st Battalion sector also included a deep salient along the Busovaca–Kiseljak road toward Kiseljak, the point of which was near Kacuni, the northern shoulder at Donja Polje, and the southern shoulder near Ocehnici.

The situation remained relatively calm in the Busovaca area in early April as the HVO and ABiH forces faced off in the area north, east, and south of the town. The Muslim roadblock at Kacuni, established on January 23, prevented direct HVO access between Busovaca and Kiseljak, but there were no major direct confrontations. On April 8–9, the commanders of the 333d Mountain and Zrinski Brigades issued a joint order addressing the plan for filling in of trenches in the area no later than April 12, and the completion of the withdrawal of outside forces by April 16 in accordance with the provisions of the January cease-fire agreement.[5] On April 8, Zrinski Brigade headquarters reported a quiet night, and on April 10 the ABiH III Corps headquarters reported a generally quiet situation with "occasional provocation by HVO forces in the Busovaca municipality" as a result of the deterioration of Muslim-Croat relations in the Travnik area.[6] The following day, April 11, III Corps HQ reported that on the night of April 10–11, an HVO platoon deployed on the Kula–BM 712–Mejdani line opened fire with small arms on ABiH positions on the Solakovici–Marjanov Kosa line.[7] Single shots and short bursts provoked no ABiH response, and there were no casualties. An UNPROFOR patrol also reported the fall of six mortar rounds in the vicinity of the UNPROFOR checkpoint near Kacuni at 12:40 A.M. on April 11, as well as heavy small arms and machine-gun fire in the surrounding area following the mortar impact.[8]

On April 12, the Zrinski Brigade HQ reported a generally quiet situation in the preceding period with no significant combat activity, stable defense lines, satisfactory morale, good logistical support, and functioning communications.[9] The Busovaca–Kiseljak road remained closed, and new ABiH entrenchments were observed in the Kula sector. On April 13, III Corps HQ reported that during the previous night HVO forces had provoked ABiH units in the Gornja Rovna area, but no one was hurt.[10] The ECMM reported progress with filling in the trenches in the Busovaca area on April 14, and ECMM representatives met with the Croat mayor of Busovaca and the Muslim president of the War Presidency of Kacuni, who agreed to form a temporary joint municipal government.[11]

Despite the relative calm and apparent progress in implementing the January cease-fire agreements in the Busovaca area, there were solid indications that the Muslim forces were preparing for offensive action. On April 11, a soldier from the Zrinski Brigade's 2d Battalion reported to the Busovaca Security Information Service office that while talking with one Vinko Ljubicic from Zenica he had learned that rumors were rampant in Zenica that the ABiH was prepared to sacrifice three thousand to five thousand men in order to capture territory in the vicinity of the Busovaca municipality.[12]

The Muslim offensive in the Busovaca area began on April 15, and for the next four days it took the form of artillery, mortar, and direct-fire attacks from a distance. There was little or no movement toward the HVO defensive lines, and thus no direct close combat. At 3:05 P.M., April 15, two HVO Zrinski Brigade soldiers were wounded in the area of Sarcevici and transported to the war hospital in Busovaca.[13] At 3:30, ECMM and UNPROFOR observers reported small-arms fire in the vicinity of the Kacuni bridge, and ECMM monitors protested to the HVO headquarters in Busovaca. The HVO authorities claimed their forces were being fired upon by ABiH troops in positions overlooking the HVO checkpoint at Gavrine Kuce, a claim that was later confirmed.[14] At about 5:30, HVO forces mounted a spoiling attack with small arms supported by artillery against ABiH units in the village of Putis. The ABiH casualties included two KIA and two WIA.[15]

The 303d Mountain Brigade's participation in the Busovaca attack provides an important indicator of Muslim intentions and the timing of the ABiH offensive. At noon on April 16, Suad Hasanovic, the brigade commander, issued his attack order based on orders received from the III Corps commander.[16] The order noted that the 3d Battalion, 303d Mountain Brigade, controlled the villages of Merdani, Grablje, and Putis from a command post in Grablje and that the 2d Antisabotage Detachment of the Zenica TO forces had organized the defense in the Saracevica-Kicin area. The 303d's 2d Battalion was ordered to move from its deployment area along the Zenica–Drivusa–Janjici–Gumanic axis to occupy defensive positions on the line Saracevica (BM 957)–Kicin (BM 921) as far as BM 567. After consolidating its defenses along that line, the units were then to "mount an attack" along a primary axis of advance from Saracevica via Jelinak to Loncari; to occupy the Obla Glava–Gradina heights; and then "mount an attack" along the Saracevica–Vrela route to reach the line BM 813–Vrana Stijena–Bakije–Katici, where the battalion was then to prepare to advance on order toward the Busovaca–Vitez communication line. After occupying the defensive area between Saracevica and Kicin, elements of the 2d and 3d Companies of the 2d PDO–Zenica were to come under the control of the 2d Battalion, 303d Mountain Brigade, which would also be reinforced by the following forces: part of the brigade reconnaissance platoon; a 120-mm mortar platoon; two squads of 20-mm antiaircraft guns; a squad equipped with a 128-mm light rocket launcher; and one Maljutka (Sagger) antitank rocket. The 3d Battalion was to designate a company to act as a reserve for the attacking 2d Battalion. Following occupation of Saracevica, the 2d Battalion was also to be reinforced by one T-55 tank from the 301st Mechanized Brigade, the employment of the tank and the Maljutka antitank weapon to be controlled directly by the 303d Mountain

Brigade commander. The brigade artillery group (minus the 120-mm mortar platoon) and other brigade elements were assigned suitable supporting tasks. As shown on a captured ABiH map, the sector assigned to the 303d Mountain Brigade ran from BM 514 just northeast of the village of Ahmici east through Loncari and Jelinak to Putis.[17]

Two important facts need to be emphasized regarding the 303d Mountain Brigade's attack order of April 16, 1993. First, it is clearly labeled an "Order for Attack," and it indeed instructs subordinate units to carry out an attack—rather than a counterattack or a defensive action. Second, the rather lengthy and detailed order was apparently issued at noon on the sixteenth, following receipt of a III Corps order dated earlier in the day. Considering the time required to prepare and issue the III Corps order and the time required for the 303d Mountain Brigade commander to conduct his analysis of the corps order, prepare an estimate of the situation, and prepare his own implementing orders, it is highly unlikely that the 303d Brigade operation was undertaken in reaction to an HVO attack in the early morning hours. Given the known defects of ABiH staff work and communications, the 303d Brigade action had to have been planned much earlier.

At 8:15 on the morning of April 16, a British UNPROFOR patrol reported heavy fighting in the area of the Croat village of Rijeka and the Muslim village of Vranjska, where many houses were burning.[18] At 5 P.M., Zrinski Brigade HQ reported that the fighting had continued during the day with a strong Muslim infantry attack launched from the Gornja Rovna and Pezici area at 5:30 A.M. on the HVO positions in the villages of Donja Rovna and Bare, to which the HVO forces responded vigorously.[19] Light combat activity was also reported in the Kuber–Obla Glava area; otherwise, the defense lines around Busovaca remained quiet during the day.[20] At 7:45 P.M., HQ, OZCB, issued orders for the Zrinski Brigade to reinforce the defense in the Kuber area with a minimum force of one company (120 men) of "your best prepared and most able forces."[21] The Zrinski Brigade was further ordered to coordinate its actions with the Viteska Brigade and "make sure that Kuber does not fall."

The ABiH III Corps HQ reported on April 16 that the intensity of operations and the movement of HVO forces directed at the 333d Mountain Brigade had been "weak to the point of non-existence," and that in the southern sector occupied by the 333d Mountain Brigade's 1st Battalion and elements of the Busovaca TO forces, "no significant HVO forces activity has been observed."[22] Elements of the 309th Mountain Brigade were also reported being introduced into the area of Sudine, and elements of the Kakanj TO forces into the area of Dusina.

The ABiH elements identified as belonging to the Muslim Armed Forces launched a strong infantry attack from the area of Dvor and Grabalje at about 5:30 A.M., April 17, on HVO forces in Kuce, Putis, and Jelinak in the Kuber–Obla Glava area.[23] The Muslim attack in that area continued with artillery support throughout the day. However, at 8:30 A.M., the Zrinski

Brigade reported that Muslim forces had lost their positions on Mount Kuber and broken contact, and that ABiH forces were in control of BM 897 and Saracevici.[24] At 11:25 on April 17, the Information Office of HQ, OZCB, notified International Red Cross, ECMM, and UNPROFOR authorities that Muslim extremists were killing civilians in the villages of Jelinak and Putis and throughout the Kuber area, with some sixty civilians massacred already.[25] The international authorities were asked to investigate the situation and act to protect civilians. At 1:56 P.M., British UNPROFOR patrols reported that the village of Kuber was under attack by ABiH forces, and at 6:15 hours, HQ, OZCB, issued additional defensive orders for protection of the Kuber area and the vital Vitez–Busovaca road to the commanders of the Viteska and Zrinski Brigades and the 4th Military Police Battalion.[26] The order, to take effect immediately, called for the formation of a defense line in the Kuber area to link forces from Vidovici via BM 514, BM 646, and Jelinak to Obla Glava in order to prevent a Muslim advance toward Kaonik and Nadioci "at all costs."

Elsewhere in the area on April 17, a general alert was sounded in the town of Busovaca at 10 A.M. as mortar shells began to land. The positions of the Zrinski Brigade's 3d Battalion in Bare and Donja Rovna were also under fire all day from ABiH positions in and around Pezici and Gornja Rovna, and the 1st Battalion's positions in Strane, Gavrine Kuce, and Podjele also received sporadic fire from Merdani. The HVO reported one KIA and nine WIA (three seriously), and morale and logistics support were deemed satisfactory.

The HVO reconnaissance elements reported late on the seventeenth that Muslim mortars were firing on the Rovna and Donja Rovna areas of the Busovaca municipality from BM 536.[27] On the morning of April 18, the Zrinski Brigade commander reported a quiet night in the brigade zone of operations and described the measures taken to increase the readiness of his forces and establish the defense lines prescribed by the OZCB commander the previous day.[28] During the course of the day, the ABiH liaison officer to the ECMM reported heavy fighting in the area of Pezici and Rovna.[29] The Zrinski Brigade also reported continued combat activity in the Kuber and Bare–Donja Rovna region as well as in the Kula area, including an intense attack launched by Muslim forces at 5:50 P.M. that unsuccessfully attempted to break through the HVO defense lines in the areas of Polom, Vrata-Skradno, and Roske Stijene.[30] Brigade headquarters also reported that an antiaircraft machine gun located in the area of Crna had fired into HVO positions in the village of Strane. All defense lines remained stable, and morale and logistics support continued to be rated satisfactory.

On April 19, even as the UNPROFOR-arranged cease-fire began to take hold in the Vitez area and the Boban-Izetbegovic agreement of April 18 became known, the fighting in the Busovaca area became even more intense. Colonel Blaskic, the OZCB commander, complained to UNPROFOR representatives that the ABiH offensive north of Busovaca centered on the villages of Kuber, Jelinak, and Kaonik contravened the cease-fire agreements.[31] Zrinski Brigade HQ reported that the ABiH launched a general attack at 6:45 A.M. on Busovaca from the direction of Dvor-Putis-Gradina (BM 650) with a force of some 500 men from the 7th Muslim Brigade. Their objective was probably to take Gradina (BM 650) and seize control of the surrounding villages.[32] In the Solakovici-Milavice sector, an attack was carried out by a force of approximately 450 men from the 333d and 309th Mountain Brigades in Kakanj. Finally, some 400 men from the 333d Mountain and 302d Motorized Brigades, supported by 82-mm and 120-mm mortars, launched an attack from the Kapak-Prosje-Polom-Ocehnici area apparently with the aim of taking the Draga barracks and surrounding buildings. Meanwhile, ABiH forces numbering some 2,000 men from the 303d and 305th Mountain Brigades, supported by a few tanks from the 301st Mechanized Brigade, were reported to be in reserve in the Dusina-Lasva-Merdani-Grablje area, poised to move along the Kaonik–Grablje–Lasva road to take HVO positions and gain full control of the lines of communication.

Zrinski Brigade HQ also reported the deployment of the thirteen hundred HVO defenders under its command on April 19. The 1st Battalion held the line Vrata–Podjele–Strane–Gravrine Kuce–Jelinak and the line Donja Rovna–Kovacevac–Roske Stijene–Busovaca–Grad–Tisovac–Polom and was currently engaged but repelling the attacks in the Dvor-Putis-Gradina and Kapak-Polom-Ocehnici areas with some difficulty. The 2d Battalion held the line Prosje–Polje–Milavice–Donja Solakovici–Krcevine–Kula–Vrata and was currently engaged on the stretches Solakovici–Milavice and Donja Polje–Prosje. Croatian Defense Council forces had pushed the ABiH attackers back some three hundred meters in the Solakovici-Milavice area, but they could not maintain the new positions due to unfavorable terrain and were thus forced to return to their starting position. The Muslim attack on the Donja Polje–Prosje sector was successfully repelled, and the attackers withdrew to their starting positions. The Dutch/Belgian UNPROFOR transport battalion based in Busovaca confirmed the fighting and shelling in the area, and noted that an M-63 Plamen multiple-barrel rocket launcher fired numerous salvos throughout the morning from a position between the villages of Kula and Skradno.[33]

The battle continued on April 20 in the Polom, Roske Stijene, Putis-Gradina-Jelinak, and Bare–Donja Rovna areas. The HVO defenders repelled the Muslim attacks, but often with heavy casualties. During the course of the day, the HVO established roadblocks north and south of Busovaca to control traffic on the vital Kaonik–Kacuni road. Both the soldiers manning the HVO roadblocks and the deputy commander of the Zrinski Brigade insisted that the British UNPROFOR battalion had been involved in black market operations and the delivery of arms to Muslim villages in the Vitez area, so UNPROFOR vehicles were denied passage.[34]

The following day, April 21, the fighting in the Busovaca area began to subside as the Muslim offensive started to run out of steam. The battered HVO defenders sought a respite from the intense combat of the previous three days. The Dutch/Belgian UNPROFOR transport battalion based in Busovaca reported that the town remained quiet throughout the day and that, although the HVO roadblocks north and south of Busovaca remained in place, UNPROFOR vehicles were permitted to pass once the local police were informed. The two HVO checkpoints were removed altogether on April 22, but the ABiH established two additional checkpoints on the Busovaca–Kiseljak road and informed UNPROFOR patrols that no UN vehicles would be allowed to pass for the next ten to fifteen days. Lieutenant Colonel Bob Stewart, commander of the British UNPROFOR battalion, personally led a reconnaissance through the villages of Poculica, Vrhovine, Kuber, Jelinak, Loncari, and Ahmici on April 22. He observed that the Muslim soldiers he encountered were not happy about having received orders to withdraw from their forward positions in accordance with the peace plan then being put into effect.[35]

On April 21, the British UNPROFOR battalion conducted an assessment of the situation in the Vitez-Busovaca area and noted that the ABiH III Corps seemed to be in the dominant military position despite having suffered heavy casualties in the fighting that began on April 15–16.[36] The assessment also noted that the III Corps estimate of the situation was that a continuation of the "present conflict" (that is, the Muslim offensive) would probably provoke increased HVO artillery shelling of Zenica and perhaps the intervention of HVO forces from outside central Bosnia. Thus, although the ABiH was in position to continue the attack in the Busovaca area and against a number of key Croat villages, the decision to not do so was made in order to avoid additional casualties.

On April 25, the situation in the Kuber sector remained generally quiet, and UNPROFOR forces reported that the villages of Vidovici, Ahmici, Jelinak, and Putis appeared to be deserted. The fighting continued unabated on the Kula front east of Busovaca, however. At around 7:30 A.M., heavy machine gun and small arms firing broke out north of the UNPROFOR transport battalion's base in Busovaca, and HVO mortar positions in the town began firing in a northerly direction, expending some 140 rounds in the course of the morning. The HVO artillery located at Mosunj north of Vitez also fired between ten and fifteen rounds into the area northeast of Kula that morning.[37] At 11 A.M., the OZCB commander complained to Dutch/Belgian UNPROFOR authorities that the Muslims had launched a large attack along the line Strane–Podjele–Kula–Donja Polje that began with the ABiH firing approximately ten mortar rounds from positions in the villages of Grablje and Merdani into the town of Busovaca at 4:30 A.M. The 9/12th Lancers ran a patrol into the area of Kula in the afternoon to investigate the HVO claims but found the village quiet other than for occasional small arms fire, although villagers reported that there had been mortar fire during the morning. At 6:37 P.M., the bridge across the Lasva River to Katici and

Merdani was reported to have been demolished.[38] The Muslim attack in the Kula area petered out on the afternoon of April 25, but the following day HVO authorities in Busovaca were still concerned, and the ABiH alleged that the HVO had launched an attack on Solakovici from Kula. The same day a British UNPROFOR liaison officer visiting the headquarters of the ABiH 305th Mountain Brigade confirmed that the brigade had in fact been committed in the Busovaca area.[39]

The lines remained stable and there was only minor combat action in the Busovaca area on the morning of April 27, although firing and troop movements occurred throughout the day in the vicinity of the village of Kazagici and Sotnice. At 7:30 A.M., HVO forces repelled a brief attack on the town itself, and at 9:30 ABiH artillery fired from the Silos area on civilian buildings in the village of Donja Polje.[40] Three 120-mm mortar rounds were fired causing great destruction but no casualties. Snipers remained active throughout the area of operations.

The Muslims mounted attacks in the Kuber and Kula sectors on April 28. The HVO responded with artillery and mortar fire as well as a tenacious ground defense. Early in the morning, the ABiH launched an attack from the area of Putis on the villages of Bakje and Jelinak as well as the Gradina feature. Dutch/Belgian UNPROFOR observers in Busovaca reported that the HVO mortar positions north of town opened fire at 6:15 A.M. and had fired some fifty rounds by 7:50, at which time small arms and heavy machine-gun fire could be heard south of the town as well.[41] The ABiH launched another attack at about ten o'clock, this time from the Dusina and Solakovici areas on the HVO line from Kula down to Milavice, with heavy small-arms fire reported in the area which intensified around 2 P.M. Heavy fighting also continued in the Kazagici village area on April 28 as the ABiH retook the village from the HVO. The fighting in Kazagici on April 27–28 resulted in heavy damage to the village, where almost every house had been set afire.

The heavy fighting in the Bakje-Jelinak-Gradina area and in the Kula area continued on April 29, even as Lieutenant Colonel Stewart escorted the senior officers of both the ABiH (Sefer Halilovic) and HVO (Milivoj Petkovic) to the lines near Kula in an effort to get the cease-fire going.[42] Their efforts were largely in vain, however, and the month of April ended with HVO and ABiH forces still engaged around Busovaca in the Kuber and Kula sectors. On April 30, British UNPROFOR patrols reported seeing about a hundred ABiH soldiers occupying the ruins of the village of Jelinak and a group of fifty HVO soldiers in the village of Loncari.[43] Although the ABiH was able to gain some ground and inflict heavy casualties on the numerically inferior HVO defenders, the Muslim offensive in the Busovaca area had failed to achieve its principal objectives, just as had the attack in the Vitez area. The stubborn HVO defense around Busovaca denied the ABiH the prized Kaonik intersection and the town of Busovaca for the moment, but the Muslims would soon resume their offensive.

The ABiH Attack in the Kiseljak Area

The April, 1993, Muslim attack in the Kiseljak area also developed much as Ivica Zeko, the OZCB intelligence officer, had predicted almost a month earlier. The HQ, OZCB, preparatory order issued at 10 A.M. on April 15 accurately forecast the details of the Muslim operational plan.[44] As expected, the ABiH focused its April attack on occupying the BM 661–Svinjarevo-Mladenovac-Gomionica area, cutting the Busovaca–Kiseljak road at the Fojnica intersection just west of Gomionica, and linking up with Muslim forces in the Visnjica area, thereby dividing the already isolated Kiseljak enclave into two parts and effectively cutting off the HVO forces in Fojnica. The ABiH offensive against Kiseljak was thus restricted to a single axis of advance from the northwest, even though ABiH forces to the northeast, east, and south of the Kiseljak enclave had been active earlier. The ABiH IV Corps was committed to the Muslim spring offensive against the HVO in the Neretva Valley and was thus unable to mount a simultaneous assault from Tarcin toward the Kresevo-Fojnica-Kiseljak area. The ABiH I Corps units to the northeast and east of Kiseljak remained heavily engaged against the Bosnian Serb Army forces surrounding Sarajevo and were thus also unavailable for the offensive in the Kiseljak area.

Having failed to cut the Busovaca–Kiseljak road at the Fojnica junction in January, despite repeated bloody assaults, the Muslim forces consolidated and reinforced their positions in the villages northeast of the road (Svinjarevo, Behrici, and Gomionica) during the uneasy cease-fire in February and early April.[45] The ABiH military police units from Visoko were brought in, and there was a steady stream of Muslim-Croat confrontations leading up to the renewal of active combat operations in mid-April. Muslim forces identified in the area north and northeast of Kiseljak in the December, 1992, through January, 1993, period included elements of the 302d Motorized Brigade from Visoko (command post near Dautovci); the 1st Battalion, 303d Mountain Brigade (command post southeast of Dautovci); the 1st and 2d Battalions, 17th Krajina Mountain Brigade; and Territorial Defense forces from the Kiseljak area.[46] As far as can be determined, the same forces remained in place through mid-April.

The ABiH forces deployed in the area of Svinjarevo and Gomionica to the northeast of the Busovaca–Kiseljak road constituted the most significant threat to the Croats in Kiseljak. The forces in that area also posed a potential threat to the HVO defense of Busovaca to the northwest. Accordingly, at 9:10 A.M., April 17, under heavy ABiH attack in the Vitez area, the OZCB commander ordered the Ban Josip Jelacic Brigade commander in Kiseljak to prepare for a preemptive attack on Muslim positions around Gomionica. He was further ordered to blockade Visnjica and other villages that could be used by the ABiH to launch an attack; to take control of Gomionica and Svinjarevo following a strong artillery and mortar preparation, the main attack to be made from Sikulje and Hadrovci; and reinforce the HVO positions

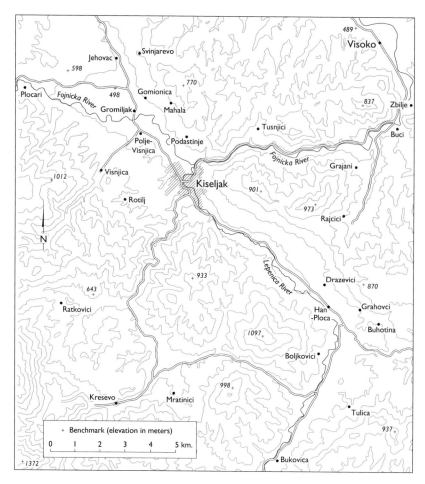

Map 4. The Kiseljak Area. *Map by Bill Nelson.*

at Badnje and Pobrdje with one company each. Finally, the brigade commander was enjoined to "keep in mind that the lives of the Croats in the region of Lasva depend upon your mission. This region could become a tomb for all of us if you show a lack of resolution."[47]

Shortly before midnight on April 17, Colonel Blaskic gave final, detailed orders to the Jelacic Brigade for the proposed preemptive attack.[48] The brigade was ordered to hold Zavrtaljka firmly and, following preparation of the objective area with mortar fire, to attack and capture Gomionica and Svinjarevo then regroup and conduct an artillery preparation for continuation of the attack to capture Bilalovac. HVO forces in the Fojnica area were assigned the mission of protecting the brigade's left flank and launching an attack on the hamlet of Dusina (south of Fojnica) or a breakthrough toward Sebesic. The operation was set to commence at 5:30 A.M., April 18.

At 1:40 A.M. on the eighteenth, the OZCB commander issued orders directly to the commander of the HVO battalion in Fojnica, instructing him to carry out the planned "combat operation" toward either Dusina or toward Sebesic, the purpose of which was to relieve pressure on the HVO defenders of Busovaca and gain control over the no-man's-land between the Kiseljak and Busovaca areas of operations.[49] Despite being issued in the most forceful terms and essential to counteract the heavy Muslim attacks in the Vitez and Busovaca areas, Colonel Blaskic's orders were not obeyed by Stjepan Tuka, commander of the Ban Jelacic Brigade's 3d (Fojnica) Battalion, who with the support of the civilian authorities in Fojnica refused to execute the operations ordered and thereby provoked a crisis in the HVO command system.

Before the HVO attack ordered by Colonel Blaskic on April 17 to clear the Gomionica/Svinjarevo area could be mounted, the ABiH forces launched an attack of their own from the Svinjarevo-Gomionica area.[50] At about 6 A.M. on Sunday, April 18, the battle for Gomionica—temporarily suspended in January—resumed when ABiH military police advanced from the village and made a frontal assault across the Busovaca–Kiseljak road.[51] The Muslim assault was brought to a halt by ten, at which time the Jelacic Brigade headquarters reported that "our forces which are fulfilling their tasks in the village of Gomionica are being attacked."[52] The same hurried situation report noted that other assigned tasks were being accomplished: the Muslim inhabitants of the villages of Jehovac, Gromiljak, Mlava, and Palez had been disarmed. The report also noted that "we have received zip from Fojnica *bojna* [battalion]."[53] At 4:45 P.M., Mijo Bozic, the Jelacic Brigade commander, reported that the conflict had spread to the villages of Rotilj, Visnjica, Doci, Hercezi, and Brestovsko, and that the HVO had lost Zavrtaljka and failed to push the Muslim forces out of Gomionica—although they had advanced about a kilometer on either side of the village.[54] Heavy fighting was still in progress, and the HVO forces reported three KIA, four WIA, and an unknown number of missing.

At 2 A.M. on April 19, Jelacic Brigade headquarters reported that heavy fighting continued in the Gomionica area as the Muslim forces reinforced their lines following an unsuccessful "counterattack"—a renewed attack launched after the HVO halted their initial attack.[55] There was a lull in the fighting elsewhere in the Kiseljak area. The stalemate around Gomionica continued on April 19 and 20, with neither side able to advance. Despite several fevered messages from the OZCB commander referring to the massacre of Croats in Zenica and the immanent destruction of all HVO forces in central Bosnia, the Jelacic Brigade was unable to move forward in the Gomionica area until April 21, when it launched a counterattack that drove the ABiH forces back some five hundred meters north of the Busovaca–Kiseljak road.[56] The lines stabilized once more, and would remain there for some time to come. The forces engaged in the Gomionica area from April 18–21 included about seven hundred ABiH soldiers and about 420 HVO troops. The HVO forces reported three KIA and thirty WIA, and estimated the Muslims had suffered some 266 casualties.

Having halted the ABiH assault at Gomionica on April 18, the HVO began to clean up the Muslim salient west of the Busovaca–Kiseljak road even before their successful counterattack on April 21. The Muslims simultaneously evacuated the entire salient. About 80 percent of the Muslim civilians in the area left on their own volition and moved to Visoko, Fojnica, and Kresevo. The Muslims in Doci and Hercezi surrendered their weapons on April 19, and the HVO arrested 120 people in Brezovena and captured two 82-mm mortars and one 120-mm mortar. They also found five 120-mm, two 82-mm, and two 60-mm mortars, as well as three 60-mm mortars ABiH troops had thrown away in a stream. The HVO took Visnjica and Polje Visnjica on April 20, and evacuated almost all of the Muslim women and children there. It is perhaps worth noting that when Fojnica fell to the Muslims on July 10, 1993, and the Croats were expelled, many of them went over the mountains to Visnjica and occupied empty Muslim houses there.

The vigorous clearing actions in the villages on both sides of the Busovaca–Kiseljak road generated a fairly large number of Muslim refugees (some 1,038 went to the Visoko area alone before April 28), and the HVO actions were subsequently characterized by ECMM teams in the area as "ethnic cleansing."[57] Undeniably, Muslim houses were burned and Muslim civilians killed in the course of clearing armed Muslim defenders from positions in the various villages in the area of operations north and south of the Busovaca–Kiseljak road. However, neither the destruction nor the loss of life was disproportionate to the necessity of eliminating active centers of resistance in the HVO rear areas. Moreover, the ECMM reports appear to be based solely on Muslim allegations and quick visits to various Muslim villages. The ECMM monitors apparently did not investigate claims of destruction in Croat villages in the area; at least they did not comment on such claims. The British UNPROFOR observers appear in this case to have been more balanced in their judgments. On April 23, elements of the 9/12th Lancers conducted a detailed reconnaissance northeast of Kiseljak around the villages of Gromiljak, Svinjarevo, and Behrici. Fighting was still going on along the ridgeline between the villages of Svinjarevo and Podastinje, and houses were burning in Behrici and Gomionica. However, the British UN-PROFOR intelligence analyst reported: "although the callsigns reported Croat/Muslim clashes there appears to be no evidence of ethnic cleansing."[58]

The village of Rotilj appears to have been of special concern to the ECMM monitors. Following the failed ABiH assault at Gomionica on April 18, some seventy ABiH soldiers occupied Rotilj.[59] The HVO offered to accept the surrender of the Muslim weapons but was told to "buzz off" by the Muslim commander, who did not want to surrender. The HVO subsequently took the village in a one-day fight on the eighteenth. The ECMM report on the affair alleges that Rotilj was attacked from 3 P.M. on April 18 to noon on April 19 (a twenty-one-hour fight!) by some twenty masked soldiers "alleged to be HVO," who supposedly destroyed all the Muslim houses (nineteen of them) in the west end of village as well as other structures. As usual, the ECMM team reported that none of the Croat houses were damaged. The Muslim men in the village were reportedly arrested and jailed in the Kiseljak HVO prison, and most of the inhabitants evacuated to the older part of town—except for seven persons who were "savagely executed." On April 25, the ECMM reported some six hundred people were in the southwest part of the village (including about one hundred to 150 refugees from Visoko) surrounded by the HVO.[60] They were still there on May 22. Apparently the HVO had a rather glacial ethnic-cleansing program.

The Muslim offensive in the Kiseljak area seems to have been launched in order to gain control of the important Visoko–Fojnica line of communications, divide the Kiseljak enclave into several smaller pieces and isolate the various Croat villages, and, ultimately, to open the area to settlement by Muslim refugees from eastern Bosnia and the Krajina. The ABiH was unable to achieve any of those objectives during the April fighting in the Kiseljak area, but it would renew its efforts in the months to come.

The ABiH Attack in the Zenica Area

The ABiH plan for its April, 1993, offensive appears to have included the elimination of HVO military forces in the Zenica area as well as the expulsion of the Croat community from Zenica and its surrounding villages. Although HVO forces and the Croat population in the Vitez, Busovaca, and Kiseljak areas came under heavy attack and suffered greatly, it was in the Zenica area that the Bosnian Croats received the most devastating blows. The two HVO brigades in Zenica were destroyed, most of the Croat population in Zenica was expelled and became refugees, and the Croat villages west and northwest of the city were attacked and "cleansed." In addition, the sole line of communication between the Croat enclaves in the Lasva Valley and those in the northern area around Zepce was severed.

Tensions in the Zenica area increased following the kidnapping of four

HVO soldiers from Novi Travnik on April 13 and the ambush and kidnapping of Zivko Totic in Zenica on the morning of April 15, but the HVO forces in Zenica appear not to have expected any major confrontation.[61] The two HVO brigades in the Zenica area (the Jure Francetic and 2d Zenica Brigades) increased their level of readiness and blocked the roads under their control, notably the Zenica–Stranjani–Tetovo and Zenica–Raspotocje routes. Nevertheless, at 6 A.M. on April 16, the Jure Francetic Brigade's headquarters in Zenica reported that the preceding night had been quiet in the brigade zone, the town was under control, and HVO units were permitting unarmed civilians to pass through checkpoints on their way to work.[62]

The situation in Zenica changed dramatically in the early morning hours on April 17. Attacking from two directions, the ABiH began to take control of the Croat areas in the Zenica municipality and to encircle the two HVO brigades (Jure Francetic and 2d Zenica) and disarm them. Able-bodied men were taken to the detention center in Zenica, but elements of both brigades escaped via Nova Kar to the HVO lines near Novi Bila, and HVO elements outside the town took up defensive positions. Vinko Baresic, commander of the 2d Zenica Brigade, then still in the process of formation, reported at 5:30 A.M. that his headquarters had been attacked from all directions and was surrounded. In the same report, issued at 10:20 hours, Baresic urgently requested instructions and assistance from HQ, OZCB in Vitez, noting that HVO forces in the village of Stranjani were completely under siege and had been given an ultimatum by the ABiH to surrender their weapons; the Muslims were progressively surrounding the villages of Zmajevac and Cajdras; and many displaced Croats were seeking refuge in Cajdras.[63] Baresic also informed HQ, OZCB, that he had issued orders for a breakout toward Janjac and Osojnica but that the morale of his forces was declining rapidly and he was unsure whether or not his orders would be obeyed. He himself was going to try to get to Cajdras.

At 1:15 A.M. on April 18, the OZCB commander appealed to the UNPROFOR battalion at Stari Bila and ECMM authorities in Zenica to take immediate action to protect the Croatian population in the Zenica municipality, particularly those in the village of Cajdras. Later that day, Colonel Blaskic telephoned Lieutenant Colonel Stewart and repeated his urgent request for the UNPROFOR forces to act to save the Croats in Cajdras.[64] In his diary Lieutenant Colonel Stewart noted: "things got worse overnight; Zenica blown up with violence and Muslims having a go at Croats who live in/around Zenica; lots of Croat refugees in Croat-held area at Cajdras; 800 civilians ethnically cleansed from Podbrezje West of Zenica by Muslims; Muslim soldiers hostile and looting; HVO had been attacked and all HVO/HOS buildings in Zenica taken over by ABiH; Boban and Izetbegovic agreed to a cease-fire."[65]

Indeed, things had gotten very much worse for the Croats in the Zenica area. At 3:45 P.M. on April 18, Vinko Baresic reported from Cajdras that although some two hundred men of the 1st Battalion, Jure Francetic Brigade, continued to man the defensive perimeter around Cajdras (running from the Cajdras crossroads–Palijike–Serusa–Strbci–Jezero–Tromnice); the 3d Battalion, 2d Zenica Brigade, had already agreed to Muslim demands; and the brigade's 1st and 2d Battalions, as well as the 2d and 3d Battalions of the Francetic Brigade, were sure to follow soon. Baresic noted that the HVO troops in Zmajevac were abandoning their positions, leaving the Cajdras defenders in an even more perilous situation. He also noted that he and some other officers did not wish to surrender because "even if we were to surrender, I am sure that we would be executed."[66] He went on to request instructions regarding Lieutenant Colonel Stewart's offer to evacuate HVO personnel from Cajdras to Vitez or Busovaca.

The destruction and "cleansing" of Croat villages in the Zenica area was widespread and thorough, despite Muslim assurances that Croat refugees could return home. On April 21, the ECMM Regional Center in Zenica forwarded a special report to ECMM headquarters in Zagreb dealing with the two hundred Croats the Muslims had imprisoned in the Zenica Prison's military section; the existence of detention centers at Bilimisce, the "Music School" in Zenica, and Nemila; and the destruction by Muslims of Croat villages in and around Zenica. Having visited and investigated the devastated Croat villages of Cajdras, Vjetrenice, Janjac, Kozarci, Osojnica, Stranjani, Zahalie, and Dobriljeno, the ECMM monitors in their usual fashion minimized the damage to Croat property and the deaths of Croat civilians caused by the Muslims and concluded that "except from Zalje the damages was [sic] less than expected."[67]

Having rid themselves of their erstwhile allies and a good part of the Croat civilian population in Zenica, blocked the road to Zepce, and "cleansed" the Croat villages in the Zenica area, the Muslims were free to concentrate on their offensive in the Vitez-Busovaca-Kiseljak area. Although the HVO forces and Croat civilians in the Lasva-Kozica-Lepenica area suffered significant destruction and casualties, Croat losses in the Zenica area were substantial, and the HVO presence and influence in the area definitively eliminated. Thenceforth, Zenica was a thoroughly Muslim stronghold. Nowhere else did the Muslims' April offensive achieve such decisive results.

The Alleged HVO Shelling of Zenica on April 19, 1993

Between 12:10 and 12:29 P.M. on April 19, six artillery shells fell in downtown Zenica, killing and wounding a number of civilians. After a hasty investigation, the ABiH authorities blamed the shelling on the HVO, claiming that it was intended as a warning to the Muslims. Numerous "experts" from the ABiH, UNPROFOR, and ECMM subsequently conducted additional analysis of the fuse and shell fragments and impact areas and concluded that the shells had been fired by HVO forces from a position near Puticevo.[68] Faulty analytical methods and ignorance of the capabilities of the various types of artillery in use in the area reinforced the assumption that the HVO had fired the six rounds. However, as Prof. Slobodan Jankovic—a bona fide ballistics expert and expert on the artillery weapons and ammunition in use at the time—has demonstrated, it was more likely that the six rounds were fired by Bosnian Serb artillery located on the Vlasic massif, just as the HVO authorities suggested at the time.[69] The essence of Professor Jankovic's technical argument is that the six rounds which fell in downtown Zenica on April 19 could have been fired either by the HVO or by the Serbs. Both had guns (122-mm and 152-mm) within range that used the type of shells and fuses of which fragments were found after the shelling. However, Professor Jankovic points out that: (1) the ABiH/ECMM crater analysis was limited to only one crater, and the allowable standard deviation (as to the direction from which the shells were fired) argues for a Serb gun rather than an HVO gun; (2) the HVO had *no* meteorological capability and could not have achieved such a tight dispersion pattern without it; (3) the two HVO guns in the best position to have fired the six rounds were reported by ABiH observers *not* to have fired during the period in question; and (4) the missing factor needed to determine definitively who fired the six shells is the tube life of the guns involved (which affects initial velocity).

Although Professor Jankovic has declined to state definitively who fired the rounds, he leans toward two Serb guns located on the Vlasic massif firing three rounds each. He discounts the use of a forward observer who provided corrections, as well as the idea that the rounds might have been fired by one HVO gun that fired several rounds and then displaced. The HVO gunners simply were not well enough trained to have gone out of battery, moved, and relaid the gun within the time available. In general, HVO artillery fire was quite inaccurate due to the absolute lack of meteorological data; substandard, black market ammunition (inconsistent performance); lack of ammunition management (use of mixed lots); lack of records of tube life (which meant most guns likely were used after their recommended tube life); and lack of gun crew training. All of this means that, even when aiming at a military target, the HVO artillery probably could not have avoided hitting nearby civilian facilities.

Actions Elsewhere in April, 1993

Ivica Zeko's predictions of March 25 as to probable Muslim actions in areas outside the main Vitez-Busovaca-Kiseljak area were remarkably accurate. Unable to mount simultaneous attacks on the HVO concentrations throughout central Bosnia, the ABiH elected to maintain the status quo with only minor actions in those Croat enclaves outside the central Vitez-Busovaca-Kiseljak-Zenica area. Tensions increased, as did the number of incidents, but there were no direct ABiH attacks in the peripheral areas. Novi Travnik, Travnik, Zepce, and Vares remained relatively quiet while the battle raged in the central area. In part, the ABiH decision to avoid open conflict outside the central area was dictated by the fact that the HVO held significant portions of the lines against the Bosnian Serb Army and could not be attacked and destroyed without crippling the Bosnian defense against the Serb aggressors.

Travnik and Novi Travnik

Conflict between Muslims and Croats erupted briefly in the Travnik–Novi Travnik area in mid-April following the dispute over the Croat flags at Easter in Travnik and the kidnapping of the four members of the Stjepan Tomasevic Brigade by mujahideen near Novi Travnik on April 13. Incidents multiplied, and there were numerous arrests and detentions of both military personnel and civilians from both sides as Muslims and Croats provoked and tested each other. On April 12, HVO forces detained a group of some forty to fifty armed Muslims, of whom twenty were ABiH soldiers in uniform, at a checkpoint in Dolac near Travnik. The detainees—including Nihad Rebihic, the assistant commander for morale, propaganda, and military police of the Vitez Territorial Defense organization—were taken to the local HVO headquarters and tied up. The civilians were released thirty minutes later. On April 14, HQ, ABiH III Corps, reported that the security situation in the Travnik–Novi Travnik area had deteriorated since the kidnapping of the Tomasevic Brigade personnel and that, although they did not engage in combat, the HVO had occupied some key points in the Novi Travnik area, abused ABiH soldiers and Muslim civilians, and reopened the Stojkovici camp. Checkpoints and roadblocks were established by both sides in the area, weapons and vehicles were seized, and the vital road link to Gornji Vakuf was severed.[70] On April 15, the intelligence sections of the ABiH 312th Mountain Brigade and OG West reported that the HVO had arrested some 150 Muslim civilians and ABiH personnel in the Travnik–Novi Travnik area between April 13 and 15, and put them in the so-called vats in the village of Stojkovici (Novi Travnik municipality). Similarly, on April 20, the Travnicka Brigade headquarters reported that its communications were being tapped and that Muslim forces were arresting Croats on a massive scale in the center of Travnik from the barracks to the entry of the town from the direction of Vitez. Also in mid-April, some 110 wounded HVO soldiers were expelled from the Travnik hospital, and a makeshift HVO field hospital was established in the church in Novi Bila. On April 25, HQ, OZCB, reported to UNPROFOR, ECMM, ICRC, and HQ, ABiH III Corps that mujahideen forces from Mehurici had entered the nearby Croat village of Miletici and taken away sixty to seventy people—mainly elderly people, children, and the sick—and maltreated the underage men, who were detained in the cellars of nearby Muslim houses.[71]

Both the ABiH and HVO drew reinforcements from the Novi Travnik area for the fight around Vitez. At 8:15 P.M. on April 16, HQ, OZCB, ordered the Tomasevic Brigade commander to take action to prevent the movement of Muslim forces from the Novi Travnik area toward Gornji Veceriska and Donja Veceriska. At 2:30 the following afternoon, the Viteska Brigade reported that information had been received regarding the movement of

Muslim forces from the village of Opara south of Novi Travnik toward the village of Zaselje—the Croat inhabitants of which were evacuating in panic in the direction of Veceriska. At 8 P.M. on April 17, the Tomasevic Brigade commander was ordered to immediately dispatch a twenty-five- to thirty-man unit to the Vitez area to prevent any further advance toward Vitez by Muslim units coming from Krcevine. Earlier, on the evening of the sixteenth, the OZCB commander ordered the 4th Military Police Battalion unit in Travnik to move to Vitez no later than 10 P.M. to reinforce HVO elements that were heavily engaged in the town.[72]

Despite the large number of heavily armed ABiH and HVO troops in the area, the high level of tension, and numerous incidents and provocations, the Travnik–Novi Travnik area remained relatively quiet even as the HVO forces in nearby Vitez, Busovaca, and Kiseljak fought desperately to blunt the Muslim offensive. For the most part, the situation remained as the Tomasevic Brigade headquarters reported on April 17: "The night was quiet on the territory of Novi Travnik municipality. We received no information on potential conflicts with the BH Army."[73]

Zepce, Zavidovici, and Novi Seher

The HVO forces in the Zepce-Zavidovici–Novi Seher area were critical to the Bosnian defense against the Bosnian Serb Army in the northern salient. They also constituted a well-organized and well-armed force that was prepared to offer significant resistance to any ABiH attempt to overcome them. Although provocations and minor incidents multiplied during the month of April, Muslim-Croat tensions did not erupt into open fighting in the area despite the fact that the HVO forces had been isolated by ABiH forces cutting the Zenica–Zepce road. On April 16, Ivo Lozancic, commander of the 111xp Brigade in Zepce, reported: "the fundamentalists [Bosnian Muslims] are constantly advocating peace whilst trying to occupy the best possible positions for conducting war with the Croatian Defence Council. Their preparation for war with Croats continues to be visible. We are under siege, unable to communicate and receive ammunition and for us it would be difficult to start a conflict. The latest information confirms that the enemy (the greens) are well armed, well equipped and have enough ammunition and they are intent to fight against the Croats."[74]

Nevertheless, Lozancic reported the following day that "relations with the BiH Army are on a satisfactory level," and two days later, April 19, he addressed another report to the HVO Main HQ in Mostar and HQ, OZCB, in Vitez in which he noted that "there have been no conflicts with the Muslims and their behaviour is odd."[75] Lozancic went on to note that

> The town of Zepce has been deserted like a ghost town for two
> days. Inns owned by Muslim owners are empty. The Islamic troops
> that have been returned from the checkpoint have left for Z. Polje.
> I am considering to issue an order on the withdrawal of our forces

from the territory of the defence of the town of Maglaj, as a warning for the attacks they are conducting on our forces in Central
Bosnia. I have been receiving some information on the mistreatment of Croats in Zenica, about the complete disarmament and
search carried out in a village above Crkvica and the confiscation of
weapons. We do not have complete information, nor has the truth
about the sufferings of Croats been sufficiently represented in the
Croatian media. . . . We have learned that the Muslims are about to
launch an attack on Zepce in five days. We are completely cut off
from the world, but we have enough reserves to be able to fight to
the annihilation of one or the other.[76]

The ABiH attack on the Zepce enclave did come not in five days. The conflict in the Zepce area did not come until the end of June—after the ABiH
had mounted a successful major attack against HVO forces in the
Travnik–Novi Travnik area.

Sarajevo and Vares

The HVO brigade in the Sarajevo area, Slavko Zelic's Kralj Tvrtko Drugi
Brigade, was nominally subordinate to the OZCB commander but generally
operated autonomously. By virtue of its importance to the defense of the
Bosnian capital, no action was taken against the Tvrtko Brigade during the
Muslims' April offensive. The same was generally true of the Bobovac
Brigade in the Vares area. Although tensions increased and a number of
brief firefights took place in April, Vares remained, as Zeko had predicted,
"too tough a nut" for the ABiH to "crack"—at least for the moment. The
ABiH units in the Vares area did increase their combat readiness, and they
reported that the HVO had reinforced Vares from Kiseljak and provoked
Muslim forces in several incidents.[77]

The Situation at the End of April, 1993

The ABiH seriously underestimated the ability and determination of HVO
forces to resist their April offensive. As a consequence, what Muslim leaders had most probably envisaged as a quick and thorough defeat of the
HVO military followed by cleansing the Vitez-Busovaca-Kiseljak-Zenica
area for settlement by Muslim refugees turned out to be a significant battle.
Moreover, the ABiH failed to achieve any of its major goals despite inflict-
ing serious casualties on HVO military personnel and the Croat civilian
population. The aggressive HVO active defense, including the selective use
of preemptive and spoiling attacks, counterattacks, and clearing operations, stalled the Muslim advance around Vitez, Busovaca, and Kiseljak.
The HVO's defensive operations—with the exception of Ahmici—inflicted
serious, but not disproportionate, damage on Muslim property and persons. At the end of the month, the two antagonists still faced each other
from lines north and south of the vital Travnik–Kiseljak road and several

smaller Muslim enclaves in the Lasva Valley, but the SPS explosives factory in Vitez remained in HVO hands, the two Croat enclaves remained intact, and the people making up the core of the Croat community in central Bosnia continued to occupy their homes and operate their businesses. Further ABiH operations would be required if the Muslims were going to realize their ambitions in the area.

9   The Continuation of the Muslim Offensive, May–June, 1993

Having failed to eliminate the HVO defenders and seize the core Croat en- claves in Central Bosnia by direct assault in April 1993, the ABiH regrouped in May and in June began a sustained campaign to reduce the Croat strongholds by attacking key points on their periphery. In turn, the Muslims took Travnik, most of the Novi Travnik municipality, Kakanj, Fojnica, and other Croat territory in Central Bosnia as well as Bugojno, Gornji Vakuf, Konjic, and Jablanica on the southern periphery. In the process more than 100,000 Bosnian Croats were expelled from their homes.[1]

The April, 1993, Cease-Fire

The temporary cease-fire in the Lasva Valley area brokered by Maj. Bryan Watters, second-in-command of the British UNPROFOR battalion at Stari Bila, on April 16 and agreed to by the HVO and ABiH commanders the following day, was a fragile reed and did little to stop the fighting in the area. However, pursuant to the military provisions of the Vance-Owen Peace Plan signed on March 3, 1993, RBiH president Alija Izetbegovic and Mate Boban, the leader of the Bosnian Croat community, signed an agreement in Zagreb on April 18 that called for an immediate cessation of all Muslim-Croat fighting; the exchange of prisoners and detainees; proper care of the wounded; the investigation of related crimes; and the reestablishment of communications between ABiH and HVO authorities. The Boban-Izetbegovic agreement also called for the return of all HVO and ABiH military and police forces to their "home" provinces; control over all forces in the proposed VOPP Provinces 1, 5, and 9 by the ABiH Main Staff and in the proposed VOPP Provinces 3, 8, and 10 by the HVO Main Staff; and the establishment of an ABiH-HVO joint command.[2]

At noon on April 21, the HVO and ABiH chiefs of staff (Milijov Petkovic and Sefer Halilovic, respectively) met at the ECMM office in Novi Bila to discuss the implementation of the Boban-Izetbegovic cease-fire agreement. European Community ambassador Jean-Pierre Thebault presided over the discussions. Although punctuated by bitter charges and countercharges by both sides regarding violations of the existing cease-fire arrangements, the meeting resulted in an agreement for an immediate cessation of combat activities; the separation of forces and insertion of UNPROFOR monitoring elements between them; unhindered patrolling by UNPROFOR units between Kiseljak and Travnik; full guarantees for the Muslims besieged in

Vitez and the Croats surrounded in Zenica; and a joint meeting of "coordination teams" at 10 A.M. on April 22. Lieutenant Colonel Bob Stewart noted in his diary, "everyone parted on good terms."[3]

Colonel Tihomir Blaskic, a participant in the meeting, subsequently recorded his own observations on the negotiations, noting that the ABiH delegation seemed preoccupied, cold, and worried about the many Croat civilian casualties caused by their offensive. Blaskic's prophetic assessment of the ABiH was that "they are either totally scatter-brained so they have agreed to everything, or they can no longer control their own actions, so now they accept everything in order to create space for a new attack, one they will not give up on." Despite his misgivings, on April 22, Blaskic ordered HVO forces in central Bosnia to implement the chiefs of staff's agreements.[4] Subordinate commanders were once again enjoined to halt all combat activities against the ABiH and to not respond to Muslim provocations unless ordered to do so by higher headquarters. Nor were they to restrict the movements of UN and ECMM teams. Colonel Blaskic also ordered the withdrawal of HVO forces from the Sljivcic–Vrhovine–BM 808–Gavrine Kuce line and informed his subordinates that the area along the Vitez–Busovaca road—from the Vjetrenica–Zenica road on the left to the Kaonik intersection on the right—was to be a demilitarized zone occupied only by UNPROFOR elements.

The high emotional level of the troops on both sides and the lack of discipline and firm control that had always characterized both the ABiH and the HVO magnified the difficulties of implementing the cease-fire agreements. In the last week of April, Colonel Blaskic attempted to rectify that deficiency by issuing a series of orders relating to the proper conduct of HVO forces, observing the cease-fire and the laws of land warfare, and avoiding interference with the operations of the UNPROFOR, ECMM, ICRC, and other international organizations in the central Bosnia area. Arson and looting were strictly forbidden, and stiff sanctions were threatened against those found guilty of such crimes.[5] Noting that the lack of military discipline evoked the condemnation of the media and the international community, Colonel Blaskic reminded his subordinates on April 23 that they were responsible for enforcing discipline among their troops and that they were to ensure that UN and ECMM patrols and teams were unhindered. He also forbade HVO forces to carry out offensive actions or to respond to isolated provocations by the ABiH, noting that they were permitted to "open fire only in case of direct attack by Muslim forces, but only after an order is issued by the superior commanders, about which the brigade commanders must inform me immediately."[6] The proper treatment of the wounded, civilians, and prisoners was covered in an order issued April 24, and a general recapitulation of the earlier instructions on the proper conduct of HVO personnel was issued the same day. Measures to reduce the spread of rumors and to raise troop morale and defensive spirit were directed on April 28. The following day, Colonel Blaskic again reminded his subordinate commanders of their obligations with respect to the release of civilian detainees.[7] Presumably, the ABiH III Corps commander issued similar admonitions to his troops, although no such orders have come to light thus far.

Following their April 21 meeting, the ABiH and HVO chiefs of staff frequently traveled to frontline areas with UNPROFOR representatives in order to stop the fighting and to personally encourage their troops to obey the cease-fire agreements. Generals Halilovic and Petkovic and their subordinate commanders also met weekly to resolve ongoing issues and work toward full implementation of the Boban-Izetbegovic cease-fire agreement. In view of the continued fighting and the fundamental distrust between Muslims and Croats, the meetings were usually full of recriminations and made little progress toward the ultimate goal. For example, on April 28, Halilovic and Petkovic met at the Spanish UNPROFOR battalion headquarters in Jablanica and discussed three special issues: the security and freedom of movement for ECMM and UNPROFOR elements; the evacuation of civilians from two Croat villages near Konjic by UNPROFOR personnel; and the establishment of a joint operational center in Mostar. From Jablanica the meeting participants traveled to Zenica by way of Tarcin and Kresevo, and then Generals Halilovic and Petkovic, accompanied by Colonels Hadzihasanovic and Blaskic, went to yet another meeting in Visoko. That meeting began "in a bad atmosphere" when General Petkovic complained about an ongoing ABiH attack against HVO positions and set "pre-conditions to any further cooperation."[8] The meeting deteriorated further when it was interrupted by a British UNPROFOR battalion report that a forty-truck UNHCR convoy carrying food for Muslims in Zenica had been "highjacked" by HVO forces in the Busovaca area.[9]

The Joint Coordination Commission (JCC) headed by ABiH colonel Mehmed Alagic and HVO colonel Filip Filipovic was established to implement the earlier January, 1993, cease-fire arrangement. It continued to function in a desultory manner even after the beginning of the ABiH April offensive.[10] However, the JCC became superfluous on April 22, when the ABiH and HVO commanders in central Bosnia took the first step toward forming the Joint Operational Center (JOC) called for in the Boban-Izetbegovic agreement by appointing their representatives: Dzemal Merdan and Vezirj Jusufspahic for the ABiH and Franjo Nakic and Zoran Pilicic for the HVO.[11] The JOC began to function from a headquarters in Vitez a few days later. On April 25, the ECMM representative to the JOC noted that the new organization had gotten off to a slow start but that the presence of experienced members from the older JCC would no doubt ensure better performance in the next few days despite the many cease-fire violations.[12]

The May Respite

The fighting between Muslims and Croats in central Bosnia died down as both sides licked their wounds and prepared for the next round. Minor cease-fire violations and even small-scale engagements between ABiH and

HVO forces occurred, but for the most part the situation remained relatively calm. Typical incidents included the killing of an HVO soldier by a sniper near Pokrajcici on May 10, and small-scale fighting between units of the ABiH 306th Mountain Brigade and the HVO Frankopan Brigade on the morning of May 11, which resulted in one KIA and one WIA on each side.[13] The continuing incidents were serious enough, however, to elicit several complaints by the OZCB commander to ECMM and UNPROFOR authorities. At the same time, Colonel Blaskic was obliged to once again remind his own forces of their obligations under the terms of the cease-fire agreement, particularly as related to the free passage throughout the central Bosnia region of UNPROFOR, UNHCR, and other international organizations.[14]

Meanwhile, the JOC sought to prevent incidents and coordinate the efforts of the two opponents to make the cease-fire work. The joint coordination concept was implemented at lower levels as well. On May 11, following talks between Mensud Kelestura, commander of the ABiH 325th Mountain Brigade, and Mario Cerkez, commander of the HVO Viteska Brigade, a joint commission was established to deal with problems surrounding the release of prisoners, care of the sick and wounded, handling of the dead, and essential infrastructure services (water, sewage, electricity, roads, and telephone and telegraph).[15] The members of the joint commission included Borislav Jozic and Stipo Krizanac for the HVO, and Refik Hajdarevic and Nihad Rebihic for the ABiH. Each side was to provide two vehicles and four military policemen with equipment to accompany the commission members. It was anticipated that the commission's work would not extend beyond June 1.

In early May, Colonel Blaskic made a comprehensive assessment of the situation in the OZCB, which he forwarded to the highest authorities of the Croatian Community of Herceg-Bosna and HVO Main HQ in Mostar. With respect to the ABiH's intentions, Colonel Blaskic characterized the situation as one of "overt hostile activity of the forces of the 7th Mechanized Brigade of the MOS [ABiH] and other extremist forces with the clear intention of settling scores with the Croats in the Lasva region" and noted that the Muslim forces "are waiting for matériel and significant logistics support and have for the time being intensified sniping, the torching of Croat houses, and provocations with the objective of making our forces respond vigorously and use up as much ammunition as possible."[16]

Blaskic went on to state that the ABiH "seriously expect 'the job to be finished' in Konjic and then regroup forces and attack Kiseljak, Kresevo and Busovaca via Fojnica." His assessment of the Muslim forces in the central Bosnia region was that they included parts of the ABiH I and II Corps as well as fifteen mountain brigades and assorted units such as the Green Legion, Patriotic League, and mujahideen under the command of the ABiH III Corps in Zenica. He characterized the opposing Muslim units as mainly poorly supplied and poorly equipped infantry forces with large numbers of snipers; frustrated by their lack of success in the Lasva region and thus highly motivated to press the offensive against the HVO; and supported by "extensive use of the media to project an image of themselves as victims." Blaskic believed the ABiH intended "To take full control of the Croatian area of the Lasva region, in particular of Kiseljak-Busovaca and Vitez with the taking of control of Busovaca being a priority. If MOS [Muslim forces in general] achieve these objectives then they would link up with the Konjic–Gornji Vakuf–Bugojno forces on the one side and those of Visoko-Kakanj and Zenica on the other side and thereby totally blockade the Croats of Kakanj, Vares and Zepce."[17]

In support of his estimate of ABiH intentions, Blaskic offered as evidence the pattern of deployment of the Muslim forces, the main body of whom—elements of some six brigades—were grouped to encircle Busovaca, "their principal task being the total blockade of this city and the cutting off of the Busovaca–Vitez road at Kaonik, to be followed by the total destruction of the city."[18] He also noted the deployment of strong Muslim forces throughout central Bosnia, most of whom were not oriented toward the defense against the Bosnian Serb Army. The 301st Mechanized, 303d Mountain, 314th Mountain, and 7th Muslim Motorized Brigades, together with MOS, Patriotic League, and Green Legion forces were stationed in Zenica; the 304th Mountain Brigade at Breza; the 302d Motorized Brigade at Visoko; the 309th Mountain Brigade at Kakanj; the 305th Mountain Brigade at Biljesevo (rather than in Zenica as UNPROFOR had guaranteed); the 308th Mountain Brigade at Novi Travnik with some three hundred mujahideen at Ravno Rostovo; the 325th Mountain Brigade at Vitez; the 333d Mountain Brigade at Kacuni; and the 306th and 312th Mountain Brigades and 17th Krajina Mountain Brigade at Travnik.

Colonel Blaskic also listed the probable avenues of attack for Muslim forces against HVO positions in the Vitez, Busovaca, and Kiseljak area, and commented on ABiH electronic warfare and intelligence-gathering activities as well as the state of ABiH morale and logistical support. As to the state of his own forces, he noted that their combat readiness was at its highest level, but they were "utterly exhausted and fatigued" and lacked weapons—some fifteen hundred to two thousand guns as a minimum. He also remarked upon the physical separation of the various Croat enclaves and the length of the HVO defense line: thirty-seven kilometers in the Kiseljak area; thirty-eight kilometers in the Busovaca area; and twenty-eight kilometers in the Vitez area—not counting the portions facing the BSA.[19]

Blaskic's concern over a probable resumption of the ABiH offensive was sufficient to warrant a special message on May 15 to Lt. Col. Alistair Duncan, commander of the British UNPROFOR battalion at Stari Bila, and Jean-Pierre Thebault, the EC ambassador at Zenica, in which he stated: "we use this opportunity to inform you that ABiH forces are gathering and consolidating from the areas of KISELJAK, BUSOVACA and VITEZ. They plan to attack the areas in the above mentioned municipalities."[20] Blaskic went on to request that UNPROFOR units immediately be sent to the agreed-upon separation lines (Kuber-Saracevici-Kula-Dusina, Kacuni, and Grablje as well as in the Han Bila–Guca Gora area) in order to forestall any Muslim offensive actions.

Colonel Blaskic's anxieties were well founded, and all of the efforts of the JOC, international organizations, the ABiH and HVO chiefs of staff, and particularly the commander of HVO forces in central Bosnia, to implement the Boban-Izetbegovic cease-fire agreement would prove largely in vain during the month of June.

The Fall of Travnik

The expected resumption of the Muslim offensive came at the end of the first week of June, when elements of eight ABiH brigades struck the HVO forces manning the defensive line against the Bosnian Serb Army in the Travnik area.[21] The Muslim attack achieved tactical surprise and was completely successful, capturing the HVO positions and driving the surviving HVO soldiers and thousands of terrified Croat civilians into the hands of the Serbs, who took them prisoner.[22]

Tensions between Muslims and Croats had been building in the Travnik area since January. Between January and April, the ABiH packed troops into the Travnik area using buses from Zenica traveling via Guca Gora to minimize observation by the HVO. The buses allegedly were engaged in rotating Muslim troops on the front lines against the Serbs, but Croat civilians frequently reported that buses were returning empty toward Zenica. Muslim troops and mujahideen from Zenica, Mehurici, and Milize were also hidden in Muslim villages in the area or in groups of two or three in Muslim houses in Croat villages. By April, the ABiH forces in the Travnik area totaled some 8,000–10,000 men under Mehmed Alagic, commander of the ABiH III Corps's OG Bosanska-Krajina (soon to be redesignated the ABiH VII Corps). The ABiH forces in the Travnik area included the 312th Mountain Brigade (about 3,300 men; commanded by Zijad Gaber); the 17th Krajina Mountain Brigade (about 3,300 men; commanded by Fikret Cuskic); the 27th Krajina Mountain Brigade (about 2,100 men; commanded by Rasim Imamovic); the 3d Battalion, 7th Muslim Motorized Brigade (about 900 men); the 1st Battalion, 308th Mountain Brigade; elements of the 325th Mountain Brigade and of the 37th Krajina Mountain Brigade; the "El Mudzahid" Detachment of mujahideen (about 400 men); some 800 men of the RBiH Ministry of the Interior Police; and two special purpose units: "Mercici" and "Nanetovi," each with around 60–80 men.[23] The town itself and the surrounding area was also packed with some 15,000 Muslim refugees, many of whom were armed.[24]

In early April, prior to the Muslim offensive against Vitez, Busovaca, and Kiseljak, the ABiH fed even more reinforcements into the Travnik area. For example, on April 15, an HVO checkpoint near the town stopped an ABiH convoy of three buses, six trucks, and thirteen other vehicles loaded with

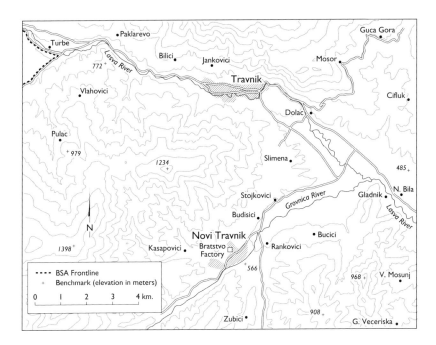

Map 5. The Travnik–Novi Travnik Area. *Map by Bill Nelson.*

troops. The Muslim convoy attempted to pass through the HVO lines three times before it was finally permitted to go through to the barracks in Travnik. On June 5, immediately before the ABiH offensive against Travnik began, the Muslim forces in Travnik were reinforced by an additional eight hundred men.[25]

From January to April, the HVO forces manning the defense lines against the BSA in the immediate Travnik area consisted of the Travnicka Brigade, commanded by Filip Filipovic, with all three of its battalions. On April 1, a second brigade—the Frankopan Brigade—was formed under the command of Ilija Nagic, and from that point onward there were five battalions in the sector. In all, there were some twenty-five hundred to three thousand HVO soldiers on the defense lines in April, many of whom were rotated in from other areas in the Lasva-Kozica-Lepenica region.[26] The HVO headquarters on the Travnik front was situated above the town of Travnik in the village of Jankovici.

On June 1, the defensive lines facing the BSA in the Travnik area were held in part by the ABiH and in part by the HVO, with the HVO holding about two-thirds of the total line.[27] The responsibility for the HVO portion of the line was divided among the HVO Novi Travnik (Tomasevic Brigade, Zeljko Sabljic commanding), HVO Travnik (Travnicka Brigade, Jozo Levtar commanding), and the Frankopan Brigade (Ilija Nagic commanding).[28] The Tomasevic Brigade held from "Sweetwater" (near BM 1182) southwest to BM 986 near the village of Petkovici, at which point the ABiH continued the line south toward Donja Vakuf and Bugojno. The Travnicka Brigade was responsible for the line from Sweetwater northwest to Kazici (a ground distance of about four and one-half kilometers), where the ABiH took up a short section of about two kilometers running northwest to Giganic. The Travnicka Brigade took over there and continued the defensive line around the Turbe salient and then east to the vicinity of BM 1109. The Frankopan Brigade, headquartered at Dolac, took up the line at BM 1109 and extended it around the Vlasic plateau and then north to the Vlaskagromila area (near BM 1919), where the ABiH assumed responsibility. The ABiH controlled Travnik, although the HVO maintained a headquarters and other facilities in the town. Muslim roadblocks at Han Bila and at the entry to Travnik near the mosque at a place called "Bluewater" controlled entry into the town itself.

On June 6, the commander of the British UNPROFOR battalion in the Lasva Valley met with Enver Hadzihasanovic, the ABiH III Corps commander, to discuss the growing problems in the Travnik area. Hadzihasanovic, taking a hard line, remarked that the Muslims were left little alternative but military action in what had become "an outright civil war." After the meeting, British UNPROFOR authorities reported, "the BiH were no longer prepared to restrain themselves, and were likely to take the military initiative in the Lasva Valley."[29] A second meeting was scheduled for the same day with Colonel Blaskic, the OZCB commander, but Hadzihasanovic refused to attend because he thought it was "too late for negotiation." The BRITBAT intelligence analyst noted that the "Corps, judging by the attitude of its commander, seems poised for further military action having clearly rejected the concept of negotiation."[30] Indeed, the ABiH was poised for further military action.

Without prior warning, Muslim troops commanded by Mehmed Alagic struck their erstwhile ally on June 6, 1993. Within seventy-two hours, the heavily outnumbered HVO forces in Travnik surrendered or were driven over the Serb lines.[31] The 303d Mountain Brigade attacked via Ovnak toward Guca Gora, while the 306th Light Brigade attacked in the direction of Pokrajcici.[32] The 312th Mountain Brigade, the 17th and 27th Krajina Mountain Brigades, and the 3d Battalion, 7th Muslim Motorized Brigade, launched attacks directly into the rear of the HVO units holding the front lines against the Serbs. Muslim Ministry of the Interior Police surrounded the "Star" headquarters in Travnik and isolated it. The fiercest attacks, which came on June 8, resulted in twenty-four HVO soldiers and sixty-eight Croat civilians killed.[33] Unable to sustain the house-to-house fighting and unable to obtain reinforcements or resupply, the HVO forces in and around Travnik broke and fled into the Serb lines accompanied by several thousand Croat civilians. On June 10, the new overall ABiH commander, Rasim Delic, ordered his troops to halt their advance.

Having secured the town of Travnik and driven the HVO soldiers from their positions facing the Serbs, the ABiH began systematically clearing the Croat villages northeast of Travnik in order to secure their line of communications to Zenica. At 3 A.M. on June 7, the ABiH attacked elements of the Frankopan Brigade holding the villages of Grahovici, Brajkovici, Plavici, Guca Gora, and Bukovica in an attempt to seize control of the road from Zenica to Travnik. As the HVO units blocking the roads withdrew, the Croat villages fell one by one into the hands of Muslim extremists who engaged in a program of very thorough ethnic cleansing.[34] By June 14, the Zenica-Travnik road via Guca Gora was firmly in ABiH hands. According to contemporary newspaper accounts, Croatian radio reported some thirty-two Croat villages had been cleansed, among which UN sources identified Brajkovici, Grahovici, Bukovica, Radojcici, and Maljine. The story of the village of Guca Gora and its famous Catholic monastery was perhaps typical. Muslim extremists, who had been hiding in nearby Muslim homes, seized the village and desecrated the church in the Franciscan monastery. They carried away the religious statuary and murdered the HVO defenders, several civilians in the monastery, and eight village guard sentinels. British UNPROFOR troops, having observed Muslim troops firing machine guns at Croat civilians fleeing into the woods, prevented an even greater tragedy by rescuing more than 180 Croats trapped in the monastery.[35]

Croatian radio reported more than 250 dead in the Travnik region, as well as some fifteen thousand Croatian refugees following the June 6–10 attack.[36] According to one contemporary newspaper account, there was "strong evidence of atrocities" as Muslim forces attempted to seize the back roads northeast of Travnik leading to Zenica. By June 9, some 8,000 HVO soldiers and Croat civilians had crossed into the Serb lines on the Vlasic massif, and 1,000 of the HVO soldiers were disarmed and taken by the Serbs to the "notorious Manjaca camp."[37] United Nations sources reported that as of June 10, 500 Croats had been killed, thirty-eight villages had been burned, and some 30,000 displaced persons were in the Novi Bila–Vitez–Busovaca–Novi Travnik area.[38] Overall, in June, July, and August, some 427 HVO soldiers and 157 Croat civilians were killed, 1,000 were wounded, 20,000 Croat civilians were displaced, fifteen hundred Croat homes and thirty-one hundred other buildings were burned, and about fifty Croat villages between Travnik and Zenica were destroyed, including Grahovcici, Donja Maljina, Guca Gora, Bikosi, Sadici, Gornja Puticevo, Rudnik, Bila, and Cupa.[39]

Although the Muslim forces had already launched two other major attacks since the beginning of 1993, one contemporary newspaper account noted on June 9: "The fighting reflected a possible new Muslim tactic. With attempts to regain territory from rebel Serbs failing, Muslim-led government troops appear to be trying to wrest territory from the Croats. 'I believe that a general (Muslim) offensive is under way,' said Col. Alastair Duncan, commander of British soldiers serving with the UN peacekeeping forces."[40]

Another contemporary newspaper account noted: "The offensive apparently was prompted by a desperate desire by Muslims for land and revenge after months of defeats by Bosnian Serbs and humiliation by Bosnian Croats. . . . By capturing Travnik, Muslim-led forces moved closer to linking their strongholds of Tuzla and Zenica to the north with Muslim-controlled Konjic in the south."[41]

Even the ECMM was forced to admit that the ABiH had indeed undertaken a military offensive against the HVO and Bosnian Croat civilians in the Travnik and Lasva Valley areas.[42]

The "Convoy of Joy"

As thousands of Croat civilians fled the Travnik area, one group had a chance encounter with a convoy en route to the relief of Muslims in the central Bosnia area.[43] With emotions in a high state of agitation, the tired, hungry, and desperate Croat refugees—primarily women and children—blocked the convoy's route in several places on June 10 and 11 and spontaneously looted trucks, killing several of the drivers in the process while the UNPROFOR troops stood by, unwilling to fire into the mass of pitiful refugees.[44] The first encounter occurred at about 7 P.M. on June 10, just north of Novi Travnik, when forty to fifty Croat women blocked the road. Shortly thereafter, the BRITBAT received reports that HVO soldiers were dragging drivers from the trucks, shooting them, and then driving the vehicles away. Throughout the night of June 10–11, BRITBAT armored vehicles provided security for the convoy, which began to move again early the next morning. As the convoy passed Novi Bila at about 7:45 A.M. on June 11, it was fired upon, presumably by HVO troops. The UNPROFOR escort returned fire, killing several HVO soldiers.[45] At about 9:00 A.M., the forward element of the convoy was halted again just short of the Dubravica intersection by a "human barricade of women and children." Ambassador Thebault, UNPROFOR Bosnia-Herzegovina Command Chief of Staff Brigadier Guy de Vere Wingfield Hayes, and senior HVO officers and political figures finally resolved the impasse.[46] Many of the convoy vehicles disappeared without a trace, the goods probably unloaded and the tractors and trailers hidden or disguised, most never to be seen again.[47]

The hijacking of the Convoy of Joy was presented in the Western media at the time as a deliberate military action by the HVO in revenge for the Travnik defeat.[48] Nonetheless, the pillaging of the convoy appears to have resulted from a chance encounter and was spontaneous—a product of the frustration and anger of the displaced Croat civilians rather than a planned HVO military operation.[49]

The Battle for Novi Travnik

Having routed the HVO forces and secured their objectives in the Travnik area, the ABiH mounted a serious attack against HVO forces in the Novi Travnik area. At 5 A.M. on June 9, the 308th Mountain Brigade from Novi Travnik (some 2,100–3,100 men commanded by Bislim Zurapi), assisted by elements of the 307th Mountain Brigade from Bugojno and the 317th Mountain Brigade from Gornji Vakuf, as well as parts of the El Mudzahid mujahideen group, the "Sosna" private army (about 100 men), a company from the 7th Muslim Motorized Brigade (around 110 men), and MUP elements (about 200 men) attacked the HVO units holding the lines against the BSA south of Travnik between Mravinjak (BM 1393) through Plani (BM 1452) to Kamenjas (BM 1310).[50] They captured the existing fortifications facing the BSA and also gained control of the Croat villages of Ruda, Jakovici, and Nokovici; those to the east toward Novi Travnik in the Pecina area; and those to the southeast in the Kovacici area. The Croat inhabitants fled.

The road through Novi Travnik, which was already held in part by the ABiH, was blocked, and heavy fighting ensued in the area on June 10. However, the ABiH failed to take the town in its entirety, and the HVO was subsequently able to establish a defensive line running from the Travnik–Vitez road northwest of the Puticevo intersection through Slimena southwest to Runjavica (BM 683) then south through the middle of Novi Travnik to the village of Zubici.[51] The HVO line then continued northeast toward Lazine, then southeast via BM 908 and BM 829 before turning east south of Zaselje to connect with the HVO defenses in Vitez near Gornji Veceriska.

On June 14–15, the ABiH cleared the Croat villages northwest of Novi Travnik toward Travnik, and HVO forces abandoned the remaining portion of their line against the Serbs southwest of Travnik to the ABiH.[52] Both HVO soldiers and Croat civilians were forced across the Serb lines to join the thousands of Croat refugees already in Bosnian Serb hands. They were subsequently permitted to transit BSA-held territory to the north of Zenica and reenter HVO territory in the Kiseljak area.

On June 18, the Muslims mounted an attack on the new Novi Travnik line with elements of the 308th Mountain Brigade and the 1st and 2d Battalions, 17th Krajina Mountain Brigade, supported by other ABiH forces. The battle for the Novi Travnik lines continued into July with the lines changing in only minor ways. The major foci of the ABiH attacks were the HVO salient south of Rastovci toward Zubici, and the important Puticevo intersection—neither of which the Muslims succeeded in taking. Meanwhile, the HVO achieved some minor successes, taking the ABiH salient around the village of Lazine. Some two thousand Muslim attackers were held off by about 150 HVO defenders.

The June Cease-Fire

On June 15, 1993, the day before peace talks resumed in Geneva, yet another general cease-fire agreement was signed, this time by all three parties to the conflict in Bosnia-Herzegovina: Maj. Gen. Milivoj Petkovic for the HVO, Brig. Gen. Ratko Mladic for the BSA, and Gen. Rasim Delic for the ABiH.[53] The agreement was to go into effect at noon on June 18, at which time all combat activities were to cease and all military activities, to include troop movements and improvement of fortifications, were to be frozen.

Even before the cease-fire was signed, pessimistic British UNPROFOR authorities opined that "the BiH appear to have no intention of surrendering their present advantage, by observing the cease-fire."[54] On June 16, Colonel Blaskic, the OZCB commander, issued detailed implementing instructions for the cease-fire in which he instructed his subordinates to issue their own signed orders for the cease-fire.[55] At the same time, Blaskic reminded his subordinates of their obligation to ensure cooperation with UNPROFOR and humanitarian organizations, allow free passage of humanitarian aid, honor the Geneva conventions, and protect human rights. Over the next several months, Blaskic issued no fewer than nine additional orders dealing with such matters as the treatment of civilians and the protection of civilian property, the passage of aid convoys, and the treatment of prisoners of war.[56] That Blaskic's orders reached the lower levels of the OZCB is attested to by the series of implementing orders issued between June 21 and September 16 by Zarko Saric, commander of the 2d Battalion, Viteska Brigade.[57] Of course, issuing orders and guaranteeing compliance with them are two different things, and the June cease-fire was observed more often with breaches by both sides.

In view of the resumption of heavy fighting between ABiH and Croat forces in the central Bosnia region and the obstinacy of the ABiH III Corps commander, Enver Hadzihasanovic, the JOC, meeting formally for the fourth time at the headquarters of the British UNPROFOR battalion at 10 A.M. on

June 28, decided that it was no longer appropriate for the body to sit. The representatives from both sides agreed to notify their commanders they were unable to make any progress and to request that new orders be issued for renewal of the cease-fire, especially in the Zepce-Maglaj area.[58] Both sides agreed to continue to send representatives at regular intervals to meet at the headquarters of the British UNPROFOR battalion, to keep the telephone lines open between Vitez and Zenica, and to continue the operations of the Joint Humanitarian Commission for the release of prisoners.

10 *The Continuation of the Muslim Offensive, July–August, 1993*

Even as the Muslim-Croat battles raged around Travnik and Novi Travnik, the ABiH intensified its efforts to sweep up the smaller and weaker HVO positions on the periphery of the Operative Zone Central Bosnia area of operations. On June 14, the ABiH overran HVO forces in the Kakanj area, and the survivors of the Kotromanic Brigade as well as some thirteen thousand to fifteen thousand Croat civilian refugees filtered southward to the Kiseljak area or north to Vares.[1] The HVO outposts south of Novi Travnik fell in late June and early July: Ravno Rostovo on June 24 and Rat and Sebesic in July. Between July 19 and 23, the ABiH attacked the HVO forces in and around Bugojno, seized control of the town, and killed or captured most of the fifteen-hundred-man HVO Eugen Kvaternik Brigade, which was defending the town. The prisoners from the Kvaternik Brigade, as well as the Croat civilians in the Bugojno area were subjected to horrible mistreatment at the hands of the victorious ABiH troops.

Continuation of the ABiH Offensive in the Vitez-Busovaca Area

Although the major ABiH assault was launched in April, the struggle for the key Vitez-Busovaca area continued with varying degrees of intensity right up to the signing of the Washington agreements in March, 1994. The fighting was nearly continuous and was marked by large ABiH attacks almost every month. Sniping and artillery/mortar exchanges were routine, and the Croat enclave within the Lasva Valley continued to be the locus of heavy fighting. Although the HVO was able to prevent a major ABiH victory, the cumulative effect of casualties, the exhaustion of HVO personnel, the consumption of supplies and equipment without replacement, and the gradual loss of ground significantly reduced the HVO's capacity to resist as time went on.

In May, 1993, the ABiH succeeded in taking the Gradina heights between the villages of Loncari and Putis, and most of the critical Kuber and Kula positions fell to the ABiH in June. In July, the 17th Krajina Mountain Brigade launched yet another unsuccessful attack on Vitez. At a press conference on August 3, HVO military and civilian authorities addressed the serious situation facing the Croat community in central Bosnia, noting the continuing Muslim propaganda campaign that accompanied the shelling of Croat population centers and assaults on HVO positions.[2] In mid-August an

ABiH mortar round landed in the center of Vitez, injuring two adults and seven children, four of them seriously.[3]

Continuation of the ABiH Offensive in the Kiseljak Area

The Kiseljak area was cut off from the Croat enclave in the Lasva Valley (including Travnik, Novi Travnik, Vitez, and Busovaca) in late January, 1993, when the ABiH seized Kacuni. Thereafter, ground communication between the Vitez-Busovaca area and the Kiseljak area was very difficult, and HVO forces in the Kiseljak enclave operated almost independently. Until the summer of 1993, most of the Muslim-Croat fighting in the Kiseljak area occurred in the north, particularly in the Gomionica area in April. After an abortive attempt to force open a line of communication at the eastern end of the enclave from Han Ploca to Tarcin in the south, the ABiH started attacking HVO forces in the Kiseljak area from the south, driving toward Fojnica and Kresevo in the west and toward Han Ploca in the east.[4] Had the ABiH offensives in the Kiseljak area succeeded, which they did in part, the Muslims would have linked the II, III, and VII Corps to the north with the I, IV, and VI Corps to the south, saving about a hundred kilometers over the Zenica–Novi Travnik–Gornji Vakuf route.

The village of Han Ploca controlled the upper end of the potential route south via Tulica-Zabrde-Toplica to connect with the road from Kresevo to Tarcin. It also controlled the eastern terminus of the Busovaca–Kiseljak–Sarajevo road and the rear of the HVO positions facing the Serbs surrounding Sarajevo. In August, 1992, checkpoints were set up, and some incidents occurred in the area of Han Ploca and the nearby village of Duhri. The HVO disarmed the Muslims in the Han Ploca–Duhri area but later returned their weapons (on the orders of Colonel Blaskic) so they could defend themselves against the Serbs. The Muslims in Duhri again surrendered their weapons to the HVO on April 22–23, 1993, following the fighting around Gomionica, but the Muslims in Han Ploca refused to do so. Fighting broke out at 10 A.M. on May 20, when the ABiH forces in the area tried to block the road. After a three-day battle, HVO forces succeeded in pushing the Muslims back to Koroska and Muresc toward Visoko. During the fighting around Han Ploca, the ABiH attempted to send reinforcements from Visoko, but they arrived too late. Most of the ABiH troops fled at the end of the battle, leaving behind those Muslim civilians who had refused to leave (or were ordered not to by the ABiH) earlier. The HVO lost four men KIA and ten WIA during the fighting, which pitted one HVO company against about two hundred well-armed ABiH troops. It should be noted that the battle did not start until the Muslims rejected the HVO forces' demand that they surrender their weapons and thus avoid a fight. Han Ploca was yet another instance in which the HVO purposefully left open an escape route for civilians.

Gomionica was the focal point of the Muslim-Croat fighting in the Kiseljak area in January and April, 1993. From May 23–25, HVO forces finally managed to clean out the Gomionica pocket and relieve the threat to the key Fojnica intersection. The Muslims subsequently evacuated the entire salient and HVO forces pushed them back toward Visoko, stopping only at the Kiseljak *opcina* boundary. Even so, the ABiH returned to the area on July 5 and, under cover of other offensive operations in the Kiseljak area, made three assaults (at 4 A.M., between 8–9 A.M., and at 5 P.M.). The attacks were unsuccessful, but HVO casualties were high: thirteen KIA and fifty WIA.

At the end of May and beginning of June, the conflict in the Kiseljak region shifted to the south. It continued to rage there until the Washington agreements were signed in March, 1994. The ABiH formed a line against the HVO in the vicinity of Toplica north of Tarcin manned by elements of the ABiH 9th Mountain Brigade supported by four tanks. The objective was to secure a north–south line of communication from Han Ploca to Tarcin, west of the line against the BSA surrounding Sarajevo, and to cut the HVO off from the BSA. The village of Tulica (in the Kiseljak *opcina*) subsequently became a focal point of the ABiH offensive from the south.

Tulica sits in a narrow corridor astride the potential ABiH route from Tarcin to Han Ploca. On June 16, the ABiH attacked the Serbs surrounding Sarajevo from the west with some success, but the Serbs reinforced with tanks and pushed back, and the HVO moved into the former Muslim positions to the east of Tulica. By the early summer of 1993, Tulica had become a Muslim enclave immediately behind the HVO lines facing the BSA ringing Sarajevo, and for that reason constituted a significant military threat to the Croats, who were obliged to take the village in order to link their lines. In his testimony in the Blaskic case, Brigadier Ivica Zeko stated that the fighting in the lower Kiseljak area (around Tulica, for example) involved Muslims trying to cut the HVO off from doing business with the Serbs as well as trying to seize the important Kiseljak–Tarcin corridor.[5] The HVO took Tulica on June 26 and subsequently repelled five major Muslim attacks on the position, losing twenty-five HVO soldiers KIA on the front by the time the Washington agreements were signed. It was a difficult position to defend, and the Muslims employed special operations forces (the "Black Swans" of the 17th Krajina Mountain Brigade) against the HVO position. Eight persons, apparently Muslims soldiers, appear to have been executed in Tulica after the HVO took the village. Their identity and the exact circumstances of their deaths are unknown. Two days after Tulica fell to the HVO, Muslims attacked the village of Bojakovic, killing three women, a fourteen-year-old girl, and a number of old people.

The Fall of Fojnica

Having been stymied in their attempt to force a passage through the Kiseljak area along the Tarcin–Toplica–Tulica–Han Ploca axis, the ABiH refocused their attacks to the west toward Kresevo and Fojnica.[6] The HVO forces defending in the Fojnica-Kresevo area included the Ban Josip Jelacic Brigade's 2d and 3d Battalions. The brigade, commanded by Ivica Rajic, had a total strength of about twenty-five hundred men. The brigade's 1st Battalion was responsible for the northern front toward Visoko. The 2d Battalion, commanded by Ivo Kulis, a former JNA infantry captain, held the eastern (Kresevo) sector of the southern front up to Crnice. The 3d Battalion, commanded by the newly assigned Branko Stanic, held the western and northern (Otigosce-Fojnica) sector up to the Busovaca–Kiseljak road with some seven hundred to 950 men.

The ABiH task force of six thousand to eight thousand men involved in the offensive on the Kiseljak enclave from the south included elements of both the III and VI Corps and was commanded by Dragan Andric, a VI Corps officer. As of August 21, 1993, the task force included the local Territorial Defense units and the 310th Mountain Brigade from the Fojnica area (normally assigned to OG Istok); elements of the 317th Mountain Brigade from Bugojno; the 17th Krajina Mountain Brigade, the 7th Muslim Motorized Brigade, and the 9th Mountain Brigade from Pazaric (VI Corps); and the 4th Motorized Brigade from Sarajevo (I Corps).[7]

The fighting in the Fojnica area began on July 2, shortly after the visit of Gen. Philippe Morillon, the UN commander in Bosnia-Herzegovina, who promised to maintain the town as a peaceful oasis. Fojnica fell to the ABiH on July 10, and the Croats were chased out and went over the mountains to Visnica, where they occupied empty Muslim houses. In the course of the Muslim attack on Fojnica, the ABiH burned part of the HVO war hospital as well as the Hotel Reumal, and the mental hospital was damaged by attacks and snipers from Muslim positions on Zvjezdice opposite the Drin and the Mal Ploca Heights opposite Bakovici.[8]

Before the conflict began in the Fojnica area on July 2, 41 percent of the town's population was Croat (about sixty-six hundred people), but the ECMM reported in October that the town was almost entirely Muslim, with only 150 Croats remaining—and they were preparing to leave because the Muslims would not provide them with food. Following Fojnica's fall, Croat villages in the area were thoroughly cleansed by the Muslims. On October 3, an ECMM team visited the former Croat village of Tjesilo, which had been completely destroyed, giving, according to the ECMM observer, "an impression of total hate and the wish to completely erase traces of former inhabitants."[9]

At the beginning of August, the ABiH attempted once more to force the HVO enclave from the northeast in the vicinity of the villages of Han Ploca, Duhri, and Lepenica by cutting across the Lepenica Valley. At the same time, they launched an attack along the Ostja–Kokoska line with the objective of separating the HVO from the BSA in that area. These attacks, too, were repelled. On August 11, the ABiH took Bakovici, but another ABiH attack by elements of the 7th Muslim Motorized, the 17th Krajina Mountain, and the 317th Mountain Brigades lasting from August 21–26 was repelled. The ABiH offensive in the Kiseljak region continued into September with the HVO slowly losing ground in some places and holding on in others.

The ABiH Attack on Zepce, Zavidovici, and Novi Seher, June–July 1993

Having successfully attacked and "cleansed" the HVO troops and Bosnian Croat civilians from Travnik and most of the Novi Travnik area in early June 1993, the Muslim-led ABiH turned its attention northward hoping to catch the isolated Bosnian Croat community in the Tesanj-Maglaj salient off guard. On June 24, the ABiH III Corps launched an attack on the town of Zepce and other HVO positions at the base of the salient.[10] The Muslim assessment of the weakness of the Croat defenders of Zepce proved to be ill founded, however, and their attack met stiff resistance and ultimately failed. The Bosnian Croat enclaves in the Tesanj-Maglaj salient thus survived until the signing of the Washington agreements in March, 1994.

The town of Zepce lies on the north (left) bank of the River Bosna about forty-five kilometers northeast of Zenica and some seventy kilometers northwest of Sarajevo. Until the municipal boundaries in the area were gerrymandered by the Communist government in 1953, Zepce's population was two-thirds ethnic Croat. The 1991 census counted 22,966 inhabitants in the municipality of Zepce, of whom 10,820 were Muslim. In the town itself, the population in 1991 totaled 5,571, of whom 3,367 were Muslim. The major road passing through Zepce from Zenica (to the southwest) to Doboj (to the northeast) was an important line of communication for both the ABiH and HVO forces manning the lines against the Bosnian Serb Army in the Tesanj-Maglaj salient inasmuch as it was the only resupply route available in the area.

The Serbian-JNA attack on the Republic of Croatia in 1991 caused great anxiety amongst Bosnian Croat residents in the Zepce area, but the Muslim-led government in Sarajevo appeared to ignore the situation. In the face of the RBiH government's inactivity, the Bosnian Croats in Zepce began organizing for defense in May, 1991, and the HVO was formed there on April 8, 1992. Muslim citizens in the Zepce area were invited to participate with the HVO in efforts to form a joint defense against the Serbs, but they persistently refused to cooperate. The local Muslim leaders seemed willing enough, but ABiH forces in the Zepce area were controlled by much more radical elements from Zenica. The HVO subsequently assumed the bulk of the defense against BSA attacks in 1992, including taking over the defense of Maglaj when Muslim authorities asked them to do so.

Although relations between the two organizations were never cordial, the ABiH refrained from direct attacks on the HVO in the Zepce area until the summer of 1992 primarily because it was the mainstay of the common defense against the BSA in the region. However, Muslim attitudes toward their Croat neighbors had hardened by that summer. The first real clash between the two communities in Zepce occurred in September, when Muslim troops were sent to take down a Croat flag in the town while all of the HVO soldiers were on the front lines in Maglaj. The Muslims were disarmed by

Croat reserve police officers. The worst that could be said about HVO forces in Zepce is that they held loud training exercises on Fridays and took control of several buildings in the town, including the Cultural Center, which housed the HVO 111xp Brigade's headquarters, and the Hotel Balkans, which became the HVO military police headquarters after the 111xp Brigade HQ moved into the Cultural Center. There was little communication or cooperation between the Muslim and Croat communities in Zepce by the fall of 1992.

When the ABiH began making probing attacks in the Lasva Valley in January, 1993, the HVO started entrenching in Zepce and on the heights of Visoka Rudia and Suhi Kriz, positions that commanded the Muslim villages of Ozimica and Golubinja. The entrenchment activity intensified in early June, and by June 24, the Croat residents of predominantly Muslim villages in the Zepce area had been evacuated to predominantly Croat villages.[11] This was done, of course, to ensure their safety in the event of a Muslim attack, which was expected momentarily.

The situation worsened in the spring of 1993 with the arrival of Refik Lendo to assume command of the ABiH's Operative Group "Bosna" in Zavidovici. Lendo, a radical Muslim from the Travnik area, began replacing the ABiH brigade commanders in the area with men more attuned to his views, the local commanders being altogether too cooperative with the HVO in his opinion.[12] Meanwhile, Lendo ordered his subordinates to prepare for an offensive against the HVO in the Zepce-Zavidovici–Novi Seher area. Hoping to reduce tensions, HVO officials met with the commander of the ABiH 319th Mountain Brigade, but they were unsuccessful.

On April 18, the ABiH III Corps cleared HVO forces and many Bosnian Croat civilians from the municipality of Zenica and cut the road to Zepce, thereby isolating the HVO forces and Croat civilians in the Tesanj-Maglaj salient. Surrounded by hostile Muslim forces, the Croats in Zepce had only one option for communicating with the outside world: through territory held by the Bosnian Serbs. The HVO thus opened negotiations with the Serbs, who for their own reasons were willing to cooperate.[13] The Bosnian Croats in Zepce were not eager to deal with the Serbs, but they had no other choice. A cease-fire between the Serbs and Croats in the Zepce area was announced on June 14.

The UNPROFOR authorities were warned of the coming attack on several occasions. On June 23, BRITBAT officers visited the Zepce and Zavidovici areas and met with Nikola Jozinovic, commander of the HVO 111xp Brigade, who—not for the first time—claimed that the ABiH was planning to attack HVO forces in the area.[14] Jozinovic also claimed that ABiH troops were assembling for the offensive in two areas: elements of the 314th and 303d Mountain Brigades and the 7th Muslim Motorized Brigade in the villages of Begov Han and Zeljezno Polje, and elements of the 309th Mountain Brigade in the villages of Kamenica and Mitrovici. The BRITBAT subsequently confirmed the presence of 150 soldiers from the 309th Brigade in

Kamenica and elements of the 303d and 314th Brigades southwest of Zepce, as well as a number of soldiers from the 306th Brigade in Cardak.[15] After the fighting in Zepce started, BRITBAT authorities commented: "At present it is not clear who was the initiator of the fighting but the balance of probability would suggest that it was the BIH who were responsible. The presence of the 314th Bde soldiers, normally based in Zenica, the number of 309th Bde soldiers (Kakanj) observed on 23 June in Kamenica and the locally dominant position of the BIH all suggest this."[16]

The HVO and ABiH forces normally stationed in the Zepce area were generally balanced. The HVO 3d Operative Group, commanded by Ivo Lozancic from his headquarters in Zepce, consisted of the 110th Brigade, commanded by Nikola Antunovic, at Usora and the 111xp Brigade, commanded by Nikola Jozinovic, at Zepce. The total number of HVO troops in the region was approximately seven thousand, with about two thousand of them in the immediate Zepce area. In addition to being heavily outnumbered by the Muslims, the HVO forces had three problems: their territory was not contiguous; they had no centralized logistics system; and they lacked adequate communications. Nevertheless, the HVO forces were somewhat better armed than the Muslims and held the bulk of the lines against the BSA, with resulting heavy casualties.[17]

Zepce became part of the ABiH III Corps in February, 1993, and was assigned to Refik Lendo's OG Bosna, headquartered in Zavidovici. The two ABiH brigades native to the area were Galib Dervisic's 319th Mountain Brigade in Zepce, and Ismet Mammagic's 318th Mountain Brigade in Zavidovici. Each brigade had some twenty-five hundred to three thousand men, but Muslim witnesses reported that most were deployed on the front lines and only about two hundred were in Zepce.

Regular ABiH forces in the Zepce area were augmented by at least two of Narcis Drocic's Green Beret platoons with thirty men each. There were also three Muslim Territorial Defense companies in Zepce, the members of which manned ABiH checkpoints in the town. Like the HVO, the ABiH forces native to the Zepce-Zavidovici area existed in isolated pockets, were poorly coordinated, and lacked good logistical support.

In order to attack Zepce and Zavidovici, the ABiH was obliged to move additional forces into the area. The headquarters of British forces in Bosnia-Herzegovina subsequently identified the ABiH brigades operating in the Tesanj-Maglaj salient as of June 28, 1993, as elements of the 301st Mechanized Brigade, 303d and 314th Mountain Brigades, and 7th Muslim Motorized Brigade from Zenica; the 309th Mountain Brigade from Kakanj; the 318th Mountain Brigade from Zavidovici; the 319th Mountain Brigade from Zepce; and the 201st Mountain Brigade from Maglaj.[18] The introduction of ABiH forces from outside the Zepce-Zavidovici area was a clear indication of the ABiH III Corps commander's aggressive intent, the more so in that several of the "outside" units were known to have been used previously for assault purposes in the Lasva Valley (to wit, the 301st, 303d,

309th, and 7th Muslim Brigades). The sudden appearance of these offensive forces in the Zepce area was foreshadowed by Gen. Stjepan Siber of the ABiH General Headquarters attempting to negotiate with Ivo Lozancic of the HVO 3d OG on May 30 to allow a 160-man mobile ABiH unit to enter Zepce. Lozancic refused to permit the stationing of the entire unit in Zepce, and half the detachment subsequently went to Begov Han, fourteen kilometers from Zepce, while the remainder stayed at the Nova Trgovina warehouses on the eastern edge of the town.

Saint Ivo's Day—June 24, 1993—was a Croat holiday, and most of the Bosnian Croats in Zepce were preparing to go to mass when the blow forecast by Ivo Lozancic was struck without warning.[19] In fact, the first burst of fighting occurred on the evening of June 23, when mujahideen advanced from Zeljezno Polje on the Croat village of Dolubina. The following morning, elements of five Muslim brigades—approximately 12,500 men—advancing in two columns from the southwest (Zenica) and the southeast (Kakanj) opened the main attack north of Brezovo Polje and soon surrounded Zepce. The Muslim forces occupied the high ground west, south, and east of Zepce, and over the next few days the Croat residents of the Muslim-dominated area on the south bank of the Bosna River fled to Croat-held areas. In Zepce itself, firing broke out at approximately 9:15 A.M. as ABiH mortars and artillery opened up on the town and Muslim Green Berets surrounded the HVO military police headquarters in the Hotel Balkans.[20]

On June 25, and again on June 26, the BRITBAT reported that HVO sources were claiming that Zepce had been attacked by the ABiH from the direction of Zeljezno Polje (that is, from the direction of Zenica) and that the fighting in the area had been sparked by the HVO's refusal to surrender in Novi Seher.[21] Inasmuch as the town was surrounded and the Muslims were firing into it from positions on the heights, the HVO forces thought it was necessary to clear the town. The resulting fight lasted six days and was very bitter, with both sides shelling their opponent's positions in the town. The HVO did, however, leave the pedestrian bridge over the Bosna clear for civilians to use to escape the fighting. Meanwhile, BRITBAT patrols reported fighting in the Zepce area at 9:30 A.M. on June 24, with smoke rising from the town and small-caliber mortar fire coming from the eastern end of the town. At 2 P.M., BRITBAT patrols reported that Zepce was under mortar and heavy machine-gun fire from the vicinity of the village of Ljubana, and that a number of buildings were on fire, including a large apartment complex that was totally engulfed in flames.[22] The BRITBAT also reported that as of 6:30 P.M. there were obvious tensions on the route between Zenica and Zepce with the number of checkpoints having been doubled and the manning doubled as well.

On June 26, COMBRITFOR reported that the fighting in Zepce continued, with heavy mortar fire being directed into the town from ABiH positions near the village of Golubinja and elsewhere to the west. The HVO headquarters in town had been extensively damaged, a large number of buildings around it were on fire, and soldiers leaving the town claimed that bitter street fighting was taking place. On June 27, the BRITBAT reported that soldiers in the area stated that the HVO and ABiH each controlled 50 percent of Zepce and that the fighting was less intense than before.[23] The BRITBAT also reported a conversation on June 27 with the deputy commander of the ABiH III Corps, Dzemal Merdan, who claimed that ABiH forces were preparing to blockade Zepce in order to suppress the HVO. Merdan claimed this tactic would subsequently be employed on Tesanj, Maglaj, Novi Seher, and Zavidovici.

Both sides shelled the town relentlessly during the battle. The ABiH units from outside Zepce held the high ground west, south, and east of Zepce but did not come down into the town itself, leaving the bitter fighting there to local Muslim forces. One witness claimed that the town was shelled continuously for seven days (presumably by the HVO) and that 80 percent of the casualties were Muslim, while not a single bullet hit the Varos area near the river, a Croat part of town.[24] The inaccuracy of both the ABiH's and the HVO's artillery fire make Dedovic's claim incredible. In fact, the destruction of the town caused by the fighting was severe, perhaps half of its buildings having been burned during the fight. The human toll on both sides was high as well, both for civilians and for military personnel.

Eventually, the HVO gained the upper hand and succeeded in pushing the Muslims to the river's south bank in the area known as Papratnica. By June 30, the HVO had cleared most of the Bosna River's west bank and the western portion of Zepce of Muslim attackers. The battle ended on June 30 with the surrender of the ABiH 305th and 319th Brigades. Galib Dervisic, the ABiH commander, had been called upon to surrender on June 25 but had refused. As the shelling intensified on June 26, the HVO slowly gained control of the town, and Muslim ammunition began to run low. Dervisic negotiated surrender terms with Bozedar Tomic on the thirtieth, agreeing to surrender the bulk of his forces in town at 5 P.M. However, some Muslim fighters held out in the eastern part of town and across the river in the Prijeko area. The Muslim forces across the river from Zepce managed to held out until September, when the HVO pushed them back from the bank toward Zenica and Kakanj, thus freeing Zepce from continued direct threat. Elements of the Green Berets in the Zenicki Put area refused Dervisic's surrender order and resisted until the next day, July 1, when they were finally forced to surrender to the HVO. Another group of 105 ABiH fighters escaped over the River Kranjace on June 18, refused Dervisic's surrender order, and held out in Zenicki Put until July 1, when they surrendered and were sent to the "silos."

Several BSA tanks, perhaps "borrowed" by the HVO, were positioned around town on June 29 and began firing on Muslim positions the next day. One eyewitness claimed he saw seventeen Serb tanks in the area while on his way to the HVO command post at Tatarbudzak, four or five kilometers from Zepce, on July 1.[25] The reports of BSA tanks in Novi Seher and moving toward Maglaj seemed to genuinely worry ABiH III Corps leaders, who on the night of June 28–29 and again the next day complained to BRITBAT officers about what they concluded was active collusion between the BSA and the HVO in the Maglaj-Zepce-Zavidovici–Novi Seher area, noting that Maglaj itself was "being attacked by BSA artillery from the east and by HVO infantry from the west.[26]

Following the ABiH surrender on June 30, approximately four thousand to five thousand Muslim civilians were detained by the HVO for seven to ten days in the area of the Nova Trogvina company warehouses under conditions that were unsatisfactory but comparable to those in which Croat civilians were detained by the ABiH elsewhere.[27] Once released, many of the civilians went to the nearby village of Kiseljak (not to be confused with the town of Kiseljak) by way of Perovic. Captured ABiH military personnel were also detained at the Rade Kondic school, the elementary school in Perkovic Han, and, most notably, at the so-called silos. The conditions under which they were held were horrific, but they were no worse than those endured by HVO prisoners held by the ABiH in other areas. The Green Berets and the 105 ABiH soldiers who surrendered at Zenicki Put on July 1 appear to have been singled out for especially harsh treatment. Many of the military prisoners were later sent to Mostar when the local HVO commander pleaded that he could not maintain them properly.

The Muslim attack on Zepce was accompanied by simultaneous attacks on Zavidovici and Novi Seher, although Tesanj and Maglaj remained quiet.[28] Elements of the HVO 111xp Brigade in Zavidovici were surrounded by ABiH troops but held their positions on the north bank of the Bosna for a week before withdrawing over the mountain toward Zepce, taking the Croat civilians with them. They then established a line against the ABiH forces attacking Zepce. Some 1,000 Croat residents stayed in Zavidovici, but only 300–500 remained by the end of the conflict. Croat villagers from other locations fled as well: 800 from Lovnica, 500 from Dijacic, and 300 from Debelo Brdo. There were about 350 Croat casualties in Zavidovici itself, many of them civilians.

According to HVO sources, the Muslim-Croat conflict in the Zepce area began with the HVO refusal to surrender to the ABiH in Novi Seher.[29] At 7:40 P.M. on June 24, the BRITBAT reported that Novi Seher was "in flames." However, the major fighting there appears to have taken place on the morning of June 25, although the BRITBAT reported continuing small-arms fire and some shelling during the afternoon.[30] The BRITBAT also reported that Novi Seher's streets appeared to be deserted and several houses were on fire, with HVO forces dug in around their headquarters in the southern part of town. The ABiH HQ in town had been evacuated, and Muslims were manning positions in the northern part of town. The HVO apparently controlled the villages of Lukici, Radjcici, Grabovica, Ponijevo, and Takal, and the former HVO headquarters was still intact with Marko Zelic in command. The front line ran from east to west through the center of town, and the ABiH 201st Brigade controlled the town center and the nearby villages of Strupina, Domislica, Cobe, and Kopice. Following the two-day fight for Novi Seher, the HVO area around the town was very compact, and HVO forces received supplies through the Serb lines. The HVO position was not continuous and consisted primarily of positions in front of the key villages.

The ABiH offensive against the HVO in the Zepce-Zavidovici area appears to have been initiated by ABiH III Corps rather than II Corps, which British UNPROFOR sources judged to be less concerned with promoting tensions with the HVO, noting that: "this interfactional fighting was probably started with the blessing of the commander, III Corps BIH. Whether it indicates a wider agenda, which might spread to II Corps BIH is hard to assess."[31] Both Enver Hadzihasanovic, the ABiH commander, and deputy commander Dzemal Merdan told British UNPROFOR officers that the II Corps did not "understand what the HVO was capable of" and thus had not acted aggressively against it. The COMBRITFOR assessment of the radical nature of the ABiH III Corps command was that "the border between 2 and 3 Corps is almost like crossing into a different country. In the Tuzla area there is a real sense of common purpose with Muslims, Croats, and Serbs serving in the same units whether BIH or HVO. In the north people join the formation nearest their home regardless of whether it is BIH or HVO. The people in this area are as unable as we are to explain the ethnic violence which is taking place in Central Bosnia."[32] Moreover, COMBRITFOR noted that this "gulf in understanding" also appeared to exist between the radical leaders of the ABiH III Corps and the RBiH government in Sarajevo.[33]

When queried by the BRITBAT commander on June 24, as to the causes of the fighting between Muslim and Croat forces in the Zepce area, the ABiH III Corps commander replied, "it was purely a case of the 'problems' of the Lasva Valley spreading north."[34] Indeed, it was; and Hadzihasanovic was himself the party responsible for their spread. On June 26, COMBRITFOR reported that a BRITBAT assessment noted that

> the reasons for the fighting throughout the area are still unconfirmed but the BIH are increasingly looking like the aggressors. If this is proven it might be regarded as a further stage in the perceived strategy of Muslim "land grab." The story of the "mujahadeen" involvement as the precursor has been noted in a number of areas. It would appear, however, that the capacity for escalation was either unforeseen or underestimated. At present, Tesanj is the only population centre unaffected and there must be a grave danger that the troubles will spread further and seriously compromise the line against the Serbs. Unlike the Travnik area, Maglaj and Zavidovici have traditionally been areas of Serb interest and they are unlikely to miss any available opportunity. . . . This HQ assesses that the BIH took any escalation of the conflict with the HVO into

consideration during their planning of the operation. It is assessed that the BIH want the HVO out of the 3 Corps area and think that they can achieve this and, at the same time, maintain the integrity of the [common front line] with the BSA in the Maglaj finger.[35]

The August Assessments

In August, 1993, both sides took time to reassess their position. Colonel Tihomir Blaskic, the OZCB commander, conducted a review of the personnel and equipment status in his command and forwarded his report to Mostar on August 11.[36] No report was available on the Bobovac (Vares), Kotromanic (Kakanj), 110th (Usora), 111xp (Zepce), or Josip Ban Jelacic (Kiseljak) Brigades due to poor communications. The status of other OZCB brigades and units was as shown in Table 10–1.

By mid-October, the HVO personnel situation in central Bosnia was becoming critical, and Colonel Blaskic took note of the rising number of desertions by issuing an order calling for severe disciplinary measures to be taken against any HVO soldier abandoning his post on the defensive lines.[37]

Leaders of the ABiH met in Zenica on August 21–22 to review the state of their forces and to plan for the continuation of the campaign against the HVO in central Bosnia and northern Herzegovina.[38] Among the matters discussed were recent losses of territory to the BSA, the confused state of the RBiH's political leadership and the lack of support for the ABiH, the question of military discipline in the ABiH, logistical support and the development of an indigenous Bosnian arms industry, and the conflict with the HVO.

The newly formed ABiH VI Corps headquartered at Konjic was a problem from the beginning. Thus, on August 29, a team from ABiH GHQ headed by the chief of staff, Gen. Sefer Halilovic, began an investigation and assumed responsibility for coordinating the efforts of the III, IV, and VI Corps. The group's report, issued on September 20, noted deficiencies in the VI Corps, notably its failure to accomplish the previously assigned tasks of "liberating" the line of communications between Dusina (the hamlet in the Kiseljak municipality) and Fojnica and the "liberation" of Kresevo as well as the Konjic line of communications and the village of Celebici, making the planned operations in the Vrbas and Neretva Valleys more difficult. Problems in the VI Corps cited by the team included the inadequacies in staff training, the high number of desertions, the defection to the HVO of a security officer, and the murders of the commander of the 47th Mountain Brigade and other officers. The involvement of the corps headquarters in the growing of marijuana in the Blagaj area and its smuggling into Sarajevo and central Bosnia was also noted. The team report also remarked upon the unsatisfactory standards in the 317th Mountain Brigade from Bugojno and the poor performance of the independent Prozor battalion, which caused the loss of the Muslim positions "liberated" in the Crni Vrh.[39] As a result of the Halilovic team's report, large-scale changes in the leadership of the ABiH III, IV, and VI Corps were recommended, and many changes were

Table 10-1. Status of Units in HVO Operative Zone Central Bosnia as of August 11, 1993

Unit	Strength	% Fill	Weapons
OZCB Headquarters	38	59.4	-
OZCB Headquarters Home Guard	7	41.2	-
OZCB Communications Company	22	19.6	-
OZCB Military Intelligence Service	38	31.0	-
Stojkovici Logistics Base	63	36.8	-
Mixed Artillery Division	87	22.2	-
Travnicka Brigade	987	67.6	750
Stjepan Tomasevic Brigade	1,592	56.0	915
Frankopan Brigade	1,031	36.3	540
Jure Francetic Brigade	517	18.2	118
Viteska Brigade	2,212	77.9	1,290
Nikola Subic Zrinski Brigade	1,920	67.6	1,400

Source: HQ, OZCB, no. 01-8-209/93, Vitez, 3:45 P.M., August 11, 1993, subj: Delivery of Report Following Order, 2, KC Z1163.

subsequently carried out. Among other changes, Mehmed Alagic replaced Enver Hadzihasanovic as the III Corps commander and Refik Lendo became the VI Corps commander.[40] At the same time, Arif Pasalic, the IV Corps commander, was replaced by Selmo Cikotic. These personnel changes marked the ascendancy of the "hard-core" Bosnian Muslim faction, represented by Hadzihasanovic and Alagic, over the ABiH's more moderate "multiethnic" leaders, and did not bode well for the Bosnian Croats surrounded by ABiH forces in central Bosnia.[41]

11 *Operations,*
September, 1993–February, 1994

The Muslim offensive in central Bosnia continued through the fall of 1993 into the winter of 1994. The increasingly desperate HVO defenders barely managed to stave off each successive ABiH assault. The February 23, 1994, cease-fire associated with the Washington agreements and the end of open warfare between Muslims and Croats in central Bosnia came just in time: the HVO defenders were exhausted, and a final Muslim triumph was perhaps only weeks or even days away.

Continuation of the ABiH Offensive in the Vitez-Busovaca Area

In September, 1993, Muslim forces made yet another strong attempt to cut the main road through the Lasva Valley. The attack began on September 5 with an assault on the village of Zabilje from the direction of Brdo. The ABiH forces succeeded in entering the village, and the HVO subsequently reported that two HVO soldiers had been killed and nine wounded, and that fifteen to twenty civilians working in the fields had been taken prisoner. The British UNPROFOR battalion at Stari Bila reported a significant rise in the intensity of local exchanges of artillery, mortar, rocket-propelled grenade, heavy machine gun, and small-arms fire beginning at 8:30 A.M. in the vicinity of Brdo. The firing soon extended to Bukve, to Jardol in the afternoon, and on toward the main road north of Vitez. According to the UN-PROFOR: "The immediate BIH objective in this area is to capture Zabilje; this will then ultimately allow their forces to push further south in order to cut the HVO MSR . . . it is a BIH long term aim to divide the Novi Travnik/Vitez/Busovaca Croat enclave into a number of smaller isolated pockets."[1]

The attack on Zabilje was mounted by elements of the ABiH 325th Mountain Brigade. Mensud Kelestura, the brigade commander, subsequently claimed he had twenty-two HVO bodies to exchange and stated that he would attack Stari Bila within ten days. The situation quieted down on September 6, but heavy firing on the ABiH positions on Bila Hill resumed around 1 P.M. on the seventh and continued into the night. On September 8, the HVO launched its own attack in the Stari Bila area. Elements of the Viteska Brigade, supported by the Vitezovi PPN, attacked Muslim positions in Grbavica in order to forestall the promised ABiH attack and prevent Muslim forces from advancing any farther toward the SPS explosives factory. By first seizing the high ground to either side of the village, including Grbavica (Bila) Hill, which dominated the area, the HVO forces skillfully ejected Muslim troops from the village itself. The BRITBAT reported both the successful HVO clearing attack on September 8 and the consequent HVO celebrating on Bila Hill the following day.[2]

The ABiH launched another attack toward Vitez along the Preocica–Kruscica axis on September 18, their aim being to cut the Novi Bila–Busovaca road and divide the existing Croat enclave into two parts. After a quiet night in the Vitez area, ABiH artillery and mortars in the Bila area opened fire at about 1 A.M. on the eighteenth. Rounds fell on HVO positions west of Novi Travnik; in Novi Bila, Vitez, and Busovaca; and elsewhere along the line of contact in the Lasva Valley. The BRITBAT subsequently reported that the ABiH had launched a series of battalion-size assaults on HVO positions in the valley and had made a number of minor territorial gains, particularly in the area north of Kruscica toward Vitez. On September 19, the BRITBAT reported that the ABiH's main thrust seemed to be in the Kruscica and Krcevine areas, with signs of infantry attacks at about 1:10 P.M. in the area around Cifluk and Brankovac.[3] The ABiH attacks continued on September 20, focusing on the Ahmici area along the Sivrino Selo–Pirici–Ahmici–Kratine line of contact in the north, and the area between Kruscica and Vitez in the south as the Muslims advanced perhaps a kilometer in twenty-four hours. The fighting in the north shifted to the Santici area the following day, while the main battle continued along the line of contact established previously in the area south of Vitez. After four days of heavy fighting, the ABiH offensive in the Vitez area petered out without gaining its principal objectives.

On September 23, ABiH forces launched a large-scale artillery and infantry attack in the Busovaca area, killing five HVO troops, including a commander. In addition, about fifteen 120-mm mortar rounds landed in the town of Busovaca, seriously injuring several civilians. Near the end of the month, on September 27, the ABiH again tried to cut the road in the Vitez area by advancing south from Sivrino Selo and north from Rijeka at the point where the Croat enclave was at its narrowest. That same day, the Croat hospital in Vitez received three direct hits by ABiH mortars. Two persons were killed.[4] The Vitez hospital was hit by Muslim shells again on September 28 as fighting continued in the afternoon in the villages north of town on a general line running from Jardol to Nadioci. The UNPROFOR reported the next day that Fikret Cuskic's 17th Krajina Mountain Brigade had established its headquarters in the village of Kruscica. A BRITBAT officer visiting the office of Ramiz Dugalic, the ABiH III Corps security officer, saw a map with arrows indicating the severing of the Vitez-Busovaca enclave in the Sivrino Selo area.[5]

The situation in the Lasva Valley remained relatively quiet throughout the month of October, but sustained fighting erupted again in early November. On November 5, the ABiH attacked laterally from Kruscica northwest toward the SPS factory, gaining control of Zbrdje and a settlement of weekend houses in the area southwest of Vitez. They established a front line extending from the weekend homes to Bijelijna and thus brought the SPS factory under direct fire for the first time since mid-April.[6]

Just over a month later, on December 8, the ABiH mounted a two-pronged attack from Zaselje and Stari Vitez with the apparent objective of taking the SPS factory.[7] The Muslims failed again, but they achieved greater success just two weeks later when the ABiH mounted another determined attack on Vitez along the Preocica–Sivrino Selo–Pirici axis toward Krizancevo Selo on December 22. The HVO defenders were surprised; Krizancevo Selo, just fifteen hundred meters from the UNPROFOR Dutch/Belgian Transport Battalion compound near Dubravica, was taken; and between sixty and a hundred HVO soldiers and Croat civilians were killed in the village.[8] The operation was conducted by the 2d Battalion, 325th Mountain Brigade, under the personal supervision of Gen. Rasim Delic, the ABiH commander, who was present in the 2d Battalion command post during the attack. In view of the determined ABiH attempts to take Vitez and the SPS factory, it is not surprising that a proposed ABiH-HVO Christmas cease-fire fell through due to ABiH intransigence.[9]

The ABiH enclave in Stari Vitez remained a cancer in the breast of the HVO forces defending the Vitez-Busovaca enclave throughout the period. The Muslim forces in Stari Vitez were heavily armed and resupplied on occasion with the help of UN forces.[10] Even women were mobilized and took an active part in the fighting, thereby giving up their status as noncombatants. The HVO closely invested the small but noisome enclave and frequently sought without success to carry it by assault, most notably on July 18. Yet the ABiH was equally unsuccessful in its efforts to relieve the enclave, principally due to the spirited HVO resistance.[11]

The ABiH attacks in the Vitez-Busovaca area continued into 1994. Filip Filipovic, the acting OZCB commander, refused to surrender a triangle of land north of Stari Vitez that would have permitted the ABiH to link up with the Muslim Territorial Defense forces in Stari Vitez and break the siege. The Muslims responded by resuming their offensive in the early morning hours on January 9, with the ABiH forces advancing in a pincer movement from the Krizancevo Selo area south toward Santici, and from Kruscica north toward the Lasva Valley road.[12] The battle continued on January 10, and Muslim forces broke through the HVO defenses the next day. They quickly established a new line at Bukve Kuce, about a hundred meters from the OZCB headquarters in the Hotel Vitez.[13] That same day, ABiH soldiers placed a flag on a telephone pole opposite the gate of the UNPROFOR transport battalion compound in Santici. It was the "closest [the] BiH ever came to cutting the Vitez Pocket in two."[14] The attack did succeed in closing the southern exit from Vitez toward Busovaca, and during the three days of fighting some thirty-six Croats, both military and civilian, were killed, and a number were listed as missing.[15]

The HVO counterattacked on January 24 and regained some of the ground lost earlier in the month. Meanwhile, Sir Martin Garrod, the head of the ECMM Regional Center in Zenica, noted in his end-of-tour report that the two large Muslim offensives launched on December 22, 1993, and January 9, 1994, with the aim of reducing the Vitez pocket, "turned out not to be as effective militarily as they appeared to be initially."[16]

Even as negotiations to end the Muslim-Croat conflict began, fighting continued in the Vitez area. In early February, the ABiH regrouped and brought in reinforcements from Sarajevo and Zenica in preparation for another major assault to cut the Lasva Valley road at Santici. An ABiH attack toward Santici on February 8 failed, and the HVO counterattacked to widen the neck of the Vitez Pocket. On February 14, the HVO succeeded in removing the ABiH flag placed in Santici on January 11, and after almost two months of heavy fighting the lines in the Vitez Pocket were back where they had been before the first Muslim offensive in the area. The fighting in the Vitez region tapered off, then resumed briefly as both sides sought a final advantage immediately before the cease-fire pursuant to the peace accords signed in Zagreb on February 23 were to go into effect at noon on February 25.[17]

Events in the Vares Area

In October and November, 1993, the focus of the Muslim-Croat conflict shifted to the mining (chrome, iron, and zinc) and metal-processing town of Vares, which lies in a narrow valley some twenty miles north of Sarajevo on the main road from Breza to Tuzla and was then just to the west of the Serb lines. Both the Muslim and Croat residents of Vares maintained relatively good relations with the Serbs, and there was a heavy traffic in smuggled persons and goods across the opposing lines east of town. Until October, the Muslims and Croats had coexisted warily in Vares. However, large numbers of Muslim refugees fleeing the fighting in northern and eastern Bosnia flooded the town, and in early October, the HVO took control. On October 22, ABiH forces seized the village of Kopljari in order to form a link with three Muslim villages in the area and open a Muslim-controlled corridor into the pocket.[18]

Stupni Do

The small village of Stupni Do overlooked Vares and the road down the valley. In late October, 1993, it was defended by a Muslim Territorial Defense unit commanded by Avdo Zubaca and consisting of about fifty men with thirty rifles and a 60-mm mortar.[19] When a two-hundred-man HVO unit from Kiseljak and Kakanj arrived in Vares on October 21, the local Muslim War Presidency ordered the evacuation of Stupni Do's civilian population, but most of the residents chose not to leave. The following day, a force of masked uniformed HVO troops, subsequently identified as the group recently arrived from Kiseljak and Kakanj, entered the village and assaulted the ABiH soldiers and Muslim civilians still there. Both UNPROFOR forces and ECMM monitors were unable to enter the village for three days to verify the claims of untoward events.[20] On October 27, elements of the UNPROFOR Nordic Battalion (NORDBAT) finally obtained access to Stupni Do and found twenty bodies by the end of day. The ABiH subsequently claimed that the HVO attackers massacred eighty or more of Stupni Do's 260 Muslim inhabitants. Ivica Rajic, commander of the OZCB's 2d Operative Group, claimed responsibility for the attack, and Kresimir Bozic, the Bobovac Brigade commander, claimed there had been a total of forty dead for both sides, most of whom were soldiers.[21] "UN sources" speculated that the attack was in retaliation for the Muslim capture of Kopljari, a nearby Croat village, the week before, but there appears to be another plausible explanation for the attack on Stupni Do.

The village indeed did have some tactical importance: it commanded the southern end of the road into Vares from higher ground. However, it was also the gateway to BSA-controlled territory to the east, which made it a lucrative center for smuggling and black-market activities by both Muslim and Croat entrepreneurs. In fact, a small clearing above the village was reputed to be a thriving marketplace at which all sorts of goods—from cigarettes to automobiles to weapons—could be obtained for a price on "market day." The former commander of Muslim Territorial Defense forces in Vares, Ekrem Mahmutovic, when asked why the Stupni Do massacre occurred, noted that the Muslim residents of Stupni Do had become quite well-to-do from their black-market dealings, although they had to pay a percentage to the HVO, and when the Croats demanded a substantially higher cut in early October, the Stupni Do residents refused.[22] The subsequent attack on the village was not an "official" HVO action, but was instead mounted by HVO personnel like Ivica Rajic, who were deeply involved in black-market operations, and was intended to "teach the Muslims in Stupni Do a lesson." The attack thus was not a sanctioned HVO combat activity; was perpetrated by individuals for personal reasons under the cover of their official HVO positions and using HVO resources; and was essentially a gang fight among criminals. This explanation of the events at Stupni Do on October 22, 1993, was generally accepted at the time by most officials—who agreed that outsiders from Kiseljak and Kakanj were the perpetrators.[23] Sir Martin Garrod, the head of the ECMM Regional Center Zenica, noted: "It is likely that the decision to mount the operation was taken at fairly low level, and it is possible that the massacre was triggered by the refusal of the Muslims in Stupni Do, so the story goes, to pay more to the local HVO from their profits from smuggling operations in the area."[24]

Garrod also noted that when he asked HVO political leader Dario Kordic about the Stupni Do matter, Kordic was surprised and had to call General Petkovic in Mostar to find out what had happened. According to Garrod, Petkovic told Kordic "nothing bad had happened," only that a lot of houses had been burned and a lot of soldiers "in and out of uniform" had been killed, while most of the civilians "had moved out and were now in Vares."[25] Although "nothing bad had happened," the key players in the event were quickly replaced by HVO authorities in Mostar. Kresimir Bozic replaced Emil Harah as commander of the Bobovac Brigade on October 25, and

General Petkovic and Mate Boban removed Ivica Rajic from his position in mid-November.

Criminal Behavior

There is little doubt that Ivica Rajic was engaged in criminal activities, the pursuit of which fell far outside his functions as a military commander in the HVO. It is clear that he used HVO military resources, including troops under his command, to pursue his criminal activities, which were in no way a part of his official HVO duties. Rajic's involvement in the Stupni Do massacre raises a question about the Muslim-Croat conflict in central Bosnia that needs to be emphasized: to what degree did common criminals play a role in events? The whole Stupni Do episode reeks of being a dispute between black-marketeers. Moreover, many, if not most, of the convoy holdups on Route DIAMOND between Gornji Vakuf and Novi Travnik seem to have been undertaken by renegade gangs (both Croat and Muslim) rather than masterminded by HVO officials, military or civilian, acting in their official capacity. Brigadier Ivica Zeko, the former OZCB intelligence officer, noted that the fighting in the lower Kiseljak area (for example, around Tulica) involved Muslims trying to cut the HVO off from doing business with the Serbs, as well as trying to seize the important Kiseljak–Tarcin corridor.[26]

On April 13, 1994, ECMM Team V3 met with Father Bozo, the Franciscan Caritas representative in Kiseljak, who talked about the influence of the Bosnian Croat gangs that had emerged as a dominant force in the Kiseljak area.[27] The two major gangs were controlled by Ivica Rajic and were known as the "Apostles" and the "Maturice." The Apostles came to the Kiseljak area after the ABiH attack there in June, 1993. They were led by a man known as "Ljoljo," had about three hundred men in their ranks, and lived in private houses in Duri Topole. The Maturice were from the Travnik and Kiseljak areas and lived in Lepenica. These gangs were equipped as soldiers but were not employed on the front lines. Instead they were employed by Rajic to promote his criminal activities (such as in Stupni Do). Due to Rajic's influence and control over the HVO civil and military authorities in the Kiseljak area, the gangs were able to act as they wished.

Increases in criminal activity are a normal accompaniment of wartime conditions, and even well-disciplined armed forces, such as those of the United States, Great Britain, and other NATO nations, have great difficulty suppressing criminal activity, particularly black-marketeering, among their own troops. The HVO had far fewer reliable resources at its command for suppressing crime in the midst of a life-or-death struggle against the BSA and the ABiH. It thus is not surprising that independent criminal activity flourished in such isolated and autonomous areas as the Kiseljak enclave. Neither the HVO civilian authorities nor the HVO military authorities had the wherewithal to prevent such activity effectively, and it surpasses the bounds of both logic and fairness to indict them for not doing so.

The Fall of Vares

The Stupni Do affair provided the ABiH with an excuse to clean out the HVO pocket around Vares, although the Muslims scarcely needed an excuse and had been planning the operation for some time.[28] On November 2, 1993, the ECMM Coordinating Center in Travnik reported that the streets of Vares were deserted, the ABiH II Corps had already begun its attack on Vares from the north, and "the VARES pocket is a military and humanitarian powder keg. The HVO soldiers appeared nervous to the point of near panic. . . . At the moment, the BIH appear very much in control."[29]

On November 3, ECMM Team V4 reported that HVO forces had abandoned Vares and were moving in the direction of Dastansko, a village northeast of Vares and one kilometer west of the BSA's front line. All Muslim detainees had been released, and the Bobovac Brigade's headquarters set on fire. In the confusion caused by the ABiH advance, Croat soldiers and civilians fled south toward Kiseljak. Some five thousand refugees actually reached the Kiseljak municipality. The Muslim troops entering Vares, particularly those in the 7th Muslim Motorized Brigade, ran amok in an orgy of looting and wanton destruction. By November 4, the ABiH had full control of Vares and had achieved a major strategic goal by linking the ABiH II, III, IV, and VI Corps, giving it the ability to move by road from Tuzla to Gornji Vakuf without passing through any HVO pockets.[30]

The Situation at the End of 1993

The fighting died down following the ABiH assault on Vares, except around Vitez, as both sides sought to conserve their strength, survive the winter, and prepare for renewed fighting in the spring of 1994. Military historian Edgar O'Ballance noted that December, 1993, was "a month of gloom and despondency in Bosnia, as factional leaders rigidly refused to come to any common agreement on its future . . . hope was at a low ebb and despair was high . . . [and] as military operations reached a stalemate sections of defensive trenches on a First-World-War pattern began to appear, symbolic of determination to prevent the enemy from seizing another foot of terrain."[31]

Both sides were near exhaustion, but the HVO forces in central Bosnia were in a particularly perilous position, having lost a considerable amount of territory and unable to replace their losses in men and matériel. From the HVO's perspective, there was a very real danger that the ABiH was about to realize its objective of devouring the remaining small, isolated Croat enclaves around Zepce, Kiseljak, and Vitez-Busovaca. The HVO leaders were somewhat disappointed in the support they were receiving from their compatriots in Herzegovina, who appeared to be more concerned with establishing the Croatian Republic of Herceg-Bosna than with the very real threat to the continued existence of the Bosnian Croat enclaves in central Bosnia. Although they were desperate for peace, they were not ready for peace at any price.[32] Zoran Maric, the mayor of Busovaca, told Sir Martin Garrod on December 30, 1993, that if the Muslims continued their offensive, the Bosnian Croats would have no alternative but to force two corridors for survival from Novi Travnik to Gornji Vakuf and from Kiseljak to Busovaca, whether by political or military means.[33]

12 *Conclusion*

Even as the situation in central Bosnia deteriorated in late January and early February, 1994, UNPROFOR and ECMM monitors began to receive an increased number of reports that the Croatian Army was intervening in the Muslim-Croat conflict in Herzegovina. Convoys and troop movements from Tomislavgrad toward Prozor and the Gornji Vakuf area were reported, and the ABiH claimed—incorrectly—that some ten thousand Croatian soldiers in seven or eight HV brigades were in the central Bosnia area. However, Croatian official Jadranko Prlic conceded only that a few former HV soldiers were there: some twenty-six hundred "volunteers" born in Bosnia-Herzegovina who had returned to defend "their country."[1]

As the Croatian Army's involvement in Herzegovina became increasingly obvious, the UN Security Council considered sanctions against Croatia. Then, despite a year of often intense conflict between the Muslims and Croats in Bosnia-Herzegovina, the United States succeeded in bringing off something of a diplomatic coup by getting both sides to the conference table, forcing them to agree to stop the fighting and once more cooperate in their common defense against the Serbs. This was accomplished by showing a bit of carrot as well as the Security Council stick as the United States offered Croatia economic aid in return for the withdrawal of its forces and assistance in bringing about a Muslim-Croat cease-fire in Bosnia-Herzegovina. The combination was effective, and the cease-fire agreed upon in Washington went into effect on February 25, 1994, thus ending the Muslim-Croat civil war. A new Muslim-Croat federation was formed that subsequently entered into a defense pact with Croatia against the Bosnian Serbs and their Serbian/Yugoslav allies.

Although the fundamental issues dividing Bosnian Muslims and Bosnian Croats were not resolved, the Washington agreements did end the fighting and allow the Muslim-Croat alliance to concentrate on fending off the principal aggressor in the region, the Bosnian Serbs. Indeed, the ABiH was able to mount an offensive against the BSA in north-central Bosnia the same month that the Muslim-Croat alliance was renewed. However, as Sir Martin Garrod noted: "There is still basic mistrust of the Muslims by the Croats, particularly in Hercegovina, who will not forget that it was they with, they say, just a small contribution from the Muslims who 'liberated' Mostar from the Serbs, armed the BiH to fight with the HVO against the Serbs and welcomed the Muslim DPs into Mostar and

Hercegovina—only to be 'stabbed in the back' by the Muslims when they attacked them."[2]

Badgered during the Kordic-Cerkez trial by Prosecutor Geoffrey Nice to reveal who had coordinated the events in Vitez on April 16, 1993, Maj. Zeljko Sajevic, the former operations officer of the Viteska Brigade, responded, "If you are referring to the attack which took place on the 16th of April, in the morning, then you have to look for that coordinator amongst the ranks of the BH army, because they were the attackers."[3] Indeed, as Major Sajevic so succinctly pointed out, the Croatian population of Bosnia-Herzegovina and their defense forces, the HVO, were not the aggressors in the Muslim-Croat civil war in central Bosnia between November, 1992, and March, 1994. While certainly suspicious and wary of their Muslim neighbors, the Bosnian Croats did not plan or execute a systematic campaign of dispossession and extermination against their half-hearted allies in the fight against the Bosnian Serbs. Focused on and fully committed to the defense of Bosnia-Herzegovina against the Bosnian Serb Army, the HVO was genuinely surprised by the planned offensive mounted by the ABiH and its radical auxiliaries against the Croat positions in central Bosnia that began in January, 1993. Consequently, the HVO was forced to react to protect the key military industrial facilities within the Croat enclaves, the vital lines of communications to the outside, and simply to preserve Croat enclaves intact and protect their inhabitants. Heavily outnumbered and outgunned, the HVO adopted a classic "active defense" and proceeded at great cost to defend its homes, production facilities, and people. Despite successful counteroffensives to clear key terrain and open internal lines of communication, as time went on, the HVO was increasingly subjected to the attrition of men and matériel even as its Muslim opponents grew stronger and pressed harder. Only the Washington agreements of February, 1994, saved the Bosnian Croats from decimation and expulsion from the territory in central Bosnia remaining under their control.

Contrary to the assertions of the Muslim-led government of Bosnia-Herzegovina, various Muslim participants, journalists, and some UNPROFOR, ECMM, and nongovernmental organization observers, the HVO, surrounded and heavily outnumbered, had neither the means nor the opportunity to engage in a planned program to attack, dispossess, and expel Muslims from the areas in which they lived. Nor did it have sufficient motive for such an improbable campaign. As Maj. Gen. Filip Filipovic noted, the HVO had its "hands full with the defense against the Army of Republika Srpska."[4] It did, however, have the means, the motive, and the necessity to defend itself—which it did, vigorously and often at the risk of being mistaken for the aggressor by observers with only an imperfect knowledge of the local situation and a distorted view of the bigger picture. In central Bosnia, what one saw was not always what it seemed to be at the time.

Whatever the larger conflict involving the Bosnian Serbs may have been, the conflict between the Muslims and the Croats in central Bosnia was clearly a civil war. Although considerable confusion was created by the wearing of Croatian Army insignia by Bosnian Croat veterans of the war between Croatia and the Serbs/JNA and by the Croatian Army's intervention in Herzegovina during the waning days of the conflict, no Croatian Army units were introduced into central Bosnia nor, as far as can be determined, were there ever any official advisers, staff officers, or the like from the HV serving with the HVO in the OZCB area of operations. The only foreign combatants introduced into central Bosnia were the radical mujahideen from various Muslim countries invited in by Alija Izetbegovic's government.

Indeed, the available evidence, taken as a whole, clearly shows that the forces of the Muslim-led government of Bosnia-Herzegovina were the aggressors in the Muslim-Croat civil war of November, 1992–March, 1994. Only the ABiH had the means, the motive, and the opportunity required to carry out a comprehensive campaign against the Croatian community in central Bosnia. At one level, the ABiH's aggressive actions can be seen as a legitimate effort by the central government in Sarajevo to control its national territory, to suppress separatist groups, and to secure vital industrial facilities and lines of communication. Insofar as the Muslim offensive adhered to those goals and utilized straightforward military means, it can be argued that its aims and methods were lawful and legitimate, the counter-claims for legitimacy of the HVO notwithstanding. However, by their own admission, the ABiH leaders, particularly those in the III Corps area, were extremists who followed a conscious policy of aggression against the Bosnian Croats while accusing the HVO of the very crimes they themselves were committing. In any event, whether by policy decision or by inability to prevent it, the ABiH allied itself with radical Muslim factions and units raised internally as well as groups of ideologically radical Muslim fighters from abroad (the mujahideen) who the ABiH could not or would not control, and whose aims and objectives were far more sinister than credulous journalists and restricted international observers could see.

Civil wars are seldom neat and clean, and the Muslim-Croat war in central Bosnia between November, 1992, and March, 1994, was no exception. In the heat of ethnic and ideological passion and in the fog of battle many things were done by both sides that cannot be condoned under the laws of land warfare agreed upon by the majority of the world's governments. Soldiers of both the ABiH and the HVO committed murder, rape, wanton destruction, and pillage, as well as unlawfully detaining and torturing people in the course of otherwise legitimate military operations. Yet such atrocities often were the result of private quarrels and animosities having nothing whatsoever to do with the "official" opposition of the two parties.[5] Indeed, the impact of criminal elements—including black-marketeers and traditional bandits, as well as individuals seeking private vengeance—has yet to be fully assessed. Thus, what might appear superficially to have been a war crime committed by the armed forces of one party on the civilian adherents of the other party may actually turn out to have been the result of a vendetta, or a criminal squabble over the division of spoils or spheres of influence. Such certainly appears to be the case with the massacre at Stupni Do, and in large part explains the frequent holdup and extortion of humanitarian aid convoys traversing the central Bosnia area.

The aims and objectives of the more radical elements of the ABiH and their mujahideen auxiliaries clearly encompassed the elimination of the Roman Catholic Croats from central Bosnia and the settlement of Muslim refugees in their place, the expropriation of Croat property, the establishment of a fundamentalist Muslim state in Europe, and even the ritual murder of both HVO soldiers and Bosnian Croat civilians. By their failure to control those radical elements, or even to condemn them publicly, the Muslim political and military leaders of the Republic of Bosnia-Herzegovina bear a heavy guilt that, with only a few exceptions, they have yet to be called upon to expiate before the international community of nations.[6]

Questions of guilt and responsibility for aggression and war crimes aside, from a strictly military point of view, the Muslim-Croat civil war in central Bosnia offers four important insights for contemporary political and military leaders. First, the Muslim-Croat conflict epitomizes the Clausewitzian dictum that "war is the continuation of policy by other means." The goals sought by both sides in the conflict were ultimately political in nature, having to do with the shape of the newly independent Republic of Bosnia-Herzegovina and who was to rule what part of it. When political solutions to the central questions were not forthcoming, the Bosnian Muslims and Croats resorted to force as a means of deciding them. Yet, in the end they were forced to return to political means to resolve what had become an intolerable conflict that threatened to destroy the new republic. At that point, the Muslims and Croats stood Clausewitz on his head, making politics the continuation of war by other means. The formation of the fragile Muslim-Croat Federation of Bosnia-Herzegovina did nothing to resolve the key issues over which the two sides were fighting. Since February, 1994, the conflict has only changed form. Political maneuvering, war crimes charges, and the character assassination of opposition leaders have replaced combat actions as both sides continue to seek their goals.

The Muslim-Croat conflict also highlights the continuing importance of logistical factors in the conduct of modern war. The conflict in large measure arose from the attempt to secure industrial facilities of military importance and the lines of communication in central Bosnia. Moreover, severe logistical limitations—shortages of arms, ammunition, and other supplies, and the embargo on such goods imposed by the United Nations—affected both the ABiH and the HVO and dictated many of their strategic and tactical decisions. Indeed, few recent armed conflicts have reflected so clearly the central importance of controlling the means of military production and distribution and the impact of logistical considerations on war making.

The conflict also reiterated the destructiveness of modern warfare, even when conducted in a limited space by relatively small and poorly armed forces without access to airpower or the latest high-technology weapons. In 1994, the International Institute for Strategic Studies estimated that some 150,000 to two hundred thousand persons were killed and an equal number wounded in the three-way conflict in Bosnia-Herzegovina between 1992 and 1994. The number of homes, businesses, public buildings, and other parts of the nation's infrastructure destroyed was enormous, and the UN high commissioner for refugees estimated that at the beginning of 1994, there were some 4.3 million people in Bosnia-Herzegovina who required relief services, 3.5 million of whom were classified as refugees or displaced persons.[7]

Finally, the Muslim-Croat civil war in central Bosnia epitomizes a new type of warfare characteristic of the last quarter of the twentieth century and the probable dominant form of armed conflict in the world for the foreseeable future: the intrastate conflict between religious and ethnic groups seeking to control a given territorial space. This new form of war resembles traditional tribal warfare or the nationalist struggles of the nineteenth century rather than the ideologically inspired "wars of national liberation" and other forms of Cold War conflict common between 1945 and 1985. The emergence of religious/ethnic-based civil war leading to the fragmentation of post–World War II nation states and their former colonies poses substantial problems for the United States and the democratic nations of Europe and Asia. This new form of conflict requires a complete rethinking of national strategy, means, and methods. Above all, it calls into question the viability of the prevailing doctrine of "stability above all." The strategy of maintaining stability at all costs has been shown to be ineffective at best, and often counterproductive in dealing with conflicts such as those precipitated by the breakup of the former Yugoslavia. Rather than seeking to maintain stability at all costs, Western leaders must devise effective methods for controlling change and directing aspirations for national, religious, and ethnic solidarity in positive rather than negative directions. As political analysts and military planners in the West search for solutions to such fundamental questions, they would do well to examine in depth the complex causes and conduct of the Muslim-Croat civil war in central Bosnia in 1992–94.

Appendix A
Order of Battle, HVO Operative Zone Central Bosnia

Unit	Location	Commander	Date	Remarks
HQ, Ops Zone Central Bosnia	Vitez	Pasko Ljubicic	4/92	Known as Central Bosnia Armed
		Filip Filipovic	5/92	Forces Command until 7/10/92;
		Zarko Tole	5/92	redesignated as Vitez Military
		Tihomir Blaskic	6/92	District, 11/93
		Filip Filipovic	1/94	
4th Light Artillery Rocket Unit	Novi Travnik	Marko Lujic		Redesignated 4th Air Defense Light Artillery Rocket Bn., 1/94
Mixed Artillery Unit	Nova Bila	Bratunac	?/93	
		Josip Ramljak	2/94	
Antiaircraft Artillery Unit	Vitez	Goran Batalija		Merged with 4th Light Artillery
		Nikica Hakic		Rocket Unit in 1/94 to form 4th Air Defense Light Artillery Rocket Bn.
Logistics Unit	Stojkovici	Franjo Sliskovic		
PPN Vitezovi	Dubravica	Darko Kraljevic		OPCON; disbanded, 11/93
4th Military Police Battalion	Vitez	Zvonko Vukovic	92	OPCON; redesignated 7th MP Bn.,
		Pasko Ljubicic	2/93	11/93; subsequently redesignated
		Marinko Palavra	8/93	4th MP Bn.
Security Intelligence Service	Vitez	Ante Sliskovic		OPCON
1st Operative Group	Vitez			Established 7/10/92
Stjepan Tomasevic Brigade	Novi Travnik	Marijan Skopljak	11/92	3 Bns.
	(Stojkovici)	Borivoje Malabasic	2/93	
		Mario Cerkez	2/93	
		Zeljko Sabljic	4/93	
Viteska Brigade	Vitez	Mario Cerkez	3/93	Formed from 2d Bn.,
		Vlado Juric	3/93	Tomasevic Bde, 3/93; 4 Bns.
Travnicka Brigade	Travnik	Ivica Stojak	10/92	Overrun, 6/93; remnants
		Filip Filipovic	2/93	operated in Bandol area
		Jozo Leutar	4/93	
		Vlado Juric	10/93	
		Robert Ramzak Berti	1/94	
Francopan Brigade	Dolac/	Ilija Nakic	7/93	Overrun, 6/93; 3 bns.; remnants
	Guca Gora	Ljupko Rajic	2/94	later operated in Kula–Nova Bila–Zaselje area
Jure Francetic Brigade	Zenica	Zivko Totic	2/93	Overrun and disbanded, 4/93
2d Zenica Brigade	Zenica	Vinko Baresic	2/93	Overrun and disbanded, 4/93
2d Operative Group	Kiseljak	Ivica Rajic	7/93	Established 7/10/92
Nikola Subic Zrinski Brigade	Busovaca	Niko Jozinovic	2/93	3 bns.; later subordinated to 1st OG
	("Sumarija")	Dusko Grubesic	4/93	
		Yuri Cavara	4/94	
Ban Josip Jelacic Brigade	Kiseljak	Mijo Bosic	2/93	3 bns.
		Ivica Rajic	7/93	
		Mario Bradara	1/94	
Bobovac Brigade	Vares	Emil Harah	2/93	3 bns.; overrun, 11/93, and
	(Ponikve)	Krezimir Bozic	10/93	remnants (ca. 700 men)
		Borivoje Malabasic	1/94	redeployed to Dastansko area
Kotromanic Brigade	Kakanj	Neven Maric	2/93	Formed from Bobovac Bde; surren-
	(Haljinici)			dered to ABiH, 14/6/93
3d Operative Group	Zepce	Ivo Lozancic	7/93	Established 7/10/92
		Nikola Jozinovic	4/94	

Unit	Location	Commander	Date	Remarks
110th "Usora" Brigade	Tesanj/Zabljak	Nikola Antunovic	2/93	Subordinate to 7th OG, ABiH I Corps,
		"Karvu" Dorsip	4/94	in 1/94?; awarded "Golden Lily" unit
				citation by HQ, ABiH III Corps,
				for defense of Maglaj pocket
111xp Brigade	Zepce	Ivo Lozancic	11/92	5 bns.
	(Bankovici)	Nikola Jozinovic	7/93	
		Drago Dragicevic	4/94	
4th Operative Group	Sarajevo			Established 93
Kralj Tvrtko Drugi Brigade	Sarajevo	Franjo Talijancic	2/93	Originally assigned to 2d OG;
		Slavko Zelic	7/93	forced to reorganize by ABiH
				on 6/11/93 and redesignated ABiH
				"Croat Mountain Brigade"
Other Units Known to Have Operated in Operative Zone Central Bosnia, 1992–93				
Alpha Force Reconnaissance-Sabotage Group	Vitez	Chris Wilson	4/92	Formed 6/4/92; ca. 35 OEM; appears to have been under OZCB control
Tvrtko II	Lasva Valley			Appears to have been a PPN under OZCB control
3d Light Assault Unit	Lasva Valley	Vlado Cosic		Formed from 4th MP Bn. in 1993?
PPN Ludvig Pavlovic	Lasva Valley			OPCON to OZCB, 10–12/92?
PPN Bruno Busic	Lasva Valley			OPCON to OZCB, 10–12/92?

Note: All data is as of July 20, 1993, unless otherwise noted.

Sources: HQ, BHC (UNPROFOR), "Bosnia-Hercegovina Warring Factions," 6th ed.; ibid., 8th ed.; 1 Cheshire MILINFOSUM no. 121, February 28, 1993, KC Z507.1; 1 PWO, "Order of Battle for HVO Operative Zone Central Bosnia," (two hand-drawn documents) n.d. (ca. July, 1993), B 378 and B 379; Brigadier Ivica Zeko, Blaskic trial testimony, September 11 and 21–22, 1998.

Appendix B

Order of Battle, ABiH III Corps

Unit	Location	Commander	Date	Remarks
HQ, ABiH III Corps	Zenica	Enver Hadzihasanovic	12/92	Formed 12/1/92; III Corps had
		Mehmed Alagic	11/93	89,000 OEM, including
		Kadir Jusic	1/94	Territorial Defense units
		Sakib Mahmuljin	9/94	
Headquarters Support Unit	Zenica			
Artillery Brigade	Zenica			
Mixed AAA Brigade	Zenica			
Light Air Defense Unit	Zenica			
Engineer Battalion	Zenica			Subordinated to OG Zenica in 1/94
ABC Company	Zenica			
Signal Battalion	Zenica			
Military Police Battalion	Zenica			
Communications (EW) Battalion	Zenica			
Logistics Brigade	Zenica			
Min. of the Interior Police	Zenica			
Muslim Armed Forces	East Zenica			Formed from members of HOS
Operative Group Zenica	Zenica			Notional HQ for units directly subordinate to HQ, III Corps
7th Muslim Motorized Brigade	Zenica/	Asim Koricic	11/92	Formed 11/17/92; highly
	Bucje	Asim Koricic	8/93	mobile assault unit; 5 bns. in
		Serif Patkovic	4/94	1/94 deployed in Travnik, Zenica, Kakanj, Maglaj, and Sarajevo
301st Mechanized (Armor) Brigade	Zenica	Halil Selimbasic	2/93	Formed 12/1/92; 6 tanks;
		Haso Ribo	1/94	deployed piecemeal
314th Motorized Brigade	Zenica	Ibro Puric	2/93	Formed 1/12/92; aka Patriotic
		Faud Smailbegovic	8/93	Bde./Golden Lilies
Operative Group Bosna	Zavidovici	Refik Lendo	7/93	Formed 3/93
318th Mountain Brigade	Zavidovici	Ismet Mammagic	2/93	Formed 12/2/92
		Haris Catic	7/93	
319th Mountain Brigade	Zepce	Galib Dervisic	2/93	Obliterated and dropped 7/93
Operative Group Bosanska Krajina	Travnik	Mehmed Alagic	6/93	Formed 2/27/93 as OG
		Fikret Cuskic	3/94	Travnik; reorganized in 8/93
17th Krajina Mountain Brigade	Travnik	Fikret Cuskic	2/93	Formed 11/18/92 from 1st and
		Ripac	1/94	7th Krajina Bdes.; aka Slavna Bde.; highly mobile; at least 4 bns.
27th Krajina Mountain Brigade	Travnik	Rasim Imamovic	11/93	Formed 6/7/93 from Krajina
		Suki Snu	1/94	refugees; aka Banja Luka
		Fazlic Mustapha	3/94	Bde.; at least 4 bns.
306th Light Brigade	Han Bila	Esed Sipic	7/93	Formed 12/22/92
		Nezir Jusufspahic	11/93	
		Milo Caric	11/93	
		Munir Coric	2/94	
312th Motorized Brigade	Travnik/	Zijad Caber	2/93	Formed 11/25/92; aka 1st
	Slimena			Krajina Bde.; at least 4 bns.
Operative Group Lasva	Kakanj	Nehru Ganic	8/93	Formed 3/93; disbanded 11/93
305th Mountain Brigade	Biljesevo	Halid Dedic	2/93	Formed 12/1/92; aka Jajce Bde.
309th Mountain Brigade	Kakanj	Dzemal Hadzic	1/93	Formed 1/5/93; 3 bns.
		Mensud Kelestura	1/94	
325th Mountain Brigade	Preocica	Esad Dzananovic	2/93	Formed 12/1/92; at least 3
		Sefkija Dzdic	2/93	bns.; subordinated to OG

Unit	Location	Commander	Date	Remarks
		Mensud Kelestura	5/93	Bosanska Krajina in 1/94
		Ibro Puric	1/94	
		Muhamed Burberovic	2/94	
333d Mountain Brigade	Kacuni	Dzevad Mekic	2/93	Formed 12/1/92; aka Brdska
		Ekrem Alihodzic	7/93	Bde.
		Farik Lusija	11/93	
		Razajic	2/94	
Operative Group Zapad	Bugojno	Selmo Cikotic	10/93	Formed 3/93
307th Mountain Brigade	Bugojno	Senad Dautoric	2/93	Formed 10/21/92; 4 bns.
		Tahir Granic	7/93	
308th Mountain Brigade	Novi Travnik/	Refik Lendo	2/93	Formed 12/1/92; 3 bns.;
	Opara	Bislim Zurapi	4/93	subordinated to OG Bosanska
		Hadic Dzemal	1/94	Krajin in 1/94
317th Mountain Brigade	East of Gornji	Farhoudin Agic "Paje"	2/93	Formed 11/20/92; at least 4
	Vakuf	Enver Zejnilovic	6/93	bns.; subordinated to OG
				Bosanska Krajin in 1/94

		Other Units Known to Have Operated in ABiH III Corps Area, 1992–93		
8th Muslim Brigade	Mehurici	Abu Haris	10/93	Formed 10/93; thought to be the successor of the "El Mujahid" mujahideen unit; area of operations: Jablanica, Konjic, Fojnica, Kakanj
302d Motorized Brigade	Visoko	Hasib Musinbegovic		I Corps, OG Istok unit attached
			2/93	to III Corps; redesignated 315th Mountain Bde. by 1/94
304th Mountain Brigade	Breza	Senad Hajovic	2/93	I Corps, OG Istok unit
		Mursad Begic	1/94	attached to III Corps
310th Mountain Brigade	Fojnica	Nihad Kamenjas	2/94	I Corps, OG Istok unit attached to III Corps
311th Mountain Brigade	Kakanj			Subordinate to OG Lasva in 1/94?
315th Mountain Brigade	Visoko			Formerly 302d Mtzd. Bde.
316th Mountain Brigade	Maglaj	Sulejman Herceg	2/93	I Corps unit? = 201st
		Basib Musinbegovic	1/94	Mountain Brigade at Maglaj?
320th Mountain Brigade				Subordinate to OG Bosna in 1/94
322d Mountain Brigade	Vares	Zijad Kamenjas	1/94	Formed 1/94; aka Vares Bde.
323d Light Brigade	Kiseljak			
330th Light Brigade	Dolac	Mirsad Ibrakovic	12/93	Formed 12/24/93; subordinate to OG Lasva in 1/94
370th Mountain Brigade	Bugojno/	Faraouk ("Yupi")	1/94	Formed 1/94? from elements
	Gornji Vakuf			of 307th Mtn. Bde.; aka 306th Bde.; subordinate to OG Zapad in 1/94
"El Mujahid" Unit	Zenica/Mehurici			Mujahideen; 400 OEM; thought to be a subordinate co. of 1st Bn., 7th Muslim Bde.; subsequently formed core of 8th Muslim Bde.
"Abdul Atif" Unit				Mujahideen
"Sosna"	Novi Travnik			Private army; 100 OEM
"Nanetovi"	Nanetovi			Private army; 60–80 OEM
"Mercici"	Mercici			Private army; 60–80 OEM
Green Berets		Ahmed Demirovic		
Patriotic League				SDA Party forces
Green Legion				
Green League				

Note: All data is as of July 20, 1993, unless otherwise noted.

Sources: HQ, BHC (UNPROFOR), "Bosnia-Hercegovina Warring Factions," 6th ed; ibid., 8th ed.; 1 Cheshire MILINFOSUM no. 121, February 28, 1993, KC Z507.1; 1 PWO, "Order of Battle for HVO Operative Zone Central Bosnia" (two hand-drawn documents), n.d. (ca. July, 1993), B 378 and B 379; Brigadier Ivica Zeko, Blaskic trial testimony, September 11 and 21–22, 1998.

Appendix C

Characteristics and Capabilities of Selected Weapons Systems Used in Bosnia-Herzegovina, 1992–94

Weapon	Effective Range (meters)	Sustained Rate of Fire (rpm)	Remarks
Infantry Weapons			
Grenade Launcher, M-57, 44-mm	200	5	Widespread use
Rifle, Assault, AK-47, Kalashnikov, 7.62-mm	300	600	30-round magazine; standard infantry weapon
Rifle, Sniper, M-76, 7.9-mm	ca. 800		Widespread use
Submachine Gun, ERO (Uzi), 9-mm	200	32	HVO only?; Croatian production
Machine Guns			
Machine Gun, Light, RPK, M60, 7.62-mm	800	650	75-round drum; 40-round clip
Machine Gun, Company, RP-46, 7.62-mm	1,000	600	250-round belt; Degtyarev
Machine Gun, Heavy, M-38/46, 12.7-mm	1,500	500–600	DSchK; range = 1,000 meters against aerial targets
Machine Gun, Heavy, KPVT–1, 14.5-mm	1,400	550–600	
Mortars			
Mortar, M-57, 60-mm	2,537	25–30	ABiH = 20; HVO = 24
Mortar, M-70, 60-mm	2,537	20–25	Widespread use
Mortar, M-69A, 82-mm	6,050	20–25	Widespread use
Mortar, Mountain, M-74, 120-mm	6,534	12	Extended range = 9,056 meters; std. inf. bn. spt. wpn.
Mortar, M-75, 120-mm	5,400	12	Extended range = 9,056 meters; used by all; std. in JNA
Artillery			
Gun, Mountain, M-48B1, 76-mm	8,750	25	"Tito Gun"; packable; crew of 6; ABiH = 20; HVO = 20
Gun-Howitzer, D-20, 152-mm	17,410	5–6	HVO only?
Gun-Howitzer, M-84AB, Nora, 152-mm	24,400	4	W/projectile OF540/R + fuse RGM-2; from Bratstvo; ABiH = 9; HVO = 9 (2 in OZCB)
Gun-Howitzer, M-65, 155-mm	14,955	4	Widespread use
Howitzer, M-56, 105-mm	13,100	16	Crew of 6; ABiH = 40; HVO = 60
Howitzer, D-30J, 122-mm	15,300	8	W/projectile OF462 + fuse RGM–2; from Bratstvo; ABiH = 12; HVO = 12 (1 in OZCB)
Howitzer, M-115, 203-mm (8–in.)	30,000	<4?	ABiH = 10
MLRS, M–92A1, Obad, 4-round, 60-mm	8,540		Man portable; crew of 2–3
MLRS, M–93A2, 40-round, Caplija, 70-mm	8,000		2.75-in. aircraft rockets; crew of 3–5
MLRS, Chinese Type 63, 12-round, 107-mm	8,500		Crew of 3–5
MLRS, M-63, Plamen, 32-round, 128-mm	8,600–12,800	4 min reload	Most used by JNA; crew of 7; ABiH = 46; HVO = 30
MLRS, M–87, Orkan, 12-round, 262-mm	50,000	1 per 2.3	ABiH = 2

Weapon	Effective Range (meters)	Sustained Rate of Fire (rpm)	Remarks
Antitank Weapons			
Grenade Launcher, AT, M-57, 44-mm	200	5	
Grenade Launcher, AT, M-80, 44-mm	400	5	
Guided Missile, AT, AT-3, *Maljutka/Sagger*	500–3,000	2	
Gun, AT, Recoilless, M60/60A, 82-mm	1,000–1,500	4	
Gun, AT, Recoilless, M-79, 82-mm	670	6?	
Rifle, AT, Recoilless, B-10, 82-mm	400	6	
Rifle, AT, Recoilless, M-65, 105-mm	600	6	
Rifle, AT, Recoilless, B-11, 107-mm	1,000	5	
Rocket Launcher, AT, *Zolja*, 60-mm	400		
Rocket Launcher, AT, *Armbrust,*	350	5	Disposable; German-made; ABiH only?
Rocket Launcher, AT, M-71, 1–round, 128-mm	800–8,564		A few
Rocket Launcher, RBR, *Hornet,* 120-mm	400		Disposable
Rocket Launcher, RBR, M-79, *Osa,* 90-mm	350	5	Widespread use
Rocket Launcher, RBR, M-80, 64-mm	250		Disposable
Rocket-Propelled Grenade, RPG-2, 82-mm	100		Tube = 40-mm; Round = 82-mm
Rocket-Propelled Grenade, RPG-7, 80-mm	300		Tube = 40-mm; Round = 80-mm
Rocket-Propelled Grenade, RPG-22	250		
Antiaircraft Weapons			
Gun, AA, Lightweight, M-75, 20-mm	1,000 (H) 2,000 (V)	650–800	60-round drum or 10-round magazine
Gun, AA, M-55A2, 3 barrels, 20-mm	1,200 (H) 1,500 (V)	650–800 X 3	
Gun, AA, SP, BOV-20/3l, 3 barrels, 20-mm	1,500	650–800 X 3	
Gun, AA, ZU-23–2, 2 barrels, 23-mm	7,000	1,000 X 2	
Gun, AA, BOV-30/2, 2 barrels, 30-mm	3,000	750–800 X 2	
Gun, AA, SP, M–53/59, 2–bbls, 30-mm	3,000	420–450 X 2	
Gun, AA, L/70 Bofors, 40-mm, auto	3,000–4,000	260	HVO = 4; ABiH = some
Gun, AA, S-60, 57-mm, auto	4,000	105–120	Range with radar = 6,500 meters
Machine Gun, AA, Heavy, ZGU-1, 14.5-mm	1,400	550–600	Mountain pack; = KPVT-1 HMG
Machine Gun, AA, Heavy, KPV/ZPU–2/4, 12.7-mm?	1,400 air	660 X 2/4	
SAM, *Strela–2* (SA-7 *Grail*), low altitude	3,700		
SAM, FIM–92, *Stinger*	>4,500		Man portable; ABiH only
Aircraft			
UTVA-75 (primary trainer/utility)	2,000 km		ABiH = 2; HVO = 4
An-2 Colt (light transport)	905 km		
Mi-8C/NTV–1 Hip (transport helicopter)	960 km		ABiH = 5; HVO = 4
MD-500 (utility helicopter)	431 km		HVO = 2

Sources: Department of Defense, *Bosnia Country Handbook—Peace Implementation Force (IFOR);* Friedrich Wiener and William J. Lewis, *The Warsaw Pact Armies.*

Notes

The materials used in the preparation of this study consist primarily of testimony and exhibits from the trials of Tihomir Blaskic, Dario Kordic and Mario Cerkez, and others before the International Criminal Tribunal for the Former Yugoslavia in The Hague from 1998–2001. Testimony in the various trials is cited by the name of the witness, the trial, and the date of the testimony (e.g., Brigadier Ivica Zeko, Blaskic trial testimony, Sept. 11, 1998). Most of the exhibits cited were presented by the prosecutor and are identified in the case of the Kordic-Cerkez trial by KC with a Z in the exhibit number (e.g., KC Z1212), or in the case of the Blaskic trial by B with no alpha designator (e.g., B 323). Other documents were presented as defense exhibits in the various trials and are identified with a D in the exhibit number (e.g., KC D123; B D234). The daily Military Information Summaries (MILINFOSUMs) produced by the British UNPROFOR units in central Bosnia—the 1st Battalion, 22d (Cheshire) Regiment; the 1st Battalion, Prince of Wales's Own Regiment of Yorkshire; the 1st Battalion, Coldstream Guards; and commander, British Forces in Bosnia-Hercegovina—are cited as 1Cheshire MILINFOSUM, 1PWO MILINFOSUM, 1CSG MILINFOSUM, and COMBRITFOR MILINFOSUM respectively. Published works are cited in the usual way.

Prologue

1. Edward Vulliamy, *Seasons in Hell: Understanding Bosnia's War,* 179–80.

2. The ABiH as it existed in late 1992 was composed almost exclusively of forces raised on the old Yugoslavian National Army Territorial Defense pattern. Its units were generally tied to a given geographical area and were not "mobile" in the sense that an American or British infantry battalion is mobile (i.e., available for deployment outside the immediate vicinity of its home station).

3. The infamous 7th Muslim Motorized Brigade, composed in part of mujahideen and the principal assault unit of the ABiH's III Corps, was formed on November 17, 1992, and the mobile 17th and 27th Krajina Mountain Brigades were formed from Muslim refugees in Croatia in November, 1992, and June, 1993, respectively and subsequently moved into Bosnia-Herzegovina.

4. The unsubstantiated opinion that the Muslim-Croat conflict in central Bosnia was precipitated by Croat insistence on early implementation of the VOPP surfaced early in the conflict. For example, Lt. Col. Robert A. Stewart, commander of the British UNPROFOR battalion in the Lasva Valley, recorded in his diary that he had expressed to the Equerry to the Prince of Wales his belief that "the HVO were causing problems in order to force the Muslims to agree to the Geneva Peace Plan" (Stewart diary, Jan. 29, 1993, sec. 3, 12, KC D56/1 and KC D104/1). It has also been promoted by journalists (e.g., Peter Maas in *Love Thy Neighbor: A Story of War,* n 286); by human rights organizations (e.g., Helsinki Watch [Human Rights Watch] in *War Crimes in Bosnia-Hercegovina,* 2:379–81); and in other Western publications (e.g., Jane's Information Group, *Jane's Bosnia Handbook,* sec. 2, 3–4).

5. Franjo Nakic, Kordic-Cerkez trial testimony, Apr. 13, 2000. Nakic was chief of staff of the HVO's OZCB from December, 1992, to December, 1996.

Chapter 1. The Operational Milieu

1. The complex and nuanced historical development of a broad and diverse region such as the former Yugoslavia cannot be covered in a short introduction with absolute thoroughness and accuracy to the satisfaction of all readers. In the brief historical sketch that follows, I have tried to present fairly the broad outlines of the development of the principal competing ethnic and political entities in the region based on standard reference works in English, principally the *Encyclopedia Americana on CD-ROM*. Readers who require a deeper and more thorough understanding of the history of the territories comprising the former Yugoslavia are advised to consult more detailed works by scholars expert in the history of the region. A few of the better general works in English include: Ivo Banac, *The National Question in Yugoslavia: Origins, History, Politics;* Stevan K. Pavlowitch, *A History of the Balkans, 1804–1945,* and *Serbia: The History of an Idea;* Marcus Tanner, *Croatia: A Nation Forged in War;* Tim Judah, *The Serbs: History, Myth and the Destruction of Yugoslavia;* Noel Malcolm, *Bosnia: A Short History;* Jozo Tomasevich, *The Chetniks: War and Revolution in Yugoslavia, 1941–1945,* and *War and Revolution in Yugoslavia, 1941–1945: Occupation and Collaboration.*

2. The Bogomil heresy arose in Bulgaria in the eighth century and combined elements of Orthodox Christianity with a heavy dose of Manichaenism emphasizing the conflict in the world between good and evil. Both the Orthodox Serbs and the Roman Catholic Croats persecuted the Bogomils, but they found many adherents in medieval Bosnia.

3. Of the 419 delegates attending the constitutional convention, only 258 participated in the final vote on June 28, 1921. Only 223 of the delegates voting, a minority of the whole, cast their ballots for the new constitution. See "YUGO-SLAVIA—6. Monarchical Yugoslavia," in *Encyclopedia Americana on CD-ROM.*

4. The Ustasha accepted Muslim recruits as "Croats of Muslim faith." The 21st Waffen-SS Mountain Division "Skanderbeg," raised in Albania, and the 23d Waffen-SS Mountain Division "Kama," raised in Croatia but dissolved in 1944, were the other two Waffen-SS divisions manned primarily by Muslims. See I. C. B. Dear, ed., *The Oxford Companion to World War II,* 1047–1049.

5. Department of Defense, *Bosnia Country Handbook—Peace Implementation Force (IFOR),* 2–3.

6. Michael O. Beale, *Bombs over Bosnia: The Role of Airpower in Bosnia-Herzegovina,* 7.

7. International Institute for Strategic Studies (hereafter IISS), *Strategic Survey, 1991–1992,* 35.

8. Following the secession of Slovenia, Croatia, Bosnia-Herzegovina, and Macedonia, Serbia and Montenegro united to form the FRY in April, 1992. The United Nations and the European Union refused to recognize the FRY, the new president of which was none other than Dobrica Cosic, the "spiritual father of Serbian nationalism in the Milosevic era" (IISS, *Strategic Survey, 1992–1993,* 91–92).

9. IISS, *Strategic Survey, 1991–1992,* 35.

10. Macedonia, which declared its independence from the FRY on September 17, 1991, also managed to avoid the worst of the civil strife occasioned by Serbian-led attempts to thwart the independence of the other Yugoslavian republics, although Macedonia has problems with a small Macedonian Muslim minority aided by Muslim terrorists spilling over from Kosovo and Albania.

11. IISS, *Strategic Survey, 1991–1992,* 36.

12. IISS, *Strategic Survey, 1992–1993,* 83. Milan Panic, elected prime minister of the new FRY, tried to reach a more permanent settlement with Croatia but was foiled by the Bosnian Serbs. Slobodan Milosevic subsequently defeated him in the Serbian presidential elections in December, 1992 (ibid., 92).

13. Ibid., 94.

14. *Jane's Bosnia Handbook,* sec. 2, 3.

15. In particular, the revolt of Serbs living in the Krajina and the JNA attack on Croatia in July, 1991, alerted the Bosnian Croats to the danger, and many of them went to fight in defense of their Croatian homeland.

16. Bosnia-Herzegovina's physical geography and climate are described briefly in *Jane's Bosnia Handbook,* §II, 18–20.

17. Department of the Army, *DA Pamphlet No. 20–243: German Antiguerrilla Operations in the Balkans (1941–1944),* 2.

18. For the French position at Dien Bien Phu, see, Bernard B. Fall's *Hell in a Very Small Place: The Siege of Dien Bien Phu.*

19. Headquarters, United States Army Europe, Office of the Chief of Public Affairs, *A Soldier's Guide to Bosnia Herzegovina,* 5.

20. Ibid. The religious preferences of the population at that time were: 40 percent Muslim, 31 percent Orthodox Christian, 15 percent Roman Catholic, and 4 percent Protestant.

21. Brigadier Ivica Zeko outlined the locations of the various factories and the items they produced in his testimony at the Blaskic trial, September 11 and 21, 1998. Zeko was the intelligence officer (S2) for HQ, OZCB, in 1992–94, and later served as a brigadier and the senior intelligence officer (G2) of the Bosnian Federation army.

22. Thorvald Stoltenberg to the UN secretary general, Jan. 9, 1993, message, subject: Talks in Bonn, KC Z354.1.

23. The principal routes in use during the conflict in Bosnia-Herzegovina were assigned codenames by UNPROFOR (see UN Military Observers, Sector Southwest, MIO [Military Information Officer] Briefing, May 3, 1994, KC D333/1). The most important of those routes were:

Designation	Route
CIRCLE	Split–Brnaze–Kamensko–Tomislavgrad–Mandino Selo
TRIANGLE	Mandino Selo–Omrcanica–Prozor
SQUARE	Mandino Selo–Jablanica–Prozor
DIAMOND	Prozor–Gornji Vakuf–Novi Travnik–Puticevo
SALMON	Prozor–Gornji Vakuf–Fojnica–Gromiljak
PACMAN	Jablanica–Konjic–Tarcin–Kresevo–Kiseljak–Busovaca–Kaonik–Puticevo
LADA	Doboj–Maglaj–Zepce–Zenica
GANNET	Split–Metkovic–Mostar–Jablanica
DOVE	Kislejak–Breza
FINCH	Sarajevo–Ilijas–Vares
TROUT	Kiseljak–Fojnica–Blodnica

24. The road was actually upgraded by the Bosnian Croats in 1991, an effort in which the Muslims refused to cooperate (Maj. Franjo Ljubas, Kordic-Cerkez trial testimony, May 16, 2000). Ljubas was an HVO battalion commander in the Travnik area in 1993 and later served as a Major in the Bosnian Federation army.

25. 1PWO MILINFOSUM no. 045, June 13, 1993, KC D201/1.

Chapter 2. Organization of the Opposing Forces

1. HQ, European Community Monitoring Mission (ECMM), "Introduction Brief for new ECMM Monitors," n.p. (Zagreb), Feb. 25, 1993, KC Z495, 6. None of the HVO's armor and only a small portion of its artillery was in central Bosnia.

2. Edgar O'Ballance, *Civil War in Bosnia, 1992–94,* 126–27.

3. IISS, *The Military Balance, 1992–1993,* 70.

4. IISS, *The Military Balance, 1993–1994*, 74–75. The BSA was believed to have sixty-seven thousand troops in 1992–93, and up to eighty thousand in 1993–94.

5. HQ, HVO Main Staff, no. 06–01–666/93, (Mostar), Feb. 23, 1993, subj: Proracun potrsonje mesnih konzervi u ishrani postrejbi HVO ze 30 dana (Ration Strength and 30-Day Supply Level), KC Z489.2.

6. Sefer Halilovic, *Lukava strategija* (*The Shrewd Strategy*), 123–24. General Halilovic was the ABiH's chief of the General Staff from May, 1992, to November, 1993.

7. Ibid., 124.

8. Zeko, Blaskic trial testimony, Sept. 21, 1993.

9. HQ, ABiH III Corps, no. 02/3–67 (*sic*), Zenica, July 11, 1997, subj: Podatke o mob. razvoju dostavlja, KC Z1477.4.

10. HQ, Vitez Military District, Vitez, n.d. (Feb. 2), 1993, subj: Assessment of the Situation (Table, "Ratios of Forces and Equipment by Locality"), 21, KC D59/2.

11. HQ, HVO Main Staff, Mostar, June 10, 1993, subj: Decision on Carrying Out Mobilization in the Territory of the Croatian Community of Herceg-Bosna in Times of the Immediate Threat of War or in Wartime (*Narodi List*, no. 11/93, June 10, 1993), B 38C/1.

12. See, among others, Zeko, Blaskic trial testimony, Sept. 21, 1998.

13. See, among others, the testimony of Nihad Rebihic, Kordic-Cerkez trial, Oct. 13, 1999; testimony of Brigadier Dzemal Merdan, Kordic-Cerkez trial, Jan. 19 and 25, 2000; Halilovic, *Lukava strategija*, 124. Rehibic was the intelligence officer for ABiH forces in Stari Vitez in 1993. Merdan was the Deputy Commander of the ABiH III Corps in 1992–1994.

14. The northern (Maglaj) front was held jointly, and the ABiH III Corps also had forces deployed against the HVO in the Bugojno–Gornji Vakuf area.

15. The ABiH's June, 1993, attack on the HVO in the Travnik area is discussed in chapter 9.

16. Zeko, Blaskic trial testimony, Sept. 23, 1998.

17. Conversation with Maj. Franjo Ljubas, Travnik area, Aug. 20, 1999.

18. Croatian Defense Council of the Croatian Community of Herceg-Bosna, Mostar, Mar., 1992 (should be 1993), subj: A Report on Work in 1992, 1, KC Z511.

19. Halilovic, *Lukava strategija*, passim.

20. Croatian Defense Council, subj: A Report on Work in 1992, 1.

21. Mate Boban, interview by Helsinki Watch representatives, Grude, Oct. 23, 1992; quoted in Helsinki Watch, *War Crimes in Bosnia-Hercegovina*, 2:297.

22. Croatian Defense Council, subj: A Report on Work in 1992, 5.

23. Brigadier Slavko Marin, Blaskic trial testimony, Sept. 24, 1998. Marin was the Operations Officer (S3) of HQ, OZCB, and later served as chief of staff of the Federation army's I Guards Corps.

24. See, among others, HQ, HVO, no. 01–93/92, Mostar, Apr. 23, 1993, subj: Order, KC Z79; and HQ, Municipal HVO Command Kiseljak, no. 11–05/92, Kiseljak, May 10, 1992, subj: Order, KC Z99.

25. See HQ, OZCB, Nov. 18, 1992, subj: Formation of the Central Bosnia Operative Zone Command, B D201; and Marin, Blaskic trial testimony, Oct. 6, 1998. The former OZCB chief of staff, Brigadier Franjo Nakic, testified that when he reported for duty at HQ, OZCB, on December 1, 1992, there were only eleven persons on the staff, and only the commander, Col. Tihomir Blaskic, had any substantial professional military training. Nakic himself had extensive experience as an infantry major in the JNA (Kordic-Cerkez trial, Apr. 13, 2000). He became the OZCB chief of staff in December, 1992, and served in that position until December, 1996, when he retired from the Federation army as a brigadier.

26. HQ, HVO Regional Staff Central Bosnia, Order no. 94/92, Gornji Vakuf, July 4, 1992, subj: Order (Operative Zones/Sectors in Central Bosnia), KC Z151.

27. HQ, OZCB, Order no. 875/93, Vitez, Oct. 7, 1992, KC Z234. Apparently, the Kralj Tvrtko Drugi Brigade in Sarajevo constituted a fourth separate Operative Group.

28. The 3d Guards Brigade, located in Vitez, was part of the HVO's newly formed professional mobile force. As of February 4, 1994, the 3d Guards Brigade had only 140 men assigned. See commander, Vitez Military District (Col. Tihomir Blaskic) to HVO Main Staff Posusje Forward Command Post, no. 01–2-87/94, Vitez, Feb. 4, 1994, subj: (report on the replenishment of units in the Vitez Military District), KC D321/1.

29. An excellent outline of the organization and employment of the village guard formations can be found in the testimony of Sgt. Fabijan Zuljevic, Kordic-Cerkez trial, September 19, 2000. Zuljevic was from the village of Krizancevo Selo and participated in the village guard organization there. He later served as a sergeant in the Federation army.

30. Sergeant Zuljevic also provides a good description of how the HVO shifts were organized and deployed. See his testimony at the Kordic-Cerkez trial, Sept. 19, 2000.

31. For example, the shifts drawn from the Vitez area usually assembled at the Motel Lovac in Kruscica. A shift was in the act of assembling there on April 16, 1993, when the Muslims launched their attack in the Lasva Valley.

32. HQ, OZCB, Order no. 1224/92, Vitez, Nov. 25, 1992, subj: Organization of brigades within the area of the Central Bosnia Operational Zone, B D240.

33. The JNA Type "R" reserve brigade was authorized 2,864 officers and men. See the testimony of Maj. Zlatko Senkic, Kordic-Cerkez trial, July 24, 2000. Senkic was the assistant commander for organization and personnel (S1) of the Stjepan Tomasevic Brigade. He later served in the Federation army's Joint Headquarters in the administration and mobilization field.

34. Commander, Frankopan Brigade, to commander, OZCB, Guca Gora–Travnik, May 17, 1993, subj: (Organization and Strength of Frankopan Brigade), B D246.

35. HQ, Viteska Brigade (Vitez), n.d. (fall, 1993), subj: Review of the Effective Strength of Combat Units (Viteska Brigade), KC Z583; HVO Defense Office Vitez, no. 02–11–4-08–867/93, Vitez, Sept. 28, 1993, subj: Assessment, KC Z1220.1.

36. Commander, Vitez Military District (Col. Tihomir Blaskic), to HVO Main Staff Posusje Forward Command Post, Feb. 4, 1994.

37. Organigramme of HVO as of July 20, 1993, HQ, BHC, "Bosnia-Herzegovina Warring Factions," ed. no. 6 (Kiseljak, July 22, 1993), KC Z1148.2; KC D27/2.

38. HQ, HVO Novi Travnik, Novi Travnik, Feb. 27, 1993, subj: List of the HVO Members Novi Travnik in the Unit: Command of the II Battalion (VP 72298), KC Z505.

39. See Article 10, item 8, of the *Decree on the Armed Forces of the HZ HB* (*Narodni List*, no. 1/92), and *Decision on the Structure of the Home Guard*, Nov. 3, 1992 (*Narodni List*, no. 7/92). Implementing instructions were issued in HVO Department of Defense, Order no. 02–1-15/93, Mostar, Feb. 5, 1993, B 768; and HVO General Staff, Order no. 01–254/93, Mostar, Feb. 8, 1993, KC Z451.

40. Assistant commander for the Home Guard, OZCB (Zonko Vukovic), to municipal Home Guard commanders, no. 20–3-538/93, Vitez, Mar. 13, 1993, subj: (Order for Establishment of the Home Guard), KC D321/1.

41. Ibid.

42. HQ, UN Military Observers Sector Southwest, SMO (Sector Military Observers) Briefing, Gornji Vakuf, June 20, 1995, KC D317/1.

43. Ibid.

44.   Halilovic, *Lukava strategija,* 166.

45.   Ibid., 57. The decree establishing the new TO organization was not published until April 9, 1992, and April 15 is celebrated as the ABiH's official "birthday." At that time, the HVO's military structure was also recognized as an integral part of the RBiH's defense forces.

46.   Ibid., 123.

47.   For example, in April-May, 1992, the TO District Staff in Zenica controlled forces in the municipalities of Donja Vakuf, Bugojno, Gornji Vakuf, Travnik, Novi Travnik, Vitez, Busovaca, Kakanj, and Zenica. The TO structure in the Zenica district is discussed in some detail in Zeko, Blaskic trial testimony, Sept. 11, 1998.

48.   Sefer Halilovic later complained bitterly of Izetbegovic's compliance with the dictates of the JNA and of the influence of Izetbegovic's close adviser, Fikret Muslimovic, who Halilovic identified as an agent of the Serbian secret intelligence service (see Halilovic, *Lukava strategija,* 57 and 73). Muslimovic subsequently rose to command of the Muslim forces that became part of the Federation army in 1994.

49.   Zeko, Blaskic trial testimony, Sept. 21, 1998.

50.   Halilovic, *Lukava strategija,* 54–55, 65, 164–68, and 215. Sefer Halilovic left the JNA in September, 1991, and from December, 1991, until March, 1992, was involved in organizing the Patriotic League military contingents and the defense of Sarajevo. In May, 1992, he commanded the defense of Sarajevo against the former JNA and stopped the coup staged by Alija Delimustafic. Passed over for appointment to head the RBiH Territorial Defense forces, Halilovic was appointed chief of the ABiH General Staff that same month, and served in that position until November 1, 1993. His authority was usurped in part by the extraconstitutional appointment of Rasim Delic to the nonexistent post of commander of the General Staff by Alija Izetbegovic on June 8, 1993 (see Halilovic, *Lukava strategija,* 247–48).

51.   Ibid., 54–55.

52.   Ibid., 120, 164–68 and 247. Halilovic led the organizational meeting of the Patriotic League at Mehurici from February 7–9, 1992, and—along with Rifat Bilajac, Zicro Suljevic, and Kemo Karisik—drafted the defense plan.

53.   Ibid., 120, 166, and 247.

54.   Ibid., 123.

55.   O'Ballance, *Civil War in Bosnia,* 29.

56.   RBiH Presidency, no. 02/1091–37, Sarajevo, Aug. 18, 1992, subj: Decision on the Establishment of Corps of the Army of the Republic of Bosnia and Herzegovina, Their Areas of Responsibility and the New Subordination Structure, KC Z191.

57.   RBiH Presidency, no. 02–011–308/93, Sarajevo, June 8, 1993, subj: Decision on the Restructuring of the RBiH Supreme Command Headquarters of the Armed Forces and the Appointment of Senior Officers, KC Z1031.2. See also HQ, BHC (UNPROFOR), Weekly Information Summary (INFOSUM) no. 34, Kiseljak, June 21, 1993, 5b(5), KC Z1090.

58.   HQ, ABiH III Corps, no. 02/33–628, Zenica, Mar. 8, 1993, subj: (Order for Formation of Operational Groups), KC Z527.1.

59.   "The Army of Bosnia and Herzegovina," *Jane's Intelligence Review,* Mar. 1, 1994.

60.   Halilovic, *Lukava strategija,* 219.

61.   Ibid., 14.

62.   Ibid., 24. The final decision was issued as RBiH Presidency, no. 02–011–308/93.

Chapter 3. Command, Control, and Communications

1.   Col. Robert A. Stewart, Blaskic trial testimony, June 18, 1999. See also the testimony of Chris Leyshon, who held a contrary view (Blaskic trial, November 18,

1998). Stewart commanded the 1st Battalion, 22d (Cheshire) Regiment, in the Lasva Valley from October, 1992, to May, 1993. Leyshon, then a captain in the British army, headed the Cheshire's military information cell (intelligence staff) during the same period.

2. Marin, Blaskic trial testimony, Sept. 24, 1998. Marin makes the point that "volunteerism" and the political influences on commanders at the village level served to soften discipline and make logistics more difficult.

3. Order no. 01–118/93, HQ, Viteska Brigade, Vitez, April 8, 1993, subj: (Ban on transfers), KC Z629.

4. Marin, Blaskic trial testimony, Sept. 25, 1998. The procedures and formal authority to appoint and dismiss HVO officers and noncommissioned officers were prescribed by Article 34 of the "Decree on the Armed Forces of the Croatian Community of Herceg-Bosna-Revised Text" (*Narodni List* no. 6/92), Oct. 17, 1993, B 36A, KC Z2298. See also HQ, OZCB, no. 01–3-839/93, Vitez, Mar. 26, 1993, subj: Clarification on persons authorized to appoint and dismiss officers and noncommissioned officers, KC Z572.

5. HQ, OZCB, no. 01–4-335/93, Vitez, 0140 hours, Apr. 18, 1993, subj: Order to Engage Unit for Combat, KC Z731.

6. HQ, OZCB, no. 01–4-417/93, Vitez, Apr. 20, 1993, subj: Order (Relief of Commander, 3rd Battalion, Jelacic Brigade), KC Z749; HQ, OZCB, no. 01–4-418/93, Vitez, Apr. 20, 1993, subj: Order Regarding Subordination, KC Z744.

7. In fact, Sefer Halilovic's memoir, *Lukava strategija*, is almost entirely devoted to the story of his differences with Alija Izetbegovic over whether, how, and why to defend Bosnia-Herzegovina.

8. Halilovic, *Lukava strategija*, 123.

9. Ibid., 65.

10. Marin, Blaskic trial testimony, Sept. 25, 1998. According to the official U.S. Joint Chiefs of Staff definition, when a commander is given OPCON of a unit he normally has "full authority to organize commands and forces and to employ those forces as [he] considers necessary to accomplish assigned missions. Operational control does not, in and of itself, include authoritative direction for logistics or matters of administration, discipline, internal organization, or unit training" (*Joint Pub 1–02: Department of Defense Dictionary of Military and Associated Terms*, 274–75).

11. 1PWO MILINFOSUM no. 101, Aug. 8, 1993, para. 7, KC Z2435.2 and KC D134/1; 1PWO MILINFOSUM no. 103, Aug. 10, 1993, para. 18, KC Z2435.4 and KC D135/1; ECMM Regional Center Zenica, Weekly Summary, Apr. 10–17, 1993, para. 1, KC Z707.1.

12. Ekrem Mahmutovic, witness statement, Kordic-Cerkez trial, Dec. 3, 1998, 4, KC D31/1. A Muslim native of Stupni Do, in 1992–93, Mahmutovic was a captain first class in the ABiH and commanded the TO forces in Vares. He frequently interacted with HVO authorities in Vares while serving in that capacity.

13. See HB HZ, HVO, "A Report on Activities for the Period January to June 1993," n.p., n.d. (Mostar, June, 1993), 17, B 457/4; and PPN "Vitezovi" (Dragan Vinac), no. 3–065/94, Vitez, Feb. 18, 1994, subj: Report, 8, KC Z1380.

14. For more general information on the Vitezovi, see PPN "Vitezovi" (Dragan Vinac), no. 3–065/94, KC Z1380.

15. Maj. Gen. Tihomir Blaskic, Blaskic trial testimony, May 11, 1999. Blaskic, who commanded the HVO OZCB from June, 1992, to February, 1994, was promoted to major general and given command of the HVO in August, 1994. On March 3, 2000, the ICTY found him guilty of war crimes and sentenced him to forty-five years imprisonment. Although often identified as brigades or regiments, the PPN

units were actually company-size elements with fifty to 150 men. In October, 1993, the Ante Bruno Busic Brigade was located in Gornji Vakuf and was commanded by Goran Cisic. In May, 1993, the Ludvig Pavlovic Brigade, created on May 5, 1992, was based at the Bozan Simovic Barracks in Capljina and was commanded by Maj. Dragan Curcic. See also 1PWO MILINFOSUM no. 177, Oct. 22, 1993, para. 11c, KC Z2439.9; HQ, COMBRITFOR MILINFOSUM no. 190, May 5, 1993, KC D317/1.

16.   Marin, Blaskic trial testimony, July 18, 1999; 1PWO MILINFOSUM no. 101, para. 7, KC Z2435.2 and KC D134/1.

17.   For the HVO Military Police, see HZ HB, HVO, "Report on Activities," 17, KC Z1134; Pavo Loncar, "The Establishment, Structure and Development of the Military Police," *Vojna policija* (*The Military Police*), Apr., 1995, 6–16, KC Z2485.1.

18.   United States Army military policemen do not normally exercise any authority over American civilians, nor are they employed as assault troops, except possibly in extreme and unusual situations.

19.   Col. Marinko Palavra, Kordic-Cerkez trial testimony, Nov. 15, 2000; testimony of Maj. Zeljko Sajevic, Kordic-Cerkez trial, July 25, 2000. Palavra commanded the 4th Military Police Battalion from August 1, 1993, to August 27, 1997, and later served as a colonel and chief of military police in the Security/Intelligence Section of the HVO component of the Federation army. Sajevic was the Viteska Brigade's operations officer (S3) and later served in the Bosnian Federation's National Security Service.

20.   Helsinki Watch, *War Crimes in Bosnia-Hercegovina,* 2:352.

21.   Many Bosnian Muslims joined the HOS to fight against the Serbs during the period when Alija Izetbegovic's government appeared disinterested in defending the RBiH from the BSA and its Serbian and JNA allies (Vulliamy, *Seasons in Hell,* 215).

22.   Helsinki Watch, *War Crimes in Bosnia-Hercegovina,* 2:352.

23.   Ibid., 2:352–53.

24.   HQ, Jure Francetic Brigade, no. 703/93, Zenica, Apr. 5, 1993, subj: (Merger of the HOS with Units of the HVO), KC Z607 and KC D17/1.20.

25.   Central Bosnia Armed Forces Command, Alpha Force Reconnaissance-Sabotage Group, document listing members of the Alpha Force, their duty assignments, and their personal identity numbers, n.d., KC Z67; HQ, OZCB, no. 1006/92, Vitez, Nov. 3, 1992, subj: List of Salaries of the Vitez Alpha Force Sabotage Group for the Month of June, 1992, KC Z265.

26.   For more on the organization, orientation, and employment of the 7th Muslim Brigade, see the rather evasive testimony of its first commander, Col. Asim Koricic, Blaskic trial, June 10, 1999. Koricic commanded the brigade from November, 1992, to July, 1993. He retired from the Federation army as a colonel in 1996. Colonel Amir Kubura, who succeeded Koricic and commanded the brigade until March, 1994, was indicted for war crimes by the ICTY in The Hague on July 13, 2001.

27.   Koricic, Blaskic trial testimony, June 10, 1999; 1PWO MILINFOSUM no. 176, Oct. 21, 1993, para. 7, KC Z2439.8. The mujahideen and their connection with various Islamic charitable groups are discussed below.

28.   Koricic, Blaskic trial testimony, June 10, 1999.

29.   See, among others, HQ, COMBRITFOR MILINFOSUM no. 200, May 15, 1993, para. 2c(4), KC D317/1; Vulliamy, *Seasons in Hell,* 168 and 258; and Blaskic, Blaskic trial testimony, Feb. 22, 1999.

30.   Zeko, Blaskic trial testimony, Sept. 11, 1998.

31.   See, among others, Marin, Blaskic trial testimony, Sept. 24, 1998; administrative assistant for the SIS (Ivan Budimir), HQ, 2d (Vitez) Battalion, Stjepan Tomasevic

Brigade, (Vitez), Jan. 25, 1993, subj: Report on the Activities of Groups and Individuals Acting without the Knowledge of the HVO Command, B D204; ibid., (Vitez, Jan., 1993?), subj: Analysis of the Work of the VP in the Zone of Responsibility of the II Battalion, KC D17/1.7 and KC D10/2; HQ, Viteska Brigade, no. 01–117/93, Vitez, Apr. 8, 1993, subj: Ban on the Movements of Uniformed Individuals and the Bearing of Arms in Inhabited Areas, KC Z630.

32.   HZ HB, HVO, "Report on Activities," 21, KC Z1134.

33.   Zarko Andric ("Zuti") was shot by the HVO in October, 1993, to curb his growing criminal activity. See 1PWO MILINFOSUM no. 177, para. 1, KC Z2439.9.

34.   1PWO MILINFOSUM no. 177, para. 1, KC Z2439.9.

35.   For the alleged HV major in Novi Travnik, see Stewart, Blaskic trial testimony, June 18, 1998. For orders of HQ, OZCB, requiring subordinate units to report any officers of the Croatian Army (HV) in their ranks, see HQ, Central Bosnia Armed Forces Command, no. 865/92, Vitez, Oct. 5, 1992, subj: Order, KC Z255.2; and HQ, OZCB, no. 01–4–171/93, Vitez, Apr. 12, 1993, subj: Order, KC Z2414. For the wearing of HV uniform items and insignia by Bosnian Croats who earlier served with Croatian units in the war against the JNA and the Serbs, see, among others, Zeko, Blaskic trial testimony, Sept. 23, 1998. Zeko noted that the veterans of the 1991 war in Croatia simply wanted to demonstrate their greater combat experience and that they were few in number. On the prohibition of the wearing of HV insignia by HVO personnel in central Bosnia, see HQ, Viteska Brigade, no. 01–81–1/93, Vitez, Mar. 31, 1993, KC Z580.

36.   ECMM Regional Center Zenica to HQ, ECMM, Zenica, 2332, June 3, 1993, subj: Report-HV Involvement in BH, 1, KC Z1012. Could it be that the HVO was simply a tough and resourceful fighting force?

37.   United Nations Secretary General to the President of the Security Council, UN Security Council doc. no. S/1994/109, New York, Feb. 2, 1994, KC Z2458. However, a close reading of this document, along with other Security Council documents, makes clear that the UN definition of "central Bosnia" included the Gornji Vakuf–Rama area, which was not in the area of responsibility of the OZCB commander, that is, not in "central Bosnia" as we have defined it here. See also Permanent Representative of Croatia to the United Nations to the Secretary General, UN Security Council doc. no. S/1994/197, New York, Feb. 18, 1994, KC Z1380.1.

38.   Statement of the Government of the Republic of Bosnia and Herzegovina, (Sarajevo), n.d. (May 13, 1993), paras. 1 and 2, KC Z912.

39.   ECMM Regional Center Zenica to HQ, ECMM, Zenica, June 3, 1993, 1, KC Z1012.

40.   Ibid.

41.   See the testimony of General Blaskic, Brigadier Marin, and Brigadier Zeko in the Blaskic trial.

42.   Stewart, Blaskic trial testimony, June 18, 1999; Lt. Gen. Sir Roderick Cordy-Simpson, Kordic-Cerkez trial testimony, Aug. 4, 1999. An officer in the British Army, Sir Roderick Cordy-Simpson was chief of staff of the UNPROFOR Bosnia-Herzegovina Command in Kiseljak from September 18, 1992, to April 10, 1993.

43.   The figure of three thousand to four thousand mujahideen in Bosnia-Herzegovina was advanced by the OZCB commander, Colonel Blaskic, but such a high figure was not confirmed by UNPROFOR. The actual number was probably closer to two thousand. See Cordy-Simpson, Kordic-Cerkez trial testimony, Aug. 4, 1999.

44.   Zeko, Blaskic trial testimony, Sept. 21, 1998.

45.   Ibid., Sept. 11, 1998. The initial increments of mujahideen appear to have been

from Iran and Afghanistan. Others came from Algeria, Egypt, Pakistan, Tunisia, Jordan, Sudan, Turkey, Saudi Arabia, and the Gulf States (O'Ballance, *Civil War in Bosnia*, 94–96; Annex A to ECMM Regional Center Zenica Daily Summary Report for April 8, 1993, in "Extracts of Political Material in ECMM Team Reports," Zagreb, Apr. 9, 1993, KC Z635; 1PWO MILINFOSUM no. 168, Oct. 13, 1993, para. 5, KC Z2439.6; "Extracts of Political Material in ECMM Team Reports 24–25 April 1993," Zagreb, Apr. 26, 1993, para. 24.4, KC Z822; Cordy-Simpson, Kordic-Cerkez trial testimony, Aug. 4, 1999).

46.   Zeko, Blaskic trial testimony, Sept. 21, 1998.

47.   1PWO MILINFOSUM no. 59, June 27, 1993, para. 10, KC Z1119.1. See also Koricic, Blaskic trial testimony, June 10, 1999. Colonel Koricic maintained that he knew nothing of the "Abdul Atif" Detachment and that the "El Mujahid" Detachment, rather than being attached to the 7th Muslim Brigade, was engaged only in "humanitarian work." In fact, Muslim authorities frequently portrayed the mujahideen as idealistic humanitarian relief workers rather than cold-blooded murderers. See, for example, the statement of the ABiH III Corps security officer to an EC monitor in "Extracts of Political Material in ECMM Team Reports 24–25 April 1993," para. 24.4.

48.   Vulliamy, *Seasons in Hell*, 259.

49.   Ibid., 64; O'Ballance, *Civil War in Bosnia*, 94.

50.   For example, in September, 1992, Croat authorities in Zagreb discovered some four thousand weapons and a million rounds of ammunition on an Iranian aircraft supposedly delivering humanitarian aid to Bosnian refugees (Beale, *Bombs over Bosnia*, 14).

51.   Koricic, Blaskic trial testimony, June 10, 1999; 1PWO MILINFOSUM no. 176, para. 7, KC Z2439.8.

52.   HQ, BHC (UNPROFOR), "Bosnia-Hercegovina Warring Factions," ed. no. 8, (Kiseljak), Feb. 3, 1994, D-24, KC D315/1.

53.   In January, 2002, Bosnian authorities arrested and subsequently turned over to the United States six Algerians with apparent connections to the al-Qaeda terrorist network. All had been in Bosnia-Herzegovina for some time, and five of the six worked for Muslim aid organizations. The incident has raised questions about the possible link to terrorism of many of the 120 Islamic humanitarian organizations operating in Bosnia-Herzegovina (Aida Cerkez-Robinson, "Bosnia Probes Aid Groups," Associated Press, New York, 2:12 P.M., EST, Jan. 21, 2002).

54.   Stewart diary, Sunday, Sept. 27, 1992; Vulliamy, *Seasons in Hell*, 227–28.

55.   Stewart diary, Sunday, Oct. 18, 1992, sec. 1, 16; ibid., Tuesday, Nov. 3, 1992, sec. 1, 27.

56.   Ibid., Sunday, Oct. 18, 1992, sec. 3, 14.

57.   Ibid., Tuesday, Nov. 3, 1992, sec. 1, 27.

58.   See, among others, Carole Rogel, *The Breakup of Yugoslavia and the War in Bosnia*, 64; Cordy-Simpson, Kordic-Cerkez trial testimony, Aug. 4, 1999; diary of Col. Peter G. Williams entitled "A Balkan Winter: War and Peace in Central Bosnia-The Significant Events-BRITBAT Commanding Officer's Diary Covering Operation Grapple 3, 12 November 1993–8 May 1994," Dec. 31, 1993, and Feb. 1, 1994, KC D167/1. Williams commanded the 1st Battalion, Coldstream Guards, the British UNPROFOR unit in the Lasva Valley from November 8, 1993, to May 21, 1994.

59.   The deployment of UNPROFOR II to Bosnia-Herzegovina is outlined succinctly in "United Nations Protection Force 1," available at http://www.un.org/Depts/DPKO/Missions/unprofor, accessed Jan. 17, 2002. See also IISS, *Military Balance, 1993–1994*, 66–67. The idea of using UN armed forces to protect the humanitar-

ian aid convoys—a concept known as "protective support"—was advanced by British foreign secretary Douglas Hurd in August, 1992. See Carole Hodge, "Slimey Limeys," *New Republic,* Jan. 9, 1995, 21.

60. See UN Security Council Resolution 824, May 6, 1993; UN Security Council Resolution 844, June 18, 1993.

61. John F. Hillen III, *Killing with Kindness: The UN Peacekeeping Mission in Bosnia.* Overall, the United Nations intervention in the former Yugoslavia from February, 1992, to March 31, 1996, was a massive undertaking involving over $4.6 million and some 167 UN fatalities. By March, 1995, the force deployed consisted of 38,599 military personnel, including 684 UN military observers; 803 civilian police; 2,017 international civilian staff members; and 2,615 local staff members ("UNPROFOR fmr YUGOSLAVIA," available at http://www.xs4all.nl/~vdrkrans/unprofor/f, accessed Jan. 17, 2002.

62. Rogel, *Breakup of Yugoslavia,* 64.

63. The Nordic Battalion also operated in the Vares area, and a Canadian battalion was stationed in the Visoko area. The HQ of the commander of British Forces in Bosnia-Herzegovina (HQ, COMBRITFOR) was collocated with HQ, BHC, in Kiseljak.

64. Maj. Roger D. Marshall (British Army), "Operation Grapple: British Armed Forces in UN Protection Force," US Army Intelligence Center, Fort Huachuca, Ariz., available at http://www.fas.org/irp/agency/army/tradoc/USAIC/mipb/1996–4/marshall, accessed Jan. 17, 2002. The successive deployments of the three battalions were designated Operations GRAPPLE I, II, and III.

65. See Stewart, Blaskic trial testimony, June 17–18, 1999. One company was placed on standby for future deployment to Tuzla.

66. See the testimony of Brigadier Alaistair Duncan, Kordic-Cerkez trial, Nov. 9–10 and 25–26, 1999. Duncan commanded the 1st Battalion, Prince of Wales's Own Regiment of Yorkshire, the British UNPROFOR unit in the Lasva Valley, from May 11 to November 8, 1993.

67. See Williams, Kordic-Cerkez trial testimony, Jan. 31, 2000, and "Balkan Winter," Dec. 11, 1993.

68. See Col. Johannes de Boer, Kordic-Cerkez trial testimony, Jan. 11, 2000, and Lt. Col. Paulus Schipper, Kordic-Cerkez trial testimony, Nov. 12, 1999.

69. See, among others, Rogel, *Breakup of Yugoslavia,* 21, and Hillen, *Killing with Kindness.* Hillen maintains that the UN intervention in Bosnia-Herzegovina was fatally flawed in that it prolonged the conflict and suffering rather than reducing them. He also charges the UN with the lack of a comprehensive overall strategy stemming from the unwillingness of the principal UN powers to address the conflict's fundamental political causes because of the costs involved. In general, the British battalions deployed in the Lasva Valley were better trained, better disciplined, and better equipped than other UNPROFOR units, although the BRITBAT commanders at times displayed an abysmal ignorance of the political and cultural situation in which they found themselves.

70. Soon after their arrival in the Lasva Valley, the Cheshires gained the nickname of "SHOOTBAT" due to their propensity to open fire on the HVO and, less frequently, the ABiH (Marshall, "Operation Grapple").

71. Croatian Defense Council commanders especially distrusted the UNPROFOR's preference for Muslim interpreters, but their complaints were usually dismissed in a most cavalier manner with such comments as, "A gentleman does not comment on another gentleman's servants." See Williams, "Balkan Winter," Dec. 11, 1993.

72. The ECCM's deployment is outlined succinctly in "ECMM: Observers in White," available at http://www.users.hol.gr/~posi/ecmm, accessed Jan. 17, 2002.

73. See, for example, the ECMM dismissal of Croat charges against the Muslims for razing Croat villages near Zenica in April, 1993 (HQ, ECMM RC Zenica to HQ, ECMM Zagreb, "Special Report on Croats in Zenica, 20–21 April 1993," [Zenica, Apr. 21, 1993], KC Z765 and KC D25/1]), and the intemperate comments of the ECMM Regional Director, French ambassador Jean-Pierre Thebault, regarding the June, 1993, incident involving the so-called Convoy of Joy (HRC, Zenica [Ambassador Thebault] to HQ, ECMM, Zenica, June 10, 1993, subj: HVO Attack on Tuzla Convoy, KC Z1041.1; and HRC, Zenica [Ambassador Thebault] to HQ, ECMM, Zenica, June 11, 1993, subj: The Tragedy of the Tuzla Convoy, KC Z1045.2). By any measurement, Ambassador Thebault was thoroughly anti-Croat in word and deed, but his successor, Britain's Sir Martin Garrod, was much more evenhanded.

74. In his testimony at the Blaskic trial on September 25, 1998, Brigadier Marin stated that the OZCB did not have any secure communications, and that the lack of it influenced the types of reports and other information reaching the commander. See also Zeko, Blaskic trial testimony, Sept. 21 and 23, 1998.

Chapter 4. Training, Doctrine, and Logistics

1. Brigadier Slavko Marin, Blaskic trial testimony, Oct. 7, 1998. Speaking of the early days of the HVO in Travnik, Maj. Gen. Filip Filipovic said that the HVO "practically had no training" (Kordic-Cerkez trial testimony, Apr. 12, 2000). Filipovic was perhaps the most experienced military officer in the OZCB, having risen to the rank of colonel and command of an artillery regiment in the JNA before leaving in April, 1992. In April-May, 1992, he commanded all HVO forces in central Bosnia and then became a staff officer under Col. Tihomir Blaskic in the OZCB and, for a short time, commander of the Travnicka Brigade. Filipovic again took command of all HVO forces in central Bosnia in April, 1994, and remained in that position until April, 1995. He retired from the Federation army with the rank of major general in January, 1997.

2. Halilovic, *Lukava strategija*, 238.

3. Koricic, Blaskic trial testimony, June 10, 1999.

4. Zeko, Blaskic trial testimony, Sept. 23, 1998. The third was Filip Filipovic.

5. The ABiH had many more officers with JNA experience than did the HVO (Filipovic, Kordic-Cerkez trial testimony, Apr. 11, 2000).

6. For a discussion of JNA doctrine and tactics, see Charles R. Patrick, *Tactics of the Serb and Bosnian-Serb Armies and Territorial Militia.*

7. Ibid., 6.

8. Ibid., 17.

9. Ibid., 38.

10. IISS, *Military Balance, 1993–1994*, 100.

11. Ljubas, Kordic-Cerkez trial testimony, May 16, 2000.

12. Patrick, *Tactics of the Serb*, 17.

13. Prof. Slobodan Jankovic, conversation with author, Zagreb, Oct. 20, 1999. Major General Filip Filipovic testified in the Kordic-Cerkez trial (April 11, 2000) that of the 2,000 weapons seized by the HVO and ABiH at Slimena, over 1,000 went to the ABiH and 500–600 to the HVO. Of the weapons seized at Bratstvo, one-third went to the ABiH in Visoko, one-third to the HVO, and one-third was split locally between the HVO and ABiH. The ABiH received no less than a hundred mortars, nine 122-mm howitzers, and two 152-mm *Nora* gun-howitzers.

14. See, for example, the list of matériel supplied by the Croatian government in 1992, 1993, and 1994 in "List of Military Equipment Issued for Special Purposes

in the Period 1992–1994," n.p., n.d., KC Z2497.2. At the height of the Muslim-Croat conflict in 1993, the Croatian government supplied the ABiH with 1,995 152-mm shells.

15.   On the transit of arms for both the HVO and the ABiH through Croatia, see Zeko, Blaskic trial testimony, Sept. 23, 1998.

16.   Beale, *Bombs over Bosnia,* 14.

17.   See, for example, ABiH General Staff, Visoko Section (Rasim Delic) to HVO Central Bosnia Headquarters, no. 01–10151/93, n.p. (Visoko), Feb. 5, 1993, subj: Agreement, B D402, which deals with a request for the movement of ABiH ammunition from Tarcin to Tuzla via Kiseljak and Vares.

18.   Cordy-Simpson, Kordic-Cerkez trial testimony, Aug. 4, 1999; Williams, "Balkan Winter," Dec. 31, 1993, and Feb. 1, 1994.

19.   HVO Defense Office Vitez, no. 02–11-4-08–867/93, Vitez, Sept. 28, 1993, subj: Assessment of Military, Political, Economic and Other Conditions in Wartime, KC Z1220.1, 11–12. The reported HVO production for a two-month period included, among other things, five thousand mortar shells, sixteen hundred shaped charge mines, seventeen hundred hand grenades, and four thousand kilograms of gunpowder.

20.   1PWO MILINFOSUM no. 161, Oct. 6, 1993, para. 4, KC Z2439.3.

21.   See Halilovic, *Lukava strategija,* 88–100, 153, 183, 195–97, 212–13, and 238–39.

22.   Ibid., 93, 94.

23.   When the war ended in February, 1994, HVO authorities in Vitez were still pleading with the HVO Main Staff in Posusje for boots, winter clothing, underwear, and socks (see HQ, Vitez Military District, no. 01–2-63/94, Vitez, Feb. 4, 1994, subj: Provision of Footwear, Clothing and Armaments Request, B 456/114).

24.   Zeko, Blaskic trial testimony, Sept. 23, 1998. See also the special report prepared by the commander, HVO OZCB, for the supreme commander of the Armed Forces of the HZ HB, Vitez, May 7, 1993, KC Z891, which characterizes the ABiH as "poorly equipped" (in comparison to the BSA).

25.   IISS, *Military Balance, 1993–1994,* 74.

26.   For ABiH tanks, see, among others, 1CSG MILINFOSUM no. 65, Jan. 4, 1994, para. 10, KC Z2447.3. Although HVO units in the OZCB had no tanks of their own, they were reported to have "rented" BSA tanks for certain operations.

27.   Zeko, Blaskic trial testimony, Sept. 11, 1998. Some of the items listed were no doubt deployed against the BSA.

28.   Beale, *Bombs Over Bosnia,* 2, 20–21.

29.   At any given time in 1993, there were perhaps eighty to a hundred wounded or sick Croats in the Novi Bila hospital. Serious casualties apparently were evacuated by helicopter from the Kiseljak area (see Medical Corps of the Ban Josip Jelacic Brigade to Dr. Ivo Sandrak, Mostar Medical Sector, HVO Department of Defense, Kiseljak, June 23, 1993, subj: Report, B D257, which discusses the delivery of medical supplies by helicopter from Divulje and provides a list of the seriously ill and wounded for whom adequate care could not be provided in Kiseljak). On the arrangements for the use of HV helicopters for medical evacuation from central Bosnia, see Drago Nakic, Kordic-Cerkez trial testimony, Sept. 18, 2000. Nakic was a midlevel executive of SPS Vitezit Cromen, the explosives firm located just outside Vitez. In October, 1992, he was sent to Split to coordinate SPS activities there. He later assumed responsibility for overseeing welfare activities to aid Croat refugees from central Bosnia using SPS resources and funds supplied by the Croat communities in the Lasva Valley.

30.   Drago Nakic, Kordic-Cerkez trial testimony, Sept. 18, 2000.

31.   At the end of July, 1993, the UNPROFOR Bosnia-Herzegovina Command

reported that "the HVO are running out of munitions." See HQ, BHC (UNPRO-FOR), Daily INFOSUM, July 31, 1993, para. 4a, KC Z2433–1. The last HVO supply line to Herzegovina, which ran through Sebesic, was cut by the ABiH on the night of July 2, 1993 (see 1PWO MILINFOSUM no. 68, July 6, 1993, KC D58/2).

32.   Zeko, Blaskic trial testimony, Sept. 22, 1998. For resupply of the HVO in central Bosnia by helicopter see, among others, Blaskic, Blaskic trial testimony, Mar. 26, 1999; 1CSG MILINFOSUM no. 65, Jan. 4, 1994, para. 2, KC Z2447.3; HQ, BHC (UNPROFOR), Daily INFOSUM, July 31, 1993, para. 4a, KC Z2433–1; and Williams, "Balkan Winter," Nov. 14 and Dec. 3, 1993.

33.   Brigadier Ivica Zeko, conversation with author, Split, Aug. 27, 1999.

Chapter 5. Prelude to Civil War in Central Bosnia

1.   Memorandum, The First Vitez Brigade, Vitez, n.d. (1992), subj: Proposal to establish the Command of the unit, B D18. The Crisis Staff was an HVO instrumentality.

2.   HZ HB Municipal Headquarters Busovaca, no. 62/92, Busovaca, 0120, May 10, 1992, subj: Order, KC Z100.

3.   O'Ballance, *Civil War in Bosnia,* 48.

4.   By prior agreement, the HVO and the TO were to share the JNA weapons and equipment, but Muslims led by Dzemal Merdan acted to seize them all. See HZ HB Municipal Headquarters Busovaca, no. 62/92, KC Z100.

5.   HQ, HVO Command Central Bosnia, Vitez, 1207, Oct. 20, 1992, subj: Report on the Situation in Novi Travnik and Travnik, KC Z241; HQ, ECMM Policy and Coordination Cell, Daily Monitoring Report for 20–21 June 1992, n.p. (Zagreb), June 22, 1992, KC Z137.

6.   Filipovic, Kordic-Cerkez trial testimony, Apr. 11, 2000; Witness V, Kordic-Cerkez trial testimony, Nov. 25, 1999. Witness V, a Bosnian Muslim, was a member of the TO forces in Donja Veceriska.

7.   Central Bosnia HQ, HVO, no. 01–513/92, Busovaca, Sept. 22, 1992, subj: Excerpt from the Minutes of the Meeting of Croatian Defense Councils in Municipalities of Central Bosnia, 22 Sept. 1992, KC Z223.

8.   Zeko, Blaskic trial testimony, Sept. 11, 1998; Vulliamy, *Seasons in Hell,* 230. O'Ballance is thoroughly confused about the incident, which he describes as a Croat seizure of "a government fuel convoy" (*Civil War in Bosnia,* 113).

9.   Ljubas, Kordic-Cerkez trial testimony, May 16, 2000; Filipovic, Kordic-Cerkez trial testimony, Apr. 11, 2000.

10.   Zeko, Blaskic trial testimony, Sept. 11, 1998.

11.   Office of the Centre of the Institute for the Investigation of Crimes against Humanity and International Law, no. 60–16.02, n.p., Feb. 16, 1994, subj: Statement of Fuad Berbic, reproduced as Presidency of Bosnia and Herzegovina, State Commission for Gathering Facts on War Crimes no. 3611/94, Statement of Fuad Berbic, 4, 5, KC D13/2. Berbic, a Muslim who attained the rank of captain first class in the old JNA Territorial Defense organization, was commander of the TO in Ahmici until September, 1992.

12.   Zeko, Blaskic trial testimony, Sept. 23, 1998.

13.   Stewart, Blaskic trial testimony, June 17, 1999. The HVO detachment involved went on to Jajce, not to Novi Travnik, once the road opened.

14.   Maj. Sulejman Kalco, Kordic-Cerkez trial testimony, Mar. 7, 2000. Kalco was deputy commander of the Muslim forces in Stari Vitez in 1993. He later retired from the Federation army.

15.   Stewart diary, end of Oct., 1992, §1, 23; idem., Blaskic trial testimony, June 17, 1999; Zeko conversation, Aug. 27, 1999.

16. O'Ballance, *Civil War in Bosnia,* 48.

17. Major Zeko, the HQ, OZCB, intelligence officer at the time, noted that although he mentioned to his superiors several times the growing disadvantage of the HVO position in the area due to Muslim infiltration and the positioning of ABiH forces to the rear of HVO units defending the front against the Serbs, there did not appear to be any urgent reaction on the part of the HVO leadership (conversation with author, Split, Aug. 17, 1999).

18. Later, both Maj. Ljubas (Kordic-Cerkez trial testimony, May 16, 2000) and General Filipovic (Kordic-Cerkez trial testimony, Apr. 12, 2000) pointed to the arrival from Croatia in June, 1992, of the Muslim 1st and 7th Krajina Mountain Brigades (commanded by Mehmed Alagic and Fikret Cuskic, respectively) as the point at which Muslim-Croat relations in the Travnik area began to deteriorate.

19. Despite their aggressive intent, the Muslim forces were incapable of mounting a simultaneous attack on all HVO enclaves in central Bosnia. For that reason, Travnik, Novi Travnik, Zepce, and Vares (and to a certain extent the Kiseljak area) were not included in the April, 1993, main attack but were left for subsequent individual attacks. On Muslim objectives see, among others, Filipovic, Kordic-Cerkez trial testimony, Apr. 11, 2000; Franjo Nakic, Kordic-Cerkez trial testimony, Apr. 13, 2000; and especially Mehmed Alagic (with Nedzad Latic and Zehrudin Isakovic), *Ratna Sjecanja Mehmeda Alagica: Rat U Srednjoj Bosni* (*War Reminiscences of Mehmed Alagic: The War in Central Bosnia*), 18, 21, 24, and 28.

20. The Vance-Owen Peace Plan canton map was not agreed upon until January 10–12, 1993.

21. Halilovic, *Lukava strategija,* 78. See also the comments of journalist Edward Vulliamy regarding the "grand scheme" of Mehmed Alagic, a senior ABiH commander in central Bosnia, for "consolidation of the 'Muslim triangle' in Central Bosnia" (*Seasons in Hell,* 257–58).

22. U.S. Joint Chiefs of Staff, *Joint Pub 1–02,* 3, defines "active defense" as: "The employment of limited offensive action and counterattacks to deny a contested area or position to the enemy." Indeed, the former commander of OZ Northwest Herzegovina used the term in exactly its American sense to describe the series of small counterattacks and other offensive actions taken by the HVO in the Lasva-Kozica-Lepenica Valleys and elsewhere (Maj. Gen. Zeljko Siljeg, conversation with author, Medjugorje, Aug. 23, 1999).

23. Zeko conversation, Aug. 27, 1999.

Chapter 6. The ABiH Probing Attack, January, 1993

1. The refugees were used first to fill vacancies in existing ABiH units and then to form new units (Zeko conversation, Aug. 27, 1999). The positioning of ABiH units in early January, 1993, is depicted on a captured ABiH map entitled "Obostrani Raspored Snage u zoni 3. korpusa kraj decembra 1992. g.-januar 1993. god," KC D189/1. The map clearly depicts the locations of the 325th, 333d, and 309th Mountain Brigade and elements of the 7th Muslim Motorized Brigade, and shows that their orientation is toward the HVO rather the BSA.

2. Zeko, Blaskic trial testimony, Sept. 21, 1998.

3. Zeko, Kordic-Cerkez trial testimony, Sept. 21, 1998.

4. HQ, OZCB, no. 01–1-184/93, Vitez, Jan. 16, 1993, subj: Full combat readiness of all HVO formations in the Central Bosnia Operations Zone, KC Z370.

5. PPN "Vitezovi" (Dragan Vinac), no. 3–065/94, 4, KC Z1380.

6. Details regarding the events in Gornji Vakuf were obtained by the author in conversations with two former HVO combatants in Gornji Vakuf, Aug. 22, 1999.

7. Stewart diary, Wednesday, Jan. 13, 1993, §3, 1.

8. Zeko conversation, Aug. 27, 1999.

9. According to the former OZCB chief of staff, Brigadier Franjo Nakic, seventeen to thirty ABiH troops established the checkpoint at Kacuni with the aim of controlling an eleven-kilometer stretch of the main supply route between Busovaca and Kiseljak (Kordic-Cerkez trial testimony, Apr. 13, 2000).

10. Zeko, Blaskic trial testimony, Sept. 11 and 23, 1998.

11. HQ, Jure Francetic Brigade, Zenica, Jan. 27, 1993, subj: Report, KC D209/1; Col. Serif Patkovic, Blaskic trial testimony, June 10, 1999. Patkovic commanded the TO in Zenica and then the 2d Battalion, 7th Muslim Motorized Brigade. He subsequently served as the 7th Muslim Brigade chief of staff before assuming command of the brigade in April, 1994. He later served in the Federation army. See also Koricic, Blaskic trial testimony, June 10, 1999. Neither Patkovic nor Koricic has been indicted by the ICTY for their war crimes in Dusina and elsewhere.

12. Zeko, Blaskic trial testimony, Sept. 11, 1998.

13. Franjo Nakic, Kordic-Cerkez trial testimony, Apr. 13, 2000.

14. Ante Juric, former commander of the Zrinski Brigade's 1st Battalion, and a former Zrinski Brigade operations officer, conversation with author, Busovaca, Aug., 1999.

15. HQ, Nikola Subic Zrinski Brigade, no. 39/93, Busovaca, Jan. 6, 1993, subj: Estimation of ALLY Forces in Zone of Responsibility, B D187.

16. Stewart diary, Sunday, Jan. 24, 1993, §3, 7.

17. Brigadier Dusko Grubesic, Kordic-Cerkez trial testimony, Dec. 6, 2000. Grubesic commanded the Municipal Staff of the HVO Busovaca from June to October, 1992, and the Zrinski Brigade from February to October, 1993. He subsequently was chief of staff and then commander of the 3d Guards Brigade and rose to the rank of brigadier in the Federation army.

18. Zeko, Blaskic trial testimony, Sept. 21, 1998, concerning an Aug. 5, 1992, document issued by Kiseljak's Municipal Defense Staff related to the conduct of reconnaissance, collection of information, and preparation for combat operations to seize the key lines of communications in the area (B D185). In that same trial session, Zeko also referred to an even earlier document from the Kiseljak TO staff regarding the preparation of units for an attack (May 22, 1992, B D184). The HVO in Kiseljak had been successful in taking over most of the facilities and weapons left behind by the withdrawing JNA, and Muslim officials in the Kiseljak area were much chagrined (O'Ballance, *Civil War in Bosnia*, 49).

19. Stewart diary, Monday, Jan. 25, 1993, sec. 3, 8. Stewart's judgments were often admittedly presumptive. For example, in his diary entry for Friday, January 22, 1993, he notes that while en route back to Vitez from Gornji Vakuf, "we noticed that many of the houses in the village of Bistrica were ablaze. We *presumed* it was HVO ethnic cleansing" (ibid., §3, 6; emphasis added).

20. 1Cheshire MILINFOSUM no. 90, Jan. 29, 1993, KC Z417.1; British Broadcasting Company (BBC) Summary of World Broadcasts, "Muslim-Croat Conflict at Busovaca; Serbian Attack on Mostar" (from Croatian Radio Zagreb at 9 P.M. GMT, Jan. 27, 1993), n.p. (London), Jan. 29, 1993, KC Z414.

21. HQ, OZCB, no. 03–1-447/93, Vitez, Jan. 29, 1993, subj: Combat report on the situation in the area of responsibility of the N. S. Zrinski Brigade Busovaca and the Ban Jelacic Brigade Kiseljak on 29 Jan. 1993, B D409.

22. HQ, OZCB, no. 02–1-471/93, Vitez, 0815, Jan. 30, 1993, subj: Report, KC Z421.

23. Stewart, Blaskic trial testimony, June 17, 1999.

24. 1Cheshire MILINFOSUM no. 93, Feb. 1, 1993, B 512.

25. Order no. 01–131, HVO Main Staff, n.p. (Mostar), Feb. 11, 1993, B 456/9.

26.   See Orders no. 02/33–431–02/33–438, HQ, HVO OZCB/HQ, ABiH III Corps, Kakanj, Febr. 13, 1993, (B D351 et seq.).

27.   HQ, OZCB, no. 01–2-05, Vitez, Feb. 4, 1993, subj: Overcoming the Current Crisis, KC Z439; HQ, OZCB, no. 01–2-134/93, Vitez, 1230, Feb. 13, 1993, subj: Organisational order for further action, KC Z464.

28.   Official Note, HQ, 4th Military Police Battalion, Vitez, Feb. 2, 1993, B D214.

29.   HQ, OZCB, no. 01–1-217/1/93, Vitez, 1100, Feb. 6, 1993, subj: Warning for failure to carry out the command no. 01–1-217/93 from 10 Jan. 1993, B D208.

30.   Public Announcement, Novi Travnik HVO Press Service, Novi Travnik, 4 P.M., Feb. 10, 1993, B D218.

31.   HQ, Viteska Brigade, Vitez, Mar. 16, 1993, subj: Report by officers on duty on 15 and 16 Mar. 1993, B D209.

32.   SIS, 4th Military Police Battalion, no. 80/93, Vitez, Mar. 1, 1993, subj: Information about the persons who organized an attack on MUP and the Military Police in Vitez, B D213.

33.   HQ, OZCB, Vitez, 1200, Mar. 17, 1993, subj: Treatment of Persons Inclined towards Criminal and Destructive Conduct, KC Z550 and KC D17/1.18. See also the implementing orders issued by the Viteska Brigade (no. 01–18–1/93, Vitez, Mar. 18, 1993, KC Z553), and the 1st Battalion, Viteska Brigade (no. 1–1/93, Vitez, Mar. 19, 1993, KC Z554).

34.   Stewart diary, Thursday, Feb. 4, 1993, sec. 3, 15. Stewart was able to reach Katici, which was held by the HVO, but observed no fighting. He was unable to reach Merdani, which was held by the ABiH.

35.   Report, HQ, 2d Battalion, Stjepan Tomasevic Brigade (Ivan Budimir, administrative assistant for the SIS), Vitez, Feb. 12, 1993, subj: Report on the arrest of HVO Soldiers, B D219.

36.   Letter no. 480/93 (handwritten), HQ, N. S. Zrinski Brigade (Dusko Grubesic) to ECMM, 1 (NL/BE) UN Transport Battalion; and HQ, OZCB Vitez, Busovaca, Mar. 13, 1993, subj: Protest because of breaking the ceasefire, B D415. Grubesic also noted that Muslim forces were firing with small arms from Peznin and Gornji Rovena at HVO positions in the villages of Donja Rovna, Bare, and Roske Stigene, as well as with an antiaircraft machine gun at the same location and at 10:30 P.M. from the direction of Merdani at HVO positions in the village of Gavrine Kuce. Tracer ammunition set fire to two Muslim houses in the latter village.

37.   Report no. 02–4/3–07–459/93, HQ, 4th Military Police Battalion (Pasko Ljubicic) to Department of Military Police–Mostar, Vitez, Mar. 18, 1993, B D509.

38.   Commander, HVO OZCB, to commander, ABiH III Corps, Vitez, Mar. 29, 1993, subj: Protest in connection with the murder of members of HVO VP, B D261. In his letter of protest, Colonel Blaskic asked the III Corps commander to clarify the status of the 7th Muslim Brigade within III Corps and that the brigade be dissolved "because it harbours confirmed enemies of the Croatian people."

39.   HQ, Viteska Brigade, subj: Report by officers, B D209.

40.   Zeko, Blaskic trial testimony, Sept. 11, 1998.

41.   Ibid., Sept. 21, 1998. The document in question is HQ, OZCB, "Minutes re Evaluation of Newly-Established Military Security Situation in the Area of Hazdjici, Jablanica, and Konjic," no. 16–8/08–62/93, n.p. (Vitez), Mar. 20, 1993, B D191.

Chapter 7. The ABiH Main Attack, April, 1993: The Vitez Area

1.   Stewart, Blaskic trial testimony, June 18, 1999.

2.   Military Intelligence Service, HQ, OZCB, no. 205–8-I/93, Vitez, Mar. 25, 1993, subj: Estimation of Possible Activities by a Potential Aggressor in the Territories

of the Central Bosnia Operative Zone, B D190. It should be noted that Zeko's analysis was contemporary and not an ex post facto rationalization.

3.   Ibid., 1.

4.   Zeko noted in his estimate that open clashes in Novi Travnik would trigger an attack on the town by Muslim forces from Kasapovici (Isakovici) and Trenica with support from Opara through Pecuj and Rastovci, while forces from Vodovod and Senkovici would attack Margetici and Bratstvo to take control of the town (ibid., 4). The attackers might also be expected to move forces from Travnik to seize the HVO logistics base as well as Bucici and Stojkovici thereby linking their forces.

5.   Ibid., 4–5.

6.   Assistant chief of the Military Intelligence Service (Zeljko Katava), Nikola Subic Zrinski Brigade, no. 241/93, Busovaca, Mar. 14, 1993, subj: Report, B D193.

7.   Ibid., no. 39/93, 1, B D 187; Zeko, Blaskic trial testimony, Sept. 21, 1998.

8.   Zeko, Blaskic trial testimony, Sept. 11 and 21, 1998; HQ, ABiH III Corps, no. 02/33–867 (to commander, 303d Mountain Brigade), Zenica, Apr. 16, 1993, subj: Order to Move Out and Occupy Positions, KC Z673 and KC D190/1.

9.   HQ, 4th Military Police Battalion, no. 02–4/3–07–677/93, Vitez, Apr. 14, 1993, subj: Report on the work in the period 1–11 Apr. 1993, B D499.

10.   Ibid., 10; Ljubas, Kordic-Cerkez trial testimony, May 16, 2000.

11.   1Cheshire MILINFOSUM no. 160, Apr. 8, 1993, KC Z623. A number of sources attribute the flag incident to a visit to Travnik by Mate Boban on April 8, but Boban did not visit Travnik on that date. See Filipovic, Kordic-Cerkez trial testimony, Apr. 11, 2000; and Ljubas, Kordic-Cerkez trial testimony, May 17, 2000.

12.   1Cheshire MILINFOSUM no. 160, KC Z623; HQ, 4th Military Police Battalion, no. 02–4/3–07–677/93, B D499.

13.   HQ, 4th Military Police Battalion, no. 02–4/3–07–677/93, B D499.

14.   HVO Travnik, no. HVO-01–582/93, to the presidents of Croatia, the HZ HB, and the HVO, Travnik, Apr. 12, 1993, subj: Report of the Travnik HVO on the armed conflicts in Travnik before and during Easter festivities, KC Z647. The letter contains a detailed account of the April 8–12 conflict in Travnik and calls upon Croatian president Franjo Tudjman to deny passage through Croatia to "foreign citizens from Islamic and Arab countries using the Republic of Croatia as a transit area to enter Bosnia and Herzegovina in order to fight in the units of the BH Army against everything that is Croatian and Christian" (ibid., 2–3).

15.   "Book of Observations of the Officer on Duty in the Central Bosnia Operative Zone, 11 January 1993–15 May 1993," entry for 4:20 P.M., Apr. 13, 1993, KC Z610.1, 64 (hereafter cited as "OZCB Duty Officer Log"). One of the kidnapped HVO officers, Zdravko Kovac, provided details of the kidnapping during a conversation with the author in Vitez, August 20, 1999.

16.   HQ, OZCB, no. 07–4-190/93, Vitez, 1030, Apr. 14, 1993, subj: Pursuit for kidnapped officers of Headquarters of the Brigade "Stjepan Tomasevic," Novi Travnik, B D263.

17.   Commander, Stjepan Tomasevic Brigade, to commander, OZCB, no. P-622/93, Novi Travnik, 0100, Apr. 18, 1993, subj: Disappearance of Stjepan Tomasevic Brigade officers, B D303. Sabljic also reported that on April 16 the ECMM representative stated his belief that the EC representative should withdraw from the joint commission and that "all further action should be taken by professional organizations."

18.   Stewart, Blaskic trial testimony, June 17, 1999.

19.   A full account of the rather bizarre exchange is given in ECMM Regional Center Zenica (Dieter Schellschmidt) to HQ, ECMM Zagreb, Zenica, May 19, 1993, subj: Exchange of Detained Arabian Foreigners and HVO Hostages, KC D79/1.

20. Grubesic, Kordic-Cerkez trial testimony, Dec. 6, 2000; Slavko Jukic, Kordic-Cerkez trial testimony, July 25, 2000. As commander of the Zrinski Brigade in Busovaca, Grubesic was responsible for the defense of Mount Kuber and its environs. Slavko Jukic, a member of the HVO Home Guard, spent ten months in HVO defensive positions on Mount Kuber after April 16, 1993.

21. Maj. Anto Bertovic, Kordic-Cerkez trial testimony, Oct. 4–5, 2000. Bertovic estimated that at the beginning of April, 1993, the overall ratio of ABiH to HVO forces in the Lasva Valley was probably four to one. A 1990 graduate of the military academy in Sarajevo, Bertovic commanded the Tomasevic Brigade's 2d Battalion from December, 1992, to mid-March, 1993, when it became the Viteska Brigade's 1st Battalion. He continued to command the battalion throughout the Muslim-Croat civil war and subsequently served as a major in the Federation army.

22. PPN "Vitezovi" (Dragan Vinac), no. 3–065/94, Vitez, Feb. 18, 1994, subj: Report, KC Z1380, 2. The total number of men in the "Tvrtko II" special purpose unit is unknown but was probably quite small. As of February 15, 1993, the 4th Military Police Battalion had a total authorized strength of eighty officers and 640 men, but the MPs were distributed throughout the OZCB and only a small portion were available in the immediate Vitez area. See commander, 4th Military Police Battalion (Pasko Ljubicic) to Military Police Administration, Mostar, no. 02–4/3–07–190/93, Vitez, Feb. 15, 1993, subj: (Military Police Payroll), found with KC Z610.1.

23. HQ, OZCB, Vitez, 1000, Apr. 15, 1993, subj: Preparatory Combat Command for the Defense of HVO and the Town of Vitez from Extremist Mudjahedin-Muslim Forces, KC Z660.1.

24. The ABiH 325th Mountain Brigade's 1st Battalion occupied Kruscica, located two kilometers south-southwest of Vitez at the southern terminus of the principal axis of advance of Muslim forces attacking from north of the Travnik–Kaonik road. Anto Bertovic, the battalion commander, managed to mobilize about eighty men and deployed them in four groups on the high ground and across the roads leading to Vitez from the villages of Kruscica, Vranjska, and Rijeka. At the Hotel Ribnjak in Kruscica, fifty HVO troops preparing to relieve the shift then on duty in the lines facing the BSA were surrounded by the ABiH but subsequently managed to exfiltrate out of Kruscica into the HVO lines (Bertovic, Kordic-Cerkez trial testimony; Capt. Vlado Taraba, Kordic-Cerkez trial testimony, Sept. 18–19, 2002; Maj. Zeljko Sajevic, Kordic-Cerkez trial testimony, July 25–27, 1993). Taraba was the operations officer (S3) of the 1st Battalion, Viteska Brigade. A graduate of the University of Sarajevo, he later served as a captain in the Federation army.

25. Sajevic, Kordic-Cerkez trial testimony, July 25–27, 2000. The Viteska Brigade's sector defense arrangement was formalized on April 21, 1993, when Cerkez formally appointed sector commanders and defined the extent of the five sectors, each of which had several subsectors. The 1st Mosunj Sector, commanded by Slavko Badrov, included Mali Mosunj, Veliki Mosunj, Stari Bila, Zabilje, Jardol, Divjak, and Brdo. The 2d Krcevine Sector, commanded by Anto Bertovic, included Krcevine, Krizancevo Selo, and Dubravica. The 3d Sljivicica Sector, also commanded by Anto Bertovic, included Sljivicica, Santici, Nadioici in depth, and Safradinovo. The 4th Kruscica Sector, commanded by Karlo Grabovic, included Kruscica, Rijeka, Previla, and Vranjska. The 5th Zabrde Sector, commanded by Ivica Drmic, included Donja Veceriska, Gornja Veceriska, Gacice, Zaselje, and Zabrde (commander, Viteska Brigade, no. 01–147–1/93, Vitez, Apr. 21, 1993, subj: Order on the appointment of sector commanders, KC Z765.1).

26. HQ, OZCB, Vitez, 10 A.M., April 15, 1993, KC Z660.1.

27. The HVO Main Staff apparently informed HQ, OZCB, of the forthcoming attack

after making a number of communications intercepts (Bertovic, Kordic-Cerkez trial testimony; *OZCB Duty Officer Log,* 70–71). Communications intercepts were a common form of intelligence collection used extensively by both sides.

28.   HQ, OZCB, Vitez, 0345, Apr. 15, 1993, subj: Order to take action, KC Z660.

29.   U.S. Joint Chiefs of Staff, *Joint Pub 1–02,* defines *Active defense* as "the employment of limited offensive action and counterattacks to deny a contested area or position to the enemy." A *spoiling attack* is "A tactical maneuver employed to seriously impair a hostile attack while the enemy is in the process of forming and assembling for an attack." A *preemptive attack* is defined as "An attack initiated on the basis of incontrovertible evidence that an enemy attack is imminent." Both are legitimate military operations, but to an observer imperfectly informed as to the overall operational situation, either might appear to be entirely offensive in nature. However, although by definition both are "attacks," both are essentially defensive operations, designed to prevent the success of a planned enemy attack and to preserve the defensive position intact (ibid. 3, 195, 355).

30.   Among those tried and convicted of war crimes related to the Ahmici incident are: Maj. Gen. Tihomir Blaskic, then commander of the OZCB; Dario Kordic, then a prominent Croat politician in the Lasva Valley; Mario Cerkez, then commander of the Viteska Brigade; Vladimir Santic, then commander of the 1st Company, 4th Military Police Battalion; and Anto Furundzija, then commander of the antiterrorist platoon, 4th Military Police Battalion. Among the HVO soldiers tried, Dragan Papic was acquitted; Drago Josipovic was convicted; and the convictions of Zoran Kupreskic, Mirjan Kupreskic, and Vlatko Kupreskic were overturned on appeal. The trial of Pasko Ljubicic, then commander of the 4th Military Police Battalion, is pending.

31.   See, among others, Filipovic, Kordic-Cerkez trial testimony, Apr. 11, 2000. The matter was apparently not even discussed at ABiH-HVO Joint Commission meetings (Franjo Nakic, Kordic-Cerkez trial testimony, Apr. 14, 2000). Even Stewart did not mention Ahmici in his diary until April 22, well after the event. See Stewart diary, Apr. 22, 1993, sec. 3, 41: "ABiH reluctant to withdraw due to claimed incident at Ahinici [Ahmici]."

32.   Even UNPROFOR officers have stated that the village had military significance. See, for example, Lt. Col. Bryan S. C. Watters, Kordic-Cerkez trial testimony, July 29, 1999. Watters was deputy commander of the 1st Battalion, 22d (Cheshire) Regiment, the British UNPROFOR unit in the Lasva Valley in April, 1993. Both the deputy commander and chief of staff of the OZCB identified the Ahmici-Santici area as the narrowest part of the Croat Vitez enclave and thus of supreme military significance (Filipovic, Kordic-Cerkez trial testimony, Apr. 11, 2000; Franjo Nakic, Kordic-Cerkez trial testimony, Apr. 13, 2000).

33.   Military Intelligence Service, HQ, OZCB, no. 205–8-I/93; assistant chief of Military Intelligence Service (Zeljko Katava), Nikola Subic Zrinski Brigade no. 241/93.

34.   In a letter to Vinko Puljic, the Catholic archbishop of Bosnia, Enver Hadzihasanovic, the ABiH III Corps commander, lied outright in stating: "there were no military formations in the village and no resistance was offered" (commander, ABiH III Corps to Monsignor Vinko Puljic, Archbishop of Bosnia, Zenica, Apr. 19, 1993, KC Z737.2).

35.   Captured ABiH map entitled "Obostrani Raspored Snaga u zoni 3. korpusa kraj decembra 1992. g.-januar 1993. god"; Enes Varupa notebook, entry for Apr. 11, 1993, B D17. Varupa was a member of the Muslim TO in the Lasva Valley. His notebook was captured by the HVO at Grbavica later in 1993.

36.   Zeko, Blaskic trial testimony, Sept. 23, 1998.

37. Statement of Fuad Berbic, 5. Berbic had commanded the Muslim TO forces in Ahmici in 1992. The fortification of Ahmici before April 16 was also confirmed by the testimony of Witness CW1 in the Blaskic trial (not seen, but cited in ICTY, *Judgement* [sic] *in the case of Prosecutor vs. Dario Kordic and Mario Cerkez* [*Case No. IT-95–14/2-T*], n.p. [The Hague, Feb. 26, 2001], 212 (hereafter Kordic-Cerkez *Judgment*).

38. For the 325th Mountain Brigade, see HQ, OZCB, Situation Report for the Area of Vitez Municipality, no. 04–135–1/93, n.p. (Vitez), Apr. 10, 1993, B D192; Zeko, Blaskic trial testimony, Sept. 11 and 21, 1998. For the 303d Mountain Brigade, see HQ, ABiH III Corps, no. 02/33–867, Zenica, Apr. 16, 1993, subj: Order—To Move Out and Occupy Positions, KC Z673 and KC D190/1; and HQ, 303d Slavna "Glorious" Mountain Brigade, no. 01/2524–1, Zenica, noon, Apr. 16, 1993, subj: Order for Attack, KC Z674.

39. Report on the Ahmici attack by Anto Sliskovic, SIS officer at HQ, OZCB, May 25, 1993, KC Z975.1 (not seen, but cited in Kordic-Cerkez *Judgement*, 203); Statement of Fuad Berbic, 5.

40. Witness AT, Kordic-Cerkez trial testimony, Nov. 27, 2000, as cited in Kordic-Cerkez *Judgment*, 213. Witness AT was a senior member of the 4th Military Police Battalion and was present in Ahmici on April 16. He testified in a private session late in the Kordic-Cerkez trial, and although referred to in the Kordic-Cerkez *Judgment*, his testimony is not available on the ICTY Internet site. The Kordic-Cerkez defense team impugned Witness AT's character and veracity, but the prosecutor and the trial chamber relied heavily upon his testimony. His allegations regarding the attack's planning and the supposed orders of senior HVO commanders are probably false, but his narration of some of the events leading up to the attack and of the assault itself is credible.

41. Ibid., 201–202. The "Bungalow" was also known as the "Swiss chalet."

42. Kordic-Cerkez Exhibit Z676, as cited in Kordic-Cerkez *Judgement*, 206.

43. According to Witness AT, Pasko Ljubicic told the assault force that Colonel Blaskic had ordered all the Muslim men in the village to be killed, the houses set afire, and the civilians spared. Given the unreliability of Witness AT on such matters, it is doubtful that Blaskic ever issued such instructions (Kordic-Cerkez trial testimony, Nov. 27, 2000 [as cited in Kordic-Cerkez *Judgement*, 203]).

44. Ibid., 207. Colonel Bob Stewart also offered the opinion that the assault probably started at the Travnik–Busovaca road or perhaps at the "Bungalow" (Blaskic trial testimony, June 17–18, 1999).

45. "When the attack commenced our guards and reinforcements in the lower part of Ahmici engaged in combat" (Statement of Fuad Berbic, 5). See also Witness AT, Kordic-Cerkez trial testimony, Nov. 27, 2000, as cited in Kordic-Cerkez *Judgment*, 213.

46. HQ, 4th Military Police Battalion, Vitez, April 16, 1993, subj: Report, B D280; Witness AT, Kordic-Cerkez trial testimony, Nov. 27, 2000, as cited in Kordic-Cerkez *Judgement*, 213. Witness AT stated that the mosque was used as a strong point and that there was an observation post and heavy machine gun located in the minaret (ibid., 207). Antitank rockets hit the mosque during the attack and the minaret collapsed. Colonel Stewart testified in the Blaskic trial that he found reports of the use of the mosque as a strong point incredible "because mosques are rotten places to defend." However, mosques were frequently used as hiding places, assembly areas, command posts, and storage areas for arms and ammunition for Muslim forces throughout the central Bosnia area. That some of the Muslim forces in Ahmici, under heavy ground attack, should have barricaded themselves in the mosque (and elementary school) is, in fact, consistent with reports from other areas during the period.

47. See director, Croatian Information Service (HIS) (Dr. Miroslav Tudjman) to

President of the Republic of Croatia (Dr. Franjo Tudjman), no. 716–2412-E-03/94–052, n.p. (Zagreb), Mar. 21, 1994, subj: The Massacre at Ahmici, KC Z1406.1. Tudjman's report noted that the behavior of two of the attackers, Miroslav "Cicko" Bralo and Ivica "Sjano" Antolovic, both recently released from Kaonik Prison where they had been serving sentences for murder, "was extremely uncontrolled." The report also exonerated Mario Cerkez, the commander of the Viteska Brigade, from any responsibility for the attack on Ahmici. Pasko Ljubicic, the 4th Military Police Battalion commander, rationalized the attack by reporting to Colonel Blaskic that the assault on Ahmici developed following a failed Muslim attack on HVO military police in the Bungalow (HQ, 4th Military Police Battalion, Apr. 16, 1993).

48.   Statement of Fuad Berbic, 5–6. Forty conscripts from the Viteska Brigade relieved the 4th Military Police Battalion's assault elements around midday on April 18. See commander, OZCB, to commander, Viteska Brigade, no. 01-4-344/93, n.p. (Vitez), Apr. 18, 1993, subj: Providing Personnel for Relief on the Line of the Military Police to Enable Rest, found with KC Z610.1.

49.   Based on the accounts of Muslims who escaped the carnage, 103 people were killed, six were missing, and forty-nine were taken to the Dubravica camp. See Humanitarian Section, ECMM Regional Center Zenica (Charles McLeod), "Inter-Ethnic Violence in Vitez, Busovaca and Zenica—April 1993," Zenica, May 17, 1993, App. 2 to Annex N, N2–1, KC Z926. See also Stewart diary, Thursday, Apr. 29, 1993, sec. 3, 48; and idem., Blaskic trial testimony, June 17, 1999, where the Ahmici casualty estimate prepared by Thomas Osorio and Payam Akhavan of the UN Center for Human Rights is stated as 103 killed and thirty-five missing. There were approximately eight hundred inhabitants in the village.

50.   On March 16, 1968, elements of the U.S. 23d (American) Infantry Division ran amok in the South Vietnamese hamlet of My Lai killing between 175 and four hundred Vietnamese civilians, including women and children (see John W. Chambers II, ed., *The Oxford Companion to American Military History,* 461–62). On June 9, 1942, Adolf Hitler ordered the destruction of the Czech village of Lidice near Prague in retaliation for the assassination of Reinhard Heydrich. The village was razed, 198 men were shot in cold blood, and the women and children were sent to concentration camps (see Dear. ed., *Oxford Companion to World War II,* 839–40). Two years later, on June 10, 1944, elements of the 2d SS Panzer Division incarcerated the inhabitants of the French village of Oradour-sur-Glane in the village church and several barns, which were then burned to the ground, killing some 642 persons (see ibid., 690).

51.   Details of the events in Donja Veceriska from December, 1992, through April, 1993, are drawn primarily from Bono Drmic, Kordic-Cerkez trial testimony, Sept. 27, 2000; and Witness V, Kordic-Cerkez trial testimony, Nov. 25, 1999. In 1993, Drmic, a Bosnian Croat, was a firefighter at the SPS factory and a resident of Donja Veceriska. It should be noted that there is an important distinction between the English words *clearing* and *cleansing,* a distinction not always reflected by the interpreters in trials before the ICTY when translating the BCS word *ciscenje.* In American military parlance, the term *clearing operation* implies a legitimate local offensive operation designed to clear enemy armed forces from key terrain.

52.   HVO Reserve Group–Donja Veceriska, no. 04/4/93, n.p. (Donja Veceriska), Mar. 14, 1993, subj: Estimate of security situation and the plan for securing the Croat population from Donja Veceriska and the evacuation of that population, B D536; HVO Reserve Force–Donja Veceriska, no. 05–5/93, Donja Veceriska, Mar. 16, 1993, subj: Decisions taken with respect to the security of Donja Veceriska, B D210. Before the deterioration of Croat-Muslim relations in Donja Veceriska, the Muslims and Croats had devised a joint plan for evacuating civilians in the event of a Serb attack, and to that end had prepositioned three tents with supplies in the nearby woods.

53.   Varupa notebook. See Zeko, Blaskic trial testimony, Sept. 22, 1998.

54.   Conversation with a Croat inhabitant of Donja Veceriska, Vitez, August, 1999. Witness V testified that the Muslim defenders numbered only forty to fifty men but that other members of the TO were manning the lines against the Serbs. Under cross-examination, Witness V also admitted that the Muslim forces in Donja Veceriska had some forty-two rifles (Kordic-Cerkez trial testimony, Nov. 25, 1999).

55.   Bono Drmic, Kordic-Cerkez trial testimony. Drmic left the SPS factory firehouse at about 7:30 A.M. and encountered the hastily assembled HVO force as he entered the village. Five Muslims (four males and one female) were in the house.

56.   HQ, Viteska Brigade, no. 01–125–23/93, Vitez, 0600, Apr. 18, 1993, subj: Operations Report for the period midnight to 0600, B D307; Bono Drmic, Kordic-Cerkez trial testimony. The UNPROFOR forces in central Bosnia routinely evacuated wounded Muslims to hospitals and Muslim civilians to places of safety but refused to perform the same services for Croats. See, among others, the complaints recorded April 17–19 in *OZCB Duty Officer Log*, 109, 112, 119, 126, 128–129, 139.

57.   At 1:06 P.M., an element of the British UNPROFOR battalion reported about twelve HVO soldiers assaulting from house to house in the village. See 1Cheshire MILINFOSUM no. 170, Apr. 18, 1993, Item I, para. 1, KC Z722.

58.   Witness V, Kordic-Cerkez trial testimony, Nov. 25, 1999.

59.   Details of the Gacice action are based primarily on Nikola Mlakic, Kordic-Cerkez trial testimony, Sept. 21, 2000; Witness AP, Kordic-Cerkez trial testimony, Mar. 7, 2000; and a conversation with Carlo Grabovac, commander of the 1st Battalion, Viteska Brigade, Vitez, Aug., 1999. On April 16, Mlakic was a member of the Croat village guards in the nearby hamlet of Kamenjace and participated in the HVO assault on April 19. He later commanded the 4th Company of the Viteska Brigade's 4th Battalion. Witness AP was a Muslim resident of Gacice who served for three years as an interpreter for UNPROFOR forces in the Lasva Valley.

60.   Filipovic, Kordic-Cerkez trial testimony, Apr. 12, 2000.

61.   Witness AP stated that during the fighting in Gacice on April 19, 1993, there were only 25 armed Muslim men in town. However, during Witness AP's cross-examination, Mario Cerkez's defense counsel noted that Nesad Hrustic, the Muslim TO commander in Gacice, had indicated that the total was probably closer to 60, including some 40 men who withdrew into the nearby forest, 15 men who surrendered to the HVO, and 3 who were killed in the course of the fight. Nesad Hrustic was not called to testify in the Kordic-Cerkez trial inasmuch as his testimony would probably not have supported the prosecution's case.

62.   Varupa notebook. During the cross-examination of Witness AP (Kordic-Cerkez trial, Mar. 7, 2000), Mario Cerkez's defense counsel referred to a statement by Nesad Hrustic that the Gacice TO had two mortars and some thirty-eight rifles.

63.   Nikola Mlakic testified that shortly before the outbreak of fighting in the Vitez area on April 16, the Muslim mayor of Gacice, Sabahudin Hrustic, taunted the town's Croat residents by saying to them in effect, "Why are you Croats hanging around here? The III Corps will be here tomorrow" (Kordic-Cerkez trial testimony, Sept. 21, 2000).

64.   A videotape of the Muslims entrenching in Gacice was reportedly made, but the tape was allegedly turned over to the ICTY and has not been seen since.

65.   Mlakic, Kordic-Cerkez trial testimony, Sept. 21, 2000. Witness AP stated that an HVO soldier told her that the 303d Split Brigade and the 125th Varazdin Brigade of the Croatian Army also participated in the Gacice fighting (Kordic-Cerkez trial testimony, Mar. 7, 2000). However, during Witness AP's cross-examination,

Mario Cerkez's defense counsel noted that Nesad Hrustic had stated that he saw no Croat forces in Gacice. In any event, no such named units ever existed in the Croatian Army.

66.   In fact, during the April fighting, the Viteska Brigade's command post received three rounds of 82-mm recoilless rifle fire from Gacice, and a number of Croat civilians in Vitez were killed by mortar fire from the village. See HQ, Viteska Brigade, no. 02–125–34/93, Vitez, Apr. 20, 1993, subj: Operations Report, KC Z751.

67.   Nikola Mlakic tried to take two wounded Muslim acquaintances to medical aid, but UNPROFOR personnel would not let them pass. See Mlakic, Kordic-Cerkez trial testimony, Sept. 21, 2000.

68.   Ljubomir Pavlovic, Kordic-Cerkez trial testimony, Oct. 5, 2000. Pavlovic was a Croat businessman in Stari Vitez.

69.   Military Intelligence Service, Viteska Brigade, Vitez, Apr. 22, 1992, subj: Report, B D195. Brigadier Franjo Nakic, the former OZCB chief of staff, said the ABiH 325th Mountain Brigade had 600–700 men in Stari Vitez and that they were well-armed before April 16 (Kordic-Cerkez trial testimony, Apr. 13, 2000). Sulejman Kalco, the deputy commander of TO forces in Stari Vitez, stated that there were 256 ABiH soldiers in Stari Vitez (Kordic-Cerkez trial testimony, Mar. 7–8, 2000). Nihad Rebihic, the Stari Vitez TO intelligence officer, put the number at 325 armed men—including 30 military policemen, 30 armed civilian policemen, and several ABiH soldiers "just passing through" Stari Vitez "on their way to the front at Visoko and Vlasic" (Kordic-Cerkez trial testimony, Oct. 13–14, 2000). The TO headquarters in Stari Vitez was subordinate to the ABiH 325th Mountain Brigade, commanded by Sefkija Djidic.

70.   Military Intelligence Service, Viteska Brigade, Vitez, Apr. 22, 1992, B D195; Kalco, Kordic-Cerkez trial testimony, Mar. 7–8, 2000; Rebihic, Kordic-Cerkez trial testimony, Oct. 13–14, 2000.

71.   Commander, OZCB (Col. Tihomir Blaskic), order issued at 1:30 A.M., Apr. 16, 1993, KC Z676, as cited in Kordic-Cerkez *Judgment*, 206.

72.   On July 18, the Vitezovi mounted a major assault on the Muslim enclave between 4:15 A.M. and 6 P.M. The unit advanced from the direction of the SPS factory behind an armored bulldozer that was hit by an ABiH rocket-propelled grenade. The assault was unsuccessful, and the HVO lost twenty-seven men in this attempt to reduce the Muslim pocket (Kalco, Kordic-Cerkez trial testimony, Mar. 7–8, 2000).

73.   Ibid. Kalco stated that Muslims in Stari Vitez purchased ammunition from HVO soldiers. A senior ABiH commander, Mehmed Alagic, boasted in his memoir that the ABiH was able to supply ammunition to the Muslims in Stari Vitez with the help of UNPROFOR (see Alagic et al., *Ratna Sjecanja,* 28). One humorous incident occurred in the resupply of Stari Vitez. In December, 1993, the ABiH extorted a truckload of coal and a truckload of food from the Croat "White Road" relief convoy before allowing it to pass Vitez. When the truck carrying food was opened, the Muslims discovered that 80 percent of its contents was canned pork. British UNPROFOR officers considered the Croat "trick" to be some sort of war crime, but the inhabitants of Stari Vitez probably ate the pork with relish as Bosnian Muslims were notoriously lax in their observance of Islamic dietary rules (Williams, "Balkan Winter," Dec. 20, 1993). Former British army captain Lee Whitworth, the BRITBAT liaison officer in the Vitez area from June until November, 1993, testified about an incident in which ammunition hidden in bandages was brought into Stari Vitez by a BRITBAT armored vehicle (Kordic-Cerkez trial testimony, Oct. 18, 1999).

74.   The Vitezovi alone lost seven KIA and twenty-two WIA from April 16–25, mostly in the lines around Stari Vitez. See PPN "Vitezovi" (Dragan Vinac),

no.3–065/94, 5, KC Z1380. Nihad Rebihic put the total Muslim casualties during the "siege" at fifty-four killed, including twenty-nine able-bodied men, and many wounded (Kordic-Cerkez trial testimony, Oct. 13–14, 2000).

75. Williams, "Balkan Winter," Feb. 27, 1994. The operation was named for Simon Gill, the UNPROFOR liaison officer in Vitez.

76. Soon after April 16, many of the Croat village guard units were inducted into the Viteska Brigade. See Mlakic, Kordic-Cerkez trial testimony, Sept. 21, 2000.

77. Some 172 Muslims were killed and 420 Muslim buildings destroyed in the fighting around Vitez (see Kordic-Cerkez *Judgment*, 218). No figures are available for Croat losses.

Chapter 8. The ABiH Main Attack, April, 1993: Busovaca, Kiseljak, Zenica, and Elsewhere

1. Zeko, Blaskic trial testimony, Sept. 11, 1998.

2. The deployment of ABiH forces around Busovaca is based on positions shown on a captured ABiH map entitled "Obostrani Raspored Snaga u zoni OG 'Lasva' kraj aprila 1993 god." B D196.

3. In early May, Colonel Blaskic, the OZCB commander, complained to ECMM representatives that when the 305th Mountain Brigade was withdrawn from the Gornji Vakuf area, UNPROFOR had guaranteed it would go to Zenica. However, the 305th's 2d Battalion was in the Busovaca area, part of the brigade was in the Silos area, and the 3d Battalion was in Solakovici. See Annex G (May 8, 1993, Meeting with Colonel Tihomir Blaskic, Commander of HVO Operative Zone Vitez [*sic*]) to Humanities Section, HQ, ECMM (Charles McLeod), "Report on Inter-Ethnic Violence in Vitez, Busovaca and Zenica—April 1993" (HS 720; Zagreb, May 15, 1993), G-1, KC Z926 (hereafter McLeod report).

4. Elements of the 314th Motorized Brigade from Zenica may also have supported the attack in the Busovaca area (Zeko, Blaskic trial testimony, Sept. 11, 1998).

5. Joint Order, HQ, 333d Mountain Brigade (Busovaca), no. 02–370/1/93, and HQ, Nikola Subic Zrinski Brigade (Busovaca), no. 689/93, Busovaca, Apr. 8–9, 1993, KC Z633. The joint order was issued pursuant to the joint orders issued on February 13, 1993, by the ABiH III Corps and the HVO OZCB commanders, as well as the agreement reached in the coordinating committee meeting at Kakanj on April 17.

6. HQ, Zrinski Brigade, no. 677/93, Busovaca, Apr. 8, 1993, B D259; HQ, ABiH III Corps, no. 02/31–390, Zenica, Apr. 10, 1993, subj: Regular Combat Report, para. 3, B 733.

7. HQ, ABiH III Corps, no. 02/31–394, Zenica, Apr. 11, 1993, subj: Regular Combat Report, 1, KC Z641.2.

8. 1Cheshire MILINFOSUM no. 163, Apr. 11, 1993, para. 2, KC Z641.1.

9. HQ, Zrinski Brigade, no. 703/93, Busovaca, Apr. 12, 1993, subj: Report on the situation in the brigade zone of responsibility at 0600, KC Z646.

10. HQ, ABiH III Corps, no. 02/31–398, Zenica, Apr. 13, 1993, subj: Regular Combat Report, KC Z652.1, 1.

11. McLeod Report, Annex R, R-1, KC Z926.

12. SIS (Zarko Petrovic, aide to the chief of the SIS), no. 137/93, Busovaca, Apr. 14, 1993, subj: Report, B D262.

13. HQ, Zrinski Brigade, no. 756/93, Busovaca, Apr. 15, 1993, subj: Special Report on Casualties, B D265.

14. McLeod Report, Annex R, R-2, KC Z926.

15. Ibid.

16. HQ, 303d Slavna "Glorious" Mountain Brigade, no. 01/2524–1, Zenica, noon,

Apr. 16, 1993, subj: Order for Attack, KC Z674. The III Corps order (HQ, ABiH III Corps, no. 02/33–867, Zenica, Apr. 16, 1993, subj: Order to Move Out and Occupy Positions, KC Z673 and D190/1), also instructs the 303d Brigade commander to "be prepared to provide assistance to our forces in the village of Putis, Jelinak, Loncari, Nadioci, and Ahmici. In the event of an attack launched by the enemy, forcefully repel it and embark on a counterattack along the Nadioci–Sivrino Selo axis."

17.   Captured ABiH map entitled "Obostrani Raspored Snaga u zoni OG 'Lasva' kraj aprila 1993 god."

18.   McLeod Report, Annex R, R-3, KC Z926.

19.   HQ, Zrinski Brigade, no. 764/93, Busovaca, Apr. 16, 1993, subj: Report on the situation in the brigade zone of responsibility at 5 P.M., B D277.

20.   Anto Juric, commander of the Zrinski Brigade's 1st Battalion and a brigade operations officer, alleged that ABiH forces used mortar shells filled with poison gas against HVO forces in defensive positions to the south of Busovaca on April 16 (Juric conversation, Aug., 1999).

21.   HQ, OZCB, no. 01–4-280/93, Vitez, 1945, Apr. 16, 1993, subj: Combat order for the defense of Kuber, KC Z682.

22.   HQ, ABiH III Corps, no. 02/31–410, Zenica, Apr. 16, 1993, subj: Regular Combat Report, KC D81/1.

23.   HQ, Zrinski Brigade, no. p-22 (?), Busovaca, Apr. 17, 1993, B D288; ibid., no. 771/93, Busovaca, Apr. 17, 1993, subj: Report on the situation in the zone of the Zrinski Brigade at 0600, B D294.

24.   Ibid., n.p. (Busovaca), 0830, Apr. 17, 1993, subj: Report, B D289.

25.   Information Office, HQ, OZCB, no. 08–4-306/93, Vitez, 2325, Apr. 17, 1993, subj: Information about a Massacre of Civilians in Kuber, KC Z698.

26.   1Cheshire MILINFOSUM no. 169, Apr. 17, 1993, para. 1, B D64; HQ, OZCB, no. 01–4-319/93, Vitez, 1815, Apr. 17, 1993, subj: Order, KC Z699.

27.   HQ, Viteska Brigade, no. 01–125–21/93, Vitez, midnight, Apr. 17, 1993, subj: Operations Report, KC Z703.

28.   HQ, Zrinski Brigade, no. 777/93, Busovaca, Apr. 18, 1993, subj: Report on the implementation of order no. 01–4-322/93 of 17 April 1993, B D314.

29.   McLeod Report, Annex R, R-4, KC Z926.

30.   HQ, Zrinski Brigade, no. 783/93, Busovaca, Apr. 18, 1993, subj: Report on the situation in the brigade zone of responsibility at 0600, B D313; HQ, Zrinski Brigade, no. 783–3/93, Busovaca, Apr. 18, 1993, subj: Report on the situation in the brigade zone of responsibility by 2200, B D315.

31.   1Cheshire MILINFOSUM no. 171, Apr. 19, 1993, para. 1F, B D65.

32.   HQ, Zrinski Brigade, no. 786/93, Busovaca, Apr. 19, 1993, subj: Report further to the dispatch no. 01–4-380/93 of 19 Apr. 1993, B D324.

33.   1Cheshire MILINFOSUM no. 171, para. 1H, B D65.

34.   The northernmost roadblock consisted of two trucks blocking the road and five TMA-5 mines. The allegations of black market activities and supplying the Muslim forces in the Vitez area by British UNPROFOR personnel have persisted. The same allegations were made to the author during a conversation with former HVO personnel in Vitez in August, 1999. When asked how the Muslim forces in Donja Veceriska were resupplied, the response was: "By the British UNPROFOR, of course! They would provide anything to anyone for gold." The czar of the British UNPROFOR black market operations was said to be a captain named Perry. He has since been identified, but no action has been taken against him.

35. 1Cheshire MILINFOSUM no. 173, Apr. 21, 1993, para. 1, KC Z776; ibid., no. 174, Apr. 22, 1993, paras. 1, 5, B D66.

36. 1Cheshire MILINFOSUM no. 173, para. 3, KC Z776.

37. Ibid. no. 177, Apr. 25, 1993, para. 2, 4, KC D73/1. The HVO artillery apparently was laying down defensive fires to protect HVO forces in the Kula area on the orders of Colonel Blaskic, the OZCB commander.

38. Ibid., para. 2, 3L, KC D73/1. The British UNPROFOR patrol also reported that the Croat village of Kula was heavily fortified. It had an infantry trench system with overhead protection running northwest to southeast through the northern part of the village so as to defend the position against a Muslim attack from the Dusina or Solakovici area.

39. Stewart diary, Monday, Apr. 26, 1993, sec. 3, 44; McLeod Report, Annex R, R-12, KC Z926; 1Cheshire MILINFOSUM no. 178, Apr., 26, 1993, para. 2, KC D73/1.

40. HQ, Zrinski Brigade, no. 822/93, Busovaca, Apr. 17 (should be 27), 1993, subj: Report on the situation in the zone of responsibility of the brigade at noon, B D292.

41. 1Cheshire MILINFOSUM no. 180, Apr. 28, 1993, para. 1, KC D148/1.

42. McLeod Report, Annex R, R-14, KC Z926; Stewart diary, Thursday, Apr. 29, 1993, sec. 3, 46.

43. 1PWO MILINFOSUM no. 001, Apr. 30, 1993, para. 5, KC Z857.2.

44. Military Intelligence Service, HQ, OZCB, no. 205–8-I/93, 1–2, B D190; HQ, OZCB, Vitez, 10 A.M., Apr. 15, 1993, KC Z660.1.

45. Two former HVO soldiers from the Kiseljak area, conversation with author, Kiseljak and Vitez, Aug., 1999. Apparently, the Muslim forces in the area were reinforced by troops from Visoko brought in by truck.

46. The deployment of ABiH forces in the Kiseljak area from December, 1992–January, 1993, is shown on the captured ABiH map entitled "Obostrani Raspored Snaga u zoni 3. korpusa kraj decembra 1992. g.-januar 1993. god." KC D189/1.

47. HQ, OZCB, no. 01–4-303/93, Vitez, 0910, Apr. 17, 1993, subj: Preparatory combat order for the tying-up of a part of the Muslim forces that are attacking HVO, B D299.

48. Ibid., no. 01–4-331/93, Vitez, 2345, Apr. 17, 1993, subj: Order for combat operations, B D300.

49. Ibid., no. 01–4-335/93, 0140, Apr. 18, 1993, subj: Order to engage unit for combat, KC Z709.

50. Unless otherwise noted, the details of the fight at Gomionica presented here are based on the author's conversation of two former HVO soldiers from the Kiseljak area, in August, 1999.

51. The question of who started the fighting in the Kiseljak area in April, 1993, is moot. The ABiH attack, whether it was the opening of a planned offensive or simply a spoiling attack, apparently came just minutes before the planned HVO preemptive attack was to be launched.

52. HQ, Jelacic Brigade, Kiseljak, Apr. 18, 1993, subj: Regular Fighting Day Report 18.04.1993, Situation at 1000, KC Z712.

53. Ibid. The report quotes what was apparently a report from the Fojnica battalion: "Everything is ready, they are asking for negotiations. At this moment UNPROFOR came to the commander."

54. HQ, Jelacic Brigade, no. 6409/93, Kiseljak, 1645, Apr. 18, 1993, subj: Report, KC Z710.

55. Ibid., no. 6420/93, Kiseljak, Apr. 19, 1993, subj: Regular combat report for 19 Apr. 1993, at 0200, B D323.

56. HQ, OZCB, sent at least two such messages on April 19 encouraging the Jelacic
     Brigade to clear the Gomionica area. See HQ, OZCB, no. 01-4-401/93, Vitez,
     6:45 P.M., Apr. 19, 1993, KC Z732; ibid., no. 01-4-406/93, 9:40 P.M., Apr. 19,
     1993, KC Z733.

57. ECMM Team V1 (Lars Baggesen) to RC Zenica, Apr. 28, 1993, subj: Daily
     Report—28 Apr. 1993, KC Z841; ibid. (Allan Laustsen and Lars Baggesen) to
     RC Zenica, Apr. 29, 1993, subj: Daily Report—29 Apr. 1993, KC Z847. Laustsen
     and Baggesen referred specifically to the villages of Visnjica, Polje Visnjica,
     Hercezi, Doci, and Gomionica.

58. 1Cheshire MILINFOSUM no. 175, Apr. 23, 1993, para. 1, KC Z795.1.

59. Conversation with two former HVO soldiers.

60. ECMM RC Zenica (Remi Landry and Dimitrios Dagos) to HQ, ECMM Zagreb,
     Zenica, Apr. 25, 1993, subj: Special Report on Alleged Ethnic Cleansing, 1, KC
     Z818.

61. Colonel Robert Stewart testified that, in his opinion, the Totic kidnapping "came
     as a severe shock to the HVO, and the HVO Brigade commander, the second
     one [Vinko Baresic, commander of the 2d Zenica Brigade], was extremely con-
     cerned," which led Stewart to conclude that the HVO authorities in the Zenica
     area were not prepared for a conflict (Blaskic trial testimony, June 18, 1999). In-
     deed, neither of the two HVO brigades was at anywhere near full strength, and
     both were physically isolated from HQ, OZCB. Moreover, the commander of the
     Francetic Brigade, Zivko Totic, was still being held captive by Muslim extremists.

62. HQ, ABiH III Corps, no. 02/31–40, Zenica, Apr. 15, 1993, subj: Regular Combat
     Report, 3, KC D80/1; HQ, Francetic Brigade, no. 560/93, Zenica, Apr. 16, 1993,
     subj: Operative report on the situation at 0600, KC Z677.

63. HQ, HVO Command–Zenica, Forward Command Post at Zmajevac, 10:20 A.M.,
     Apr. 17, 1993, subj: Request, KC Z696.

64. HQ, OZCB, Vitez, 0115, Apr. 18, 1993, subj: Protest, KC Z708; Stewart, Blaskic
     trial testimony, June 17, 1999.

65. Stewart diary, Sunday, Apr. 19 (should be 18), 1993, sec. 3, 39.

66. HQ, HVO Command–Zenica, Forward Command Post at Cajdras, 1545, Apr. 18,
     1993, subj: Report (marked URGENT! URGENT!), B D311.

67. HQ, ECMM RC Zenica to HQ, ECMM Zagreb, "Special Report on Croats in
     Zenica, 20–21 April 1993," n.p., n.d. (Zenica, Apr. 21, 1993), KC Z765; KC
     D25/1.

68. See, among others: HQ, 303d Mountain Brigade, no. 01/3219–1, Zenica, June 5,
     1993, subj: Expert opinion (of Husein Hajdarevic) on the shelling of the town
     of Zenica on 19 April 1993, issued by the Zenica Security Services Centre, B
     D591/126; John Gerard Brendan Hamill, witness statement, Apr. 4, 5, and 6,
     1997, KC Z2816; District Military Court–Zenica (Judge Mladen Veseljak),
     no. 146/3, Zenica, Apr. 19, 1993, subj: Record of the On-Site Investigation of
     the Shelling of the Zenica Town Centre, KC Z728.

69. Prof. Slobodan Jankovic, Zagreb, written statement, Aug. 10, 1999; idem., con-
     versation with author, Zagreb, Aug. 28, 1999. Professor Jankovic examined all
     of the available documents regarding the shelling and applied his own knowl-
     edge and scientific calculations to arrive at a conclusion regarding the validity of
     previous analyses and the probable location from which the six rounds were
     fired on April 19. See also HQ, OZCB, no. 01-4-494–1/93, Vitez, 2125, Apr. 22,
     1993, subj: Re: Retracting the Verbal Protest, KC Z784.

70. HQ, ABiH III Corps, no. 02/31–356, Zenica, Apr. 12, 1993, subj: Regular Combat
     Report, B 735; ibid., no. 02/31–402, Zenica, Apr. 14, 1993, subj: Regular Combat
     Report, B 737. Ibid., no. 02/31–402, noted that the HVO had established a

checkpoint at Poluka (the Sebesic crossroads) on the Novi Travnik–Gornji Vakuf road and was not allowing ABiH forces to pass. In reality, both sides established checkpoints on the vital artery and denied access to each other. Fighting between ABiH and HVO forces around Gornji Vakuf at the southern end of the route blocked access at that end as well.

71. HQ, ABiH III Corps, no. 02/31–403, KC D80/1; HQ, Travnicka Brigade, no. 06–1315/93, 1345, Apr. 20, 1993, subj: Extraordinary Combat Report, B D328; Ljubas, Kordic-Cerkez trial testimony, May 16, 2000; HQ, OZCB, no. 01–4-606/93, Vitez, 1610, Apr. 25, 1993, subj: Information on the arrest of Croatian nationality in the Travnik Municipality, KC Z815.

72. HQ, OZCB, no. 01–4-282/93, Vitez, 2015, Apr. 16, 1993, subj: Order for increased control of the territory, B D283; HQ, Viteska Brigade, no. 02–125–18/93, Vitez, 1430, Apr. 17, 1993, subj: Combat Report, B D293; HQ, OZCB, no. 01–4-324/93, Vitez, 2200, Apr. 17, 1993, subj: Command for Reinforcements to Vitez Forces, KC Z700; ibid., no. 01–4-280/93, Vitez, 1940, Apr. 16, 1993, subj: Withdrawal of Troops of the Travnik VP Company to Vitez, KC Z682.

73. HQ, Tomasevic Brigade, no. 588/93, Novi Travnik, 0600, Apr. 17, 1993, subj: Regular Combat Report, B D285.

74. HQ, 111xp Brigade, no. 02/3–35/93, Zepce, Apr. 16, 1993, subj: Report, B D275.

75. Ibid., no. 02/4–191/93, Zepce, Apr. 17, 1993, subj: Report on situation within units of 111xp Brigade, B D286; ibid., no. 02/3–36/93, Zepce, Apr. 19, 1993, subj: (Situation Report), KC Z727.

76. HQ, 111xp Brigade, no. 02/4–191/93, B D286.

77. HQ, ABiH III Corps, no. 02/31–403, KC D80/1; ibid., no. 02/31–410, KC D80/1.

Chapter 9. The Continuation of the Muslim Offensive, May–June, 1993

1. ICTY, *Brief of Appellant Dario Kordic,* vol. 1, *Publicly Filed,* case no. IT-95–14/2-A. See Pavo Sljivic, Kordic-Cerkez trial testimony, May 16, 2000. Sljivic was a Croat municipal official in Kakanj.

2. HQ, HVO Main HQ, no. 02–2/1–01–648/93, Mostar, Apr. 18, 1993, subj: Cessation of conflict between the BH Army and HVO, KC D84/1; 1Cheshire MILINFOSUM no. 170, Annex B. The cease-fire order was passed on to HVO forces in central Bosnia by HQ, OZCB, no. 01–4-363/93, Vitez, Apr. 18, 1993, subj: The cease-fire between the HVO and ABiH units—Command, KC Z715. The HQ, OZCB cease-fire instructions were repeated in HQ, OZCB, no. 01–4-435/93, Vitez, 1115, Apr. 20, 1993, subj: Bilateral cease-fire Order, KC D85/1.

3. HQ, OZCB, no. 01–4-471/93, Vitez, 2300, Apr. 21, 1993, subj: Negotiations between the ABiH and the HVO Chiefs of Staff, B D335; Stewart diary, Wednesday, Apr. 21, 1993, sec. 3, 41.

4. HQ, OZCB, no. 01–4-471/93, B D335; ibid., no. 01–4-473/93, Vitez, 0910, Apr. 21 (should be 22; see sequence number of other messages and reference in this message to the April 21 chiefs of staff meeting in the past tense), 1993, subj: Implementation of agreement between units of the ABiH and (HVO) Order, KC Z768.

5. Ibid., no. 01–4-480/93, Vitez, 1300, Apr. 22, 1993, subj: Treatment of citizen's personal property, KC Z781. Special orders with respect to free circulation and operation of the ICRC were issued by HVO Main HQ on April 20 (see HVO Main Staff, no. 01–659/93, Mostar, Apr. 20, 1993, KC Z755), and implementing instructions were issued in HQ, OZCB, Vitez, Apr. 21, 1993, subj: Order, KC Z767.

6. HQ, OZCB, no. 01–4-537/93, Vitez, 2000, Apr. 23, 1993, subj: Behaviour of HVO members and the level of military discipline, KC Z791.

7. Ibid., no. 01–4-546/93, Vitez, 1000, Apr. 24, 1993, subj: Treatment of the

Wounded Order, KC Z805; ibid., no. 01–4-542/93, Vitez, 0920, Apr. 24, 1993, subj: Elimination of arbitrary acts by commanders and individuals, KC Z804; ibid., no. 01–4-700/93, Vitez, 1615, Apr. 28, 1993, subj: Visiting soldiers on the primary defense lines, B 456/30; ibid., Vitez, 1940, Apr. 29, 1993, subj: The release of detained civilians Order, KC Z852.2.

8. HQ, ECMM Regional Center Zenica (Ambassador Thebault) to HQ, ECMM Zagreb, Apr. 28, 1993, subj: Peace Process in Middle Bosnia 28/04, para. 1, KC Z840. The UNPROFOR declined to evacuate the two Croat villages near Konjic after the UNHCR representative stressed that international organizations did not participate in ethnic cleansing. The Spanish UNPROFOR battalion was assigned to "monitor" the situation instead.

9. Ibid., para. 3.

10. See, for example, ECMM Representatives–Busovaca Joint Commission (Erik Friis-Pedersen and Hendrik Morsink) to ECMM Regional Center Zenica/ UNPROFOR HQ, Kiseljak, (Busovaca), Apr. 20, 1993, subj: Daily Operational Report, KC Z754.

11. Joint Announcement, HQ, ABiH III Corps/HQ, HVO OZCB, Zenica/Vitez, Apr. 22, 1993, subj: (Establishment of Joint Operational Center), KC Z787. See also HQ, OZCB, no. 01–4-473/93.

12. ECMM representatives to JOC Vitez (Erik Friis-Pedersen, Torbjorn Junhov, and Allan Laustsen) to ECMM Regional Center Zenica, Apr. 25, 1993, subj: Daily Operational Report, KC Z817; KC D86/1. The ECMM representatives continued to make daily reports on JOC operations.

13. ECMM Team Z3 (Stavros Kynigopulos and Lars Baggesen) to ECMM Regional Center Zenica, May 11, 1993, subj: Daily Report—11 May 1993, B 97.

14. See, among others: HQ, OZCB, no. 01–5-349/93, Vitez, 1130, May 15, 1993, subj: Notice about the probable activities of ABiH forces, B 301; ibid., no. 01–5-689/93, Vitez, 1800, May 26, 1993, B 622; and ibid., no. 01–5-704/93, Vitez, 1030, May 27, 1993, subj: Securing free passage for UNPROFOR forces, B D367.

15. RBiH, BH Army, and HVO Joint Command, Vitez, May 11, 1993, subj: Joint Order, KC Z903; RBiH, Vitez Municipal Assembly, Commission for Exchange and Release of Prisoners, Vitez, May 22, 1993, subj: Powers and Competence of the Commission, KC Z965.1.

16. HQ, OZCB, no. 01–5-160/93, Vitez, 1230, May 7, 1993, subj: Special Report on the Situation in the Central Bosnia Operative Zone of the HVO of the Croatian Community of Herceg-Bosna, 1, KC Z891.

17. Ibid., 3–4, 5.

18. Ibid., 5.

19. Ibid., 9–11.

20. Ibid., no. 01–5-349/93.

21. The following account of the ABiH attack on Travnik is based primarily on the Kordic-Cerkez trial testimony of General Filipovic (Apr. 11, 2000) and Major Ljubas (May 16–17, 2000) and in part on the author's conversations with Major Ljubas at Travnik–Guca Gora, Aug. 19, 1999, and Vitez, Aug. 20, 1999. See also Zeko, Blaskic trial testimony, Sept. 11, 1998; Annex B (Summary of Recent Events in Travnik and the Western Lasva Valley), 1PWO MILINFOSUM no. 041, June 9, 1993, KC D201/1; and the successive COMBRITFOR MILINFOSUMs no. 220 (June 4, 1993) through no. 228 (June 12, 1993), KC D317/1.

22. The degree to which the HVO was again surprised by an ABiH offensive may be seen by the fact that on June 1, the OZCB commander ordered a reduction in the readiness level of his units in order to decrease the manpower burden. See HQ, OZCB, no. 01–6-3/93, Vitez, 0900, June 1, 1993, subj: Order for Combat

Readiness of Units re: Combat Order no. 01–5-816/93 of 31 May 1993, KC Z1003.

23. Ljubas, Kordic-Cerkez trial testimony, May 16, 2000; Father Branko Neimarevic, conversation with author, Guca Gora, Aug. 19, 1999. See also Zeko, Blaskic trial testimony, Sept. 11, 1998.

24. McLeod Report, Annex F, F-3, KC Z926.

25. Ibid., Annex G, G-1; COMBRITFOR MILINFOSUM no. 221, June 5, 1993, para. 2c(2), KC D317/1.

26. Ljubas, Kordic-Cerkez trial testimony, May 16, 2000.

27. Ibid.; Filipovic, Kordic-Cerkez trial testimony, Apr. 11, 2000. Despite its much greater manpower resources, the ABiH had only fifteen hundred to seventeen hundred troops actually manning positions against the Serbs in the Travnik sector (see Zeko, Blaskic trial testimony, Sept. 23, 1998).

28. The description of the deployment of ABiH and HVO forces in the Travnik sector is based on Ljubas, Kordic-Cerkez trial testimony, May 16–17, 2000; Zeko, Blaskic trial testimony, Sept. 11, 1998; and Ljubas conversations, Aug. 19 and 20, 1999.

29. COMBRITFOR MILINFOSUM no. 222, June 6, 1993, para. 2B(1), KC D317/1.

30. 1PWO MILINFOSUM no. 038, June 6, 1993, KC D164/1. The lack of cooperation by Enver Hadzihasanovic, the ABiH III Corps commander, was confirmed by Brigadier Guy de Vere Wingfield Hayes: "The BiH were no longer prepared to restrain themselves and were likely to take the military initiative in the Lasva Valley, where they enjoyed a tactical advantage over the HVO" (Kordic-Cerkez trial testimony, Mar. 8, 2000). Hayes was UNPROFOR chief of staff from April 7 to October 13, 1993.

31. See, among others, COMBRITFOR MILINFOSUM no. 223, June 7, 1993, KC D317/1, para. 2, and ibid., no. 224, June 8, 1993, para. 2, KC D317/1. Contemporary newspaper accounts reported the HVO was outnumbered four to one. See "'Atrocities' Cited as Muslim Rout Croats," *Toronto Star,* June 9, 1993, A16. HVO leaders later reported that the HVO was outnumbered eight to one (Ljubas, Kordic-Cerkez trial testimony, May 16, 2000; Franjo Nakic, Kordic-Cerkez trial testimony, Apr. 13, 2000).

32. The deployment of ABiH forces in the Travnik attack is described in Zeko, Blaskic trial testimony, Sept. 11, 1998.

33. Ljubas, Kordic-Cerkez trial testimony, May 17, 2000.

34. Annex B, "Summary of Recent Events in Travnik and the Western Lasva Valley," 1PWO MILINFOSUM no. 41, June 9, 1993, KC D201/1; 1PWO SITREP, 082000B June 1993, para. 2b, KC D316/1. See also Ljubas, Kordic-Cerkez trial testimony, May 17, 2000.

35. "'Atrocities'," A16; Neimarevic conversation; 1PWO SITREP, 091800B June 1993, para. 2b, KC D316/1; 1PWO SITREP, 101800B June 1993, para. 2b, KC D316/1; COMBRITFOR MILINFOSUM no. 225, June 9, 1993, para. 2c, KC D317/1. See also "'Atrocities'," A16; "Muslim Forces Push Offensive in Bosnia," *Toronto Globe,* June 10, 1993, A10. On the desecration of the Guca Gora monastery by the mujahideen, see, among others, UNPROFOR Weekly INFOSUM no. 34, June 21, 1993, para. 4a(2), KC Z1090; and COMBRITFOR MILINFOSUM no. 233, June 17, 1993, para. 2c(3), KC D317/1.

36. HQ, ECMM, "Excerpts from Political Material in ECMM Team Reports," Zagreb, June 9, 1993, 7, 9, KC Z1034. See also "Croat Town Falls to Muslims," *Toronto Sun,* June 9, 1993, 8.

37. "'Atrocities'," A16. The Bosnian Serbs took many of the civilians all the way around the northern half of the encircled RBiH and allowed them to reenter

HVO-held territory in the Kiseljak area (Ljubas conversations, Aug. 19 and 20, 1999).

38. COMBRITFOR MILINFOSUM no. 227, June 11, 1993, para. 2c(2), KC D317/1. Major Franjo Ljubas reported that the ABiH expelled some twenty thousand Croats from the Travnik area. He also denied the canard that the Croats left Travnik in response to HVO propaganda (Kordic-Cerkez trial testimony, May 17, 2000). Brigadier Franjo Nakic stated: "no propaganda could have driven these people away. They were forced to flee by the [ABiH] onslaught" (Kordic-Cerkez trial testimony, Apr. 13, 2000).

39. Ljubas, Kordic-Cerkez trial testimony, May 17, 2000. See also Koricic, Blaskic trial testimony, June 10, 1999.

40. "Croat Town Falls to Muslims," 8.

41. "Muslims Push Offensive for Bosnian Land," *Toronto Star,* June 10, 1993, A13.

42. HQ, ECMM, "Excerpts from Political Material in ECMM Team Reports," Zagreb, June 10, 1993, 8–9, KC Z1040.

43. The story of the so-called Convoy of Joy (also known as the "Convoy of Mercy" or the "Tuzla Convoy") has been told in several different versions. ECMM authorities, led by EC ambassador Jean-Pierre Thebault, have promoted a version that portrays the incident as a planned HVO operation (see HQ, ECMM, "Excerpts from Political Material," 5–7; ibid., 7–8, 11–12; message, HRC Zenica [Ambassador Thebault] to HQ, ECMM, Zenica, June 10, 1993, subj: HVO Attack on Tuzla Convoy, KC Z1041.1; ibid., June 11, 1993, subj: The Tragedy of the Tuzla Convoy, KC Z1045.2). The version told by British UNPROFOR sources is somewhat more balanced and more credible (see, among others, "'Convoy of Joy': A Summary of Croat/HVO Interference" annex to 1PWO MILINFOSUM no. 043, June 11, 1993, KC Z1044; 1PWO SITREP, 111800B June 1993, para. 2b, KC D316/1; COMBRITFOR MILINFOSUM no. 229, June 13, 1993, para. 2C[5], KC D317/1).

44. British UNPROFOR authorities anticipated just such an eventuality. See 1PWO SITREP, 101800B June 1993, para. 2b, KC D316/1.

45. Brigadier Hayes, the UNPROFOR chief of staff, said that BRITBAT soldiers killed three HVO soldiers and that some of the Muslim convoy drivers were killed by Croat women armed with pitchforks (Kordic-Cerkez trial testimony, Mar. 8, 2000).

46. "'Convoy of Joy'" annex to 1PWO MILINFOSUM no. 43, KC Z1044; Hayes, Kordic-Cerkez trial testimony, Mar. 8, 2000. Brigadier Hayes went to the scene with Ambassador Thebault to try to resolve the situation.

47. The HVO apparently diverted some forty trucks to the Mosunj quarry and another twenty-five to the timber yard in Vitez. See "'Convoy of Joy' " annex to 1PWO MILINFOSUM no. 43, KC Z1044.

48. See, for example, Mark Thompson, "The Bosnian Victims Fight Back," *New Statesman and Society,* June, 1993, 14. Thompson's reliance on Muslim sources and his accuracy regarding the facts leave much to be desired. For example, in the same article he asserts that "from January to May, the HVO 'cleansed' a belt of territory between Travnik and Busovaca" and "the HVO tried to seize weapons factories still working in Novi Travnik, Vitez, Bugojno, and Konjic." In fact, it was the ABiH that tried to cleanse the Travnik to Busovaca area, and it was the ABiH that seized and controlled the arms factories in Novi Travnik, Bugojno and Konjic. The Vitez explosives factory remained in HVO hands from beginning to end. Thompson's bias and inaccuracy is not untypical of Western media reports of the Muslim-Croat conflict in central Bosnia.

49. Among others, Filipovic, a senior HVO officer who was certainly in a position to know the facts and whose veracity is generally accepted, denied the HVO had

plans to attack the convoy (Kordic-Cerkez trial testimony, Apr. 11, 2000). There is no question, however, that HVO troops were caught up in the violence and took advantage of the situation to divert vehicles from the convoy.

50. The following account of the ABiH attack in the Novi Travnik area is based on Zeko, Blaskic trial testimony, Sept. 11, 1998; Ljubas, Kordic-Cerkez trial testimony, May 16–17, 2000; COMBRITFOR MILINFOSUM no. 229, 2c, KC D317/1; and Ljubas conversations, Aug. 19 and 20, 1999; and 1Cheshire MILINFOSUM no. 160.

51. The HVO lines around Novi Travnik were described to the author and drawn on a map by Maj. Franjo Ljubas (conversations with author, Aug. 19 and 20, 1999).

52. COMBRITFOR MILINFOSUM no. 233, para. 2c(4), KC D317/1. See also HQ, OZCB, no. 01-6-370/93, Novi Bila, June 15, 1992 (should be 1993), subj: Battle Order Op. no. 13, KC Z134; UNPROFOR Weekly INFOSUM no. 34, June 21, 1993, para. 4a(1), KC Z1090.

53. COMBRITFOR MILINFOSUM no. 231, June 15, 1993, para. 2c, KC D317/1.

54. Ibid., no. 229, para. 2c(6), KC D317/1. See also ibid., no. 231, para. 2c(6), KC D317/1.

55. HQ, OZCB, no. 01-6-441/93, Vitez, 1640, June 16, 1993, subj: (Cease-fire Order), B D370.

56. See among others, HQ, OZCB, orders: no. 01-8-441, June 19, 1993, KC Z1076; ibid., no. 01-6-442/93, June (19), 1993, B D372; ibid., no. 01-8-443, June 19, 1993, B D374; ibid., no. 01-8-444, June 19, 1993, KC Z1077; ibid., no. 01-6-486/93, June 21, 1993, B D373; ibid., no. 01-7-356/93, July 21, 1993, B D376; and ibid., no. 01-9-241, Sept. 13, 1993, B D384.

57. See among others, HQ, 2d Battalion, Viteska Brigade, Bila, orders of: June 21, 1993, B D375; July 12, 1993, B D377; Aug. 7, 1993, B D370; Aug. 27, 1993, B D381; Aug. 30, 1993, B D383; and Sept. 16, 1993, B D387.

58. ABiH-HVO Joint Command (Lt. Col. Alastair Duncan), Vitez, June 28, 1993, subj: Fourth Meeting of the Joint Command—June 28, 1993—Record of Decisions, B 389. See also COMBRITFOR MILINFOSUM no. 231, para. 2c(4), KC D317/1; and ibid., no. 233, para. 2c(7), KC D317/1.

Chapter 10. The Continuation of the Muslim Offensive, July–August, 1993

1. Sljivic, Kordic-Cerkez trial testimony. See also COMBRITFOR MILINFOSUM no. 226, June 10, 1993, para. 2c(13), KC D317/1; ibid., no. 227, para. 2c(7), KC D317/1; ibid., no. 229, para. 2c(7), KC D317/1; and ibid., no. 231, para. 2c(8–9), KC D317/1. The Kotromanic Brigade, commanded by Neven Maric, was subsequently dissolved. The ABiH takeover in the Kakanj area resulted in as many as 120 Croats killed—mostly women and men aged fifty to eighty— and twenty-five hundred Croat homes, thirty chapels, and thirty cemeteries destroyed.

2. Extracts from the press conference were distributed in HQ, Nikola Subic Zrinski Brigade, no. P-1202/93, Busovaca, Aug. 4, 1993, subj: Information for Soldiers, KC Z1154.

3. 1PWO MILINFOSUM no. 103, Aug. 10, 1993, para. 2, KC D135/1.

4. Details of the fighting in the Kiseljak area are derived in part from two former HVO soldier conversations with author, August, 1999.

5. Zeko, Blaskic trial testimony, Sept. 11, 1998.

6. Unless otherwise noted, details of the battles for Fojnica and Kresevo are drawn from ECMM Team V3, "Background Report: Fojnica (YJ 3272)," n.p., n.d. (Tomislavgrad, Oct. 13, 1993), 2, B D153.

7. After September 6, the ABiH VI Corps's area of operations was extended to

include the entire Vares-Breza-Visoko-Ilijas-Kiseljak-Fojnica-Kresevo area and was commanded by Salko Gusic. See ibid.

8.   HQ, BHC (UNPROFOR), Weekly INTSUM no. 39, July 26, 1993, KC Z2430–6, para. 4g; two former HVO soldier conversations, Aug., 1999; HVO chief of medical services, 3d Battalion (Fojnica), Nikola Subic Zrinski Brigade (Dr. Bogomire Bar-bic) to HVO Department of Defense Medical Sector in Mostar (Col. Dr. Tugomir Gveric), no. 07–60–1/93, Fojnica, Aug. 21, 1993, subj: (report), B D256.

9.   ECMM Team V3, "Background Report: Fojnica," 2, 3. According to Stjepan Tuka, former commander of the HVO battalion in Fojnica (Kordic-Cerkez trial testimony, Nov. 22, 1999), the ABiH destroyed about 70 percent of the Croat villages in the Fojnica area, and some 5,500 Croats became refugees.

10.   The following account of the ABiH attack in the Zepce-Zavidovici–Novi Seher area in June and July, 1993, is based on three principal sources: the prosecutor's summary, witness statements, and other materials included in the so-called Zepce binder submitted by the ICTY prosecutor in the Kordic-Cerkez trial and subsequently admitted by the trial chamber; HVO artillery commander in the Zepce area, conversation with author, Zepce, Aug. 22, 1999; and contemporary MILINFOSUMs produced by COMBRITFOR.

11.   Some ten to fifteen days before the conflict in Zepce erupted, the HVO moved Croats living in the Muslim villages of Begov Han, Golubinja, and Brezovo Polje to the Croat villages of Tatarbudzak and Osova.

12.   COMBRITFOR MILINFOSUM no. 240, June 24, 1993, para. 2C(2), KC D317/1.

13.   For example, the Serbs in Ozren, northeast of Zepce, were eager to cooperate since they were not to be included in the Serbian area under the Vance-Owen peace plan. The Serbs offered to allow Croat civilians and wounded HVO per-sonnel to pass through their lines as well as to provide the HVO with artillery support.

14.   COMBRITFOR MILINFOSUM no. 240, para. 2C(1), KC D317/1.

15.   Ibid.; no. 241, June 25, 1993, para. 2C(1), KC D317/1; and ibid., no. 244, June 28, 1993, para. 2B(1), KC D317/1.

16.   COMBRITFOR MILINFOSUM no. 241, para. 2C(3), KC D317/1.

17.   HVO artillery commander conversation. One HVO civilian official stated that 116 HVO soldiers from Zepce died in battle against the Serbs while only twenty-nine Muslim soldiers from Zepce perished. Overall, the 111xp Brigade suffered some 450 casualties from 1992–94.

18.   COMBRITFOR MILINFOSUM no. 244, para. 2B Comment, KC D317/1. The 301st Mechanized Brigade was the ABiH III Corps tank unit. Its participation in the Zepce attack was probably minimal inasmuch as it had only about six tanks in all.

19.   Saint Ivo was the patron of Vrankovici Parish in the municipality of Zavidovici, but he was honored in Zepce as well. In fact, the Muslim forces attacked two days earlier than the written attack order from Zenica specified.

20.   COMBRITFOR MILINFOSUM no. 241, para. 2C(3), KC D317/1; HVO artillery commander conversation; Esad Dedovic, witness statement, July 14 and 16, 1996, 3, KC Z2291.1. According to Dedovic, "It was the 'Green Berets' and the HVO soldiers who shot on each other."

21.   COMBRITFOR MILINFOSUM no. 241, para. 2C(3), KC D317/1; ibid., no. 242, June 26, 1993, para. 2C(2)(c), KC D317/1.

22.   Ibid., no. 241, para. 2C(1), KC D317/1; ibid., no. 242, para. 2C(1), KC D317/1.

23.   Ibid., para. 2C(2)(d), KC D317/1; ibid., no. 244, para. 2B(2), KC D317/1.

24.   Dedovic, witness statement, 3. Page 2 of the OTP summary in the Zepce binder incorrectly states that the HVO occupied the surrounding hills and fired artillery

into the town. However, the ABiH occupied the hills west, south, and east of Zepce. As a result, the artillery fire from the direction of Papratnica and Zeljezno Polje at 9 A.M. on June 23(?) could only have come from ABiH forces occupying those areas (OTP Summary, "Zepce binder," 7). Known ABiH firing positions were in Ljubna, Bljuva, and Vorosiste, all to the northwest of Zepce. See COMBRITFOR MILINFOSUM no. 242, para. 2C(2)(d), KC D317/1.

25. What the eyewitness apparently observed were seven tanks and ten armored fighting vehicles from the BSA Teslic Brigade's 1st Battalion.

26. COMBRITFOR MILINFOSUM no. 246, June 30, 1993, para. 2B(2), KC D317/1.

27. HVO artillery commander conversation. It appears that some Muslim civilians were also detained at the Rade Kondic school, the elementary school in Perkovic Han, and the silos.

28. COMBRITFOR MILINFOSUM no. 242, paras. 2C(1) and 2C(2)(a).

29. Ibid., KC D317/1; ibid., no. 241, para. 2C(3), KC D317/1.

30. Ibid., no. 241, para. 2C(2), KC D317/1; ibid., no. 242, para. 2C(2)(b), KC D317/1.

31. Ibid., no. 241, para. 2B(1) and Comment, KC D317/1.

32. Ibid., no. 242, para. 2C(5), KC D317/1. The ABiH 201st Mountain Brigade in Maglaj resisted becoming part of the III Corps because it reputedly was very "mujahideen," that is, radically Muslim and not "multicultural." The issue was not resolved until commanders more in tune with the III Corps philosophy replaced the old commanders in the Maglaj area (see Alagic and others, *Ratna Sjecanja*, 41).

33. COMBRITFOR MILINFOSUM no. 246, para. 2B(3), KC D317/1.

34. Ibid. no. 242, para. 2C(3), KC D317/1.

35. Ibid., para. 2C(2)(f), KC D317/1.

36. HQ, OZCB, no. 01–8-209/93, Vitez, 1545, Aug. 11, 1993, subj: Delivery of Report Following Order, 2, KC Z1163.

37. Ibid., no. 01–10–249/93, Vitez, Oct. 11, 1993, subj: The Implementation of Disciplinary Measures for Deserting Positions and Defense Lines, KC Z1242.

38. The discussions held during the ABiH leadership conference are laid out by Sefer Halilovic in *Lukava strategija*, 236–39.

39. Ibid., 242, 243–44.

40. Ibid., 244–245. Mehmed Alagic did not assume command of III Corps from Enver Hadzihasanovic, who replaced Sefer Halilovic as the ABiH chief of staff in Sarajevo, until November, 1993.

41. Sir Martin Garrod (head, ECMM Regional Center Zenica) to HQ, ECMM, Apr. 18, 1993, subj: HRC Zenica—End of Tour Report, para. 11, KC D119/1.

Chapter 11. Operations, September, 1993–February, 1994

1. 1PWO MILINFOSUM no. 130, Sept. 6, 1993, para. 2, KC D122/1; 1 PWO SITREP, 051800B Sept., 1993, para. 2b, KC D316/1.

2. 1PWO MILINFOSUM no. 130, para. 2, KC D122/1; 1PWO SITREP, 061800B Sept., 1993, para. 2b, KC D316/1; ibid., 071800B Sept., 1993, para. 2b, KC D316/1; Zeko, Blaskic trial testimony, Sept. 22, 1998; Vitezovi PPN "Vitezovi" (Dragan Vinac), no. 3–065/94, 5, KC Z1380; 1PWO SITREP, 081800B Sept., 1993, para. 2b, KC D316/1; ibid., 091800B Sept., 1993, para. 2b, KC D316/1.

3. 1PWO SITREP, 181800B Sept. 1993, para. 2b, KC D316/1; ibid., 191800B Sept. 1993, para. 2b, KC D316/1.

4. Drago Ljubos (Busovaca Police Station commander) to HVO President of the Busovaca Municipality, no. 03–9/4–235–202/93, Busovaca, Sept. 23, 1993, subj:

Report, B D450/19; 1PWO MILINFOSUM no. 152, Sept. 28, 1993, B D139; B D591/117.

5. 1PWO MILINFOSUM no. 155, Sept. 30, 1993, para. 3, KC D45/2.

6. ABiH forces from Kruscica, assisted by troops from the Opara area, attacked Zbrdje on April 18–19, 1993, killing and wounding several HVO defenders, and burning the hunting lodge. See Ljubo Calic, Kordic-Cerkez trial testimony, Sept. 21, 2000. Calic was a Croat member of the Kruscica Hunting Club, which owned the lodge and participated in its defense from April 18–20. See also HQ, Viteska Brigade, no. 02–125–34/93, Vitez, Apr. 20, 1993, subj: Operations Report, B D330.

7. UNPROFOR SITREP for the period 090001 to 092359A Dec., 1993, Kiseljak, 0300, Dec. 10, 1993, KC D335–1/1.

8. Williams, "Balkan Winter," Dec. 22, 1993. Estimates of the Croat casualties, many of whom are believed to have been massacred after surrendering, vary widely. Colonel Williams put the HVO casualties at 60–70. Major General Filip Filipovic put them at 100 (Kordic-Cerkez trial testimony, Apr. 11, 2000). Dr. Miroslav Tudjman, director of the Croatian Information Service (HIS) put the total HVO and civilian casualties at Krizancevo Selo and nearby Buhine Kuce at 80 (see Miroslav Tudjman to Franjo Tudjman, no. 716–2412-E-03/94–052). See also Zeko, Blaskic trial testimony, Sept. 11, 1998. As a result of the disaster at Krizancevo Selo, Colonel Blaskic relieved Mario Cerkez as commander of the Viteska Brigade, and "kicked him upstairs" by making him deputy commander of the Vitez Military District.

9. Williams, "Balkan Winter," Dec. 23–24, 1993. Colonel Williams reported that Rasim Delic, the ABiH commander, remarked that a cease-fire was impossible because there was "too much unfinished business in Central Bosnia."

10. Alagic and others, *Ratna Sjecanja,* 28. Alagic wrote: "Through connections in the UN, we succeeded in getting some means [weapons] into Stari Vitez, so that they could defend themselves."

11. Mehmed Alagic claimed in his memoir that ABiH leaders feared the Muslim defenders of Stari Vitez would be massacred if the HVO took the enclave. Nevertheless, they decided to not succor the Muslim garrison there lest such action impede the ABiH's receipt of supplies from Croatia (*Ratna Sjecanja,* 26, 28).

12. Williams, "Balkan Winter," Jan. 9, 1994.

13. The attack began at 5:45 A.M. See 1CSG MILINFOSUM no. 75, Jan. 14, 1994, para. 37, KC Z1357.1; ibid., no. 70, Jan. 10, 1994, para. 7, KC Z2449.2; UNPROFOR SITREP for the period 100001 to 102359A Jan., 1994, Kiseljak, 3:15 A.M., Jan. 11, 1994, KC D335–1/1; and Zeko, Blaskic trial testimony, Sept. 11, 1998. The ABiH simultaneously attacked Novi Travnik with small arms and machine-gun fire, and on January 10 fired forty mortar and/or artillery rounds into Busovaca (see UNPROFOR SITREP for the period 110001 to 112359A Jan., 1994, Kiseljak, 3:30 A.M., Jan. 12, 1994, KC D335–1/1).

14. Williams, "Balkan Winter," Jan. 11, 1994.

15. General Filipovic says the HVO lost twenty KIA at Bukve Kuce alone (Kordic-Cerkez trial testimony, Apr. 11, 2000).

16. Williams, "Balkan Winter," Jan. 24, 1994; Garrod to HQ, ECMM, Apr. 18, 1993, para. 13, KC D119/1.

17. UNPROFOR SITREP for the period 030001 to 032359A Feb., 1994, Kiseljak, 3 A.M., Feb. 4, 1994, KC D335–1/1; ibid., for the period 110001 to 112359A Feb., 1994, Kiseljak, 3:15 A.M., Feb. 12, 1994, KC D335–1/1; ibid., for the period 110001 to 112359A Jan., 1994, KC D335–1/1; Williams, "Balkan Winter," Feb. 8, 14, and 23, 1994.

18. Sir Martin Garrod, Kordic-Cerkez trial testimony, Feb. 1, 2000. Garrod was a former lieutenant general and commander of the British Royal Marines. He succeeded Ambassador Jean Pierre Thebault as director of the ECMM Regional Center Zenica on October 14, 1993, and later served in various high-level EC and UN posts in the Balkans. The village was destroyed during the ABiH attack that began at 5:30 A.M. on October 22, but the ECMM later claimed that nothing happened. See ECMM Regional Center Zenica, Daily Report for Mar. 21, 1994, KC D175/1.

19. Witness AO, Kordic-Cerkez trial testimony, Mar. 7, 2000. Witness AO was a former Croat member of the HOS. In addition to the Territorial Defense forces, an ABiH special purpose unit—the "Lasta" from Dabravine—may also have been in the village in late October.

20. ECMM Team V3 (Oscar Meyboom and Karsten Carstensen) and Team V4 (Rolf Weckesser and Etienne Begue) were sent to investigate on October 24, but were denied entry to Stupni Do by Emil Harah, then commander of the HVO Bobovac Brigade. See Garrod, Kordic-Cerkez trial testimony, Feb. 1, 2000. Team V4 subsequently reported that Ivica Rajic was present and seemed to be in charge in Vares.

21. The HVO GHQ subsequently transferred Ivica Rajic to Caplinja, where he changed his name to "Victor Andric." He later disappeared and is believed to have taken refuge in Serbian territory, where he is relatively immune to capture and trial for his crimes. Kresimir Bozic took command of the Bobovac Brigade from Harah on October 25, immediately after the Stupni Do attack, and apparently had nothing to do with the affair.

22. ECMM Coordinating Center Travnik, "Daily Summary," Travnik, Nov. 2, 1993, para. 1, KC D117/1; Garrod, Kordic-Cerkez trial testimony, Feb. 1, 2000; Ekrem Mahmutovic, witness statement, KC D31/1.

23. According to Garrod, "The clear understanding that we had was that the attack was done by the HVO from Kakanj and Kiseljak, not the HVO from Vares" (Kordic-Cerkez trial testimony, Feb. 1, 2000).

24. Garrod to HQ, ECMM, Apr. 18, 1993, para. 5, KC D119/1.

25. Garrod, Kordic-Cerkez trial testimony, Feb. 1, 2000.

26. Zeko, Blaskic trial testimony, Sept. 23, 1998.

27. ECMM Team V3, Daily Report, Apr. 13, 1994, KC Z1417.

28. According to Garrod, on November 6, 1993, Jozo Maric, the mayor of Grude, told Philip Watkins, head of the ECMM Coordinating Center at Mostar, "the massacre was the excuse the ABiH wanted, and the coordinated attack by the 2d and 3d ABiH Corps on VARES proved they were prepared." Garrod added, "this certainly would accord with my assessment of what transpired, and appears to be a shift of the previous HVO position" (see Sir Martin Garrod, witness statement, Feb. 17–19, 1998, 10, KC OTP Vares binder). Mehmed Alagic signed the order for the Vares offensive (see Alagic et al., *Ratna Sjecanja,* 31).

29. ECMM Coordinating Center Travnik, "Daily Summary," Travnik, Nov. 2, 1993, paras. 1, 7, KC D117/1.

30. Ibid., Nov. 3, 1993, KC Z1284.2; O'Ballance, *Civil War in Bosnia,* 221; Garrod to HQ, ECMM, Apr. 18, 1993, para. 7; idem., Kordic-Cerkez trial testimony, Feb. 1, 2000.

31. O'Ballance, *Civil War in Bosnia,* 232.

32. Garrod to HQ, ECMM, Apr. 18, 1993, para. 20, KC D119/1.

33. Garrod, Kordic-Cerkez trial testimony, Feb. 1, 2000.

Chapter 12: Conclusion

1. Garrod to HQ, ECMM, Apr. 18, 1993, para. 14, KC D119/1; quoted in Garrod, Kordic-Cerkez trial testimony, Feb. 1, 2000.

2.   Garrod to HQ, ECMM, Apr. 18, 1993, para. 31, KC D119/1.

3.   Sajevic, Kordic-Cerkez trial testimony, July 27, 2000.

4.   Filipovic, Kordic-Cerkez trial testimony, Apr. 11, 2000.

5.   Helsinki Watch, *War Crimes in Bosnia-Hercegovina,* 2:7: "Most of the abuses attributable to Bosnian Croatian and Muslim forces are perpetrated by individuals and do not appear to be part of a premeditated plan of the Bosnian government or the authorities of the self-proclaimed 'Community of Herceg-Bosna.'"

6.   To date, the ICTY has indicted only four senior ABiH officers (Sefer Halilovic, Enver Hadzihasanovic, Mehmed Alagic, and Amir Kubura), and the offenses for which they have been indicted are relatively minor and restricted in scope. No Muslim political leaders have been indicted.

7.   IISS, *Strategic Survey, 1993–1994,* 104. Although the rebuilding of central Bosnia and the return of refugees to their home areas is proceeding, progress remains slow nearly a decade after the conflict began.

Glossary of Common Abbreviations

AAA	Antiaircraft Artillery	209
ABC	Atomic-Biological-Chemical	
ABiH	Armed Forces of the Republic of Bosnia and Herzegovina	
BHC	Bosnia-Hercegovina Command (UNPROFOR)	
BiH	Bosnia and Herzegovina	
BRITBAT	British Battalion (i.e., the UNPROFOR unit in the Lasva Valley area)	
BSA	Bosnian Serb Army	
COMBRITFOR	Commander, British Forces in Bosnia-Herzegovina	
EC	European Community	
ECMM	European Community Monitoring Mission	
EU	European Union	
EW	Electronic Warfare	
GHQ	General Headquarters	
Green Berets	Muslim paramilitary group	
Green Legion	Muslim paramilitary group	
HDZ	Croatian Democratic Union (Croatian political party)	
HDZ-BiH	Croatian Democratic Union of Bosnia-Herzegovina (Bosnian Croat political party)	
HMG	Heavy Machine Gun	
HOS	Croatian Defense Association (or Forces)	
HQ	Headquarters	
HSP	Croatian Party of Rights (extremist political party)	
HV	Republic of Croatia; also used to designate the Army of the Republic of Croatia	
HVO	Croatian Defense Council	
HZ HB	Croatian Community of Herceg-Bosna	
ICRC	International Committee of the Red Cross	
ICTY	International Criminal Tribunal for the Former Yugoslavia, or, more properly, International Tribunal for the Prosecution of Persons Responsible for Serious Violations of International Humanitarian Law Committed in the Territory of the Former Yugoslavia since 1991	
JCC	Joint Coordination Commission	
JHC	Joint Humanitarian Commission	
JNA	Yugoslavian National Army	
JOC	Joint Operational Center	
KIA	Killed in Action	

LMG	Light Machine Gun
LTRD	Light Rocket Artillery Unit
MOS	Muslim Armed Forces (extremist Muslim paramilitary group); also used to refer to the Bosnian Muslim armed forces in general
MTD	Mixed Artillery Unit
MUP	RBiH Ministry of the Interior Police
NATO	North Atlantic Treaty Organization
NCO	Noncommissioned Officer
NGO	Nongovernmental Organization
NORDBAT	Nordic Battalion (UNPROFOR)
OEM	Officers and Enlisted Men
OG	Operations (or Operative) Group
OZCB	Operative Zone Central Bosnia (HVO)
PDO	Antisabotage Unit (ABiH)
PPN	Special Purpose Unit (HVO)
RBiH	Republic of Bosnia and Herzegovina
RPG	Rocket-Propelled Grenade
SDA	Party of Democratic Action (Bosnian Muslim political party)
SDS	Serbian Democratic Party (Bosnian Serb political party)
SIS	HVO Security Information Service
TO or TD	Territorial Defense Forces
UNHCR	United Nations High Commissioner for Refugees
UNPROFOR	United Nations Protection Force
VP	Military Police
VOPP	Vance-Owen peace plan
WIA	Wounded in Action
Young Muslims	Muslim paramilitary group

Sources

The materials used in the preparation of this study consist primarily of testimony and exhibits from the trials of Tihomir Blaskic, Dario Kordic and Mario Cerkez, and others before the International Criminal Tribunal for the Former Yugoslavia in The Hague from 1998–2001. The prosecutor presented most of the exhibits cited to the court. A smaller number of documents were presented as defense exhibits in the various trials. No exhibits presented in closed or private session have been used, and I have made every effort to verify that the trial chamber admitted a given document (thus making it a matter of public record) before using it here. The state of the finding aids available to me made this difficult at times, but verification was necessary because many of the documents—the very useful Military Information Summaries (MILINFOSUMs) prepared by British UNPROFOR units in central Bosnia, for example—were obtained from national governments that impose security classifications and time restrictions on the release of official documents, except insofar as they are entered into evidence in a public trial.

The reliability of documents presented as exhibits before the ICTY varies somewhat. Aside from the MILINFOSUMs and periodic reports prepared by UNPROFOR units and the European Community Monitoring Mission, which were provided directly by the British government and the European Community respectively, many of the HVO and ABiH documents presented at trial by the prosecutor were obtained from the Secret Intelligence Service of the Muslim-dominated government of the Republic of Bosnia-Herzegovina. There is substantial reason to believe that not only was the process of identifying and turning over the documents selective, but that there was perhaps some tampering with documents in order to ensure that the ABiH's actions were presented in the most favorable light and those of the HVO in the most unfavorable light. In fact, few ABiH documents of any kind were presented in either the Blaskic trial or the Kordic-Cerkez trial, thereby leaving a significant gap in our knowledge of ABiH plans and actions. By and large, the HVO documents presented at trial, whether by the prosecution or the defense, are contemporary with the events described and are, in my judgment, fairly reliable, particularly with regard to dates, times, and actions, insofar as they may be judged authentic. Some of the HVO documents presented in the Kordic-Cerkez trial were obtained from the Croatian government archives in Zagreb, and the government of Bosnia-Herzegovina supplied many others. Of course, one must always consider the possibility of tampering, so it is always useful to compare the contents of a given document with other contemporary sources whenever possible. One is also well advised to remember that not all orders were issued on paper and that some matters (or documents) may not have been openly recorded.

Even UNPROFOR and ECMM documents must be studied with some care. For the most part, UNPROFOR documents such as the MILINFOSUMs report events accurately and without obvious bias toward one side or the other in the conflict. However, UNPROFOR military units in central Bosnia were not always aware of what was happening and thus had a propensity to misinterpret some events. In general, UNPROFOR documents increased in reliability as time went on and the UNPROFOR units better understood what was happening around them. Thus, the MILINFOSUMs produced by the Coldstream Guards' 1st Battalion in late 1993 and early 1994 are much more evenhanded and reliable than those produced by the Cheshire Regiment's 1st Battalion in late 1992 and early 1993.

The various reports and other documents generated by the ECMM present something of a problem. They are often blatantly biased toward the Muslim side in the conflict, and so go out of their way to blame the HVO for everything that happened and absolve the ABiH of any wrongdoing. I believe that this bias was the result of several factors. First, ECMM monitoring teams were often denied access to the scene of events by both the ABiH and HVO and thus did not directly observe what was going on. Second, ECMM teams seem to have relied heavily on what they were told by the ABiH authorities in Zenica and elsewhere, much more so than was prudent. Third, most of the interpreters and translators employed by the ECMM (and by UNPROFOR) were Muslims, leaving the accuracy and thoroughness of their translation in any given situation open to question. Fourth, testimony in both the Blaskic and Kordic-Cerkez trials clearly demonstrated that many ECMM monitors were put out with the HVO for what they considered to be personal insults and affronts to their dignity. Denied access to a given area of conflict by HVO troops, many ECMM monitors were quick to assume that the HVO had some heinous crime to conceal. More likely, the HVO commanders were concerned about the strength and disposition of their forces being reported to the ABiH by garrulous ECMM monitors.

The bias of European Community ambassador Jean-Pierre Thebault in favor of the Muslims and his eagerness to blame every incident on the HVO was particularly noticeable and appears to have stemmed from something deeper than mere ignorance or personal affronts. His words and actions suggest that he was perhaps acting on private instructions from the French government that were not made public and which obliged him to favor the Muslim side on every issue. Indeed, the French government had substantial reasons to act in favor of the Bosnian Muslims and to ignore the plight of the Bosnian Croats: namely a large and restive Muslim population in metropolitan France and extensive French business interests in the Muslim world. In any event, Ambassador Thebault's bias is perfectly obvious in his judgments and reports. His successor, Sir Martin Garrod, was far more evenhanded.

The knowledgeable reader will note the omission of many of the most familiar books, articles, and journalistic accounts of the conflict in Bosnia-Herzegovina from the selected bibliography that follows. This is by design rather than neglect, as most of them focus on political and diplomatic matters and the situation of the Muslims in Sarajevo, Mostar, Srbrenica, and other areas outside central Bosnia. I have studied many of them, but they generally contain few useful details on the military aspects of the Muslim-Croat conflict in central Bosnia and are often inaccurate in the details they do provide. Even the work of such recognized military historians as Edgar O'Ballance must be read with care, having been prepared before all the pertinent facts were generally known (as was this present study, as it will no doubt be revealed in time). The published memoirs of ABiH leaders such as Sefer Halilovic and Mehmed Alagic should, of course, be used with some caution. Unfortunately, the HVO leaders have not yet published any accounts of their participation in the conflict.

In many cases, I have relied on my own informal conversations with participants in the 1992–94 conflict—conducted during a trip to central Bosnia in August, 1999—for details about the fighting in specific areas. Almost all with whom I talked were former HVO military personnel, and I have made due allowance for the fact that they were naturally eager to present their actions— and those of the HVO in general—in the best possible light while inflating the perfidy of their Muslim opponents. For the most part, however, I found their version of events compelling, particularly inasmuch as it generally squared with the available documentary evidence presented before the ICTY. Most of the persons I talked to consented to be identified by name, but in several cases I have omitted the names of the individuals concerned. Readers may give such testimony whatever weight they may wish.

Selected Bibliography

Alagic, Mehmed, with Nedzad Latic and Zehrudin Isakovic. *Ratna Sjecanja Mehmeda Alagica: Rat U Srednjoj Bosni* (War Reminiscences of Mehmed Alagic: The War in Central Bosnia). Zenica: Bemust, 1997.

"The Army of Bosnia and Herzegovina." *Jane's Intelligence Review,* March 1, 1994.

"'Atrocities' Cited as Muslim Rout Croats." *Toronto Star,* June 9, 1993, A16.

Banac, Ivo. *The National Question in Yugoslavia: Origins, History, Politics.* Ithaca, N.Y.: Cornell University Press, 1984.

Beale, Michael O. *Bombs over Bosnia: The Role of Airpower in Bosnia-Herzegovina.* Maxwell Air Force Base, Ala.: Air University Press, 1997.

Chambers, John W., II, ed. *The Oxford Companion to American Military History.* Oxford/New York: Oxford University Press, 1999.

"Croat Town Falls to Muslims." *Toronto Sun,* June 9, 1993, 8.

Dear, I. C. B., ed. *The Oxford Companion to World War II.* Oxford/New York: Oxford University Press, 1995.

Department of the Army. *DA Pamphlet No. 20–243: German Antiguerrilla Operations in the Balkans (1941–1944).* Washington, D.C.: Department of the Army, August, 1954.

Department of Defense. *Bosnia Country Handbook—Peace Implementation Force (IFOR).* Washington, D.C.: Department of Defense, December, 1995.

Encyclopedia Americana on CD-ROM. Danbury, Conn.: Grolier Electronic Publishing, 1995.

Fall, Bernard B. *Hell in a Very Small Place: The Siege of Dien Bien Phu.* New York: Vintage Books, 1966.

Halilovic, Sefer. *Lukava strategija* (The Shrewd Strategy). Sarajevo: Marsal, 1997.

Headquarters, Bosnia-Hercegovina Command, UNPROFOR. *Bosnia-Hercegovina Warring Factions.* 6th ed. N.p. (Kiseljak): Headquarters, Bosnia-Hercegovina Command, UNPROFOR, July 22, 1993.

———. *Bosnia-Hercegovina Warring Factions.* 8th ed. N.p. (Kiseljak): Headquarters, Bosnia-Hercegovina Command, UNPROFOR, February 3, 1994.

Headquarters, U.S. Army Europe, Office of the Chief of Public Affairs. *A Soldier's Guide to Bosnia Herzegovina.* N.p. (Heidelberg): Office of the Chief of Public Affairs, HQ USAREUR, n.d. (ca. 1996).

Helsinki Watch (Human Rights Watch). *War Crimes in Bosnia-Hercegovina.* 3 vols. New York–Washington–Los Angeles–London: Human Rights Watch, April, 1993.

Hillen, John F., III. *Killing with Kindness: The UN Peacekeeping Mission in Bosnia.* Cato Institute Foreign Policy Briefing no. 4. Washington, D.C.: Cato Institute, June 30, 1995.

Hodge, Carole. "Slimey Limeys." *New Republic,* January 9, 1995.

International Criminal Tribunal for the Former Yugoslavia. *Judgement* [*sic*] *in the case of Prosecutor vs. Dario Kordic and Mario Cerkez.* Case no. IT-95–14/2-T. The Hague, February 26, 2001.

———. Brief of Appellant Dario Kordic. Vol. 1, *Publicly Filed.* Case no. IT-95–14/2-A. The Hague, August 9, 2001.

International Institute for Strategic Studies. *The Military Balance, 1991–1992.* London: Brassey's for the International Institute for Strategic Studies, 1991.

———. *The Military Balance, 1992–1993*. London: Brassey's for the International Institute for Strategic Studies, 1992.

———. *The Military Balance, 1993–1994*. London: Brassey's for the International Institute for Strategic Studies, 1993.

———. *Strategic Survey, 1991–1992*. London: Brassey's for the International Institute for Strategic Studies, 1991.

———. *Strategic Survey, 1992–1993*. London: Brassey's for the International Institute for Strategic Studies, 1992.

———. *Strategic Survey, 1993–1994*. London: Brassey's for the International Institute for Strategic Studies, 1993.

Jane's Information Group. *Jane's Bosnia Handbook*. 1st ed. Alexandria, Va.: Jane's Information Group, 1996.

Joint Chiefs of Staff. *Joint Pub 1–02: Department of Defense Dictionary of Military and Associated Terms*. Washington, D.C.: Joint Chiefs of Staff, March, 1994.

Judah, Tim. *The Serbs: History, Myth and the Destruction of Yugoslavia*. New Haven, Conn.: Yale University Press, 1997.

Maas, Peter. *Love Thy Neighbor: A Story of War*. New York: Alfred A. Knopf, 1996.

Malcolm, Noel. *Bosnia: A Short History*. New York: New York University Press, 1994.

"Muslim Forces Push Offensive in Bosnia." *Toronto Globe,* June 10, 1993, A10.

"Muslims Push Offensive for Bosnian Land." *Toronto Star,* June 10, 1993, A13.

O'Ballance, Edgar. *Civil War in Bosnia, 1992–94*. New York: St. Martin's Press, 1995.

Patrick, Charles R. *Tactics of the Serb and Bosnian-Serb Armies and Territorial Militia*. Sandhurst, U.K.: Conflict Studies Research Centre, Royal Military Academy Sandhurst, March 2, 1994.

Pavlowitch, Stevan K. *A History of the Balkans, 1804–1945*. London: Longmans, 1999.

———. *Serbia: The History of an Idea*. New York: New York University Press, 2002.

Rogel, Carole. *The Breakup of Yugoslavia and the War in Bosnia*. London/Westport, Conn.: Greenwood Press, 1998.

Tanner, Marcus. *Croatia: A Nation Forged in War*. New Haven, Conn.: Yale University Press, 1997.

Thompson, Mark. "The Bosnian Victims Fight Back." *New Statesman and Society,* June, 1993.

Tomasevich, Tomo. *The Chetniks: War and Revolution in Yugoslavia, 1941–1945*. Stanford, Calif.: Stanford University Press, 1975.

———. *War and Revolution in Yugoslavia, 1941–1945: Occupation and Collaboration*. Stanford, Calif.: Stanford University Press, 2001.

Vulliamy, Edward. *Seasons in Hell: Understanding Bosnia's War*. New York: St. Martin's, 1994.

West, Rebecca. *Black Lamb and Grey Falcon: The Record of a Journey through Yugoslavia in 1937*. 2 vols. London: Macmillan, 1946.

Wiener, Friedrich, and William J. Lewis. *The Warsaw Pact Armies*. Vienna: Carl Ueberreuter, 1977.

Index

"Abdul Latif" Detachment, 52
ABiH (Armed Forces of the Republic of
  Bosnia and Herzegovina): battles listed,
  167–68; matériel estimates, 17–18, 59–63,
  182n13; organizational structure, 34–39;
  personnel estimates, 21–24, 34, 189n21,
  201n27; predecessors, 32–34; role in civil
  war, 159–63; Sept. '93 status report,
  148–49; strategic plan, 65–66, 70–72;
  supply routes, 18–20, 173n23. *See also*
  command/control systems, effectiveness
  barriers
ABiH Corps, organizational structure, 34–35
ABiH I Corps: Fojnica area operations, 140;
  headquarters, 35
ABiH II Corps, headquarters, 35
ABiH III Corps: aggression policy, 161;
  command/control challenges, 44, 48;
  Fojnica area operations, 140; Kacuni area
  operations, 75–76, 186n9; Novi Travnik
  kidnapping, 88, 89; personnel estimates,
  23, 24; structure of, 35–36, 37f; weapons
  estimates, 62; Zepce area operations, 141,
  142, 147
ABiH IV Corps, Fojnica area operations, 82,
  140
ABiH VI Corps, 35, 39, 140, 148–49
ABiH VII Corps (ABiH), headquarters, 35
ABiH operations: battles listed, 167–68; before April '93, 67–70, 81–82; Blaskic's
  May '93 concerns, 126–28; Bosnian Serb
  conflicts, 3, 23–24, 66–67; Busovaca area,
  75, 76–77, 101–10, 137–38, 152–54; effectiveness, 121–22; Fojnica area, 139–40,
  204n9; Gornji Vakuf area, 73–75; Kacuni
  area, 75–76; Kiseljak area, 77, 111–15,
  138–39, 186n18; Novi Seher area,
  120–21, 146–47; Novi Travnik area,
  118–20, 133–34; strategic plan, 65–66,
  70–72; Travnik area, 118–20, 128–33;
  Vares area, 154–57; Vitez area, 151–54,
  206n6; Zavidovici area, 120–21, 146;
  Zenica area, 115–18; Zepce area, 120–21,
  141–46. *See also* Vitez area, April '93 ABiH
  attack
active defense, defined, 190n29
Ahmic, Muniz, 69
Ahmici village, 68–69, 92–95, 109, 190n34,
  191–92n47, 192n49, photo #13
Alagic, Mehmed: cease-fire agreement, 125;
  command responsibilities, 24, 149; photos

#1, #10; on Stari Vitez fighting, 206nn10,
  11; Travnik operations, 128, 131
Alexander I, 9–10
Alpha Force, 46, 48
al-Queda, 52, 180n53
Andric, Dragan, 140
Andric, Victor (Ivica Rajic), 49, 155, 156,
  207n21
Andric, Zarko "Zuti," 49, 81
Ante Bruno Busic Brigade, 177–78n15
Ante Starcevic Brigade, 75
Antolovic, Ivica, 191–92n47
Antunovic, Nikola, 143
Apostles (gang), 49, 156
Armed Forces of the Republic of Bosnia and
  Herzegovina (ABiH). *See ABiH entries*
arms embargo, 17, 60–61
arms supplies, overview, 59–64
Army of the Republic of Croatia, 49–51, 159,
  161
Arnauti village, 52
Arnold, Derek, 53
attacks, types defined, 190n29
Austro-Hungarian Empire, 6, 8–9

Badrov, Slavko, 189n25
Bakje village, 110
Bakovici village, 140
Ban Josip Jelacic Brigade, 32, 43, 77, 111,
  113–14, 139–40
Baresic, Vinko, 89, 116–17
Bare village, 106, 187n36
Barica Gaj, 95
Battle of Kosvo-Polje, 7
battles, listed, 165–68
Bayazed, 7
Begue, Etienne, 207n20
Behrici village, 78, 111, 115
Berbic, Fuad, 184n11
Bertovic, Anto, 189nn21, 24
Besici village, 78
Bikosi village, 132
Bilajac, Rifat, 71, 176n52
Bilalovac village, 76
Bila village, 79, 132
Bistrica village, 186n19
black market operations. *See* criminal activity
Blaskic, Tihomir, 41, 80, 89; on 7th Muslim
  Brigade, 187n38; Ahcimi operations,
  94; Aug. '93 report, 148; Bila talks, 79;
  Busovaca conflict, 107–108; cease-fire

ISBN 1-58544-261-5